R P Durrett
sept 01
WASH DC

milking

*A Southerner's
Story of Life on
This Planet*

The moon

EUGENE WALTER

as told to Katherine Clark

FOREWORD BY GEORGE PLIMPTON

 Crown Publishers   New York

Published by Crown Publishers, New York, New York.
Member of the Crown Publishing Group.

Random House, Inc. New York, Toronto, London, Sydney, Auckland
www.randomhouse.com

CROWN is a trademark and the Crown colophon is a registered trademark of Random House, Inc.

Printed in the United States of America

Design by Barbara Sturman

Library of Congress Cataloging-in-Publication Data
Walter, Eugene, 1921–1998.
    Milking the moon : a Southerner's story of life on this planet /
by Eugene Walter as told to Katherine Clark.
    1. Walter, Eugene, 1921–1998. 2. Walter, Eugene, 1921–1998—Friends and associates. 3. Authors, American—Southern States—Biography.
4. Authors, American—20th century—Biography. 5. Food writers—United States—Biography. 6. Mobile (Ala.)—Social life and customs.
7. Americans—Europe—Biography. 8. Southern States—Biography.
9. Europe—Biography. I. Clark, Katherine. II. Title.
PS3573.A47228 Z475   2001
818'5409—dc21
    [B]   00-064530

ISBN 0-609-60594-1

10 9 8 7 6 5 4 3 2 1

First Edition

Contents

Foreword

Eugene Walter is one of those personages who turn up in life and leave, well, an indelible impression in which all personal characteristics—manner, speech, dress, and so on—are memorably distinctive. The first time I saw him was in the spring of 1952—an apparition standing in the doorway of the cramped *Paris Review* office on the rue Garancière. He was wearing a faded linen suit, the kind plantation owners traditionally wore, at least in the movies, set off with a white panama hat. Actually, I don't recall a hat, but the rest of the ensemble was exact. He posed in the doorway to let all this sink in. He was there because he had submitted a short story to the fledgling literary enterprise—indeed it was one of the first submissions received—and to our delight it was quite wonderful, a Eudora Welty-ish tale entitled "Troubadour."

We had summoned him to give him the news. His first words on hearing our delight were, "Ah, Tum-te-tum" . . . a curious, drawn-out triad of sounds that stuck in one's mind. Indeed, we referred to him as such ("Tum-te-tum is coming in to confer") and I wrote notes and letters to him as "Dear Tum-te-tum," though in fact he preferred to be known as Professor James B. Willoughby. That was how he signed his letters, under the phrase "mille fleurs." The reference to flowers was appropriate since he was an expert on the decorative arts—costume and set design. He pressed a number of his drawings on us at the *Paris Review,* including one of courtiers illustrated as different vegetables; his influence was such that Archibald MacLeish, who had taught a number of the editors and early contributors in his famous English S course at Harvard, wrote me in his capacity as an advisory editor, wondering if the magazine was getting a bit fey. He might have been even more concerned had he known Eugene often spoke about starting up a magazine entitled *The Druids' Home Companion.*

The monkey was his favorite animal. The highest accolade he pressed on the girls around the Café Tournon, across from the Hôtel Helvétia where he lived, was that they were just a step or two below being "Queen of the Monkeys." They adored him. He invited them in for candlelit suppers in his tiny one-room apartment, the light reflecting on the gold stars he had pasted on the walls. He knew a lot about Southern culinary delights, gumbos, and so forth, but he was poor, and so for all the intended elegance of these little suppers, he did miracles with no more than an onion, a carrot or so, and some oysters. A remarkable stew would come of this, not much of it for sure; one truly learned that taste was far more important than volume.

In the room he had a stuffed monkey under a glass bell jar that he packed and took with him whenever he moved. It went with him when he left Paris to take up residence in Rome. I saw it there when I visited him on the way to Africa one year. His rooms were quite substantial—cats and plants everywhere in the moist rain-texture of the place—certainly substantial compared to the little room in the Helvétia, where there wasn't enough room, as he put it, "to swing a cat . . ."

I saw him once or twice in Mobile when I was in the area doing research for an oral biography on Truman Capote. He knew Truman as a boy, of course, and had stories about him. He knew some of the folks up in Monroeville where Truman spent his early life—Harper Lee, of course, and he had stories about her. What I remember especially about my trips to Mobile, though, was his despair at the ruination of Government Avenue, the sea captains' houses that stood in rows torn down to make way for malls and gasoline stations, and especially the disappearance of the shade trees, which he said were a requirement in the summer because it was always ten degrees cooler when you went and stood under them.

Anything of beauty or antiquity (the two were synonymous) being threatened was to cause him anguish. Modernity, the future seemed of little interest. One of the reasons he wrote less than he could have, and perhaps should have, was his suspect view of what was going on around him; playing in movies, and there were so many of them, especially roles with exotic costumes, provided him with a wonderfully agreeable escape. I remember asking Louis Auchincloss, who wrote Jamesian novels, which century he would revert to given the chance, and he said, wisely if somewhat surprisingly, "Anything after novocaine." I think Tum-te-tum would bypass the threat of pain to eagerly embrace an era of seventeenth-, even sixteenth-century gentility and grace, at least as long as troubadours were about, and harlequins, and courtiers wearing vegetable hats, and surely a monkey dressed in red pantaloons sitting in a golden cage.

GEORGE PLIMPTON
New York, New York

Eugene in the Details

I first met the extraordinary Eugene Walter when I moved to Mobile, Alabama, in 1987. I remember a plump, avuncular figure with a cheerfully protruding belly and missing teeth who beamed at me through glasses that magnified his eyes into giant jelly beans and paid me much more attention than I had expected him to. Eugene was, after all, Mobile's reigning "character," the city's Grand Old Man. I knew of his illustrious past, the decades spent in Europe as a bon vivant, the involvement with the *Paris Review,* and the roles in Fellini films. But he seized on me as if I were the celebrity: "Honey chile, tell me all about yourself." I later learned that, for Eugene, the capacity to be interested in others was one of the hallmarks of a truly great individual. Eugene himself had a boundless curiosity for the other people with whom he shared "life on this planet." That first night he quizzed me endlessly about my Alabama background, my Harvard education, and the upcoming publication of my first book, *Motherwit,* which was an oral biography of a black granny midwife.

Soon after, Eugene invited me to lunch at his house. Despite our previous encounter, the invitation took me by surprise: Eugene Walter and I really did not know each other. But this was precisely why he invited me. I have since realized that Eugene operated on this particular principle of hospitality all his life, and this is one reason his life was so full of interesting people, whether in Mobile, where he grew up, or in New York, Paris, or Rome, where he spent a combined total of over thirty years. He knew few people when he first arrived in these cosmopolitan capitals, but by the time he left, his friends and acquaintances included some of the more extraordinary individuals of the time in each of those places. In Rome, where he lived for over twenty years, he "kept the nearest thing to a salon," the writer Muriel Spark tells us, and "all roads led to him." Wherever he lived, Eugene sought out people the way others seek money or career advancement. If he happened to meet someone who struck his fancy, he did not wait for chance to provide a second meeting. He quickly planned either a lunch, a dinner, a picnic, or a party. And so I found myself, a young woman in her mid-twenties, going to have lunch at the house of a gentleman in his late sixties whom I did not know.

I had been told the experience would be unique, but little did I realize just how much so. Now, after working so closely with Eugene's account of his life, I know that what I felt when I crossed the threshold of his house had been experienced by hundreds of others in all the different places where Eugene had lived. It was like entering another world, a magical universe of Eugene's creation. It wasn't just the books everywhere, cramming the shelves and piling up on the floors; or the cats draped over the sofas and chairs and lounging among the dishes on the dining room table; or the paintings and objects of art accumulated from a lifetime, jamming the walls. It was also the absence of any sense of time. I had stepped out of the nine-to-five workaday world where a living must be earned and so many things must be done, into a place where good food, good wine, good conversation, and human companionship took precedence over anything else. Eugene would have called the otherworldliness of his environment simply "civilization."

I was immediately handed a glass of sherry to "whet the appetite." There was an hour of conversation, interrupted occasionally by Eugene's stirring of pots in the kitchen while I absorbed the exotic atmosphere of the cat-free room, filled with Eugene's most treasured relics, off-limits to the cats' prying claws. As the conversation evolved (and the sherry went to my head), a strange transformation seemed to take place. The soul expanded. The worries and anxieties of daily life now seemed trivial and far away. I found myself discussing transcendent subjects, like my favorite books or Eugene's memories of Europe. Throughout the lunch, of Southern food and French wine and cats crawling on the table, I felt as if I had entered a higher level of existence, where the transcendent had superseded the everyday. This was made possible not so much by the unaccustomed alcohol I was consuming at midday as by the clock-free rhythm of Eugene's household, which allowed a person to slow down and thus achieve depths of thought and feeling not possible in the nine-to-five race to get things done.

After lunch there was a glass of port, "to aid the digestion, dahlink." By the time I left, a wonderful new friendship had been formed. Actually, I now felt closer to Eugene after just one visit than I did to some of my so-called close friends I had known for years. Instead of just grabbing a drink or a quick bite to eat, we had spent real time together and had been able to truly share our different selves. As I stepped back outside, that workaday world was in my face again like an unexpected brick wall. For one thing, it was still so bright. Lunch had lasted three hours, which is long for lunch, but it seemed longer. Was it really the same day? Was I really the same person as when I first arrived? No. All was changed. Not only was there a new friendship, but there was a new world opening up, a slightly new me.

From that moment on, my friendship with Eugene progressed rapidly. He called me often for small favors, usually rides to the grocery store, since he didn't have a car. I was always happy to oblige; indeed, I was flattered to be asked. There were many others he could call on to perform these services. I felt chosen. And I was always rewarded, if not by a lunch or one of his "squiggle" drawings, then just by the sheer pleasure of his company. And it was such a pleasure. Taking Eugene to the grocery store was not just a trip to the grocery store. For that matter, taking Eugene anywhere or just being with Eugene was, again, like inhabiting a different universe.

His conversation was his greatest gift, the means through which he transformed the everyday world into a comic spectacle for anyone in his presence. It might just be a running commentary on the passing landscape: "Have you ever noticed how the Baptist churches have the smallest steeples? I hate those little-prick Baptist churches." It might be a tragicomic tale of woe about a recent visit to the dentist or a run-in with a benighted city official. Or it might be a reminiscence about an important event or personage from his years outside the South. But just to greet Eugene with a conventional "How are you?" was to invite the unexpected. "Oh, I don't know, darling," he replied to me once. "I'm fat, I'm bankrupt, and I've got fleas." Eugene was nothing less than a walking one-man show, always on, always delivering an impromptu dramatic monologue that never failed to amuse, delight, challenge, stimulate, fascinate, and educate all at the same time.

The qualities and characteristics that made Eugene so special are the same ones to be found in his favorite animal: the monkey. A creature of subtropical climates, the monkey is noted for its capering, its chattering, its mischief making, and its high jinks, frivolity, and caprice. Eugene was just such an animal. Throughout his book of poetry, *Monkey Poems,* he celebrates life as lived by the monkey. "I'll celebrate all wayward things," he proclaims in the first poem. In the last, he declares, "O, I am monstrous proud / This life to live, this joy to laugh out loud." He was, like the title of one of these poems, "The Socrates Monkey, seen dancing in midair, amidst Sun, Moon, Stars and Field Flowers." He was bawdy, funny, irreverent, mischievous, flamboyant, and impish; at the same time he was shrewd, incisive, learned, and knowing. He was a rare combination of sage philosopher and monkey clown.

The many of us who knew and loved Eugene always assumed that he would one day write a memoir about the remarkable life he had lived in and out of the South. After all, Eugene was a writer who had won a Lippincott Prize and an O. Henry citation, among other awards for his poetry, short stories, and novels. Eugene himself assured us regularly that he had every intention of writing such a memoir. But as the years went by, it gradually dawned on me that no such book was forthcoming. Part of the reason, I'm afraid, is that Eugene engaged in too many daily sessions with a certain "Dr. Jim

Beam." But the larger reason, I think, is that Eugene's true artistic genius went into creating the moment—into living life itself—and for him, capturing those past moments in print would have been only a second-best achievement. As for Oscar Wilde, so for Eugene: he put his genius into his life and only his talent into his writing. I think he knew this.

So, gradually, the idea of doing an oral biography with Eugene dawned on me. It was exactly the kind of project that appealed to my love of Southern culture. Unique though he was, Eugene's personality and voice were so classically Southern as to be archetypal. And in Southern literature, the autobiographical narrative of a native Southerner's coming of age in the South and then embarking on a journey of exile and return is no less an archetype. To me, Eugene was the living embodiment of so much of Southern culture that should not be allowed to pass away with him. It had to be preserved. When I tentatively broached the subject with him, he said, "Darling, I can see it on your résumé now: *Motherwit* and *Daddyshit*."

Happily, this was Eugene's way of saying yes. As I planned for our project, the beauty of it struck me more and more. An oral biography was really the ideal medium for Eugene's life story. This was the way to capture Eugene's ability to create the moment through his conversational genius and the power of his personality as he performed his stories for an audience. It was not Eugene the writer, but Eugene the consummate Southern raconteur who needed to recount his autobiography. So, in the summer of 1991, I spent three hours every day from the beginning of May till the end of August tape-recording the stories of Eugene Walter in that same cat-free room where I had awaited my first meal with him.

The mere facts of Eugene's life are quite impressive. Born in Mobile in 1921, he was virtually orphaned in his early teens. He embarked on life with no family, no money, no connections, no college education. Yet in the course of his seventy-six years, he was a writer, a poet, an actor, an editor, a translator, a cryptographer, a puppeteer, and a gourmet chef. The list could actually go on. His 1954 novel, *The Untidy Pilgrim,* was awarded the Lippincott Prize by judges Jacques Barzun, Bernard DeVoto, and Diana Trilling. *Monkey Poems*, published in 1952, won the author a Sewanee-Rockefeller Fellowship. He also wrote the bestselling cookbook *American Cooking: Southern Style,* compiled for the Time-Life *Foods of the World* series. He was one of the founding contributors to the *Paris Review;* his short story "Troubadour" appeared in the magazine's first issue and was later awarded an O. Henry citation. For many years he served as editor for the important multilingual journal *Botteghe Oscure,* published in Rome by the American-born Princess Marguerite Caetani. As an actor, he appeared in over a hundred films, including several by Fellini, most notably *8½.*

Despite the apparent drawbacks of his background, Eugene lived a charmed existence. By pure serendipity, he always managed to be at the right place at the right time. In the late forties he lived in Greenwich Village when it was coming alive as a famous community of artists. He was in Paris in the early fifties, when the second wave of American expatriatism was sweeping the city. And he was in Rome in the sixties, during the golden age of Italian cinema. In each of these places, Eugene was a part of what was happening and knew the people who were making it happen. He was one of those people himself.

But Eugene and I did not put together his oral biography in order to document his achievements or provide an exhaustive portrait of the postwar period in New York, Paris, and Rome. What we are offering is the madcap narrative of one happy-go-lucky Southerner's adventures of "life on this planet."

The themes of Eugene's own life story are the same ones generated by his prize-winning novel and best-known work, *The Untidy Pilgrim.* In the novel, the protagonist is a young man from a small central Alabama town who goes to Mobile to work in a bank and study law. But after this unnamed pilgrim arrives in "the kingdom of monkeys, the land of clowns, ghosts and musicians, and sweet lunacy's county seat," he is soon seduced away from his beaten career path and set on what he calls a "zigzag course" through life.

Eugene's notion of "the untidy pilgrim" is juxtaposed against the image of those industrious Puritan pilgrims who arrived in the bleak world of New England to found our American society. They imparted to our culture its grim, inexorable work ethic, along with a certain nose-to-the-grindstone singleness of mind and purpose. It is they who spawned that Yankee breed of "cutters and dryers who already have their lives mapped out when they're six years old." In the "green and crazy land" of the South, however, there are only "untidy pilgrims" and "monkeys."

An untidy pilgrim is a product of a culture which is cut off from the mainstream of American society and the iron grasp of the Puritan work ethic. An untidy pilgrim is one who has been transformed by the lush, sensuous, prodigal landscape of the South, where life is erratic, erotic, eccentric, and exotic. The ruling forces are those of "chaos, craziness, and caprice," which Eugene calls "the Three-Eyed Goddess." In his novel's Mobile, which lays claim to the oldest Mardi Gras in America, the permanent atmosphere of Carnival takes the place of any work ethic. Throughout the novel, the author celebrates this culture and its inhabitants, who inevitably forsake the straight and narrow, conventional and predictable road to Success in order to embark on an untidy pilgrimage of adventure and exploration through life and the world at large.

This is exactly what Eugene Walter did throughout his own life. He eschewed any straight and narrow career path and spent his life wandering from one place to another without clear direction or a fixed destination. Not only did he never obtain a college education, but he never even formed any definite plans for his life. He simply set out and went wherever his whimsy led him. Yet his life was one of extraordinary excitement and fulfillment. His life story is the flip side of the traditional American success story, which involves achieving money, power, and status. For Eugene, success meant the ability to enjoy and celebrate life. It is probably no coincidence that the kind of success he did achieve was more possible in Europe than in America. His is the tale of someone who simply followed his heart and lived in the moment and was rewarded with a transcendent life of art and culture. The book's title, *Milking the Moon,* is intended to convey just that image of someone who traveled far and wide to squeeze all the life out of life. This title was inspired by a song Eugene wrote called "Go Milk the Moon" for Fellini's film *Juliet of the Spirits.*

Milking the Moon traces Eugene Walter's life from his childhood in Mobile, to his three years as an air force cryptographer in the Aleutian Islands during World War II, to his years in New York, then Paris, then Rome, and then back again to Mobile. Fittingly, the trajectory of Eugene's life did not follow a straight line from one fixed point to another, but formed an untidy circle, which ended up almost, but not exactly, where it had begun, as the Mobile Eugene returned to was not the same Mobile where he had grown up. In part one, "Mobile," Eugene describes with poignant lyricism his beloved hometown of banana trees and oak trees, subtropical heat and humidity, old houses and front porches. His evocation of the porch life and the Southern household routines of gardening, cooking, shopping, eating, napping, visiting, and gossiping forms a classic portrait of Southern life. This first section is also a portrait of the artist as a young man in his small but exotic Southern town. In its concentrated description of the special hothouse environment which produced our untidy pilgrim, the first section differs somewhat from the others, which trace the "zigzag" path of that pilgrim after he leaves his Southern home and launches himself into the world at large. In their episodic progression from one adventure to another, these sections become a picaresque narrative depicting our rogue hero in action as he meets important people and becomes involved in important events. Again, this progression does not have a climactic or culminating moment, but travels a circular course where there is always another adventure right around the bend.

Knowing that the journey was all, Eugene relished every detour and seized every opportunity for being sidetracked along the way. "Sagittarians are interested in so many things," he says of himself, "that when we head out for California, we end up in Florida." Eugene's stories are the same way. He says of Alice B. Toklas that she "had the true classical gift of the parenthesis"—she always finished her parenthesis, and she always returned to her original subject. According to this definition, Eugene Walter also had "the true classical gift of the parenthesis." Readers of this quintessentially Southern narrative by this quintessential Southern storyteller must assume the virtue, if they have it not, of a Southern audience, which has all the time in the world and, of course, absolutely nothing better to do than sit out on the porch and swap stories.

One of the first things readers will want to know as they encounter Eugene's fantastical tales about real people like Tallulah Bankhead, Judy Garland, T. S. Eliot, and many more is: "Are they true?" This was the same question I was asked repeatedly before I began my collaboration with Eugene: "Do you think he will tell you the truth?" Invariably, my reply was: "I certainly hope not." I was not after "the truth" of Eugene's life, whatever that was or might be. I wanted his stories. The ones I had been hearing, and he had been telling, for years and years. After all, these stories were the central and most important "truth" of Eugene's life. It was through storytelling that he invented himself and created a life for himself out of nothing. Therefore, I felt, his life story should reflect this storytelling and its central truth.

So in response to inevitable questions like "Did Eugene Walter really get three pubic hairs from Tallulah Bankhead?" I answer with some questions of my own which indicate my approach to fact-checking Eugene's anecdotes. How can we ever know? I also have three words of advice for the reader of this narrative: Just enjoy it. Eugene is best understood and appreciated as a mythmaker, as a teller of tall tales, as a yarn spinner from the Southern oral tradition. As such, he never allowed the facts to get in the way of a good story.

However, this is not to say that Eugene had no regard for factual accuracy. When I arrived at his house every morning for our daily interview, it was not so much the "Monkey Poet" who welcomed me as it was a sober and earnest schoolboy intent on making all the right answers on his upcoming exam. Eugene approached our project with more seriousness than I thought he possessed. Throughout the summer, he made a monumental effort to recall the events of his life with as much accuracy as possible. But when it came to his favorite stories, he was like a great jazz improvisationist. These were familiar riffs and staples of his repertoire, and he never played them the same way twice.

Eugene's own philosophy of storytelling can be pieced together from various things he said over the years. One of his grandmother's favorite sayings, which he was very fond of quoting, was, "Gossip is no good if it doesn't start from fact." This was Eugene's conviction as well: A story was no good if it didn't start from fact. My very strong sense is that Eugene's stories are essentially accurate in their basic foundation. He met the famous people he says he met; what he says transpired is probably a fair approximation of what really happened. In other words, Eugene was not primarily a fabricator. He embroidered. He embellished. At a certain point in his very best stories, the actual gives way to the apocryphal. This isn't the mark of a fraud; it's the mark of a great storyteller.

In one of our interviews, Eugene himself said, "The mark of a good storyteller is: Have a whole shelf full of shoeboxes of details. Take out one detail one time, one detail another. Otherwise, if you tell the same story over and over, it gets stale. You have to have a new detail which you bring out each time. It's like those ballad singers at the Scottish lords who improvised new verses for those ballads every night and forgot some others."

A case in point would be Eugene's oft-told tale about the time he had dinner in Paris with William Faulkner and Katherine Anne Porter. At the end of a spectacular meal at one of the finest Parisian restaurants, Eugene says, Faulkner leaned back in his chair and observed wistfully, "Back home, the first butter beans will be coming in." In the most classic version of the tale, Katherine Anne Porter replies with the same wistfulness, "Blackberries." The title of a recent Southern cookbook, *Butter Beans to Blackberries*, was inspired by this story of Eugene's. I have heard that well-known version, but the version Eugene recounted to me on tape is slightly different. After Katherine Anne Porter says "Butter beans," Faulkner says, "The baby speckled ones." "Blackberries" had been put into a shoebox, and "the baby speckled ones" had been taken out.

Although I know of no feasible way to verify this story, I don't doubt that Eugene attended such a dinner with William Faulkner and Katherine Anne Porter. I have no trouble believing that they had an exchange afterward which inspired the dialogue Eugene has attributed to them in his retelling. But clearly Eugene has been doctoring that dialogue for some time. The anecdote has a basis in fact, but Eugene is in the details. I think this is the case for many, if not all, of Eugene's stories.

In another interview, when I was pressing Eugene to supply a specific name or date in one of his stories, he finally replied in exasperation, "Oh, darling, I can't remember. That's a research detail for a novelist. I'm a ballad singer." This was the second time he had referred to himself as a ballad singer, and the analogy is as instructive as it is appropriate. Eugene's narrative is often lacking in specific names, dates, and other dry facts not particularly relevant to the heart of a given story. So be it, I say. When Eugene later recalled such information, or corrected an error or inconsistency, I have changed the text accordingly. Otherwise I have let the lapse of memory, the contradiction, or the error stand. As I see it, my role was to let Eugene be Eugene in print as he was in person and thus capture his character as I knew it and his voice as I heard it. In putting together the final manuscript, I have strenuously avoided any editorial meddling which would violate the integrity of either that character or his voice. Inevitably, I have not been able to include every story Eugene told me or cover every aspect of his busy life. This book is representative of those stories and that life, but it is by no means comprehensive.

There is a Cast of Characters at the back of the book which provides biographical information about many of the people Eugene mentions. Of course, some of them have not yet made it into the reference books. Others are too far-flung to be tracked down by even the most diligent researcher. I hope the reader will approach it with the spirit in which it is offered: as a helpful, though not exhaustive, appendix to the text.

The last time I saw Eugene Walter alive was on March 28, 1998, when he lay in a coma in the hospital a few hours before he died. He could not know that I had just driven over from New Orleans, where I now live, to pay my final respects and say farewell. I'm sure he wanted it that way. Farewells and final respects were not really in his line. To the last, Eugene Walter was a man of comedy, not tragedy, or even serious drama. Nothing illustrates this point better than my encounter with him just two months earlier, the last time I saw him truly alive.

My husband and I were to pick him up at seven o'clock on a Saturday night in late January for a dinner party at a friend's house. We rang the doorbell right on time. I knew immediately that something was wrong. The mail, which was one of the loves of Eugene's life, was still in the mailbox outside the door. Nor did I hear the faint sounds of the classical music that Eugene kept on for the cats whenever he left the house. The familiar sounds of his feet shuffling to the front door also failed to materialize. There were no sounds of any kind. The house was all silence, stillness, and darkness. There was no Eugene.

We rang the doorbell repeatedly, to no avail. We tried the front door and the back door without success. We went around the side of the house and hollered for Eugene through the windows. No answer.

Finally we got back in the car and drove down the block to the pay phone at the Circle K. There was no answer at Eugene's house. Then we called our host to see if Eugene had perhaps contacted him or canceled for the evening. But no, our host replied that he had spoken with Eugene at noon, and Eugene was most enthusiastic about attending the dinner party that evening. In desperation we dialed Eugene's number again. This time we got a busy signal. We hopped in the car and raced back to his house.

But the same thing happened all over again. No answer when we rang the doorbell. No answer when we shouted through the windows. We took our second trip back to the pay phone at the Circle K. And this time Eugene picked up the phone.

"Eugene, are you okay?"

"Darling," he said, "I'm perfectly fine. I just can't get up off the bathroom floor."

"You can't get up off the bathroom floor?"

"I'm flat on my back on the bathroom floor."

"What in the world has happened?"

"I just stumbled and lost my balance and fell."

"Are you hurt?"

"Darling, I could dance a jig if I could just get up, but I can't get up. I've been trying all afternoon."

"All afternoon?!"

"Yes, darling. Luckily there's a phone in the hall right outside the bathroom, and I've been trying for hours to get hold of the cord. Finally I managed to grab it and pull it over to me."

"You know, Eugene, the line was busy when I called you earlier."

"Oh," he said, "that was Nell."

"Well, is she on her way over? Does she have a key to your house? Did you tell her what happened?"

"No, darling. Of course not."

"But Eugene—why not?"

"Because, darling, it was none of her business."

Nell was one of his best friends—someone he'd known for over fifty years.

We had no choice but to call 911, and a few moments later firemen broke into Eugene's house and retrieved him from the bathroom floor.

"Mr. Walter," one said, "are you on any medications, sir?"

"Oh, yes," he said. "Let's see. Ah—honey, peanut butter, British orange marmalade, and Jim Beam."

"May we see your driver's license, Mr. Walter?"

"I don't have a license. I don't drive a car, I don't wear blue jeans, and I don't go to football games."

It was during that episode at his house that I finally acknowledged something I'd been denying and suppressing for months: Eugene Walter was dying. Yet I was laughing.

With almost anyone else, what had just happened would have created a sad, somber, serious scene. With Eugene, however, it was comic. It was as if the tragic could not even gain a toehold in the presence of Eugene Walter. There was no room for it, no oxygen for it. It was not just that Eugene had been able to "maintain a sense of humor" after spending what we later figured was at least six hours on the bathroom floor. It was something more than that. The sheer force of his personality had turned a potentially tragic scenario into a comedy.

With his aching back and his evident discomfiture, he was not trying to be funny, any more than I was being callous by laughing. He was just being Eugene, and I was just doing what I always found myself doing whenever I was with him—I was laughing. Even in the face of death.

Afterward I came to understand and respect Eugene's comic genius more than I ever had before. Eugene saw life through the lens of his own antic wit. He loved to quote Aristophanes' claim that "God is a comic poet." Paradoxically, his whimsical response to life was so powerful that he forced others to see the humor in any given situation, including death. This vision was not one that denied the serious or the tragic, or merely anesthetized us to that part of life. Rather, his was a spirit that could find and affirm the joy of life in the midst of the terrible, the horrible, the traumatic, and the catastrophic. To know Eugene was to know that joy. He helped to show us the joy and fun of living when we might have seen nothing but a grim reality. Not only that, but he could transform a grim reality, like a bad spill onto the bathroom floor, or a dull chore, like going to the grocery store, into an occasion for hilarity.

Eugene stands as an important and rare counterpart to the many people, especially in America, who are so caught up in some serious purpose that they have no ability to enjoy the tiny details of daily life. Indeed, anything that does not pertain to that serious purpose or pursuit is only an irritant for such people. For them, the world is just an interference, a place of small daily torments. Too late, they often learn that achieving that goal or dream was not the key to happiness they thought it would be, and they've missed out on life along the way.

Those without such a driven or "serious" approach to life are the ones for whom, like Eugene, the world opens up in all its infinite beauty and enchantment. A trip to the grocery store could give him no end of pleasure, as he cruised the aisles, humming happily to himself, pushing his basket, inspecting the shelves, and then, inevitably, going into a paroxysm of delight as he discovered some new item, like, say, lingonberry jam.

Not only would he be transported, but in turn, his presence somehow transfigured the store from a modern-day wasteland of fluorescent lights and Muzak into a magical universe of surprises and possibilities. And from him I learned a lesson that few teach us in a society so consumed with success: It is not necessarily the most important or significant things that can give us the most intense happiness in our daily lives. It's the stray cat, the purple wildflower, the lingonberry jam.

When Eugene died that Sunday night a few hours after I left the hospital, I was at first distraught that I had not been able to say my final farewells. Now I'm glad that my final encounter with him was on that night in January, when he dusted himself off and said, "Of course I'm still going to the party, darling. I wouldn't *dream* of missing it."

When Eugene Walter died, one of the few remaining vestiges of a bygone Southern culture died also. As Eugene himself once remarked, "They don't make them like they used to," even in the South. The Southern psyche and Southern voice that Eugene exemplified have virtually disappeared along with the South itself. I am proud to have been a part of putting together a book which attempts to preserve Eugene Walter for posterity. I will be the first to say that the experience of reading his stories and encountering his personality in print pales tremendously in comparison with the experience of actually being in Eugene's company and watching him perform his stories with gestures and pantomime and facial expressions and eye movement and accents and mimicked dialogue. But I think those who knew and loved Eugene will find that this book comes as close as anything possibly could to capturing our dear old friend between two covers. And I know that the many others who never knew Eugene Walter will find in this book great cause to wish they had.

KATHERINE CLARK
New Orleans, Louisiana

Mobile

PART ONE

Monkey Was I Born

You may think you don't know me, but you have probably seen me on late-night television playing either an outlaw or a hanging judge. During those twenty-three years I lived in Rome, I must have been in over a hundred of those crazy Italian films. I've been a crooked cardinal, a lecherous priest, and a female impersonator, just to name a few. I was Velvet Fingers in Lina Wertmüller's *Ballad of Belle Starr.* If you've ever seen Fellini's *8½,* I'm the tacky American journalist who keeps pestering Marcello Mastroianni with obnoxious questions. And if you haven't seen *8½,* you need to: it's one of the great films of this century.

But to begin at the beginning.

I was born, at least this time around, in little ole Mobile, Alabama, in my grandmother's house on the corner of Conti and Bayou Streets. Downtown Mobile. 1921. The first thing I remember is a big gray face staring down at me. I learned later from my nurse, Rebecca, that it was one of my grandmother's twenty-three cats. When someone suggested to my grandmother that it might not be in the best interests of the newborn baby to have a cat in its cradle, my grandmother said, "Nonsense." The cat is much more likely to catch something from the baby, she said. So perhaps that is why I belong much more to the world of cats than I do to the human race.

And like most poets, I was born with my thumb attached to my nose in that ancient gesture of disrespect toward all authorities, establishments, institutions, and shitfaces. It has taken long and arduous operations to disattach it. In certain weather, and in certain circumstances, it jerks back to its original position.

The moment I was born, my sun, my moon, and my ascendant planet were all in the same sign of Sagittarius. The effect is that I am triple everything. Triple Sagittarius. Sagittarians are basically happy, don't like to settle down, like to travel, are of an inquiring mind, basically generous, can be real mean and snotty if crossed, have lifelong feuds—the good Mobile stuff. We are the ones who gallop ahead two hundred miles and then stop and say, "What country is this?" If we could organize, we could have taken over the world way back, but we are interested in so many things that when we head

3

for California, we end up in Florida. You know. Our emblem is the centaur: half animal, half man. And shooting that arrow at the moon. Centaurs have all four feet on the ground, but that arrow is whizzing off to a distant planet.

I'm supposed to, by ancient tradition, get along with all Geminis because that's the opposite sign. I get along perfectly well with Aquarius. They don't understand us, and we don't understand them, but we get along. So many of my lady friends have been Aquarius. Leontyne Price, Muriel Spark, Ginny Becker are all Aquarius. If I don't show too much exuberance, I get along very well with Capricorns. Fellini is a Capricorn. All of the Italian film directors except Zeffirelli are Capricorns. But there are no fish signs anywhere in my life. Sagittarians do not get along with Pisces.

This is all part of an ancient body of knowledge that we have simply dumped, because the early Christians were opposed to it. But those cave age darlings were onto something. They knew that if that dead stone the moon can affect us the way *it* does, then those big things like Jupiter *have* to affect us. The movement of the planets, the influence of the planets on weather, on crops, on childbirth, animal husbandry, on everything—it was practical knowledge. Don't underestimate those cave age people. We like to think they were just sitting around grunting and throwing dinosaur bones over their shoulders, but they had the rouge pot, the mascara pot, and the pet cat. They had everything. They knew what they were up to.

It's not that I believe that thing in the daily paper that says you're going to get a letter from Aunt Minny tomorrow. That's not what I'm talking about. What I'm saying is that once upon a time, astrology and astronomy used to be one subject. As alchemy and chemistry were. They were part of one core of knowledge and quest. In the precise imparting of known facts, there was always that open window toward the unknown, the uncharted, the unstatistified. Logic was not God, and statistic was not God. There was always a sense of quest. And that first horoscope done by the old lady in Mobile when I was a child proved exactly true. I quivered when I came back from Rome after all those years and found it in a box in Aimee King's attic, along with the first marionettes I ever made. What she had predicted was, "You will never be rich, but you will travel widely and everything you really want you will have." I read it again after all those years and just quivered. Triple Sagittarius.

And anyone who knows me knows I'm more monkey than man. (Actually I'm a rare cross between cat and monkey.) Monkeys can carry on two or three conversations at once. And while looking over their shoulder they are perfectly aware of what is happening in front of them. It's the awareness, the total awareness of everything and the sense of mystery and creative mischief. Monkeys realize that many people die of boredom. More people die of boredom than die of diseases, since activity is the human norm. So many people get bogged down in marriage, business, church, property. So monkeys like to create mischief. That is to say, they eventually smash a few windows. People who stand upright in the usual way approach life in the usual way. But I'm more likely to be found upside down, swinging from the chandelier. And that's why I have—shall we say—a different perspective. Monkey was I born, monkey am I, monkey evermore to be.

But after all, if, as a child, you saw, every Mardi Gras, the figure of Folly chasing Death around the broken column of Life, beating him on the back with a Fool's Scepter from which dangled two gilded pig bladders; or the figure of Columbus dancing drunkenly on top of a huge revolving globe of the world; or Revelry dancing on an enormous upturned wineglass— wouldn't you see the world in different terms, too?

South of the Salt Line

The South of every country is different, and the south of every South is even more so. I come from that stretch of Gulf Coast South which is another kingdom. Mobile is a Separate Kingdom. We are not North America; we are North Haiti. Because we are so different from the rest of the United States. The spirit is closer to the Caribe than it is even to Montgomery. I mean, with so many black people, banana trees, Carnival, corrupt politics, and all the little cottages in every color of the rainbow—pinks and corals and purple and turquoise—like Southern belles in ball gowns. It's the Caribe. It's another climate.

Someone driving southward will note a change about fifty miles before reaching the coast: a change in vegetation, a whiff of something in the air. It's called "the salt line," that invisible frontier between the Black Belt and the coastal plains. Coming south, at a given moment, you suddenly finish with hills and you're on flat, level ground, and then you will begin to see palmettos and you begin to see certain large-leafed swamp things, and if the wind is right, you smell the salt air from the Gulf. You smell the salt. Then you know you're south of the salt line.

And of course my dear friend, the writer Elizabeth Spencer, wrote a novel called *The Salt Line*. I met her in Rome. She had a fellowship at the American Academy, and she was writing that book about Rome they made into a film. *The Light in the Piazza*, or whatever it's called. But she also wrote *The Salt Line*, where she revived that nineteenth-century phrase. It's the idea that attitudes change, life is different, when you cross over the salt line. She is

5

from a small town in Mississippi, and she is Something Else Again. She is not the usual Southern belle. She is not the amusing, intellectual Southern maiden lady. She is not the domestic Southern lady. She is not the socially conscious Southern lady. She is a little law unto herself. For many years she lived in Canada, and I think she got Canadized a little bit. Miss Elizabeth. She was very jolly when I knew her in Rome. We had many laughing evenings together.

But that's an ancient Gulf Coast concept, the salt line. It's probably Indian. Because you know the Indians used to come down to get salt. They dug salt from somewhere around this part of the world because there was a salt deposit here. And I guess when they did their little expeditions from up there to come get salt, they could smell the Gulf and knew they were crossing the salt line. And the sailors on the riverboats, you see, they would know they were getting close to the coast because they could smell it.

It's a genuine frontier. It might be the frontier between a somewhat Anglo-Saxon South and a world which is a mélange of French, Spanish, English, and Confederate, with a thoroughbass of African and Indian. Or an invisible defining line between the Sunday South and the Saturday-night South. It means Mardi Gras and parties on this side, and it means Sunday school on the other. On that side of the line you have the plantations and the slaves and the cotton and all that. It's the landed gentry with a rather British country house style. This group goes to call on that group. And that group goes to call on this group. They ride horses or carriages or whatever twenty miles for dinner. All that English country life—Southern country life ain't so different. But when you get to the coast, you see, you've got pirates and drama and Carnival and fishing fleets and smuggling and so many different skies and thunderstorms, like this constantly changing pageant in the background. It's another country. And that's where I come from.

I feel like I've overlapped several civilizations and several centuries. When I was a small child, there were still Confederate veterans marching down Government Street on Memorial Day—men who'd been teenage boys in the War Between the States. There was one old gentleman my grandmother would take me to visit, who had a chamber pot with a picture of U. S. Grant in the bottom. And my first history lesson with Miss Maude Simpson, whose daddy was killed at Second Bull Run: Columbus discovered America, George Washington chopped down a cherry tree, and then this War Between the States broke out.

But the Mobile I grew up in during the 1920s was still a French port city.

milking the moon

Mobile was French, Spanish, and English, but the French were strong. You would never know it now except for the street names and the fact that the old downtown is laid out on a grid. It is not laid down according to where the bayou flowed. It is Bienville Square, things going east and west, things going north and south—it's a French layout. When I was a child there were still more French names. A lot of them are still around, but somehow there is no feeling of it being a French city. First World War, Second World War, all those peasants in the fields came to work in the shipyards and built Baptist churches on every corner. But back then Mobile was quite a place. The twenties were roaring here like they were everywhere. There were rumrunners on the Bay and moonshiners in the woods. And seventeen bordellos on State Street and St. Anthony Street.

And how I wish I could really have known Mobile, not just as a child, in the days of those great restaurants—and they were great: the wine lists went on forever—and all those bars, those theaters going full blast, *and* the circuses, *and* the tent shows, *and* the magicians, *and* the fortune-tellers. I think I'd like that.

My cousins the Schimpfs had a restaurant on Dauphin Street. There were 280-something dishes on the menu, and they were all cooked to order. They had the first refrigerator anywhere on the Gulf Coast. There was always a whole side of venison in there, thousands of hams, guinea hens. And they had a wonderful wine list. They got cases off of ships from here and ships from there because Mobile was an old-fashioned port. And the customs inspector—if you gave him a bottle of wine, he would look upriver when you came in with cases of wine.

And of course there were the whorehouses. Nobody said "whorehouse"; they said "Miss Edna's place" or "Miss Minnie's place." Now most ladies—three or four children, two dogs, one servant, household to clean, laundry—they were so glad if the boys went and got it off before they came home at night. Boys have to get their rocks off every eight to twenty-four hours. It's not my idea—Mother Nature made them that way. And the Gulf Coast understood that in a way the Baptist country does not. The minute a woman realizes the way Mother Nature has made all healthy male creatures, then the expectations of romance, courtship, marriage, shared real estate, or vacations in the mountains take on a more relaxed air. But the bordellos were not just for copulation. It was where the boys went to shoot dice and play cards. And do the political gossip of Mobile. Because the gentlemen couldn't shoot dice at home with mothers or wives. Even some card games were forbidden. So they were clubs where you went to play cards or shoot craps or talk politics or just drink moonshine.

7

The bordellos were really one of the greatest deterrents to crime because if those sailors had been on those boats a month, they were ready to copulate. And instead of finding a town with no bordellos, nothing but bars where they would get drunk and fight and kill each other or kill whoever was passing, in Mobile they could have a good fuck and then drink and be happy. Then there are all these mad country boys dying for a blow job. And their born-again Baptist wives wouldn't give them one. So the bordellos kept everything in balance. Otherwise you'd have all these mean rednecks running around killing each other.

And some of them just wanted female company. The fat ladies, the ample ladies who were mistresses, were strange combinations of mother superior, mother, grandmother, doctor, nurse, female notary. They were all kinds of functions, those madams. They knew everybody's little perversions. They might know that the president of the bank liked to have two young teenage girls to bite his buttocks simultaneously. And they would always find the proper little girls. Because the president of the bank would call and he would say something like "Two for tea." It was a French city. It was Bordeaux. It was Marseilles. It was a French city.

And how I wish I could have played bridge in one of those whorehouses and just talked to those country girls. These country girls who were from families with eighteen boys and fourteen girls and just wanted to get some money together to buy themselves a piece of property in their county. And having seen dogs, cats, cows, horses, pheasants, and guinea hens copulating, there was no news to them about copulation. It was just something boys wanted to do. So they would come to town and work for three or four years in a bordello and save every penny. Go home and buy themselves a pocket handkerchief, find 'em a guy and marry, and raise eight children. Pillars of the church. Modest downcast eyes. They never told all they knew.

Lord, Lord: the facts of life.

milking the moon

King of Cats and Onions

My grandfather Walter, from whom I get my name, came to America as a young man, and he came to Mobile because Mobile was this little cosmopolitan port with an enormous Bavarian colony. Just as Mobile had interesting French and interesting Spanish and highly interesting Jewish, it also had an educated Bavarian population. My grandfather Walter came from this town in Bavaria where his family had had property since the Middle Ages because they were scribes. They were given land for helping somebody in some crusade because they could read and write and the Bavarian prince couldn't read and write. So that's how they got land. Walter means noble but without a title, means you've got a certain amount of real estate. But he was, my grandfather, maybe the youngest child, the youngest son, so everybody else had gotten the land, naturally, and he had to get up and go, and so he came to America, to this Bavarian city that had for forty years a German-language daily newspaper of great excellence.

My grandmother was French-Swiss, of a family that had been asked to leave Austria in the eighteenth century because they were too liberal in their views, so they went to Switzerland. So my grandmother, who was this amusing tiny lady with clanking amethyst beads, spent her childhood in Switzerland. And then my mother's father was a Norwegian ship captain. A family that had been in mercantile shipping for centuries. They all had this "get up and go" thing, and one of the ports that my grandfather came to was Pensacola, Florida, which had been a Spanish and English big-deal port. The Norwegian ship captain fell in love with that city and met this Miss Layfield—it's a French name that got anglicized. They married and had five children.

So these four grandparents were highly interesting. Perhaps the reason that I have basic good humor and a healthy liver is that I'm just a little ole League of Nations, I'm just a little ole United Nations without any wars.

Life was rather European, and I did not realize to what extent until I went to live in Europe. Now, I was raised with this idea that you were American. Fourth of July was red, white, and blue—eat your watermelon and behave. But somehow, everything looked toward Europe; we were always aware of Europe. Part of it was that quality came from Europe. The china, the porcelain, the silver, the crystal on the table, the damask, the good furniture. The good china, the good crystal, came from France. A certain amount of books, the Christmas magazines, came from London. It was just the idea that certain things of fineness came from over there. There was no belittling of the United States at all. It was just the idea that we don't make that—it was made over there. Well, naturally I felt I had to get over there and see what it was all about. I grew up thinking: *When* I am in Paris . . . *When* I am in London . . . Not *if*. When. So that when I got off the train at the Gare du Nord in Paris, I was at home. Same in Rome. I mean, I just was at home. The only place on this earth where when I first arrived I was absolutely an alien was New York City. It was an alien land, another planet. I never, never was able to adjust to it. Whereas when I went to Europe, that was just like going home.

My grandfather Walter owned an import-export house in the old port of Mobile—F. Walter and Company—which brought mangoes, guavas, plantains, and bananas from Central America and the Caribe, to ship to the northern United States, bringing Jonathan apples and Concord grapes from up there to send to the Gulf of Mexico. He had a three-story building with the front on Water Street, where there was a railroad track and the freight cars could pull right up in front to be loaded. On the other side of the building was the wharf where the freighters pulled in from the Caribe. So my grandfather would get the bananas and the guava and all that and just run straight through his place and get them into the ice cars on the train so they would go right away to New England. Then they would come back loaded with Jonathan apples and Concord grapes, which were sold all through the Gulf Coast.

F. Walter and Company was this wonderful place with old-fashioned—like in Dickens—high desks with high stools where the clerks were scratching with pens in big ledgers. At five o'clock they slammed them. Bang! Set out for wherever they could get a drink. What I loved to do was to sit at one of those high stools and write checks for millions of dollars. I would have been three or four, and that was like Saturday.

Then there was this huge, high-ceilinged darkened storage room filled with huge bags of onions. Sitting in the middle of these tons of onions was a throne. An enormous Renaissance-type throne with antelope-colored velvet plush, carved for the visit of the crown prince of Norway—a naval cadet—to the port of Mobile, where he was fêted. My grandfather had been the chairman of a committee of downtown merchants who welcomed the prince. So here was this beautiful throne that was made for the occasion. Some fifteen or so cats who guarded the produce house against rats occupied this throne, and curiously enough, they never clawed it. I used to love to go and sit on that throne and be the king of cats and onions.

Little Gene

As a small child I lived on Bienville Avenue near Mohawk, in a bungalow of the twenties. My father worked for his father as a purchasing agent. He went to farms all around this part of the world to buy the things my grandfather shipped, either to Central America or New England. My mother was highly educated mathematically. Her father wanted her to have mathematics because all the females in this Norwegian clan had languages and mathematics, unlike Southern belles. So my mother began as a bookkeeper at the Cawthon Hotel, which was a very elegant hotel built about 1898, right across from Bienville Square, where there's a parking lot now, of course. It had a rooftop restaurant called the Vineyard with some of the first art nouveau chandeliers. They were honey-colored glass and had glass grapes climbing on them. My mother was one of the chief bookkeepers there and later became the registry clerk. She met all kinds of fascinating creatures like Billie Burke and James O'Neill, father of Eugene, who came every year playing the Count of Monte Cristo. I believe Sarah Bernhardt stayed there once.

I think that is where my parents met. In Mobile, everybody went to the Cawthon Hotel sooner or later. It was like a meeting place. It was a restaurant and it was new and it was fashionable, and people when they went downtown would meet there, to lunch or have dinner on the top floor at the Vineyard.

I saw my parents in the morning when they set out. Then I had these two attendants. One was a black nurse who had raised my father—her name was Rebecca. She was a highly intelligent, charming person. She and my grandmother were great friends. My grandmother gave her up for a couple of years for her to be my nurse. Then there was this dog named Michael, this huge golden yellow Airedale. Michael would not let me out of his sight. If I went too near the curb on the sidewalk—even if Rebecca was right next to me—Michael would come and nose me back, nose me back. So these were my two guardian angels.

After we moved to the house on Old Shell Road, my grandmother Layfield, who was until the end of her life quite dotty, lived with us. She had one side of the house with an old bathroom and bedroom. And she just wandered about in there quite dotty. She used to have these long conversations with the mirror about life in Milton, Florida, where she was born. And she never forgot that her brother, Hillary, went home drunk from some champagne party and froze to death in the woods. He was distinguished as being one of the few people ever to freeze to death on the Gulf Coast in Florida. My grandmother Layfield would look in the mirror and say, "Hillary, poor Hillary. They found him, but he was frozen." In moments of lucidity she had some crazy stories to tell about the Layfield family. A distant relative from England who wanted to study the wildlife of the Gulf Coast was allergic to mosquitoes, and he just couldn't go into the swamp. He almost died because of the bites. So he made this merry-go-round. He had a big English bicycle that he rode to make this central axis go around to turn the platform which had these four wooden animals. If children would bring him frogs, snails, and birds, he would give them a ride. That's how he conducted his naturalist studies.

There was another black servant who took care of my grandmother. Not very bright but good-natured and sweet, and she took good care of my grandmother and Rebecca took good care of me. Because, you see, my parents worked.

<img style decorative flourish>

My mother obviously adored me—I was her only child, and I adored her. But our relationship was Norwegian. In Europe, you see, the sons are not mothered. The sons are always raised by the fathers, the uncles. In America it's different. There is the heavy mama. You know: "Randall, you certainly *are* going to Sunday school today. Now get up and get yourself ready. Wash your face. Comb your hair. Where are your shoes? You certainly *are* going, and if you don't behave and get yourself ready, I'm going to call your father. You know what he does when you don't behave." That's a heavy mama. Well, see, my mother would say to my father: "I don't know what's eating on little Gene today, but he wouldn't touch his breakfast." Then my father would come to me and say: "What ails you, son?" It was like that. Nobody ever said brush your teeth, do your homework, get up, go to bed. It was done in a kind of offhanded way. They would say, "Well, isn't little Gene sleepy by now?" And I would say, *"No!"* And they would say, "Well, maybe he will be sleepy in twenty minutes."

Being Scandinavian, my mother knew how to handle men. Scandinavians know. When the guy comes in the door at the end of the day, they never say, "Oh, you won't believe what's happened today. Oh, God, it's been so terrible." They say, "Hello, darling, come in. We're having something you like for supper." And a long time after, when the wife sits in front of her mirror brushing her hair one hundred times, she says, "Incidentally, the sheriff was here today." That's the style.

I think so many Anglo-Saxon American mothers came as frontier women, and they didn't know what they were getting into. How many miles they would have to travel, that they were going to have to cut the umbilical cords themselves, on a bumpy wagon going west or in some smoke-filled cabin, with nobody else, no woman around. And of course, thousands of men who were unmarried and living alone who might do anything to a child. He could roast it and eat it. You know. So I think these women became furiously protective, and a certain kind of bulldozer female developed in America. In America, where there's a mother there's a bulldozer.

With a Bavarian grandfather, a Norwegian grandfather, a French-Swiss grandmother, and another grandmother from England by way of France,

I escaped so much that is typically American. I just wasn't put through it. I didn't have the heavy mama. I think in my case, since my grandparents came to a basically civilized city—much more civilized then than now, of course—they were able to be more relaxed and maintain a certain formality from the European tradition. The French-Swiss grandmother had another idea about relations of mothers and sons because she was more Latin. Mother was the matriarch. Never pried into the private life of the son, but she was the matriarch, and if she said, "I want you here for Sunday dinner," he'd be there. We went every Sunday to Bayou Street. And we usually went every night for supper, because the house on Bayou Street was like the family seat.

My mother worked very hard, and toward the end she was really having an awful time because she was female in an all-male office. Then, at a given moment, she went down to City Hall and spoke her mind to some people there about the state of things in Mobile. Then she was put into the psychiatric ward in Tuscaloosa.

She had written some letters to the city officials about how schoolchildren should be fed lunches. She had seen starving children at school who had no lunch, so she made some terrible scenes and got my father in trouble. People who owned restaurants and shops didn't like the wives of their produce salesmen telling them what to do. She *had* been ill, but she did not have psychiatric problems. She had a moment of desperation. The doctor in Tuscaloosa realized she was not at all mad and put her in charge of the archives at the hospital. She was a very intelligent, efficient lady. She was definitely a liberated lady, but of course, the Scandinavian ladies were raised in that fashion. She had all the latest books, and she was a great reader. After a time she was quietly released. They hated it when she left because she was a very amusing, weird lady.

When she came out of there she moved to New Orleans where she had friends and cousins. She had a very happy life in New Orleans with the bohemian set, and that's the last I heard of her. She may still be alive, for all I know. I thought, This lady is doing what she wants, I do not wish to bother her. She did not bother me, I did not bother her. Nobody can understand that unless you can understand the European perspective. And my father was often out of town because he traveled all over this part of the world as a purchasing agent for my grandfather's business. So I was raised by the family at large, you might say. Truman Capote, whom I knew as Bulldog Persons from Monroeville, and I have that in common. We were both raised by grandparents and uncles and aunts and cousins.

The Minuet of Daily Life

My grandparents' house at 50 South Bayou Street was a single-story Victorian cottage with high ceilings, a wide hall down the middle, and a lot of Victorian froufrou on the front porch. Lots of little finials and little knobs. A lot of old Mobile had that more delicate gingerbread style. Lots of little knobs and finials. The house was pale gray with some white and darker gray trim, and there were flower beds all along the front. Cut flowers for the altar at St. Joseph's and for the dining table. My grandmother was a passionate gardener.

On one side of the house there was a little chicken run where we always had a few chickens. The little girl across the street and I used to love to sit on the back steps when Rebecca was going to kill a chicken. She'd go get it and wring its neck. She'd cut the neck off and it would walk around for a while, you know, with its head off, as chickens do. That's how you know they're brainless, because they keep on walking after their head's cut off. With the natural bloodthirstiness of children, we used to love to see that.

On the other side of the house was a big lawn with flower beds and a little path that led through a gate into the backyard where the garden was. Across the back of the yard was a series of little sheds. There was my uncle's little mechanical shop, which was this extraordinary place with lathes and grinders and tools and a work counter. My uncle Francis lived with us until he was married, and he could do anything. (If he'd been as clever with patents as he was with inventing, I'd have my white grand piano by now.) Then there was a wood and coal deposit, then there was a storage area, and then a stable. My uncle parked his Model T in there. There hadn't been any horses since World War I, but there was still straw in the mangers, and mice. I loved to run around that empty stable because of the acoustics. To scream and make horse noises, dog noises, and cat noises.

Right next to this little row of buildings was a courtyard paved with flagstones. It had a wooden counter with slats, and this faucet came up out of the ground and leaned over it. That's where they cleaned fish and plucked chickens. Underneath was a kind of miniature pond where all the mess went. It had a filter and a runoff so the water went alongside the house and out to the street in a little ground gutter. When they finished cleaning the chickens or the whatever, they would wash it all off and clean up the blood. After the water had run off, they'd take up this filter and wrap the mess in newspaper and put it in the garbage and put the little filter back. There was a whole life in that courtyard. Almost every house had some form of that. And some still had outside johns, wooden toilets with holes underneath in the ground. We

milking the moon

forget how young our country is. We've gone from privies in the backyard to perfumed toilet paper in a very short space of time.

The little garden in the back was very small when all was said and done, but there were vegetables, vegetables, vegetables, and the herb patch, of course, and the compost heap. The compost heap was where *every* fallen leaf, *every* plucked faded flower, *every* scrap from the kitchen, *every* onion peel, everything except animal fat and citrus went. Once a week, on Saturdays, my grandfather would turn the compost. In those days everybody had a little patch of garden somewhere in the back.

Everything in my early life was concerned with fine foods and wines, with gardening. I was in a kitchen and at a table forever. My grandmother and grandfather were really passionate gourmets, being European and both coming of small-town families who spent two and a half hours at the table for each meal, between wine, food, and conversation. And if you want to be a good cook, you have to be a good gardener; it all works together. My grandfather would pick the salad two minutes before it was going to be washed and dressed for the table. If we were going to have corn on the cob for lunch, my grandfather would go out in the garden and my grandmother would put the water on to boil and watch the pot. She would never let Rebecca cook that corn. When she saw bubbles forming on the bottom of the pot, she would go to the window and say, "Now." My grandfather would grab those ears off the stalk and shuck 'em and pass 'em through the window, and she would throw 'em in. Then: everybody at the table. The country butter lady would have arrived on Monday with the country butter, and my grandmother would get the crock from the icebox, where we kept the blocks of ice, the white wine, and the country butter. Then everybody would have their fresh corn on the cob with fresh butter. It was a religious experience. As my grandmother never ceased to explain, the minute you shuck it, the flavor, the sweetness, starts to go. It's something you can't measure or see, but it's there. So that's why it should be dropped into not overboiling but boiling water the minute it's undressed. I haven't had corn like that in a long time because I haven't been near corn plants.

We did fresh radishes the same way. My grandfather said, "Their soul flies to heaven within an hour after they're picked." So they were brought and plunged into a bowl of cold water with perhaps a sliver of ice. Then they were washed off. Quite often we ate them as the French do, with the leaves. And this was to experience the truth of the radish. "Sad as a store-bought radish" was one of my grandmother's favorite expressions.

Then, the first speckled lima beans, the first speckled butter beans, the first little snap beans, was like a little rite. The first spotted limas—those pale

15

green limas with purple spots—were considered one of the high points of the season. Whoever got to market first would grab enough for a friend because they didn't last long. The first ones were gone in a minute. They came in a covered dish to table, a first course by itself, with butter and the pepper mill. It's that French thing of *la première,* or the first little carrots, the first little turnips. It's a little festival all on its own.

The table was terribly serious, and the garden in the back was terribly serious. My grandmother lived for her kitchen and dining room. She believed in setting a superior table.

I never heard "We don't have anything for supper" or "I don't know what we're going to do for lunch." There was always something. And plenty of it. Because there was a garden. And there was a butler's pantry with bottles of wine and bottles of beer and bottles of preserves and big jars of rice and big jars of grits and big jars of flour and big jars of brown sugar. And there was this sense of a household.

At my grandmother's house there was a daily ritual which began when the cock crowed. My grandmother would get up in her wrapper and these flat-bottomed bedroom slippers. When the morning started, the first sounds you heard were these bedroom slippers. Slap-slap. Slap-slap. Slap-slap. Down the main hall of the house. Down the little hall from the dining room to the kitchen. Then you'd hear the iron stove being rattled. Rattle, rattle, rattle. Shaking the ashes down. You could hear this from every house in the neighborhood. The whole neighborhood would go rattle, rattle, rattle. I wish someone had recorded it. This was before radio and television had taken over the world, so what you heard were these household sounds. And you'd hear some kindling wood going in. Clink, clink. And you'd hear a couple of pieces of a big oak going in. Bong-bong. And you'd hear a match struck, and then you'd hear this delightful sound that a fire makes in an iron stove—a little gentle good-morning roar. A sort of "There you are, here am I, another day is beginning." So you heard this little symphony. Some composer should write a symphony of all those kitchen sounds.

One of my chief memories is the sound of the coffee mills in every household. Since there was no air-conditioning, the windows were all open, so you could hear those coffee mills cranking all over downtown Mobile at six in the morning. Nobody would dream of coffee that was already ground up, and they may have even roasted the beans that morning, because coffee was a ritual. In very cold weather, my grandfather always gave everybody in the household a thimbleful of the best cognac with the morning coffee. You could dump it in or have it alongside, whatever you liked. It warmed the bones.

A lot of people kept iron cookstoves even after they had gas stoves. My grandmother had both, side by side in her fairly big kitchen. All of those ladies who were serious about baking swore that really good biscuits, really good breads, really good cakes and pies, had to be done in that slow-burning, wood-fueled iron stove. And they all knew, having learned from black cooks as a child, how to put their hand in the oven and say, "Not yet." Put in another piece of wood, and after a few minutes put their hand in again and say, "Not yet." Go on about their business and finally put their hand in and say, "Now." It was that old school. They'd say, "Not yet," "In a minute," "Now," and put in the pies, the biscuits, whatever. They didn't need thermometers. They didn't need dials. They just knew. They could feel it. And I guess that's why they always took off their rings when they were baking. Their rings always sat in a little dish, like a porcelain saucer or butter dish, on the kitchen table. And when they finished baking, they put their rings back on.

When Rebecca arrived to make the biscuits for breakfast, the stove would be ready. You'd hear this car—chug-a-chug-chug—outside, hear a door slam, and hear Rebecca saying good-bye to her husband. He was a minister in a church in Prichard, and he'd bring her to work and come pick her up at the end of the day. Then you'd hear this whup-whup-whup from the kitchen. That was biscuits being beaten with a wooden spoon and elbow grease. Pies were also made early in the morning, covered with cheesecloth to keep the flies off, and put in the butler's pantry.

My grandfather would have his breakfast at the big wooden table in the kitchen before walking down to his office on Water Street, but my grandmother and I would be served at the dining room table in the dining room. Breakfast was a serious meal, as was the midday dinner. Quite often we had fried plantains and hot biscuits or some hot sweet roll. And then we'd have little bits of fish, little ham steaks, bacon, scrambled eggs, soufflé, or grits. Quite often a little tiny breakfast steak wrapped in bacon, and something sweet, like a peach pie.

You had to eat. Because people walked and worked and gardened. I think part of the problem with cholesterol now is that people don't do anything. They don't bend and stretch and dig. So all this about eating light is quite right if you live in New York and the most exercise you get is pushing the elevator button. But if—as we all did, as I still do—you really work in the garden in the hot sun, you don't want a salt-free diet. Because you sweat it out. And you want salt. I think that's why the Southern diet of pork sausage and pork chops and roast pork and ham and bacon obtained. I have this little song I sing about cholesterol: "Without you, darling, where would I be?" You know the famous Southern saying "We eat everything of the pig except the squeal." Well, you can do that if you go right out in the garden after breakfast and work for an hour, as my grandmother and I did.

Then Rebecca and Ma-Ma, as I called my grandmother, sat down and had coffee and did family. I never wanted to hear it. They did a lot of that "You can't understand anything men do. Men are not to be understood. Oh, well. Men." You know. "Men. They're all alike. Oh, men are all alike. Men are all alike." Rebecca's line was: "Ain't that like a man?" And my grandmother's was: "Well, you know what men are like." My grandmother would say, "I wonder if there's ever been a man who picked up his dirty drawers off the floor?" And Rebecca would say, "Men won't do it. Can't train 'em. Won't do it. You can train 'em to do a lot of things," she said, "but you can't train 'em to pick up their dirty drawers off the floor. Same with dirty socks," she'd say. "They'll hide their dirty socks on you. Now why would they hide their dirty socks? Just like a dog with a bone, they'll hide those dirty socks. Find one under the chair and one under the bed. Ain't that like a man?" I suppose it's true: a great many divorces are based on the fact that ladies think men should learn to pick up their drawers. It's one of those things that men can never learn to do. It's not in the nature of the male to pick up his dirty drawers. But I didn't want to hear it. I thought that was their game.

Then she and my grandmother would consult seriously about lunch. "First crowder peas is come, Miss Annie," Rebecca might announce. "Well, Franz says there'll be a boat from Ecuador today, and we're going to have some fresh bananas," my grandmother might say. "And we got those little pork sausages from Conecuh County, those baby ones that Millydew brought back last week, that are on ice. We shouldn't let them sit around too long. So we might have baby onions, steamed, with a clove in each one, and Conecuh County sausages, and those crowder peas. That'd be a real good lunch."

But if a fishing boat had pulled up, my grandfather would telephone from downtown. Often my grandmother would have something cooking, and the Bell system would ring, and my grandfather would say, "Anne-Elizabeth, I got a wonderful red snapper from a fishing boat that just came in." There were a lot of little fishing boats then, and whoever had offices or businesses downtown would come out to see what was in the fishing boat, because they would sell their catch to anybody. So right away my grandmother would get the pan ready, get the lemon, get the butter. Plans changed. She would put aside whatever. I remember once a boat came in with some huge deep-sea crabs, and my grandfather just closed his office and said to his first in command, "Do this, do that, answer the telephone," and he just came home with that crab. That was the event of the day. So there was all this serious to-do about what should go on the luncheon table. And if you are raised with that kind of interest and enthusiasm for both gardening and good food, you can't help but end up at the stove. I've always been a greedy-guts. Diet is a four-letter word. There'll be a voice from my tomb after they've closed it saying, "What's for lunch?"

After lunch was decided, my grandmother went to her desk, where she would do her household accounts and her grocery lists and write her letters. But by ten o'clock every morning she was sitting on the front porch in her rocking chair with a palmetto fan.

In my childhood, the porch was a concept as well as a place, and people used them. Everybody would sit on their front porches shelling peas and exchanging the neighborhood gossip. Nowadays, nobody is friends with anybody. You never see anybody gossiping on the front stoop because there is no front stoop. There are no front porches. We have air-conditioning instead. And there's no neighborhood gossip because nobody knows their neighbors and everybody's watching television. And worst of all, nobody has time to shell peas anymore. But the Mobile I grew up in was a place where human relationships were all-important—before the almighty dollar had taken the place of God, and where, above all, people had time to talk and tell stories, where people grew things and had animals. The old downtown front porches were like open-air parlors.

And there was furniture: a whole world of wicker or rattan chairs and divans and tables and plant stands and swings big enough for three people. How I wish some young composer had heard, as I, the different sounds of porch swings. Everything from rattle-squeak to crunch-budge-tink. With a bass accompaniment of shuffling feet, often bare.

If my grandmother sat facing the street, that meant that she would "receive." Other ladies across the street, next door, or passing by could come up on the porch and talk to her.

"Mary Winston, get off that hot sidewalk. Come up here and rest in the shade a minute. Want some iced tea?" my grandmother might say.

If she sat sideways, in profile to the street, it meant that you could greet her and speak to her from the sidewalk but not come up on the porch. If she sat with her back to the street, she was invisible. It meant that she was reading the paper or hadn't done her hair yet. You wouldn't say anything to her. That was the whole downtown code. Nobody knows how it developed—that was just how it was. All the ladies were like that.

And there was a whole lady language of gestures and pantomime because ladies don't shout from across the street. I can see old Mrs. Marx passing—"I'll call you at two o'clock"—she would say without words, only gestures. There was an entire gesture language dealing with stoves, ovens, telephones, shopping, the end of yesterday's rumor. I remember Mrs. Austin appearing once in the porch of the house catty-corner from us and, after waving for attention, simply nodding vigorously. It turned out she was affirming yesterday's rumor of a pregnancy.

One of the Bayou Street favorites was the ebullient Melanie Marx, a remarkable creature of endless energy, enthusiasm, and sheer good humor. A prankster, a punster, a puncturer of pomposity. I remember, when I was very small, the first time I saw her. She had a handful of Lilliputian zinnias, a form new at the time. "Did you *ever* see such colors?" she cried, rushing up the front steps. I was under the swing, making something out of matchboxes. "Just *look!*" I hope that's the phrase engraved on her tombstone, blessed lady. "Just *look!*"

Miss Minnie J. Cox was another character. She always wore black, black. Black hat and a walking stick. And she always had some tale of woe. She'd come by saying, "Well, say a little prayer for Miss Minnie J. Cox." She'd tell her tale of woe, and then she'd leave to go tell the neighbors on the other side. She'd say, "Well, say a little prayer for Miss Minnie J. Cox," as she'd leave.

There was the most effective telegraphy system from porch to porch. Two Model Ts could bump in Bienville Square, and in ten minutes that news would have reached Spring Hill. Who had crashed into who in Bienville Square.

"Oooo, Miss Annie, did you hear?"

"What's that?"

"Bienville Square! Judge So-and-so ran into the back of that lawyer's new Model T, right there in Bienville Square!"

She's on her way with some fresh eggs to the lady next door, who's in bed with fever, and over the back fence she says, "Tell Miss So-and-so that Judge So-and-so busted into So-and-so's new Model T right there in Bienville Square."

Downtown to Spring Hill in ten minutes. And that's how they did hurricane news, too.

For me, every morning on the front porch was Carnival. There was a passing parade of street vendors and peddlers of all kinds pushing their wagons and carts down Conti Street. Their cries would fill the air. You have to remember, there were no sounds of radio. No sounds of television. There simply was no racket. Between passing cars, a silence fell that would only be broken by certain wonderful sounds, like the cries of the street vendors.

"Got the good sweet melonnnnnnnnnnnnnnnns!"

"Corn! Corn! Too sweet to eat!"

"Snap beans that snap themselves. Soft and tender!"

"Waterme-e-e-e-e-lonnnnnns! Ripe just right! Ripe just right!"

The oysterman came down the street with his pushcart full of ice and oysters covered by a great burlap flap that smelled part wet dog and part rowboat, an umbrella on a pole quaking over all. His cry was the best of all.

"Oy-oy-oy-oy-ster-man, manny-man, manny-man, manny-man! Get your fresh oy-oy-oy-oy-oy-sters man, manny-man, manny-man, manny-man!"

You'd hear all these cries from every direction. Gershwin did a little bit of it in *Porgy and Bess.* It was just heaven. We used to rush down to the curb just to hear it.

If you wanted to serve crawfish, you called some of the little po' boys in the neighborhood. Ma-Ma would call and she'd say, "Now day after tomorrow I want four dozen crawfish." Broad Street had a ditch down the middle then for the crawfish. And those po' boys would deliver them. See, everything was mixed together. I mean, people who were wealthy, people who were modestly endowed, people who were working hard, people who didn't have anything, and blacks, who were servants. They were all sort of mixed up in downtown Mobile. Miss Minnie J. Cox had a huge house on Broad Street. Sitting in this avenue of oaks, you know. Facing the ditch. And then next to her was a ship captain who wasn't anywhere as well-off as she was. Then a block away on the other side of Spring Hill Avenue were all tiny little houses of black servants, who only walked a couple of blocks to work. So it was all social classes and colors together. And if you wanted crawfish, you just called the little po' boys.

The lightwood man who sold pine knots for the stove and fireplace sang out, "Liiiiiid-ud! Get yo' liiiiiid-ud!" These were oily pine knots for starting fires in stoves and fireplaces because all you do is put a match to them and they blaze. We had to have them year-round because of that wood-burning iron stove.

Then came the iceman. He had a huge wooden truck lined with zinc and filled with huge blocks of ice, pulled by a white horse. He had this bell and you'd hear him from miles away down Conti Street, this tinkle-tonkle, tinkle-tonkle, tinkle-tonkle. It was hanging on a little loop of iron, and he'd pull this little rope. The icebox was on the back porch, and it was this huge oak chest with another oak chest inside lined with zinc. There was a colored disc one could leave in a window which showed how many pounds of ice were needed that day. The horse-drawn ice wagon would stop at the back gate, and the iceman would saw off the blocks and carry them with his great big iron tongs to the wooden chest on the back porch. Always a drama. Every child for blocks followed the iceman to catch the "snow" which rained down when he sawed the ice. Some ate it right there, others ran home, hands cupped, to put either vanilla or lemon extract on it, or grenadine or molasses.

The country butter lady came in an old Chevrolet with a rumble seat filled with straw baskets full of ice and pats of pale sweet butter wrapped in green leaves. Miz Mimms made a proper entry with much ado and was always invited to sit and rest a moment, have a glass of iced tea, and share those details gleaned from other households. She was a master of gossip and never forgot that "gossip is no good if it doesn't start from fact," as Ma-Ma always said.

"I do feel sorry for her living alone," Miz Mimms would say. "But who owns those men's socks she hangs on her back porch?"

Tells everything.

Miz Mimms was a real character. She wore a cabbage leaf on her head to protect her from sunstroke. She said it was the only thing that would keep you cool. The sun won't go through a cabbage leaf. Never boil your brains if you wear a cabbage leaf.

Old black men with sugarcane stalks over their shoulder would come passing by. Children selling cut flowers, stolen from that morning's funeral wreaths at Magnolia Cemetery. The scissors grinder with his fascinating emery wheel-on-wheels. The pot mender with his bits of lead and solder and strange tools and a spirit lamp. The postman always stopped for a word. Conversations went on, corn was husked, beans hulled or snapped, rice picked over, coffee ground, beads restrung, paper wicks folded for next winter's fireplaces— somehow a whole world was encompassed, seized, dealt with before noon.

A lot of sloppy household stuff was done on the back porch. The back porch had the huge icebox and a series of Xs that held brooms and mops and a dustpan and an ash scoop, and all kinds of household tools. And there was this huge meter box that the meter reader came to read once a month.

And he was a strange character, wearing a cap with a big green celluloid visor. He never said anything. If you said, "Hey, Mr. Meter Man!" he wouldn't look to left or right. He would just march up onto the back porch and read that meter.

If you had green peas or the first butter beans, you often shelled them on the front porch. But peeling shrimp, or cutting the tips off okra, or husking corn for corn pudding was messy. That was done on the back porch. And then some days my grandmother would just stay in her wrapper till time to dress for lunch. She didn't want to sit on the front porch. Hot August. She'd have her hair all pulled straight back with eighteen thousand hairpins so not one hair was touching her neck. She had this loose garment of dotted blue swiss that she'd just float around in during really hot weather. With her slop-slop slippers.

One of the moments I can recollect so clearly is reading *Little Nemo*, the comic strip, out of the Sunday *Register* to my grandmother and Rebecca as they sat in these rocking chairs on the back porch, shelling the peas or snapping the beans or husking the corn. I had to describe the action of each frame as well as do the dialogue.

So now Little Nemo is on the deck and he says to Captain Flip, "Well, Cap'n, how long is it going to take to cross this channel?" And Captain says, "Why don't you climb the riggin's and see?" Then Little Nemo climbs to the top of the riggings with his telescope and carefully eases back down, and Captain Flip says, "Can you see land?" And Little Nemo says, "I can see land."

Whenever I read, they used to roar with laughter, and I was always rewarded. That was considered a job.

Then suddenly there might be a silent presence on the back porch. The boboshillies. These were old Indian women from the backwoods. They never knocked. They never cried out. Always dressed in white. They had their hair under a white turban, almost like a nurse or a nun. And sometimes a colored apron with these big pockets that they carried all kinds of things in, like gumbo filé powder, bay laurel leaves, sassafras root. They had all kinds of strange things from the swamps, like powdered this and powdered that. They sold medical, medicinal herbs to black people, things for childbirth, fever, and all that, but I don't think they sold those to white people. And I was scared of one very old lady who was a boboshilly. I don't think I ever heard her utter a sound, and she moved like a shadow, completely silent and seemingly weightless. For me, silence was everything frightening. I couldn't care less about darkness, but silence . . . My grandmother was fascinated by them. I think she bought gumbo filé, ground sassafras leaves to put in the gumbo. But the boboshillies would never sit and never stay.

When the cathedral bells rang eleven o'clock, there was a shuffle of feet, of chairs being pushed back. Everyone on all downtown front porches said in civic unison, "Gettin' hot, time to go inside." But during that morning hour, the front porch was the universal agora, the outdoor parlor, the message post, the echoing chamber for countless unofficial town criers, the first act of an opéra bouffe, endless source of gorgeous and useless information for a child.

Porch life turned neighborhoods into augmented families or familial groups. It was a formal relationship—you never intruded—but the important events of birth, death, illness, engagements, weddings, and birthdays were absolutely known. You knew them before being told, just from seeing what was happening on the other front porches. If you were outside on the front porch, you saw what was being delivered. Or not being delivered. You knew who got groceries and who didn't get groceries. You saw the druggist's boy come up on his bicycle bringing medicines, and you knew that Mrs. Allen was not so well over there or had had one of her attacks. If you saw the doctor come, and saw everybody wringing their hands, you knew someone was gravely ill. Everybody helped everybody else, and everybody shared. You couldn't watch the life taking place on someone else's front porch and not be a part of it. And if you needed this, that, or the other, all you had to do was ask two of your neighbors, and one of them would have it.

That is the good aspect of gossip. If you are in trouble, serious trouble, friends sort of happen to pass by often, happen to telephone, or put in a good word behind the scenes. In the South, gossip is a full-time occupation. That's why our roads are in bad condition, the bridges that were due ten years ago aren't built yet, the mail doesn't work. People are too busy tracking down versions of the story. "I heard she went to New Orleans alone." "Oh, no, her husband followed her." "Oh, no." "Oh, yes." But there is a humane dimension to gossip. In New York, you know, you could drop dead and the next-door neighbor wouldn't know it for ten years. Here, if the cat cries at the back door longer than two hours and it's not let in, someone will check.

If there was a death, everybody stayed home to do whatever had to be done, because funerals were at home. The neighbors always gathered—even if you loathed some of your neighbors and had been battling and feuding for years—all neighbors got together. It was that old-fashioned thing. Someone would always get the widow or widower out of the house while the undertakers were clobbering the corpse in the bedroom, doing the embalming, cleaning up afterward. The ghastly smell of formaldehyde and whatever in the house.

Porch life made everybody cousins. You may not like all your cousins, but you helped out anyway, because they were family. And that is something we have almost totally lost, along with porch life itself.

≈

Everybody came home for midday dinner in those days. Then there was always a fuss to see what my grandfather might bring home in the middle of the day. You never knew what might turn up from one of those boats. Once my grandfather brought home this bunch of plantains, and we found a baby spider monkey in it. The midday meal was a serious occasion, the dining table a sacred altar where everybody worshiped at noon. There was always a cold consommé or a cold cream soup to start. No ghastly globby dressings on raw salad to insult our innards at the beginning of the meal. My grandfather never allowed water on the table; there was always wine, which he made himself and stored under the house. There were always two meats or one meat and one seafood. Little lamb chops and then ham. Or broiled fish and then pork chops. Always at least two starches. Rice and potatoes and barley. There were always hot breads. My grandmother made wonderful crunchy-crust bread, or little muffins, or cornbread, or fresh biscuits. Then usually it was salad and cheese and fruit. Beautiful cheeses; I don't know where my grandfather got some of those cheeses. He loved Limburger. We called that "dirty socks cheese." Afterward some small sweet thing like a pickled peach, and there was always some splendid dessert. My grandmother made these wonderful aniseed cookies. They had to age for a week. I'd come home from running around the neighborhood and I could smell them in the house. She would have hidden them in a different place every day. The minute I came in I'd start that room-by-room search. I often found them. And I learned to take one and rearrange the others. Or there might be some glorious bit of chocolate from George's Chocolate Shop. Or a sherbet made of Karo syrup and blackberries. All glorious foods. But you see, everybody was active. By the time I had climbed the pecan tree and gone under the house and skipped around the block and dug holes and gotten into Uncle Francis's wood shop, I needed to eat. And my grandfather walked down to Water Street and then walked up and down the street, talking to the other produce people. He couldn't have had a sandwich and a cup of tea after all that.

Then: Close the shutters, pull the drapes, lie down, and Take A Nap. During that time of day when it was too hot to do anything, people just didn't even try to do anything. There was no air-conditioning, and people just didn't fight the climate then the way they do now. They closed the shutters, pulled the drapes, and took a nap. Our brains only function for two weeks out of the year in this climate anyway. Weariness, bone laziness, gets in the blood because we ain't adapted to this climate yet. Even if we *are* born here, we don't realize that three million generations of something more northern is suffering subtropical languor. We *are* in the subtropics down here, and that means a constant battle between humanity and humidity. We just ain't adapted. It is only by conscious efforts we keep the motor running during the six months of August. One reason I believe in the nap is, if you can't lick 'em, join 'em. Alligators nap, possums nap, cats nap. Everything in this climate naps. Not even monkeys come out in hot weather like we have. They're sitting in the trees picking little flakes of skin off each other's shoulders. Quietly. During the heat of the day.

Between one-thirty, say, and four o'clock, which was nap time, there was not a sound. Nobody would dare make a sound. If someone was awake, he or she would be very silent and move barefoot through the house so as not to wake up those who were napping. Nap time was sacred. I think that's why people lived longer and were mostly in a better humor. I can remember when, at three o'clock in the afternoon on a summer day downtown, there was no sound. No motion. There was total silence and stillness. Our society would be better off if that were still the custom: fewer divorces, fewer murders, fewer nervous breakdowns, fewer bankruptcies. Because in our climate, people change their minds constantly and are quick to take offense, so lifelong feuds are born.

So after lunch, everybody just crawled into some corner and fell asleep. Rebecca would retire to a rocking chair on the back porch and doze. She might have darning in her hand, but she wasn't darning. I loved to sleep in the front parlor, which was used only for the official visit when the priest came to dinner. It was very cool in there because it was kept closed always. Of course, the moment the sun was going to hit the house they would close the shutters and close the curtains to keep everything cool inside. There were glass transoms over all the doors between the rooms which could be flipped open by a long metal rod that came down and rested on the door frame near where the doorknob was. You could push that up or push that down to open and close the transoms. Usually the windows in the front room would be left up, with the shutters closed, so that what air was moving—and we were close enough to Mobile Bay that there was always some air moving—came in the lower part of the window and went through all the open transoms in the house. If you moved intentionally at a slow pace, got everything done before ten o'clock, and took a nap after lunch, you wouldn't even have dreamed of inventing air-conditioning.

At night, porch life went on forever. All ages and colors sat together on the porch, rocking and fanning and telling stories. When the gossip got really good, my grandmother would switch from English to French.

"And nobody knew where she was, they looked high and low, nobody could find her, and then she was seen in New Orleans with—"

And the rest would be in French, so that little eavesdroppers couldn't hear the rest of the story. I knew then that one day I would learn French, because French was the gossip language. All the good parts happened in French. When the going got really good, it was in French, not English. So I knew one day I had to learn that language and find out all I'd been missing.

Children played hide-and-seek, and those were the sounds you heard for blocks around at twilight. "Five, ten, fifteen, twenty, twenty-five, thirty. Coming, ready or not!" Then you'd hear these giggles as people were found. We also played statues, where somebody puts their head against a tree and says, "Five, ten, fifteen, twenty, twenty-five, thirty, thirty-five, forty, stop," while the rest are running around. When you hear "stop," you have to stop and be a statue. The one who was counting gets to choose who is the best statue. Then that person gets to do the counting and all of us have to run around again and be a statue when we hear "stop."

On special nights the children from several houses would get together and play steamboat. Steamboats were when you took an old shoebox and first cut out crescent moons or star shapes or flower shapes. Then you lined the box with scraps of colored tissue paper that came from candies or oranges. Then you filled the shoebox halfway with sand or ashes and you had two little vigil lights from the church and a long string attached to the front, and you'd go up and down the sidewalk pulling your steamboat. The procession of steamboats would be one block long, going up- and downriver. And you'd be saying, "Toot-toot! Ding-ding! King's Landing! Demopolis!" And it was a pretty sight, those little illuminated colored boxes moving along. Playing steamboat. You didn't do it every night. You'd sort of check with the other children: "Are we going to do steamboats tonight?"

The other thing children did was the penny poppy show. You saved odd things, like an unusual wine cork which came out of a bottle of port from a Portuguese ship, say. Or you saved a lizard skull that had been found somewhere. You saved a piece of colored glass. You saved a broken mother-of-pearl comb. And you would dig a little hole which you lined with either broken mirror or tinfoil. Then you arranged all your unusual things in that. You covered it with a piece of wood or a piece of cardboard or maybe some banana leaves. Somebody had to pay, either two banana caramels, or one penny, and you'd let them see your penny poppy show, just for a minute. You'd pop it open and pop it shut. For a penny or two banana caramels. That's a penny poppy show.

I remember once, somebody in the neighborhood had put a used condom in one. She didn't know what it was. She had found it in the shrubbery near the Baptist church. And she didn't know what it was. This was a little girl who always had fresh roses in her penny poppy show and dolls and antique mirrors. And then a used condom. She'd washed it and had it lying out. Of course, the little boys knew what it was, and she was about to burst into tears because she thought we were laughing at her penny poppy show.

Most people went in around ten-thirty. If it was really hot, the men would stay out forever. They'd be drinking juleps, or there was a drink called Cuba libre—very fashionable during the twenties and thirties—which was Coca-Cola with dark rum in it, about half and half. Very cold. Coca-Cola then was not sweet, and it was said to have a pinch of real cocaine in it. It did give you a lift in a hot climate, on a hot August day. It was called "the pause that refreshes"—that was the ad—and it was. Everybody at around ten in the morning, and in midafternoon when they woke from their nap, wanted a Coca-Cola. The more old-fashioned wanted iced coffee with a slug of black rum in it, but most people wanted Coca-Cola because it really gave you a lift. After all, it was a chemist in Atlanta who invented it, boiled it up in his backyard. A Southern drink for a Southern climate. So the men would stay out on the front porch, rocking and talking and sipping their Cuba libres.

I come from a vanished world of big dinners at high noon, afternoon naps, suppers at twilight, and long evenings of hide-and-seek and rocking on the front porch. It was a different world. I can never remember being bored. I never knew what boredom meant until I had my first office job in New York City. In Mobile, it seemed to me that everything was so exciting. A thousand details to consider. A thousand details. And everybody was so busy, they didn't have time to quarrel or feud. They might frown and snap at each other, but that was the end of it. There were no hours of solemn crankiness. That's a recent thing. Everybody had their tasks to keep the whole show going. So nobody had time to have their liver irritated by concealed frustrations. Everybody had their little tasks, and everybody contributed. It was understood. Everybody instinctively took up their tasks, so they could sit around on the front porch and giggle in the evenings. No radio. No television. Not much traffic. So the minuet of daily life was a rhythmic thing. You did the same thing every day at the same time.

⚜

Now this was not a fixed, Yankee, do-or-die schedule. If anything out of the ordinary happened—STOP—and consider it. Southerners will stop everything, but *everything,* even a war, to hear a funny story or a juicy bit of scandal. And of course, if there was going to be a parade, *everything* stopped and everyone rushed to Government Street to see the parade. There were so many parades, not just at Mardi Gras. When the circus came to town, there was a parade. I mean elephants, and red-and-gold cages with lions and tigers and baboons and marching bears. When the beverage called Nehi came out, in a tall bottle "as high as your knee" (it wasn't), there was a float I'll never forget. It was a well-turned female leg in a high ankle-strap sandal covered in gold leaf and a bottle of cream soda as tall as that knee. There was a tall female leg and a tall bottle, and that was all there was on that float. And it said, "Nehi has come to town." Then on Memorial Day, the Confederate veterans marched down Government Street in their gray uniforms to the Confederate section of Magnolia Cemetery. And sometimes a bunch of neighborhood children would get together and make their own parade.

If a dancing beggar came through the street, everybody stopped everything to watch that beggar do that shuffle dance and collect in his tambourine. Even in the height of the Depression, people found pennies for anybody who entertained. And if the pie man came—he had this little thing full of hot ashes and had these apple turnovers that were so good. Everybody stopped everything to get an apple turnover. If a special boat was coming in—let's say a Greek boat was coming in—everybody went down there to see this Greek boat coming in and the goodies that came off the boats.

In those days, in Mobile, people weren't as serious about the eight-to-five world. In fact, there was no eight-to-five world. There was only the twenty-four-hour, "live this life on this planet" world. And it's why I haven't lasted very long in the eight-to-five world. I tried it in New York, but I couldn't take it.

I think of the carefully ordered lives of so many people that I see much younger than myself. Get up in the morning and they turn on the weather report and then they have their breakfast and then the children are taken to school. And then they go to their offices. And the wife gets to the washing machine. And goes to shop. And then he goes to some greasy spoon downtown for lunch. She either meets other ladies at some place or she heats a can of soup at home. Then she goes to pick up the children. And it's all of them, rows and rows, house after house, of them all, and at night they turn on the TV. They are all living what I consider the kind of boredom that causes cancer. Or murder within the family. Or early divorce. Or children who turn out to be either sex maniacs, thieves, drug addicts, or dedicated archivists.

But boredom was unknown to me as a child in Mobile. Life was a dazzling, ever-changing kaleidoscope of colors and movement and sound and different flavors juxtaposed. You know art is the juxtaposition of unlikely objects. Boy, we have a lot of that in Mobile. Examples: a goat coming down the stairs of the house in town; English, rare English roses growing in a mud bank above where the alligators are sleeping. The relics of Mardi Gras that are in every attic. Mobile has more of this surreal quality than the rest of the South.

High Tide and High Wind

There were three maiden sisters in this big two-story house across from us on Conti Street. The Misses Nana, Evelina, and Jessamina Ebeltoft. In the parlor they taught music: Chopin, Schubert, and Schumann. They also taught ragtime. I often think, wouldn't it be wonderful to have a film of Miss Nana in her tight corset and that pale face, not one drop of makeup, playing ragtime? Then they taught painting on cloth. A lot of grand young ladies, for their wedding dresses, had white moiré taffeta with white lilacs and white roses painted on them. Seamstresses who were going to make wedding dresses took these classes from the Ebeltoft sisters. They didn't have anything to do, and they thought, What could I do? Then, you painted on cloth. Now, you might study computer science.

On the side of the house, there were all these oleanders and wax privet. Along the Conti Street side there were these little steps going up to the second floor, where they had a bootleg school. They taught shorthand and typing secretly upstairs. The Southern belles were taught music and painting on cloth in the parlor downstairs. Southern belles heavily veiled were taught typing and shorthand secretly upstairs.

My grandmother was best friends with those Ebeltoft sisters. They were a little dotty, and she was their source of information. They'd run over and ask the damnedest things.

"Oh, Miss Annie! Miss Annie! Do you brown your stew meat in bacon fat or butter?"

Whenever there was news of a storm coming, these three sisters would come wringing their hands and say to my grandmother, "Oh, Anne-Elizabeth, what are you going to serve for the hurricane?"

"Same as ever," Ma-Ma would say. "I'm going to bake a ham, roast some chickens, make a lot of bread and cookies. I have some new potatoes, a lot of dried beans and rice, some beautiful pearl barley."

The other lady across the street, Mrs. Allen, would say, "I don't keep potatoes in the house during a hurricane. They might ferment. Sometimes I'll loosen the corks in the good wine—you just don't know what will happen—those pressure changes. Things can blow up and potatoes will ferment."

A hurricane was party time. You couldn't go to school, you couldn't go to church, you couldn't go to work, you had to sit there and hope that nothing would blow in. So, what do you do? You have a party. Children, of course, love a hurricane. Children like anything that breaks monotony, because they are basically wild little animals, and they haven't been shoed yet, they haven't been spayed, they haven't been neutered, taught to heel with a ball and chain. So they are basically wild little animals, and any breaking of routine they love. During the '26 hurricane, the high tide and the high wind coincided and blew water as far as Broad Street. There was a boat with a beautiful dead lady lying in it floating up Dauphin Street. I remember thinking, How exciting.

Back then when there was no radio, people watched for the Coast Guard warning signals, the little flags that flew. They would stroll down to the wharf, and when they saw the hurricane warning, they closed up everything and went home. There were other signs that people knew then, apart from the storm warnings in the port. There was bird activity. When all the little birds left town, that's how you knew there was going to be a hurricane. And that's how I made my name as a weather prophet four years ago. They announced a hurricane, and I said there was not going to be a hurricane. The little birds were still out there picking on the lawn. When there is going to be a hurricane, the bluejays are the only birds too dumb to leave. Those are the only dead birds you find after a hurricane. They are so busy quarreling over territorial rights, they don't notice the storm.

We had twenty-three cats at Bayou Street—four social classes—and they all came in for the 1926 hurricane. Stable cats, courtyard cats, back porch cats, and house cats. And they did not mingle. The stable cats went to the servants' bathroom, stayed right there except in the tub. The courtyard cats took the butler's pantry. The back porch cats took the hall, and the house cats went in the parlor. The hurricane went on for three days, and every baking pan in that house was full of torn-up newspaper. On the third day all the cats stood in line without fighting to get out the back door. That's how we knew the hurricane was going to end.

Baroque Roman Catholic Reformed Druid

All the family was very Catholic, and by that I mean Baroque Catholic. Catholicism in the French or the Italian sense is like a very comfortable but loose garment. Very comfortable. It is tight enough that it will keep you warm in the winter and loose enough that you can be aerated in the summer. Baroque Catholic means that you don't go to church; you sit in a bar across the street and slip in for the last amen. That's how they do it in France. In Italy. It's a Mediterranean thing. Now the ladies might go to church, but the men would be in the bar across the street. It meant that you drank—didn't mean that you got falling-down drunk—it meant that you would not have good food without good wine. When I was christened at St. Joseph's Cathedral, the minute the priest let the holy water hit me, my grandfather stepped forward with a bottle of pear brandy and touched my lips, as his father had done for him and his grandfather had done for his father. It's to counteract the holy water. It is usually pear brandy, which is clear. My grandfather had made this pear brandy himself from those old sand pears. It's not antichurch. It's just the idea that you should learn to be worldly at the same time the church says learn to be spiritual.

During the dark days of Prohibition, my grandfather, this gentle, smiling creature who never allowed water at the table, just built this thing under the house where he made beer and wine. Our house rose high off the ground, you see, with latticing between the brick supports. The drip-drip-drip from the icebox on the porch made a permanent puddle of cold water under the house, and this was as close to a wine cellar as my grandfather could arrange. When there was going to be a hurricane, the first thing my grandfather boarded up was the wine cellar under the house. That came first. Then the pantry, then the parlor and all that. A little door was cut in the lattice under the pantry window. I used to love to go and just sit quietly on a stool under the house where there were all these vats working under that cheesecloth. I would just sit and listen: plop, plop, plop, plop. I loved to listen. Music of the spheres. Spherical grapes, spherical blackberries, spherical plums. Music of the spheres.

Just as almost everybody had a little patch of garden out back, they also had some kind of wine cellar under the house. That was how Mobile got through Prohibition. I remember once during the Depression, like maybe just before the repeal of Prohibition, I went with my grandfather under the First National Bank, where there were ruins of old Fort Charlotte that the British

milking the moon

had built. It had all been torn down, but the old huge, heavy brick arches were still underground where they stood out. Underneath everything there were still these storage halls where it was all kegs of Madeira wine belonging to the officers of the bank. I mean it was half a block long, kegs of Madeira and the smell of the oak. Baroque Catholic.

I used to love to go under the house, because it was so cool underneath the icebox with its huge blocks of ice that the man brought every other day. Mary Agnes Wolf, this darling girl, the daughter of Dr. Wolf across the street, was one of the few children in the neighborhood, and we played together a lot under the house. Her family was Catholic as mine was Catholic. And we had found a granite rock with a flat top and we'd put it by this underground lake—the puddle of ice water from the icebox under the house. In the bottom of this icebox was a pair of holes. They both had corks. But at some time of the day or some time of the night, you take the corks out and the drip would go down so that under the house under the back porch was like a tiny little icy lake. I had some funny pieces of cut glass and some tinfoil. We had a white porcelain statue of the Virgin standing in the little lake, and we always brought fresh flowers. It was Our Lady of Lourdes, or Our Lady of Mud, really. Our own little miraculous spring. And we used to sneak away with crackers and peanut butter and sit by it with our feet in that puddle and cool off on summer afternoons.

Because I went to church every morning, I had a proprietary sense of church. I went every morning at dawn, after the stove was heated, to help my grandmother arrange flowers on the altar at St. Joseph's. I carried the buckets of water; I was the water boy. So the smell of incense and the sound of Latin is somehow as much a part of me as traffic on Government Street or television is for a child growing up in Mobile today. It was just part of my day. The Gulf Coast was more Catholic then, and everybody had thousands of children, and everybody gave a daughter and a son to the church. I don't think there was any parental forcing, it was just the idea that one of the boys and one of the girls would most likely want to go into that field of endeavor. There were worldly priests and worldly nuns, and they were great teachers.

But then came these potato famine Irish Jesuits, whom I loathe because they are peasant Catholic, puritan Catholic. They are as bad as the Baptists. That terrible story of the last century when the Irish didn't do any varied farming—they latched onto the potato. Then there was this plague or raw weather or something for several years and there was the great potato famine when thousands of people died of hunger. A lot emigrated. Just shiploads. So there was a certain kind of sad, skinny Irish Jesuit. We had never seen anything like that before. Their descendants came to Mobile late, late, but a lot of the dry-as-dust type did get in.

In general, the Jesuits are great educators. What they say is, "We teach you to think, and when you learn how to think, the first thing you do is question the Roman Catholic Church." That's what the great Jesuits always say. That's what they're famous for. When you apply logical thought, you think yourself out of the church. But when my grandmother saw these potato famine Irish Jesuits inking in fig leaves on line drawings in textbooks of the classical statuary of gods and goddesses in the Vatican Museum, she said, "Little Eugene is not going to school with them!" That's why I went to public school. Of course, my grandmother was an emancipated lady in many ways. I can remember when she would go to the doctor, who was a friend of ours. He would say, "How are you feeling today, Anne-Elizabeth? Are you low in spirits?" "Oh, I'm very low in spirits," my grandmother would say. So then he would pull out a bottle of bourbon and pour two glasses.

After school I went to the Polish nuns with mustaches for catechism. But I refused to learn it because it was written on cheap paper. Some aspect of me was born snob in a certain way. I knew the life of Christ had to be on all-rag paper. I just knew it. Catechism was printed on the same paper as the comic section of the *Register*. I knew that wasn't right. So I wouldn't learn it, and I got beaten across the hand with a ruler. I still have it. I stole it from Sister. The Coca-Cola Company came to every Sunday school, and the first day they gave every child a Bible, a red pencil, a green pencil, and a ruler that says "Drink Coca-Cola." So I got rapped on the knuckles with a ruler that says "Drink Coca-Cola" by a Polish nun with a mustache who smelled like a wet collie dog for not learning my catechism.

I wouldn't say that I have thought myself out of the church, but I don't know that I believe in the conventional God as that silly ole boy in a white nightgown moving around in the sky. And I think Jesus was probably a pretty nice guy and obviously a wonderful carpenter, but let's not take it too far. I mean, I think he was a boy with some pretty good ideas. He was antigovernment, antichurch. But no one yet has ever followed his two main ideas, which are Do unto others and Love your neighbor. When people come to my door and tell me they want to share a few thoughts about Jesus, I say, "Honey, don't talk to me about Jesus—I'm a Baroque Roman Catholic Reformed Druid, and on Sunday mornings I go out in my garden and contemplate the lizards." It works every time.

But now if I thought I was going to do a deathbed scene, I would get on that phone to the archbishop, and I'd want the archbishop and twenty-four altar boys swinging their censers. I'd want a full production number. I do believe that there is some light, some blinding light, or some deafening noise, or some inconceivable dimension, up, out, way up, way out, way off, way down. We don't begin to understand anything about it. So, religion should be, for the intelligent person, a conscious seeking to understand everything. Even to understand a little of everything. And I suppose for me *RC* doesn't stand so much for Roman Catholic as it does for Rare Comprehension.

Saturdays

On Saturday mornings I would often go shopping with my grandmother. She'd put on her white gloves and clanking amethyst beads, because ladies, when they went downtown, even though it was just a few blocks away, wore their white gloves. They could go up the block to the neighbors' without their gloves or hats, but you didn't go more than a few houses away from where you lived without your hat, your demiveil, and your gloves. Two buttons or three. White gloves.

The first stop was a seed store. They had these wooden drawers filled with loose seeds, and there was this wonderful smell of onion and garlic and celery seeds and God knows what all. We'd stop and gossip. Then we went to the grocery store, although there was not an awful lot to get there, maybe a certain number of tinned things and dried beans. You had an account and paid once a week. When you paid you got "nappe," from *lagniappe,* a Creole word meaning something extra. That meant that if you bought twelve, you got a thirteenth, or if you bought a pound, you got an extra ounce.

Then we'd continue down to the fish place. After you chose it, you'd leave it there on ice to pick up on your way back. Then you went to the shop that had pheasants and ducks and guinea hens (oh, the blessed and forgotten guinea hen!) hanging in the window. They'd just been killed that morning, and their feathers were still clinging to them. You'd say, "I like the looks of that one," and boy, those feathers would fly. And you left that to be picked up on your way back.

If I close my eyes, I can still smell the heady aroma of Kress's five-and-ten-cent store. It was a blend: one could recognize some kind of pine oil solution used to clean the wooden floors (all the downtown stores had wooden floors) as well as the smell of the yellow and orange corn candy and the faint odor of the cardboard boxes used to pack all the "Made in Japan" stuff.

There were dishes and tea sets of either white or pale green. An endless number of toys. Dozens of inch-high towers, bridges, stone lamps, figures of fishermen, ladies with parasols, to make "dish gardens." Dozens of different kinds of yo-yos. Unbelievable roses made of waxed paper. And the "switch" counter: racks of switches—strands of real human hair—hanging limply from stainless-steel racks. I used to stare at them. They were uniform in length, uniformly marcelled, arranged in color gradations, and I never, in a decade of every-Saturday visits, saw anybody buy one.

Then the counter of cardboard signs: DIPHTHERIA, MEASLES, BAD DOG, INFORMATION, FOR RENT, FOR SALE. And, back in the days when people read books, a surprising book counter. There used to be a publishing company in Racine, Wisconsin, called Whitman Co. which published ten-cent books in vast quantities, and then went highbrow with twenty-five-cent books with colored illustrations. I still remember one ten-cent series about a boy who ran away from home and joined the circus and toured the world. His name was Joe Strong, and there was this endless series about him. *Joe Strong the Boy Magician, Joe Strong with the Circus, Joe Strong Goes to Sea.* I'd buy one every Saturday and read it in time to finish the next Friday. I still have a very fine anthology of American poetry put together by Harriet Monroe. Ten cents at Kress. And the picture books had illustrations by the likes of Willy Pogany and Maxfield Parrish.

Most little girls bought their first lipstick, their first perfume, from the toiletries counter at Kress. I loved the tool counter with different-size monkey wrenches and screwdrivers neatly lined up. Twenty-five cents would get you a good hammer. There was a shoe department with a very attractive smell of leather and the faint warmish aroma of coarse white tissue paper. The frame sections specialized in lurid reproductions of Scottie dogs, American Beauty roses, *Light of the World, Blue Boy,* and the Grand Canyon at sunset. But the frames were wooden, and the gold leaf was real. You'd have to get a bank loan to even touch one of those frames nowadays.

Mary Jane Scruggs and Margaret McAllister and Carolyn Cowden could be found gossiping and giggling at the soda fountain every Saturday afternoon. They all studied music, and they'd go to Jessie French Music Shop in the Saenger Building and buy their sheet music of "Clair de Lune," "Whispering Silver Birches," "Girl with the Flaxen Hair," "Moccasin Dance," then sail unswervingly down Dauphin to Kress for the "tutafo." Every Saturday Kress had a five-cent special from tutafo (two to four). Some of them would probably be forbidden by the Department of Health nowadays, but we loved them. Imagine a mixture of neon artificial orange and root beer.

One Christmas, Agnes Griffith played tunes on an upright piano in the record department. She was a delightful lady who played the mighty console organ at the Saenger every matinee before the film. She specialized in "Peanut Vendor" with variations, but she played Christmas carols at Kress, and when she went to have lunch at the counter, they put on a record of Maurice Chevalier singing "Every little breeze seems to whisper Louise . . . ," and a whole gaggle of sorority girls leaned on the counter and went all moon-cow.

The chicken salad sandwiches were famous, and I once talked to an old black cook who made them. "We puts a little mustard in the dressin'," she told me, "and we uses *all* the chicken. . . . I cuts up the skin really small and uses the livers and the guzzards too . . . cut up little-bitty . . . that's what gives the flavor. . . ."

Then the candy counter! Permanently stocked: cinnamon hearts, jelly beans (the black licorice ones separate), the chewiest gumdrops ever, heavenly hash, peanut brittle, chocolate-covered peppermints, and peppermint sticks. Those peppermint sticks were rather porous, and all the children then used them as straws in a glass of lemonade. About 1939 Kress suddenly stocked another kind of peppermint stick from some other manufacturer. They were solid, not porous. So long, peppermint lemonade. If only they'd bottled that taste.

There was also Fischer's Toy Shop. I saw some things there—I still wish I had them. It was the toy theaters that threw me. Oh, those toy theaters. There was one that had the five settings for Balfe's opera *The Bohemian Girl* and one extra set of an art nouveau hotel lobby not unlike the Cawthon Hotel. I wanted that. In the middle of the stage was a trapdoor. And there was a red velvet curtain with gold fringe you could pull. I must have written three thousand plays for that theater I didn't have.

At that time, children were given nice toys, but you were expected to make things, and I used to turn the fire screen around for my theater. On the street corners in Mobile, there were Punch and Judy shows just like in England, exactly the same figures. When I first saw that Punch and Judy show, almost immediately I began making marionettes. I made marionettes, made up plays, and just turned the fire screen around for my theater. EVERYBODY was expected to attend my productions.

And life being what it is, after I recovered from scarlet fever, I was still frail and so I was given a week before going back to school. And Mr. Marsh had bought that theater for one of the Hempstead girls and given it to her as a Christmas present. Now the Hempsteads were cousins of the Marshes. And my uncle Francis married Martha Marsh. Well, Martha Marsh borrowed that theater and turned up at my grandmother's house. "See, I thought little Gene might enjoy playing with this." It was that theater with the five settings of *The Bohemian Girl.* So I had plays every night. Boy, if you didn't sit down and watch my play, you were on my shit list.

And then, of course, it went back to the Hempsteads' household because Louise Hempstead said, "Well, I'd give it to you, little Gene, but I'm keeping it for when I have children of my own." When I got back from the Second World War, the first house I went to was the Hempsteads' over on Dauphin Street. And I said, "Oh, Miss Louise, you know, Miss Margaret," and then finally I said, "Well, you know, incidentally, you all had that toy theater." "Oh," she said, "we threw it out." She said, "You know, it was under the stairs, and every time the stairs were mopped, we didn't realize it but the dirty water got on it and we just threw it out." And I went out of that house and never went back.

Often my grandmother would send me to the Lyric Theater for the matinee of the vaudeville. Rebecca would take me—she loved it, too. We'd sit there and just aah. I was like five or six. It was a wonderful theater with this huge painted backdrop of the old square. It was painted to be broad daylight, but there were these little twinkling stars from where the performers had punched in to see how the audience was filling up, and the lights backstage would shine through the drop. One of my earliest memories is of staring at that curtain and wondering how the stars could be twinkling in broad daylight. There was a full orchestra in the pit, and a very good one.

All the shows were wonderful. I can remember a British comedian who sang Scottish songs, a pair of Russian dancers, Italian acrobats, W. C. Fields, Mae West. I'll never forget Mae West, the singing comedienne with the long cigarette holders and this lamé dress. She sang, "I'm just wild about Har-ry, and Har-ry's wild about me." Or that grand mad star Eva Tanguay, in her high frizz wig and skintight silver lamé, who sang, "I don't care, I don't care, I don't care what people think of me," ending her number with a high kick which sent her flying over the footlights and into the sponge-lined bass drum in the pit. Oh, Lord.

And the intermission was nothing like Coca-Cola and popcorn. Why, they wouldn't have allowed popcorn in that velvet theater, with red velvet curtains with gold fringe and this polished marble foyer. What they had was a little counter with a little striped awning that sold George's Chocolates. Rebecca always had a napkin in the pocket of her apron so she could unsmear me afterward.

One of the numbers—it was the only time I ever peed in my pants. It started very low, this music, with a lot of pizzicato. "Shine, little glowworm. Shine, little glowworm, glimmer, glimmer . . ." Then there was this very pretty girl singing it. And it was this gorgeous backdrop of forests, a kind of eighteenth- or nineteenth-century operatic backdrop. You know, green and tangled trees, and all across the back were little lightbulbs twinkling. And she sang, "Shine, little glowworm, glimmer, glimmer . . ." That was okay.

But then came four big green velvet frogs. And they picked her up and she sang the last verse sitting on their shoulders, and they put her down and she curtsied and then vanished somehow. Then they took their heads off and started tumbling like acrobats dressed as frogs with no heads, and I couldn't take it. I peed in my pants. Lord, how I loved it.

On Saturdays at the Lyric Theater there would be a matinee for children. That's where I met Truman Capote. We were never pals. We were acquaintances called Southerners. He came to Mobile on Saturdays to have his teeth straightened and go to the doctor and various things like that. He was Truman Persons from Monroeville, but he was called Bulldog. He had some funny underbite where the lower jaw sticks out, and he looked exactly like a bulldog. One night at this party in New York, suddenly, I looked across the room and there was Truman. And I said, "Bulldog! What are you doing here?" And he said, "Sh, sh. I'm Truman Capote now." Well, see, I knew him as Bulldog Persons.

We both belonged to the Sunshine Club, which sponsored free matinees at the Lyric Theater for children. In the Sunday *Register* there was the Sunshine Page. This lady called Disa Stone had this children's page and this Sunshine Club where children wrote and sent in what they wrote and vied for prizes. The grand prize was a pony. For his contribution to the Sunshine Page and for the contest, Truman had spied on this old man who lived up the street in Monroeville and was a real old crank. Even then he was already mixing fiction and reportage. Why not? But let's not say he *invented* the reportage-fiction, fiction-reportage style. Daniel Defoe would be giggling in his grave at the thought, not to mention a dozen French writers. And some of his things are so full of Gothic narrative impossibilities that one wants to say, "Now, Cousin Truman, come down outa that tree!"

Anyway, he wrote this rather long piece called "Old Mr. Busybody, by Truman Persons." His aunt, when he told her, rushed to Mobile and went to the *Register* and said: "You cannot publish that. It is too true a description of our neighbor. He'll sue us, he'll smash our windows, I don't know what he'll do. I want to take that back." And she did. Years later when I saw him in

Paris, the first thing Truman said to me was, "Oh, Eugene, I so wanted to win that pony."

I thought he was a hoot. He was this tiny little thing with a tough little bulldog body and a high squeaky voice. But there was this bully boy, J. L. Bedsole, who was very tall, a basketball player, and had a good opinion of himself. His family was very wealthy—the Bedsole Drugs and all. J.L. was always teasing this little thing and doing crazy things to him. Truman would just say, "Leave me alone," but one day he had had enough of it. One day Bulldog backed all the way across the lobby—he looked exactly like an English bulldog—and he put his head down and charged, hitting J.L. right in the genitals. J.L. never went near that bulldog again, ever.

I saw him off and on in Mobile, and I saw him a couple of times in New York. Then, when I was in Paris, where I helped start the *Paris Review,* I heard he was coming to town. I thought that would be a great interview for our interview series. So I sent a note to him and said, "I've got to interview you." He said, "Okay, fine, come on over to my hotel, we'll talk for a while and go have dinner." I went to his hotel, and a sort of servant or something took me into this sitting room, and suddenly here came Truman, this small bulldog. What I saw had nothing to do with the famous chaise-longue, checked-vest photograph that amused half of America and made the other half nervous in 1948. I said, "Bulldog! You haven't changed a bit!" I hadn't seen him in six years. Then out of the bedroom behind him came this white bulldog, looking just like him. I said, "Bulldog!" It was too much. The two of them, looking just alike.

He was a charming person. He was an imp. He was a real imp. His sense of humor was unbelievable. After he got into New York and all that thing of drink and drugs and fancy New York society—that wasn't the Capote I knew. I remember one typical Bulldog story. We had lunch in New York in a restaurant that was upstairs. You went into a kind of bar, and then the dining room was upstairs. We were very late and I called and said, "How late do you serve?" and they said you can order until so-and-so and you can stay until—I don't know—four o'clock or something. So we went there and we started talking about the South and about Mobile and about Monroeville. We just got going as Southerners always do. Got going on the South. You know, Southerners together in New York City: Lord. It got very late, and the waitress came up and she was making comments—hinting—that it was time for us to leave, but we still hadn't overstayed. So he said, "All right." He was very courteous, very sweet. And with a haste that I shall never forget, he went to every table and loosened the metal cap on the salt shaker. She was coming up the stairs with the bill. He got back to his table and was sitting there. He did all of the tables in about two minutes. A very Bulldogian joke.

He was not a bitch. He became that after so many people had made fun of his being small, and the fact that he had an early success made a few other writers nasty toward him. We always got along well together. But he and Gore Vidal had a strange feud. Gore Vidal's mother was the daughter of an Oklahoma senator, and he was a snob. He always thought that Truman was kind of poor white trash. They feuded from day one. It was verbal more than anything: rival writers, rival Southerners. The two biggest backbiters I have ever known are Truman Capote and Gore Vidal. And they were both back-biting each other. Mention one to the other and right away they would start in. I don't feel that way. I feel that we're all in this fight together. Don't you bite my ass, and I won't bite yours.

Not a Usual Childhood

T hen came a moment of confusion and funerals. My grand-father's business failed just after the 1929 crash, and not long after that, he died. Then a few years later, my grandmother died. About two or three years after my grandmother's death, my father died of a heart attack. That began this other period of my life, when I lived with Mr. Gayfer at Dog River and was chauffeured to Murphy High School in a limousine. I took three hundred–something stools and set them up at thirty-something tables to earn my breakfast and lunch because Mr. Gayfer thought I needed that experience. Then after school I was picked up by the chauffeur and driven home.

There are at least sixteen stories about how Mr. Gayfer got me. One, of course, is that I was his illegitimate child. One is that he was a wicked old queer and I was his lover boy. Another is that he bought me from my grand-mother because he wanted someone to live in his house and keep him amused. God knows I kept him amused. Some say that my grandmother left me to Mr. Gayfer in her will as a surprise. But the truth is, Mr. Gayfer came forward when my grandmother died because her family, the Luenbergs, had taken on his three orphaned great-aunts from Switzerland in the 1870s.

Mr. Gayfer's father was Charles J. Gayfer from England, who came to Mobile and started a quality department store of the sort they have in Lon-don. It was clothes for men, women, and children and china, glass, silver, and linens. It was right on the corner of Bienville Square. A delightful set of people worked there, little ladies and maiden aunts and spinster daughters of good but poor families. My Mr. Gayfer, Hammond Gayfer, did not actively run the department store. There were all kinds of partners and lawyers—he wasn't interested. After he got to London and Paris, all he wanted was the arts. I think Mr. Gayfer was—cheated—shall we say? I don't know by whom. I think he was not as wealthy when he died as he was before.

He was a rare bird, a rare creature, and a real charmer. He could charm the paper off the walls. He had studied with some of the most famous magicians, and I can remember on my birthdays, he would say, "What's that in your nose?" And he would pull a five-dollar piece out of my nose. If I ever asked him for a dime or a nickel, he would say, "What's that in your ear?"

He had been to Sewanee and was a classical scholar. Then his father gave him a couple of years in Europe. He had lived in London and lived in Paris. He wrote that wonderful play that was in print until a few years ago called *The Subsequent History of Mr. Jonah*. It's a long one-act about the divorce proceedings of Mrs. Jonah against Mr. Jonah. Her complaint is, "I just don't believe that fish story. He was gone from home forty days—I just don't believe that fish story." It's a very amusing play. It has a black cook who talks in dialect—I guess that's one of the reasons it's not performed anymore. There is a judge trying to make everything okay for everybody, and then there is a traveling salesman. It is very funny. He wrote other plays and a lot of poetry.

Mr. Gayfer always encouraged me to write and paint and to do marionettes and to act. He never suggested what I should do, but he said, "Stay at home from school if you want to do that." In Mr. Gayfer's household, nothing was ever forbidden, nothing was ever encouraged too strenuously. He never said, You must do this or you must do that. He was this delightful person with whom I shared a house. He lived on that side, I lived on this side. We met at the breakfast table. We met at the luncheon table. We met on the porch to talk about books. I was a guest in his house.

The house had been built to his own design. You came onto this huge screened porch which faces Dog River. Instead of a hall, there was a living room through the middle. You go straight through and then three steps up there was the dining room, which he built to be like a little salon theater. It had a stage, a red piano, one of the most advanced kind of phonographs, and a tremendous record collection. He often had entertainers there, little concerts or little readings. The Children's Theater did performances there on occasion; I played King Midas there once.

Outside, he had jungle. He didn't like lawns. There were all these kinds of crazy trees and big magnolias. They had a hard time keeping me out of the trees, monkey that I am. There was one huge, ancient magnolia, and by starting in the camphor tree next to it, I could get to the first big limbs of the magnolia and get right to the top. The three huge limbs at the top were just made to sit in with your feet up and read. That was my secret place.

And I used to go exploring back in the woods. There were woods and woods and woods, with this little creek going through. And oh, the wildflowers. And snakes and birds and coons and possums and tortoises. And of course, all of that river. One of my favorite escapades was to get in this inner tube with my feet over and just float a mile down the river to this fishing bay. I'd go in and call and Mr. Gayfer would send the chauffeur to bring me back. Then there was this flat-bottomed canoe. At dawn I used to get in that flat-bottomed canoe and paddle myself across that huge stretch of Dog River and up Halls Mill Creek. Then it was all just wilderness. There were very few houses. The birds and animals, butterflies and flowers—oh it was beautiful. They would have to pry me out of that canoe. I loved that sense of skimming over the water. The chauffeur had this megaphone he finally got, and he would call out, "Where is Eugene?" all over Dog River.

And I told Mr. Gayfer about the toy theater I longed for. So he had a carpenter make this rather wonderful reproduction. Then I made these marionettes. But there were also some made by Madame Alexander, the famous doll maker. Mr. Gayfer, for some reason, was in touch with her to get dolls for Gayfer's Department Store. So he got from her a set of characters which he gave me. And I had made, more or less invented, a control you could operate in one hand, so I could do one-man shows. That's what I did in prisons and oyster camps and schools and out in the middle of nowhere. I did all those for free. And then when I did birthday parties for well-heeled Mobilians, I charged. They loved me at birthday parties because I could keep the children absolutely quiet for thirty minutes. So the parents were always delighted to have me. I did *Little Red Riding Hood, Hansel and Gretel, Tom Tic Toc, The Child That Cried for the Moon, Sleeping Beauty,* and then I had a little thing called *The Clown in the Hat,* where there was this normal-size opera hat, a man's evening hat, and there was something in it. The children would just know there was something in it. Because there would be something moving, and finally there were two eyes that came up out of it and then this face. It was a clown. It was all very slow, and finally the children would be just about to pee in their pants. Then he puts one leg up very carefully and climbs out. He would run around the hat and come down to the audience, and he'd say to the children, "Boobaloobaloobaloo!" and run and jump back in the hat. Children love any sign of disrespect. That was one of my greatest numbers. That's all there was to it. The clown in the hat.

When I said, "Mr. Gayfer, I don't want to go to school today. I have a performance with the marionettes on Friday, and I really want to make some new scenery."

He would say, "You don't have to go to school. It is much more important that you paint the scenery. You don't learn anything from school. School is just something invented to keep children away from home so their parents can have some peace. If you want to find out anything, it's all here." His house was papered with books. He had *The Complete English Poets*. That's where I first read Robert Herrick and Andrew Marvell. I just discovered them on my own and fell desperately in love with those poems. "The Garden" by Marvell: "What wond'rous life is this I lead! / Ripe apples drop about my head . . ." I just flipped.

Mr. Gayfer was a true patron of the arts. He was one of the people who gave money to restore the old ceilings of the Bethel Theater on Church Street across from City Hall. That was the Little Theater, which became Aimee King's Children's Theater. He helped all kinds of painters and writers and black singers—any black singer. He paid their tuition. One of his friends was Marie Stanley, who wrote that scandalous novel of the twenties called *Gulf Stream*, in which the black heroine commits suicide. She started a national debate: Do blacks commit suicide?

There were all kinds of people, famous singers and entertainers, passing through. He knew all kinds of people from his *Wanderjahre* in Europe. Alexandra Dagmar, a famous variety actress from England, lived in Mr. Gayfer's house the same time I did. She had danced in the chorus of the original *Pinafore* as a girl. While in England she had invested in some sort of real estate near Grand Bay or Theodore. It was supposed to be a peach orchard. When she retired and decided to come here, she discovered that the peach orchard she bought was underwater. It was a swamp. Mr. Gayfer took her in, and she lived with him for a while. He opened his house to all sorts of people. She was three thousand years old when she lived with us, but she was still a variety actress. She got up at six o'clock every morning and had the blackest of black boiled black coffee. You could smell it a mile away, that hard-roasted coffee and hard toast with marmalade. Then at six-thirty A.M. she went to that red piano and sang one of her hit tunes. I loved it.

When I was a sophomore in high school, Mr. Gayfer had these friends in for the summer, and one of them was this very young man with bright red hair and greenish white skin named Robert Penn Warren, who was writing his first novel, *Night Rider*, in the backyard, in the Chinese pagoda, where the pheasants had lived until the cats ate them. The pagoda had a card table, a folding chair, and Robert Penn Warren writing *Night Rider*. Then on the

milking the moon

front porch, Conrad Albrizio, the Italian painter, was painting a view of the river from the porch. And his wife, who was Imogen Inge, was writing her first novel, *The Breath*. I was dyeing cloth for the Children's Theater. So it was like a little art colony.

Then, of course, years later I knew Robert Penn Warren in Rome, when he was a Fellow at the American Academy. Ralph Ellison and I interviewed him together for the *Paris Review*. Ralph Ellison brought his tape recorder, and I brought my notepad. Ralph printed a literal and scrupulous transcription of his portion of the interview, and I—re-created—from my notes my portion of the interview. Life being what it is, Robert Penn Warren quarreled with Ralph Ellison over his part of the interview but had only the kindest things to say about mine.

Mr. Gayfer was in love with Aimee King, who was this tiny little lady, and an actress, a great actress. Had she not been of a strict Presbyterian household, poor darling, she would have gotten to New York and become a sensational actress. Her story is another novel. She married David King from King's Landing, and he came down with tuberculosis on the honeymoon. She nursed him for twenty-something years. Finally she left him in Sante Fe, which is where you went in those days if you were tubercular. Some said she was Mr. Gayfer's mistress, but I think they were merely engaged to be married. She and her husband had agreed to divorce. Then he died. Then Mr. Gayfer died two weeks later.

Aimee King started this Children's Theater at the Little Theater downtown, after school. Gifted rich children paid double, gifted no-money families had scholarships. Cross section of Mobile society. She did scenes from the classical mythologies of all civilizations: Greece, England, Persia, China, *Arabian Nights*, and "Snow White and the Seven Dwarfs." We had to look at pictures from the period and learn a little bit about the play. Then we would improvise scenes from the story. Then she would give us a script, and we learned it and rehearsed it and did it with a full orchestra.

I did a lot of scenery for the Children's Theater, dyeing cloth for the costumes. I had learned from a Frenchwoman who came to Gayfer's, a representative of some fabric firm in New York, that the most beautiful fabrics were double-dyed. You dye a cloth one color and then dip it in another. You can mix the two dye vats together and dip it once, but then something else happens. All the great French silks are dipped first in one color and then overlaid with another color. I must have dyed three thousand miles of unbleached domestic for Aimee King. She was a great costume designer. She could take an old doormat and make it look like mink. She could take cheesecloth—that soft cheesecloth they sell for dust rags—and make floating ladies like you wouldn't believe. I remember once she had a scene of Joséphine and her ladies, and even from the second row you would have sworn that was a rare and precious fabric, but it was three layers of that cheesecloth, each one a different color, cut on the bias. The figures just floated. Most women, I would say 101 percent of all females, look better in skirts cut on the bias. When it is cut like that, it has the possibility of movement, and no one can see your old ass moving.

To me, if you are going to make theater, you've got to know how to dye cloth, you should design costumes, and paint scenery. To get it the way you want it. And you have to write the plays to get the plays you want.

I often stayed alone on school nights in this little studio above the Children's Theater on Water Street in downtown Mobile. A port city was marvelous all night every night. A wonderful carnival of restaurants and bars. Then on the weekends I would go to Mr. Gayfer's house on Dog River. That was my childhood.

Not a usual childhood. I was always turned loose. I was accepted as an individual entity. Not as a child, not as a little boy, not as a state, not as a student, not as a little beast. I was an entity. No one ever told me that I was a child, you see.

I never really liked school, but I was fortunate in some of the teachers I got. I liked kindergarten, because we made things out of paper and glued things and dressed up as things and played music. I can remember having wonderful lunches in a brown paper bag. They were bacon-and-tomato sandwiches made on Smith's bread. They were always on the top inside the paper bag. But we always repacked our lunch the minute we got to school and put the sandwich on the bottom so the tomatoes would squash with the mayonnaise and go into the bread. So you'd have this squashy tomato sandwich with the crisp bacon and mayonnaise. It's divine.

I went to first grade on Old Shell Road and had Miss Jones. I already knew a little bit about how to read because my grandmother had taught me to read from the names of the colors in the watercolor box. I could read *ultramarine, indigo, rose madder, mocha,* and all that. So I didn't like the first-grade textbook that said "Baby Ray had a dog. Baby Ray loved the dog. The dog loved Baby Ray." Well, for me, how could that compare to *ultramarine, indigo, rose madder, and mocha?* So I was mostly bored in grammar school. I was always way ahead of my classes, because I could read far more advanced things than the assignment. And I just couldn't listen to some of that yuck. I was so lucky with my teachers because they more or less turned me loose and just let me sit in the back of the room at my desk and draw.

milking the moon

When I was a sophomore at Murphy High School, I had Miss Annie Lou White. We all, if we're lucky, remember a teacher who "opened the door" for us. They're not teachers. They don't teach. They huff and they puff, they squeal and they squeak, they grasp and they hasp, and they open doors and windows, and they slam doors and windows, and they suddenly say, "Oh, dear, next week is the last day of school. Write a paper." They're the great teachers. I call them lid lifters. In everybody's life, there are teachers like that. She was mine.

She was a doctor's daughter from the backwoods of Mississippi. And she, like myself, had never been recommended a book or forbidden a book. She had a natural curiosity about everything. She never married, but she was not like some of the mean-natured frustrated American old maids. She was like some of those English spinsters—just a jolly soul interested in flowers, wildlife, books, everything on earth. She would say, "Of course, I don't really expect you children to understand much of Chaucer's language, even though they've modernized it here. You have to remember that French and English were very close. And speaking of French, I want to play an Edith Piaf song for you all." She'd wind up the phonograph, and here comes Edith Piaf in English class. That was our Chaucer lesson. But of course, you think, Well, Chaucer. I'm going to look up that damn Chaucer, you know. She would say, "That reminds me, there's a book by Jules Renard, in French. You must notice this drawing by Degas. Did you see the color of the sycamore leaves this morning?"

The minute she saw that somebody was perking up at something and not doing the usual head-on-the-elbow, she would give something special to that person. Or call them up afterward and say, "Have you read this?" On her famous little three-by-fives in this clear little hand she'd write down the name of some strange book. On the blackboard she was always writing titles and names, and she'd say, "Oh, there's a book that hasn't yet achieved the status of classic, but the young men should perhaps read it." Then she'd say, "Now there's a poet who explains a lot about the female mind. And, oh, I don't imagine boys would enjoy it, but the girls should all read Edna St. Vincent Millay and Sara Teasdale." Of course, the boys couldn't wait to get their hands on it. Sometimes she'd come in and sit at her desk and say, "I'm rereading the unfashionable poets. None of these are in the textbook, but you can be sure that when they make a new textbook in ten years' time, what is there now will be out. Some of these will be in." She had this casual way of indicating the vast world of ideas we might investigate.

Everybody who studied with her loved her, because she had this absolute radar. She understood unruly Southern boys going through the first ghastly phase of adolescence, not certain whether they were men or boys, men or children. She had this wonderful way of dealing with people. I can remember her saying, "Now Herbert, you look real tired today. Why don't you just go sit in that empty seat in the back row and put your head down on the desk." Herbert would have been up all night doing God knows what, and you could see it in his face. She could tell at a glance when girls were having what we used to call their first moments of femininity. She never would say anything outright in class. God, no. But she would say, "Now, Mabel Ann, come here." Mabel Ann would come. And she'd say, "Mabel Ann, would you take this to the principal's office?" And she would give her a note which said "You just sit down in the waiting room at the principal's office until you feel better." The real proof is that some of those unruly Southern boys who sat in the back and hated English class have come forward and written to her years later from remote places saying, "I remember your class. And I remember what you said about blah, blah, blah. I remember how you made us read blah, blah, blah. I just wanted to say that I remember your class and appreciate it." She gets letters like that constantly from all over the world. When I think of her, I think of windows, doors, screens, shutters, all flying open, and cross-currents carrying me away.

But except for her class, I failed everything. I just didn't study. And I couldn't take what was called physical education. I just couldn't take it. I loathed basketball and football and baseball. I loathed all that. The very idea. I didn't like balls coming toward me, and the stench of those shoes was too much. Those sneakers smelled so bad. It wasn't the smell of sweat. If you live around horses and dogs and all that, a little human sweat doesn't do a thing to you. But there was something nasty about those woolen socks inside those Keds, that kind of infinitely souring, sweaty foot in sweaty Keds. And the Keds keep that stink. Stinky feet in stinky socks in stinky Keds—I just couldn't do it. So after I went to the gym twice and smelled those Keds, I sat under the stairs during physical education. They had monitors in the halls then. You had to have a pass card to be roaming in the corridors between classes. So I stole a big monitor's chair with a wide arm to write on and put it under those stairs. I sat there for three years during gym class and no one caught me. I was a monitor. On a couple of occasions when somebody would come, I would say, "Where are your pass cards?" Of course, I always let them go. "Next time be sure you have your pass card."

At the end of my senior year, they called me into the principal's office and said in wonder, "We can't graduate you. You have not enough credits, and you have never had any physical education." I got out of high school because I had won a national prize, a state prize, and two local prizes for my drawings and my poems. They said, "Well, you don't have enough credits, but you're on the graduation program for all your honors. So we'll graduate you, but you've got to come back this summer and study the Constitution and commercial geography." That's how I got my high school diploma.

There was this old guy who fancied himself a professor teaching commercial geography. It was the principal products of the Nile Valley. What is the source of rubber? How many cubic yards of raw steel does the United States export every year? Things of passionate concern to me. He was one of those teachers who flipped a key ring as he talked. Since I have the poet's memory where nothing is lost and the right stimulus, the right smell, the right unexpected sound, will bring back two encyclopedias' worth of recollections, sometimes a certain key ring—not all—it must be a high B-flat—will bring back the chief products of the Nile Valley. Because he did it throughout the class. He'd pick up the key ring and clink, clink, put it down. So for me, commercial geography is a series of key clinks.

When I was just out of high school, I went to work painting Mardi Gras floats under Edmond de Celle. His mother was the famous variety actress Alexandra Dagmar, the one who lived with Mr. Gayfer when the peach orchard she bought turned out to be a swamp. He was this wonderful half Belgian, half Danish painter, a professional, who came here as a young man and stayed on to design Mobile's Mardi Gras parades. The preparation for the parade took a full year; a brief two hours of glory trundling through the downtown streets, then back to the warehouse to be dismantled. The locations of the warehouses were secret, the themes of next year's parade a dark secret.

Edmond de Celle did the double-O Ms [OOM], the most snobby and the oldest of the parades. And they had their den, as it was called, this corrugated tin warehouse where the parade was built, in the north part of town which was close to the city dump. The dirt track leading to it had this row of houses, these fantasy structures built by the people who "worked" the dump. There was one little house built entirely of Coca-Cola signs. And there were several that had bottle trees, with bottles tied on trees to catch the bad spirits. There were others that had little garden beds edged entirely with Nehi bottles turned upside down.

The warehouse was huge, big enough for the eight wagons which were the emblem float and seven subsequent floats of the parade. The walls were hung with life-size horses, dragons, giants' heads, urns, arches, wings, and cloud formations which could be used again.

The wooden substructure for the float would take shape over this chicken wire, cunningly bent, stretched, and curved to make the basic forms. Then a long two or three weeks of weaving strips of brown paper through all the chicken wire to give a base for the papier-mâché which came next. A great cauldron bubbled over a pile of pine knots: a vat of flour paste was cooked with cow-hoof glue and bluestone added. The sheets of brown paper were dipped in, wrung out, then smoothed over all the surfaces of the figures. What a stink! Several months of this, then the prime coats of paint were brushed on. This was made up as we used it, of dry powdered pigment, water, boiling cow-hoof glue, and was even stinkier than the paste. Maestro de Celle painted all the details and important bits. In spite of the Depression, pounds of Dutch gold leaf were used on the floats. Sometimes crowns and thrones or certain details would be covered flatly, but usually the squares of gold leaf were applied onto a dab of glue so that the four corners were left fluttering. Mules drew all the floats then. When the float moved down the street, the hundreds of moving scraps of gold leaf caught the light of the torches, and the float seemed literally to burn. Everything remembered from childhood always seems grander and better, but my, when one looked down Government Street and saw the rose red glow on the overhanging oaks and heard those distant drums, it was very exciting indeed. For me, just to see the bare platforms suddenly covered with strange, mysterious-looking skeletons of chicken wire molded in the beginning of something, then weeks of papier-mâché, dipping brown paper into flour paste, molded in on the wire, then the grand coat, then the gold leaf, then the float, then the parade: it was a thrill.

Anything to Avoid a Nice Christian Household

The summer I graduated from high school, Mr. Gayfer died of a heart attack or stroke, very unexpectedly. Arrangements had been made, we thought, for me to go to LSU and be under a sort of protectorship of Robert Penn Warren, who taught down there. But Mr. Gayfer never got around to making a will. So one morning I woke up and had no home, no family, no guardian, and that's when these social workers wanted to put me in a nice Christian household. When Mr. Gayfer died, everybody said, "Poor little Eugene, poor little Eugene, what will we do with poor little Eugene?" All these people were saying I must be put in a nice Christian household, and I heard them. I got to the social services thing downtown, and I said, "Look, I've got to find out how to get into the Civilian Conservation Corps." The lady said, "Usually it is for boys who have gotten into trouble and are sent away from home." So in a sense, I ran away and joined it. Anything to avoid being placed in a nice Christian household.

The one I joined was a forestry camp in Richton, Mississippi. I was the only non–reform school boy in my group of fifty. They had all either tumbled some farmgirl down in the hay or stolen from the collection plate in church. Most of them were illiterate, totally. They were from the backwoods of the backwoods, where they sit playing poker all day on the front porch and then finally the mama appears at the front door and says, "You varmints, get out of here and get me some meat. There ain't no meat in this house. Go on. Git." Their rifles are leaning in the corner of the house, and they would get their rifles, get the shells, and say, "Oh, Ma, shut up." They go out in the woods and get Mama some meat, then go back to playing poker. Then they might say, "Is Joe tending the still today? Who's tending the still?" Back in the back even farther back—moonshine.

I was terrified of those boys at first. There was a bully, of course. It was the huge feeble-minded boy who saw right away that I was Something Else. I sized him up. I realized they were looking askance at me because they found out the first day I could read and write. So I didn't say anything to anybody at all. On the third night, I climbed on top of my locker and swung by my knees from a beam in the ceiling. They stopped everything. There was a silence. I just swung by my knees, and then I got down, got into bed, and went to sleep. The next night when it was time to put the lights out, I did it again.

There was this one really very pleasant guy who had a good sense of humor. He was one of those whose eyes made wrinkles when he laughed. He said to me, "Walter, are you going to tell us what you're doing?" I said, "I do this every night before I go to bed. It gets the cobwebs out of my brain." Then this boy said, "I told you he weren't like nobody else." Then they became friendly. Again it was that respect for the monkey. You don't know what the monkey is going to do. He moves too fast and can strangle you with his strange tail if you're too mean to him.

They fascinated me because they had a body of weather lore and weather knowledge, as the illiterate do, that we don't have. They would look at the sky and say, "About three o'clock this afternoon, rain, I reckon, coming from the north." They would look at a patch of woods and say, "Well, it looks like rabbits been in there this morning early." And they would say, "Deer in there, and deer in there." I couldn't see anything at all, but they could see a series of twigs or a series of trampled leaves on the ground, and they knew. They loved when it rained because they could stay in the barracks and play poker rather than go out and plant trees. They had a rain god named Raymond, and they would look at the sky and say, "Come on down, Raymond!"

Those backwoods boys also had some stanzas of "The Jolly Tinker" that had never been recorded before. It's a folk song that came from Elizabethan England to the mountains of Virginia, then to the mountains of Carolina, then to north Georgia, then to north Alabama, then to Mississippi. And it's a good song.

> *There was a Jolly Tinker,*
> *He came from France,*
> *All he wanted to do was fiddle, fuck, and dance,*
> *With his long lean liver flopper, kidney whopper, belly rubber*
> *Long lean baby maker hanging to his knees.*

And it goes on for three hundred stanzas.

> *The Tinker he died, he went to Hell,*
> *Swore to fuck the devil if he didn't treat him well,*
> *With his long lean liver flopper, kidney whopper, belly rubber*
> *Long lean baby maker hanging to his knees.*

> *There was an old lady, age of ninety-three,*
> *Said let the Jolly Tinker get to me!*

I was able to sit down with Alan Lomax in Paris and thrill him with some stanzas of "The Jolly Tinker" he had never heard. His father was the great expert on American folk songs who did all the collections in the thirties and forties that are now in the Library of Congress. This was Alan Lomax the son, who was continuing Daddy's work. I had some stanzas of "The Jolly Tinker" they didn't have because I had been in the CCC camp in Mississippi. This was 1953 in Paris. We sat at the Café de Tournon, and afterwards Alan Lomax said, "Isn't it wonderful? Thinking of the troubadours, the tradition of French chanson— Isn't it wonderful to be sitting here singing 'The Jolly Tinker' in Paris?"

I never planted any trees when I was in the CCC camp. The minute they saw that I had actually been through high school and had an IQ, they put me to work teaching. I taught beginner's arithmetic. Of all the things for me.

I also helped in the forestry office making the identity cards for all the guys who couldn't read or write. Then they realized that I could paint. We had had a couple of storms, so they needed these "Bridge Out" signs. They had these rules—Corps of Engineers Specifics, I think it was called—and it showed how to paint a Corps of Engineers sign. The capital letters had to be precisely so many inches high, and the boards had to be so many feet. The background was orange, and you could only use black letters. Not my kind of creative work. They put me in this open shed—cold—my God, was it cold. I had sixteen layers of wool underwear and gloves painting "Bridge Out" and "Turn Left" and "Detour 3 Miles." The one I really liked—"Soft Shoulders."

Then I painted baby coffins. They had a terrible infant mortality rate in the backwoods, you know. So there was always some guy who would come in with a wooden box. They were all shy. In the way of the backwoods, they wouldn't take a seat, they would just squat down. When they go to town, to talk on the front porch of the store, they just squat like Orientals, like Hindus. They just squatted. Then they would take a little cotton bag of tobacco out of their back pocket and roll a cigarette, pulling it closed with the corner of their mouths somehow. They would squat there with this coffin and this cigarette and say, looking at the ground, not looking in my eyes, "Howdy, Painty." I was known as Painty. I would say, "Well, hey. How are you doing?" They would say, "He died early this morning." And there would be pauses that lasted for centuries. "I thought maybe you'd do like you did for Jim, m'brother." I said, "Sure, I'll paint it for you. Just come back tomorrow morning and it will be ready." So, after I finished my things, I would paint the baby coffin white. I had some tubes of colors, so I could paint a little raise of flowers and the baby's name. They thought that was great. I must have painted a hundred baby coffins between "Detour" and "Soft Shoulders."

I could have renewed in the CCC, but I was homesick for Mobile. So I came back and got a job ushering at the Saenger Theater. I had this dapper red, rather military uniform, sort of like a brown-and-tan version of West Point. Tight trousers, stripes. I had to have my hair cut short and parted, very prissy proper, with a bow tie. Once when I was walking in my usher's costume across Bienville Square, I heard this voice say, "Jesus Christ, if it ain't Painty." There was this boy called Biggun from the CCC. He had a phenomenal penis. I mean, when he went into the shower everybody just came and stood around. We just wanted to see what it looked like. It was something. He had sort of a slight body build—all his strength had gone to one place. It was rather sad because the whores in Laurel wouldn't have him. They took one look and ran screaming. So the CCC boys had to take turns masturbating him

53

when he came back from town desperate. They would say, "It's your turn this week," "No, it was my turn last week." But they would take him in the shower and soap him up.

He told me he had joined the navy and was glad he had been asked to go to Panama because he'd heard about these nightclub acts in Panama where the girls are humped by donkeys. And he thought if there were girls in Panama who could take donkeys, they could take him. I said, "I hope you have a grand time in Panama." Had he known how to write, I would have given him my address so he could tell me everything. I thought of him often. I hope some kind soul introduced him to the showgirls in Panama.

❧

I worked at the Saenger Theater for a year. I watched Joan Crawford in *Strange Cargo* twenty-seven times. I saw Vera Zorina in *The Goldwyn Follies* twenty-two times. And as for Fred Astaire and Ginger—oh, Lord—you know.

Then I went to work for the U.S. Corps of Engineers. This was the beginning of what was called preparedness. The Corps of Engineers was at an office downtown, and it turned out that the man who was running one of the departments was an old friend of Mr. Gayfer's and also an old friend of mine. We had known him forever. He had even known my grandparents. Charming guy. He said, "Well, I have a job for you. You know how to wrap packages, don't you? This is kind of a special thing. You are going to be in that cellar. You will wrap secret, confidential materials because we send the plans for these airports we are building all over Alabama—we send them double-wrapped. They are wrapped as tacky packages to go in the post. Inside they are waterproof and secret." The outside had to look like something Granny would mail to her son in construction work in Huntsville. So I did artistic packages. I made them all look tacky and took them to the post office.

That was when I lived in the ballroom of the Rubira house. This was a beautiful old downtown house of the Spanish family Rubira. Built after the Civil War, I think, or maybe just before. This was the first house to have gas because the Rubira family brought gas to Mobile. They had this ballroom with these huge mirrors hanging from the ceiling in chains at each end of the room reflecting each other so you had infinity if you stood in the middle of the room. And these bronze statues of Italian artists: Michelangelo, da Vinci, Raphael. And it had these fabulous chandeliers with bronze lilies and birds and vines and bronze chains. There were two doors that went onto a back porch that had been all enclosed, with a little bathroom built in and a gas stove in the corner. One door I closed off from floor to ceiling with an old

milking the moon

velvet theater curtain. That was the closet. I had a double mattress on the floor, and I built a theatrical four-poster bed made of florist ribbon left over from a ballet. I had a marionette theater at that end and a grand piano. I gave some good parties. I still have a program from one of them. There were no chairs, so I had sheets of red blotting paper on the floor and had this wonderful buffet as you sat on your red blot of paper.

A Proper Salon

One day on Conception Street as I was passing by, I saw these jolly souls taking cardboard boxes full of secondhand books into a store. I went in and discovered these darlings were starting a bookshop. It was Cameron Plummer, who was the son of a famous Episcopal minister here, Dr. James Plummer, from Virginia. Cameron had had a disease, some sort of fever—I don't think it was polio—as a child and had a long convalescence. He was one of the few persons I know who can claim to have read the *Encyclopaedia Britannica* from the first page of *A* to the last page of *Z*, straight through. The other was Adelaide. Adelaide and Eleanor were these two extraordinary sisters who went to the convent. Their original French ancestor was a nobleman, a Colonel Demouy, who came to Dauphin Island in 1690. They could have all the coats of arms hanging on the front door, clanking in the wind, if they wanted. But that's not their idea of grand. Their idea of grand is you do not go outside of the house unless your hair is kept and you are properly dressed. Their grandfather and their great-uncle, the Rapier brothers, owned the *Register* and the *Times-Picayune*. They were very distinguished publishers in their day. Very advanced in their ideas and very insistent on good writing. Both girls had been raised as book-ies.

Anyway, Cameron Plummer and Adelaide Marston got together and just said, Well, Mobile hasn't had a bookshop in a long time. I think in the twenties there were maybe some bookshops, but during the Depression there was only the book department in Hammell's Dry Goods Company down on Royal Street. All it had was a book section which sold textbooks for the schools. Adelaide and Cameron were able to get this house, the old Rapier house which belonged to Adelaide's relatives, on Conception Street. It's a beautiful double house with a carriage drive through the middle, which is a law firm now. And Adelaide had filled it with Victorian furniture from the family attic. They called it the Haunted Book Shop, because both Adelaide and Cameron loved a book that came out in 1919 or 1920 by Christopher Morley, a forgotten American writer. He wrote two novels about a bookseller. The man called his shop the Haunted Book Shop. He said it's haunted by the ghosts of all great literature.

Everything worked for the bookshop to be a great success. Paperbacks had just begun again when the New American Library was founded in 1938 and published five paperback books. It was a revolution, because people who had heard of Shakespeare thought for twenty-five cents they might take a chance on it. Then the war was starting, and all these people who came to town to work for the shipyards—none of them knew anything about the jobs they were doing, so there was a tremendous market for technical books. At the same time, in wartime, people always read better books. Thornton Wilder once said in conversation that in peacetime people want a more comfortable life. In wartime people want a better life. That's what happened. People kept coming back to the shop.

It was a proper salon. Adelaide had coffee going an hour before it opened and two hours after it closed. And hidden behind books were all the bottles that Cameron got off various ships. People would leave their children in Adelaide's care. Park their cars in front. There was one man who came to town every Saturday, would tether his horse to the front ironwork. It was a message center. You know, ladies in their white gloves and hats would be there and say, "Oh, Adelaide, if Enola May comes by, tell her I'm going to be late, but I'll meet her here at twelve-thirty." There was a bulletin board with thumbtacked messages. If you wanted to start a rumor, you could say something in the Haunted Book Shop, and it would have reached Mt. Vernon, Alabama, by noon.

And everybody was there. There was a wonderful lady, a great scholar who was doing the French and Spanish papers at Spring Hill College. She would come in the Haunted Book Shop on her cane and she'd sit down and say, "Oh, I really feel faint." And Cameron would say, "Oh, I've got just the thing for you." And he'd whisk some Spanish cognac to her immediately. He finally went to keeping it behind the technical books. And she always sank in this little Victorian chair, and he would just say, "Oh, I know just the thing for you."

There were the most extraordinary characters. At the end of the day, those who were left over, like Adelaide and Cameron and the bookkeeper and sometimes myself, would go through the characters of the day. Laughing at them, what they said, what books they wanted. It was like, I imagine, Shakespeare & Company in Paris in the twenties. What the Gotham Book Mart in New York was when that crazy lady was running it. There were writers and painters and the whole human traffic. They would come for wedding presents. She'd want a cookbook or household hints. Or a King James version for the new household. And stay just to listen to conversations going on in there. I was in there because there were so many books I wanted.

I met Harper Lee there, because Truman sent her to every bookshop in the South when his first book, *Other Voices, Other Rooms,* came out. So she came to the Haunted Book Shop and told us she was the original of the little girl in the book. Well, apparently she is. I've never seen her since. I've talked to her on the phone. She's got this gin-and-Chesterfield voice now. She was a small-town Southern girl when I first met her, and now she's Miss Gin. She's lived too long in New York, and that's why she's never written another book.

Finally, of course, I started working odd hours at the Haunted Book Shop. I lived there. When I wasn't at work, I was living there. I mean, I just went through every shelf. It was full of furniture, and people sat on little low chairs, lower than the usual Victorian chairs. And there were ashtrays everywhere, and along about four-thirty sherry came out. The eight-to-five world had not yet taken over. It is what I suppose in some moment we will call civilization.

The Arctic Circle

PART TWO

Edgar Allan Poe and "The Gold-Bug"

When I was nineteen I was drafted and went off to basic training at Fort McPherson, Georgia. When I got to Georgia, they immediately put me to work. They had all these second lieutenants from New England who were supposed to be doing the registration. Of course, they didn't know how to deal with those backwoods boys. They would ask direct questions, like "What is your name?" "Where are you from?" and the backwoods boys wouldn't answer those direct questions. So they got Private Walter, and they gave me an office. These boys would come in, and I'd say, "Well, howdy. I'm from Mobile. Where are you from?"

"Possum Hollow."

"Whoa, you-all got good hunting there. I been near Possum Hollow. I was at a place up the road called Richton. I was a CCC boy."

"You were a CCC boy?"

"I was a CCC boy at Richton."

"My cousin went to Richton. He was a CCC boy."

And then I could say, "Now what's your name?" So I'd get the last name and I'd say, "Now I knew a J. T. Wideman up at Richton. That any kin to you?"

"I'm Billy Bob."

"What about your daddy? His name the same as yours?"

"No, Daddy's named John Ed."

"What was your mama's name before she married Mr. John Ed?"

"Well, she was a Muskrat."

Then they needed what church they go to, so I said, "Oh, Possum Hollow. They got that pretty little white church, got all the privet bushes around."

"Oh no, no, I went to the Methodist on the other side of the tracks."

So I could finally build their entrance form, from a conversation, you see, not from direct questions. But all those second lieutenants from New England were having nervous breakdowns because these boys would just sit there. They wouldn't talk to those Yankee boys.

And I'm going to tell you, some of those boys were brought directly from the backwoods, where the sheriff's department had to go out and tell them they were wanted for the army. And those boys would grab their rifles and say, "Who we fightin' this time, the Yankees?" So when they got to Atlanta, they thought they'd been captured already.

Then they called me one day and said, "You got a high grade on this intelligence test when you came in, so you can choose what you are going to do. Here's the list. These are the fields in which we are desperate. You can check off your preferences one, two, three, what you'd like to study, go and do." Of course, it was radar, chemical warfare, bomb making, it was dah, dah, and cryptography. And when I saw cryptography, I thought Edgar Allan Poe and "The Gold-Bug"! So I put that for first choice, and they said, "Oh, nobody asks for that for first choice," and they sent me right off to the Pauling Institute in upstate New York. And going from Fort McPherson, Georgia, to a group of high IQs at Pauling, New York, two hours north of New York City, was another cultural shift.

And that was terrific. They were short of cryptographers in every theater of war. And we had to cram. I mean cram, cram, cram. We got up at six and went straight into class because you had to memorize combinations of numbers, combinations of phrases, and combinations of letters that made no sense. They had to be in your brain. You had to have the thing to decode in your brain. I had to know which one nulls and which were live and which to use only in great emergency, and which were the ones that gave you the code for the day. Then we began learning these complex machineries. I don't think I'm breaking security because they've changed the name by this time, but there was one called the Cigarbo. And I just loved it.

I wasn't very good at the training. We had an old West Point fool general, who had been in the First World War, running this academy. He said, you know, twirling his white mustache on this bright red face, "All boys need some discipline. You can't have those boys sitting around at the Cigarbo all day and learning those things they learn out of books. They need some exercise. Get out in the snow and have some maneuvers out in the snow." He loved to play war games. When he led us in these charges, we used rotten potatoes for hand grenades. He had bags of rotten potatoes. We'd be out in the snow, charging through the snow, throwing rotten potatoes after we'd gotten up from our Cigarbo machines.

milking the moon

Alabama Meets Alabama

After I'd passed all my cryptography exams, I was allowed a weekend in New York. So I caught that train through the snow, through the slushy streets of New York, and I went right away to the Plymouth Theater. Because two weeks earlier, the Thornton Wilder play *Skin of Our Teeth* had opened. With Tallulah Bankhead in the starring role. And on the train with me, coming from some other radio school or something, I heard this boy who was in a private's uniform just as I. And I said, "What part of the South are you from?" He said, "I'm from Greensboro, Alabama." I said, "That's not too far away from where I live." So we went together to the theater. He'd never been anywhere. So I went to the box office and I said, "I declare, I know it's pretty late to get seats for tonight, but we are from Alabama and we just love Miss Tallulah." And she looked at me and found two tickets. I've always said, if you can't put your southernisms to good use, don't use them at all.

Then I wrote a note and gave it to the usher, a very charming older lady, at intermission. It said, "Dear Miss Tallulah, I'm from Mobile, Alabama, and you might remember my name. I'm a friend of the Sledges." That was old Dr. Sledge. And see, Tallulah's mother was Eugenia Sledge. The old doctor was a first cousin of Eugenia. And I said, "I'd love just to come backstage and say hello afterward." I signed it "Private Eugene Walter." When the show was over and I was in the lobby, the usher to whom I had given the note was waiting for me. She said, "Miss Bankhead would be delighted to see you. Just go on backstage. Send in your name." So I went backstage, and oh, you know, what a thrill to go in that alley. Just the idea of the stage door. New York, New York.

I was met by a snotty doorman who said, "No, no, no." And I said, "Miss Bankhead is expecting me. I'm from Alabama." He said, "Oh." So I went in and there were all these high-ranking naval officers and some very distinguished older people there. I stood very shyly with my new friend from Greensboro right there in the corner behind these navy officers who were very know-it-all types.

Suddenly this English lady appeared at the top of the stairs. You could tell she was English because she was wearing a tweed skirt that had a pleat with little inner pleats in it. And a sweater set in a pale color and one string of pearls. Her hair was in a thirties sort of bob. And no makeup except a little bit of rouge. She appeared at the top, and now I won't swear that she had a lorgnette, but it was the impression of one. Maybe she just extended her glasses to read this note, but maybe she did have a little lorgnette. She said, "Is

63

Private Walter here? If you'll come this way, sir." Then they parted like the Red Sea. Or the navy blue sea. And I went through, you know, "Excuse me, excuse me," as I went up the stairs. I allowed myself to turn and look over my shoulder and go ha-ha-ha to those officers.

Then I went in, and there she was. With this honey-colored hair. She was one of the one-hundred-brush-strokes-a-night Southern girls. And it shone. It shone. And she had these twinkling eyes, and she still had her cheekbones. She said something like "Good evening, darling. Did you enjoy the show?"

And I said, "Oh, Miss Tallulah, I did enjoy the show." In the second act she runs down the aisle for her first entrance, you see. It's the convention of the Rotary or something in Atlantic City, and she is a bathing beauty. She runs down the aisle of the theater in this red bathing suit, twirling this red umbrella. I said, "Oh, Miss Tallulah, when this show is over, you ought to send that red umbrella to the state of Alabama because we ought to make a shrine over that like they made over Buddha's tooth in Ceylon."

She went, "Ho-ho-ho." She was behind a little screen getting into slacks and a blouse. She said, "I'll give you—ho-ho-ho—something much better for the shrine." Woh, woh, woh. And she gave me three pubic hairs. One of which I still have. I traded one for a beautiful leather-bound translation of Ovid's *Metamorphoses* by various people like Addison, Ben Jonson, et cetera, et cetera, printed by the very famous Jacob Thompson, the famous typographer and bookbinder. I traded one pubic hair to an Englishman for that book. I've forgotten what I traded the other one for. The last one is in my reliquary by Zev. It's got the horn of the last known unicorn that was killed the day Voltaire was born. And in the bottom, I have a 1926 rare English porcelain of a lady with a bob and striped pajamas. It's called *First Cigarettes*. She's smoking her first cigarette. Inside that porcelain, inside a plastic bit, is that pubic hair of Tallulah. When you go over there you feel this warmth. I get the electricity.

I saw her again after the war. It was 1946. I went to the theater and sent her a note, and again she received me. And this is the image I really retain of her. It was snowing outside—she didn't have a hat. She was wearing black velvet slacks and a white satin blouse and a big mink thrown over her shoulders. She never put her arms in the sleeves. And this honey-colored hair was full of snowflakes. She was going to a party, and I was going to meet some friends at a restaurant nearby. So I was going to escort her to her limousine. We were just chatting away about Alabama. And we looked down Shubert Alley, and at the other end of Shubert Alley, there was the Salvation Army girl with her tambourine, her scarf, and her hat with the bonnet, freezing to death, and she had this tripod with a little cauldron covered with chicken

milking the moon

64

wire. Tallulah said, "Oh, my God. Come with me, darling." We went all the way down Shubert Alley. She reached into her slacks' pocket and pulled out a wad of dollar bills and stuck them in there. And she said to the Salvation Army girl, "There, there, darling, I know it's been a perfectly ghastly season for you Spanish dancers." I just loved it.

The last time I saw her was at a party in New York. It was an interesting group of people, actors and dancers and all that. And Thelma Carpenter was there, the black singer who comes from someplace up the road from Jasper, Alabama, where Tallulah comes from. Tallulah had never met her. She'd never met Tallulah. And they just fell into each other's arms, you know. "Oh, Possum Hollow. Oh, Boogaloo Junction. Oh, Jasper. Oh, Coconut." And all that. Alabama meets Alabama. Tallulah was being escorted by this Harvard boy. I don't think he was a football player, but he was a big Harvard boy with wide shoulders and beautifully tailored clothes. Just smelling of money. A young guy. He kept saying, "You know, oh come on, Tallulah, you said we'd go to your place, come on, Tallulah." He was just itching. She said, "I lived for many years near Jasper, but the family house was not in Jasper." Then Thelma said, "Well, I went to high school in Possum Hollow, you know." This boy was sitting there going mad, and finally Tallulah said, "Oh, darling." She carried a little purse just like the queen of England—basics. I thought, Well, she's got a few thousand-dollar bills and a little mother-of-pearl comb, and a lipstick, and that's all she's got in there. She opened it up, click, and took out a bunch of keys, and said, "Here, darling, you go on over to my place. If I'm not there in an hour, start without me."

But you see, they made Tallulah what is called camp. She was not. She was a Southern lady who was frank in her speech. As real Southern ladies always were. All the puritanism came late in the game. And you see, Tallulah used to come to Mobile on the sly every two or three years and buy cases and cases of this one postcard showing azaleas blooming at the entrance of the Bankhead Tunnel. She used to send that to everybody on earth for Christmas. They never knew that there was a tunnel here named for her father or uncle, whichever it was. They thought it was some bawdry that she'd invented. Bankhead Tunnel. Anyway, she was a great actress. And an elegant Southern lady with a down-to-earth quality. She really was a marvelous creature.

Writing in the Snow

Well, as I said, they were short of cryptographers in every theater of war, so they told me I could have my choice. "Send me to the eastern theater," I said. "I have cousins in every country of Europe. But I have no black or Japanese cousins." So I went to Seattle. And I was issued tropical equipment, camouflage costumes and green and brown makeup to wear in the jungle. I thought, What fun, I'll have a fern leaf here, and a bramblebush there. But unh-unh. As we were going toward the gangplank, we quietly checked all of our tropical equipment and were given parkas instead. We went off on this eight-day cruise up the inland waterway to Alaska. It was a ploy so various underground intelligence would not know that a large body of soldiers was going to the Arctic Circle and Alaska.

So then I went right away to Elmendorf Field, the airport at Anchorage, Alaska, where they broke in the graduate cryptographers. Everybody monitored every single thing you did to see if you did it right. You were monitored for a month before you were turned loose. And you were turned loose on simple things like encoded supplies. They never told how many boxes of Coca-Cola they were ordering because they didn't want the Japanese to know how many soldiers were drinking Coca-Cola. I graduated from supplies to very high command and then to inventing air-ground codes, which had to change every hour because the Japanese were very clever at breaking the codes. When I was out in the Aleutian Islands, I was in intelligence, specifically air-land codes for airplanes, bombardiers, and all. There were three categories of information—secret, confidential, and restricted—and I dealt with all three.

I used the second line of Mother Goose rhymes always for codes that only lasted an hour. And I always liked "its fleece was white as snow." Then the person in the plane knew to jumble up "Mary Had a Little Lamb." And then take his secret code and take every third letter from "Mary Had a Little Lamb" after he'd unscrambled it.

One day at Anchorage I met this poor little guy off a minesweeper. He was crying. He had this little adorable puppy he'd found wandering around the pier in San Francisco. It must have been three months old by then, this little fur thing. You couldn't see which end was which. It was just this gray-and-white fur and these curls. I said, "Oh, for Christ's sake." He said, "The commander of the minesweeper said if I come back on the ship with this animal, I'll be court-martialed." Some real shitface second lieutenant, of course. So I said, "Oh, for Christ's sake, I'll take it. I'll find a way. I'll do something." And of course, I smuggled it in. That animal was clever. It knew to make no noise. That became my beloved Ragzina Gadzooks. A Maltese terrier. She went everyplace with me, the Arctic Circle, the Aleutian Islands.

On that island where I was most of the time, Atka, one of the four big islands of the Andreanof between Siberia and Alaska, I mean the wind blew. In the three years I was there, I saw the sun five times, five days. It was fog, mist eternally, and the wind called the williwaw, that blows straight from the north. And you walk against it, you lean on it. Then if you are coming away from it, you have to crawl. I worked in this underground vault that was bombproof, where we had our Cigarbos and our various machines and somebody who would relay the Morse code messages from the place with an area where they received the Morse code. There's not a whole lot more I can say about it, because when I left they made me swear on the Bible and the Constitution and Emily Post that I would never reveal confidential information.

We lived six each in these Quonset huts that were buried—an underground dugout. Down these steps into an underground hole. They were camouflaged with tundra grass. And the eternal wind—you heard that wind day and night. The tour of duty was six months: it was considered a hardship post. A lot of people were suicidal, and there were suicides; some boys didn't even finish their six months. But I was there three years. I volunteered to stay on because for me it was exotic. I mean, it was so unlike Mobile. As a Southerner, I had never had that cultural advantage of writing in the snow with the fountain pen. Yankee boys get to write in the snow. So I liked to go and write words, peeing in the snow late at night. Dirty words. When I was a child, it snowed once in Alabama, and they closed all the schools instantly, so the children could just go out and go aah. Of course, the snow melted as soon as it hit the ground. But I saw real heaps of snow in Alaska. And everybody else was saying woo, and I was saying: That dry cold. There was a part of my lungs I had never used before. I didn't realize I had an antechamber and a back room in my lungs. I loved it. And there was no marching. There were no calisthenics. There was no saluting. I'd had basic training, six weeks of shooting rifles at targets and left, left, left . . . Forward, march. Turn left. Present arms. Clack. And I just loathed it.

I was just outside the Arctic Circle the first time I saw the northern lights. I went to Umnak, which is in the Yukon, where they were setting up a new message center. I was to go and help the boys who'd just come from the Pauling Institute to set up. One night, I went out of this place where I lived just under the Arctic Circle, and there was this silence that was so heavy, you could hear it. I can't explain it. It was like a repeated vibration that had no sound. Total silence. If you've never heard total silence, you can't imagine it. So heavy a silence, it actually hummed. White velvet snow and a black velvet sky. There was no sound at all. Just the music of the spheres. Vibration. And I was sitting there thinking, Gosh, wouldn't it be wonderful if I could see the northern lights? And honey, it was as though God said, "Well, there's that awful brat again." And they lit up. I mean: boom. Suddenly the whole sky lit up with a crazy display in rose, pale green, and gold, splinters of dancing light. I almost peed in my pants.

It was pinky green, pale pink, pale green, and pale yellow. There would be these beams that would just come up and would fade slowly away. And here come some more. That side of it would fade out and this side would go strong, and it would go up and go down. I'm going to tell you, I almost died. I almost died. And my dog, Ragzina, was sitting next to me, and she was listening to the silence, too. And when those lights started, she looked at me like, Daddy, Daddy, what are they doing? I thought, If she could sing, she'd sing "Scotland's Burning."

It was in the Aleutian Islands that I first began to cook. It was self-salvation that got me going, because I couldn't take some of the mess of the mess hall food. It was things that were brought up there frozen, chickens that were two years old. When we had anything fresh, it was always cabbages. I didn't eat cabbages for about three or four years after the war. Well, we all had some kind of little stove in that dugout to heat up the place and have water boiling so the humidity didn't go down. But I quickly got a little two-burner alcohol stove going and learned how to steal from the mess hall. Sometimes I would say to the guys in my dugout, "Don't eat that steak. Bring it back." They were just hunks of plain steak. I would get garlic and the pepper mill and cook up a stew, and everybody loved it. Sometimes I would put a little oil and butter in this pan I had, put in little slices of that big soggy mess hall bread with some paprika and some pepper, and just turn it until it was crisp. We would sit around and drink beer and eat that. Then I used to go digging clams in the black sands of the Bering Sea. Beautiful clams. Huge, tender clams. So I'd dig these clams and I'd make creole sauce out of whatever I could make it out of and have dinner parties. I was always going into the kitchen in the mess hall and stealing onions. I made a candelabra, classical goddesses out of papier-mâché, and I went to the navy and stole target cloth. Dyed it bright yellow. And that was my tablecloth. Seated on the floor Chinese style around this table with candles as the williwaw went woooooo, we sat there in a room stinking gloriously of clams creole.

～

In our time off, we used to climb up to this plateau where there was a hot spring. So that the whole year you could see the tundra grass. It wasn't green because it was arctic weather, but you could see the tundra grass. And of course, since spring is only two weeks, summer is two weeks, and autumn is two weeks, the tundra grass never completely decays. So it's like two thousand years of mattress stuffing on top of the rocks. And I invented this game called suicide. We all had these fur parkas, and we'd go to this plateau and say, "Farewell, cruel world!" and just jump over the edge. You bounce on that tundra grass right to the bottom. So we used to go up there and have suicide every day when we got finished with our work.

One day we were on this place that was lower down near this hot spring, and here were these two newborn baby caribou. I knew enough never to touch anything wild, because if the mother smells anything foreign, she will just ditch it. But I saw that it had been a difficult birth because caribou never have twins. It is extremely rare. And it must have been very difficult; there was a lot of blood. I saw one was dead and one was alive, and I heard her making little sounds. I thought, The mother has probably gone off to wash or something, she'll be back. And I went on climbing around on the tundra, and when I was starting back about an hour later, I went to see and the mother had not come back. So I took off my wool scarf. I just wrapped up that baby caribou and took it back and washed her with some warm water and took a clean undershirt and made a little teat and heated some Carnation milk. I'm afraid that I already had the reputation of being different, so they just thought it was another of my moments. I never dreamed she would survive, but she did. Hedy Lamarr. She had these black eyes just like Hedy Lamarr in the film *Algiers*, where Hedy just looks at the camera, you know, and the whole audience goes wild.

But I had these three dogs. One of Ragzina's daughters belonged to someone who lived in the same underground dugout where I did. And then there was another dog. I would go strolling up and down the Bering seashore with these three dogs and this caribou. And I always took apples. They all loved apples, and the dogs would do this little dance. I'd make them stand on their hind legs and turn around. The caribou stood on her hind legs and turned around to get the piece of apple. Then she was growing and growing, and one day—I'll never forget this—the dogs wouldn't dance. They just looked at this caribou who'd gotten a little bit bigger, and they said, "That is not a dog. What is it?" All three of them. They wanted the apple, but they said, "What's that?"

Then when her horns came out, they were covered with velvet. As the horns grow, the velvet itches them in some way. They just want to go and rub their horns and get rid of that velvet. So I would scratch her horns, and those dogs would sit in a row in the underground and they would just watch me as I scratched her horns.

She stayed, I think, eighteen months. I found her in early spring. The next spring the caribou herd came down from the mountains to eat some of the fern tops that grew along the low part. They loved those fern tops. She looked out of the little door that I had opened in this dugout and said, "Oh, my God, Daddy, what are those awful things coming down the mountain?" And I said, "It's all right, they're okay, they're okay. Those are car-re-bous, car-re-bous. You'll like them." And she said, "Oh, I'm afraid. I'm scared." And I said, "Well, come on back in." Then she came back in and had her Fig Newtons.

She stayed on milk for a long time. But after she started to need something solid, I had to go and dig under the snow to get fern tops to feed her. I tried bread dipped in milk, and she would spit. Then I started digging in the snow for the little sprouting fern tops in the tundra. And then one day I was sitting eating a bowl of Fig Newtons in a very bored fashion. The PX only had Kleenex, aspirin, shelf upon shelf of quart containers of black pepper, and three million cases of Fig Newtons. So I was sitting rather bored with a Fig Newton and she came up and said, "What's that? Oh, my God, it smells good." And I said, "Do you want to try it?" And she would go through a case in like a day. Saved from snow digging. I thought: Nabisco forever.

But when the caribou herd came down the next time, in the fall, she said, "Daddy, who are those gorgeous things going past?" And she ran off with them. Then a strange and wonderful thing happened. The night before I was going to leave, I heard this bang, bang, and this voice: she had come to say good-bye. She came down alone. She knew I was going. How can you explain it?

❧

When I was coming back, the big thing was smuggling my precious dog into the United States. The day after that first atom bomb, I knew that things were going to change. So I started training Ragzina to sit on my shoulders perfectly still as a fur piece. I also trained her to stay in a barracks bag with just her nose in an airhole. So when we left up there, I had ripped the fur collar off my parka and I wore this gray-and-white curly fur onto the ship.

milking the moon

70

We were two hours loading, and that girl didn't move. She was with me. I was with her. She knew how to stay right by me. Then we got in, I put her down, gave her a towel to piss on, and fed her. And I would walk her on the deck at night. Keep her in my stateroom in the day. Then I had this empty barracks bag with an empty cardboard box in it and these airholes. And I'd open the bag up for two hours unloading at Seattle. I got her right to that army camp. The next day I had a pass into Seattle. Got her straight to a vet and I said, "I want you to build her a little wooden cage. Ship her to Mobile, Alabama." I hated the idea of shipping her, but I'd worn this long woolen undershirt all those seven days coming back so that her cage would stink of me. Aimee King met her at the train station. And I was reunited some two months later. Boy, did that dog wiggle.

I left her with this childless English couple because I couldn't take her to New York. They were friends of the de Celles, and this woman said, "I never saw anything so adorable in my entire life." And Ragzina took to them right away. I said, "Don't tell me anything about her. I don't want to hear anything about her. I want her to be happy, and I want you all to be happy." So I never heard anymore about her. But, oh, God, for a year I missed that beast.

I was a week in Seattle being debriefed. And I had been in hospital at the very end with a wool rash. I had been wearing thick woolen drawers next to my skin for three years, and having never had wool next to my skin, I finally just had this pink rash all over. So I was in this mud pack in a hospital for a week to get rid of that. Then I was sent to San Diego to be released from the forces. You have to fill out three million forms to get out. The minute I got out, I took that khaki uniform down to the Pacific Ocean and threw it in. Got into seersuckers and fled to Los Angeles. Well, I got off the train and looked around at Los Angeles and an hour later jumped back on the train for San Francisco. Got off the train in San Francisco and thought, Wow, I'm home. I could smell something French and something Spanish, just like Mobile and New Orleans. I was at home. There were vibrations. I went to the opera, and Ruth St. Denis, an old dancer, was then seventysomething and still dancing. Couldn't bend her ankles at all, so she did everything with her hands and floating scarves. She was sensational. And I would just lie in bed. That's when I was adjusting to civilian life.

I already had a job in New York because I had ordered books before the war from the Chaucer Head Book Shop, which was owned by an Englishman and was in the East Fifties. When Mr. Gayfer was my guardian, he had given me so much that I could spend, and I had an account with E. Heffer &

Company in Cambridge, England, and an account at Chaucer Head in New York. It was like $5 a month or so at each place. And I would save up until I could get a $15 book. That was extravagant in those days. Chaucer Head was old and rare books, a few new books. And I corresponded with this guy. Then I didn't correspond during the war, but I think toward the last year of the war I was ordering books and corresponding. I had this nice letter from a secretary there saying, "Well, what are your plans for after the War? We have all your letters and see how you love books and what you have to say about them. And we are going to need a couple of new clerks, we've moved to Fifth Avenue. Would you like to come to work here after the War?" I wrote back and said, "Yeah, I'm going to be in New York, I guess." I had no plans. I had no plans at all. I was just thinking, Well, I do want to go to Bayou La Batre and have fried oysters. So I stayed a couple of months in Mobile, saw everybody and had some good parties, and then left for New York.

milking the moon

New York

PART THREE

The Break-Your-Balls-and-
All-for-the-Dollar World

When I first moved to New York, I took only the bare essentials: my Remington typewriter, my stuffed monkey in a bell jar, and a box of gold paper stars to sprinkle on the stairways of my apartment building. The place was gray walls with that sense of grime. I couldn't stand it. After I got there I found some place downtown where you could buy stuff for window displays, so I just bought bales of gold stars. Every two or three days I'd freshen them.

As for this monkey in a jar, I've had it in my life since before I was born. It was a christening gift that came two weeks before me, sent by my grandmother's family, the Luenbergs, in Switzerland. A monkey in a little red uniform. I thought it was a bellhop costume, but I was told later it was a hussar outfit. His name is Coco. A lot of monkeys are named Coco. It's a term of endearment, like cutie or dearie. Coco. It's what the French call their children.

He was my Sunday toy. I played with him only on Sunday. In the South, everybody has a Sunday toy. And, of course, a Saturday night toy, too. His dueling scars are from my very first tooth. I bit him. He has no ears because I ate them. I loved him very much.

He went with me through the war; he was in my barracks bag. I thought, If he goes with me, nothing's going to happen. And bless his heart, he is my oracle. He answers anything that can be answered with a yes or a no. If it requires gradations or definitions, he just looks into space. Whenever I have serious things to ask myself—should I or shouldn't I?—I always ask him for a yes or no. Like should I really clean this house out? You know. And if you have a monkey, it attracts other monkeys. Just as if you have a cat, it attracts cats.

Later, when I was going to go to Paris, Aimee King of the Children's Theater, who also dressed queens and kings for the Carnival and did the greatest of the masquerade costumes, said, "You can't take that monkey to Europe in that shabby costume with his ears gone." She said, "I'll dress him."

So she put him in an eighteenth-century French costume made of antique velvet from before the Civil War, and he traveled with me like that. These are serious matters.

And everybody just likes that monkey. How can you not like him? How can you not like someone whose ears have been bitten off by a poet? He has some interesting things that have been given him over the years. I have several boxes of his possessions. He has a bagpipe that Muriel Spark gave him. An engagement diary for 1962. The famous Danish lady who does invisible stitches made him a cushion by invisible stitches. A bookbinder in Paris made a little sketchbook for him. I love his little wallet; he's rich in one-lira pieces from before the devaluation of the lira. And being a well-dressed monkey, he has his opera glasses and his dance card. His hats come from Paris, naturally, and he has his gloves. He has some very beautiful jewelry and his little jewelry box. His portrait was done by Domenico Gnoli, the great Italian modern artist who died when he was thirty years old. He did this portrait of Coco which I still have.

He has traveled with me everywhere. I wouldn't dream of going anywhere on earth without Coco.

I went right away to work the second day I was in New York. The Englishman who'd owned the Chaucer Head Book Shop had gone back to England when the war was beginning. It had been bought by the heir of the Rheingold breweries, and he was this impossible spoiled, rich New York Jewish boy with a cast in one eye. "Ah, but of course." And she, the other partner, was poor white trash, Irish Catholic, from Baltimore. Rheingold fortune, rich Jewish New York, and white trash, Irish Catholic, from Baltimore. They were fighting the whole time, and I loathed them both. And of course, they didn't understand me at all.

I realized I would hate the job when they had given me instructions like "Now be sure you stand where you can see between the customer and the shelves. You don't know who will steal what, especially if they are wearing coats." They said, "Remember that priests and military men are the most famous book thieves." They said, "Never go in the record booth with a customer. You don't know what might happen."

I said, "What might happen?"

And they said, "Oh, don't go in."

"What might happen?" Then I said, "Well, who's going to put the record on the turntable?"

"Well, you put it on first, but keep the door ajar so they can't get in.

76

Then you go out and open the door for them and say politely, 'Oh, do come in.'"

I kept thinking: He's Harvard, she's self-made. Surely they should enjoy books more. But no. And I don't think they realized how vicious they were to all of the hired help. There was a black boy who worked in the basement, and he was really having a nervous breakdown. They were so bitchy and mean. "You are seven minutes late." You know. Then there was a very sort of plumpy, not very masculine boy from Connecticut. They made a nervous wreck out of him. I took refuge in Southern idiocy whenever they got onto me. But they were really destructive without realizing how much. I guess he was proving to his wealthy Rheingold family that he could make it on his own. And she was just climbing to the top from the slums of Baltimore. Now she was on Fifth Avenue.

But I couldn't take it. The minute I left there at the end of the day, I gulped and took some fresh air and forgot them until the next morning. But I didn't like it. It wasn't just the nine-to-five world. It was the "break your balls and all for the dollar" world.

So I lasted there about a year. One day I finished all my rare-book stuff and wrapped and addressed some packages down in the basement. It was twelve o'clock, and I left for lunch. It was a sunny day, and then these white clouds floated over Fifth Avenue. I put out my arms and I flew down Fifth Avenue to the Village and had lunch in an Italian restaurant. And never put foot one in the Chaucer Head Book Shop again. I saw those white clouds racing over that spring air on Fifth Avenue, and I smelled green from Central Park across the street. And I just spread my wings and flew down Fifth Avenue, never to return. Never. They are still looking for me. I am on the police missing list in New York City.

After I freed myself, I lived off unemployment insurance. It was called the thirty-two-fifty club. You got $32.50 a week. I lived off that for a couple of months while I was making my way about New York.

Then I went to work in the foreign exchange section of the New York Public Library, down on 28th Street, where they have a building eight stories high. They had something like six thousand miles of running shelving. I mean, floor after floor of shelves with only enough space between these floor-to-ceiling shelves for somebody to go slightly sideways. If you were fat, you didn't dare get in there. They had the archives of the WPA music program; they had a braille library for the blind. It was a kind of catch-all archive for the New York Public Library. So many people in New York, when they would die off, their relatives would clean out the apartment and send all the books to the New York Public Library. So they ended up there for us to sort and see if there was anything of great value. Every department would look at what was available, and if they wanted something, they would take it. Otherwise it just stayed at the foreign exchange section.

My job was to make up packages to send to South Africa, East Pakistan, wherever they were on the exchange program for books. There were exchanges where we would send a bundle of American publications and they would send a bundle of local things. They would send us their few and rare publications, say from Guandaruba, and I would send them crates of books, because we had too many. Everybody, especially the Africans, loved my foreign exchange packages. I always put copies of *Sunshine and Health*, the American nudist magazine, in the bottom as though it were padding. If I were packing a package for say, Scandinavia, I always put in things about tropical plants. If I were sending something to Africa, I always had white nudity. I can just see them: "Yeah, gee, we got our Socrates and here's the New York Architectural Board minutes for 1890, but gee, look here, *Sunshine and Health*."

If I Spread My Wings and Fly, I Always End Up in the Middle of Something

I lived with the reader's adviser of the New York Public Library, who'd been in my outfit. I shared an apartment with him for about three or four months. Then I met Randolph Echols, one of about ten people that I had introductions to. He was an actor, playing with the Maurice Evans Shakespeare Company. And I said, "Well, I've got to find a place to stay. I have to have my own place. I can't live with people." And he said, "Well, you ought to look in Greenwich Village." And I said, "No, I really want to live in New York City." Because I didn't know that Greenwich Village was part of Manhattan. Greenwich Village was a name I'd heard, but I thought it was a little town near New York City. Because we never looked toward New York from Mobile; we looked toward London and Paris.

He just giggled. And he said, "Well, you come with me. I think I know of a place." He knew a bartender who had had enough of New York and was going back to Arizona or something. He had this three-room apartment just above Sheridan Square. Being a bartender who got off at three or four A.M. and slept late, he had painted the entire apartment black. Floor, ceilings, and walls—black. With white footprints painted from the door to his cot. And the windows—he had squeezed tubes of colored oil paint on them so that no light came through. In the refrigerator, there were yogurts that must have been there a couple of weeks that had long blue whiskers. It was that primitive 1870s housing. Just two big rooms and one little room, and a john which you shared with your next-door neighbor in a little room out in the hallway. Randolph said, "Well, I can get you this at $18 a month." I said, "I'll take it."

So I gave a party for about eight people. And we scraped paint and scraped paint and scraped paint, and then I painted everything pale yellow. It took three coats over some of that black we couldn't get off. When we scraped the windows, what did I see out of my back window but the little garden of the Evangelical Lutheran Church on Christopher Street. It had a neatly clipped lawn and these wisteria vines under my fire escape. So that's where I lived. That was 194 West 10th Street.

Just up the street from me, like a few feet, there was this dead-end alley called Patchin Place. e.e. cummings had created this dead-end alley and lived in it. He was the next-door neighbor or across-the-street neighbor of Djuna Barnes. She lived there forty years. He lived there thirty-five years. And there was somebody else there. Whenever anything went vacant, some writer or painter grabbed it. He was very nice and sort of sardonically humorous. She was nervous. I used to see her in the early morning in her dressing gown and curlers at the same bakery I went to. We went to get these coffee rolls they made. They were sticky-finger coffee rolls, and they were so good. She'd become rather a recluse except for running to that corner bakery to get those sticky buns every morning, sometimes even when the bakery first opened at the Sixth Avenue corner.

Djuna Barnes wrote a key novel that came out in 1937 from Harcourt, Brace with an introduction by T. S. Eliot. He caused it to be published. I give him credit for that. When everybody was writing WPA novels—sharecroppers and drunks in New York City—she published this nineteenth-century novel. *Nightwood*. It's about this heroine who can't decide whether she's totally female or a daughter of Sappho. She lives in Paris, and she ends up on all fours in a ruined chapel in Virginia. It has one of my favorite twentieth-century lines: "Children know something they can't explain. They like Little Red Riding Hood and the wolf in bed together." I met the original of the doctor in the novel. He was still alive when I was in Paris. I went to a party where there was Greta Garbo and Mercedes de Acosta, her friend and lover. There was also this old doctor who'd been a friend of everybody in Paris. Especially if they had delicate wounds. He was made up with chalk white makeup and a lot of mascara. He took care of Americans in Paris. In the novel, after these unhappy love affairs, and she's Oh, Oh, Oh—so in the middle of the night, in a moment of absolute desperation, she goes to the doctor's apartment and bangs on the door and bangs on the door and gets in. And he's sitting up in bed with a long blond Mary Pickford wig and a frilly nightgown and little spots of rouge. Anyway, it's a great novel. And nobody was prepared for it. This last-gasp Victorian with modern frankness. It failed miserably. Not advertised or reviewed. Height of the Depression. So it was remaindered at Macy's, and there were millions of copies. My copy is a first edition from Macy's. Thirty-nine cents. I had read it just before I went off to the war.

But I never had a conversation with her. She was always in her dressing gown and curlers, and I guess I was just observing that old downtown code that all the Mobile ladies went by. You know, when my grandmother's back was to the street on her front porch, she was invisible. It might mean she hadn't done her hair yet. You didn't speak to her. So I never spoke to Djuna Barnes. We had a kind of "Good morning," "Good morning" relationship.

My apartment which I took to live in during the summer was the old kitchen and servants' dining room of a big old brownstone mansion on West 9th Street, behind the Fifth Avenue Hotel. I sublet my apartment on 10th Street and stayed on 9th Street in the summer. It was half a level below the street and had a little courtyard paved with flagstones where I could sit in the evenings and hear Jane and Paul Bowles quarreling in their nearby apartment or watch Madeleine L'Engle combing her hair at her window. I always had flowers and a fig tree from Mobile so I could look out and think, Mobile ain't that far away. The dirt it was growing in was from Mobile—black alluvial soil—so I could go touch it when New York got to be too much. But one day, the poet Howard Moss said, "That thing's dead," and picked it up, bucket and all, and threw it into the next courtyard. It was not quite spring, and the leaves were off. He was so New York, he didn't know that things dropped leaves and came back in the spring. So I never spoke to him again from that day till this. And I walked on the other side of the street to avoid him because I was afraid of him, if he thought that you killed trees because there are no leaves on them. I never shouted at him, didn't say a word when it happened. I just took him out of my telephone book that night.

❦

The year after the war, 1946, was like taking the cap off of an old-fashioned Coca-Cola. There was a big fizz all over America. And they fizzed to New York. Something like 10 percent of the intelligent, somewhat educated, or at least gifted, if uneducated, young people went to New York.

A wave of youth swept New York clean just after World War II. So when you went down the street, you saw these charming people—boys and girls from all over. The theater was full of young people attending. The library was full of young people. There was this brightness of spirit. And the city was clean.

Greenwich Village was still a village. Everybody knew everybody. Those who lived in the Village went to the same restaurants and bars and shops. We just automatically saw each other. When I began working in the theater—when I did *Master Builder* at the Cherry Lane—I'd go into shops to buy paint, go into shops to buy sequins, and somehow you'd get in with all those people. The Village was a great place for artists because the rents were so cheap. The Italians who had the wine store and the darling Viennese Jewish man who had a famous delicatessen across the street at the corner from me where Djuna Barnes went every morning to get the sticky coffee rolls she was queer for—they would let you charge. I could buy things on credit there after they knew where I lived and what I did. I could buy on credit there for a year if I needed it.

There was a restaurant in the Village called Charlie's Gorden: "garden" misspelled on the awning. He had an open-air place in the back where I used to lunch with Alison Lurie, who was a gorgeous thing. She wore green at her wedding and carried one white flower. Then there was a funny little Village restaurant in an old carriage house on a side street where it was always budding writers, or budding painters, or budding sculptors, or budding actors who were waiters. No order ever got right, but the place was fun.

I don't think anything like that exists now. The Village had such good parties and such amusing people that after a while people said, Gee, Greenwich Village. So a lot of nonentities came. The rents went up. The restaurants were no longer family-type restaurants. And that was it. It just changed. I probably wouldn't know it now.

There were several crowds that I had the great good luck to fall into. I'm centrifugal. If I spread my wings and fly, I always end up in the middle of something. It's vibrations. Many lives before this one. Friend of cats and monkeys. Pure instinct. It's because I never went properly to school. My childish instincts were never battered out of me.

In New York at that moment, there was a wonderful magazine called *Wake*, done by a boy who had just come out of Harvard or something, named Seymour Lawrence. He must have been moneyed. He was very slim and very beautiful with black, black hair. And oh, the ladies just fell over Seymour. He would come into a cocktail party and they'd go, Wow. You could hear them. The Filipino poet José Garcia Villa was the editor. He had just published his first volume of poems by New Directions. It was much made over, because his little gimmick to get attention was to put a comma between every word. To slow down the reader, he said, because people read poetry too fast nowadays. If you forget about the commas, they're some nice poems. And if I'm not mistaken, Seymour also started at New Directions. That must be how they met. There was that crazy, wonderful creature named James Laughlin who had started New Directions. He was a wealthy guy and just wanted to do it and did it. Right after the war he did that new classics series which was one of the greatest things ever done in America. He published so many of the modern writers for the first time. And reissued things which nobody knew, like Djuna Barnes's *Nightwood*. He published so many translations from French. It was just this fabulous publishing house. Distinguished design, beautiful typography, gorgeous jackets. So there was a New Directions/*Wake* crowd in the Village at that moment.

There was also a magazine called *View*, a surrealist quarterly financed by Helena Rubenstein. I had read *View* magazine all through the war; I had it sent wherever I went. I always write my comments—or did then, having nothing better to do—about any magazine like that which was something special, so I corresponded with Charles Henri Ford from Mississippi, the editor. And John Meyers, who now has the John Meyers Gallery at 57th Street. They were among the first people I saw when I moved to New York because I went to their office. It was there I met Alexander Calder and Joan Miró—all these famous refugee artists were in New York. Pavel Tchelitchew was one of those who had rushed from Paris to New York when it looked like the Germans were to take over Paris. He had rushed, as had Eugene Berman. They were all busy around *View*.

And I'll never forget going to that tiny little cinema in the East 50s somewhere that showed foreign films and special films. Once I went to see the very first Walt Disney natural history film. Not a cartoon, but one of those first films of animals and flowers and plants photographed in their natural habitat. Suddenly this tall, lanky guy somewhere in the front stood up and said, "Oh, Mrs. Nature! Mrs. Nature, she is wonderful." And that was Tchelitchew.

The *View* crowd did this avant-garde once-a-month thing at the Knickerbocker Music Hall. That was how I got to do Charles Henri's marionette play, which was designed by the artist Corte Seligmann. I executed the scenery and the marionettes from his designs for the Knickerbocker Music Hall production. John Meyers and I operated the actual marionettes. The music for violin and piano was the first Ned Rorem composition done publicly at the Knickerbocker Music Hall.

José Garcia Villa also knew the *View* crowd. So there was always a link among all the crowds: *View, Wake,* New Directions. All the different communities overlapped and impinged on each other.

I cannot remember how I met José Garcia Villa. I've known him forever. I mean, the people I really get along with, I can never remember how I met them. We met in the eighteenth century or in the Renaissance. Or on some Greek island early on. We're just remeeting years later. Anyway, José Garcia Villa was one of those nosy people who come in your apartment, you know, and if there was a table with a drawer in it, he would open it and see what was in it. One evening I was fixing dinner for him, and he just went through this pile of papers and said, "Well, I like these poems. I want to publish them." So I had these six poems in *Wake,* and they attracted a certain amount of attention. It wasn't a splash, but it was a speck.

Hazel McKinley, like her sister Peggy Guggenheim, was quite genuinely interested in young writers, young painters. They were both quite genuine. They weren't cutesy. They weren't collecting names in the news or anything. They were genuinely interested in people who were doing things. And so one of the great parties I was invited to after my poems were published in *Wake* was at Hazel McKinley's when she was coming out of her depression a year after the death of her children. She was still in very bad reputation. They said she'd thrown her two children out of this fiftieth-story window. But the truth is—which I learned from people who knew her—they went to the dentist and the window was open and nobody thought anybody would go on this little iron rail for flowerpots. It was like a little would-be verandah, an architectural detail, high above the street, to break the monotonous façade. It had not been properly attached, and her mad children went climbing out of the window and the whole thing fell fifty floors. They had to get a lot of sponges to clean up what was left of them. Of course, she never recovered. She was out of her mind with grief and became quite dotty. Then people said she threw them out because she was estranged from the husband and had always been sort of cranky with the children. She's still quite gaga, but worth meeting.

That was a good party. A very fancy apartment. I mean, the ashtrays were by Picasso and the doorknobs were by Alexander Calder. You know. Everybody that was in New York at that moment was there. That man who published the first Truman Capote short story in *Mademoiselle.* Rita Smith, the sister of Carson McCullers. Guy Pène duBois, the old painter, and his daughter Yvonne, who was also a painter. His son, William Pène duBois, was the art editor of the *Paris Review* later.

I had met Peggy Guggenheim at her gallery Art of This Century. I was there the third day after a new show opened. I had no idea who she was. All I know is that I was looking at a great big painting which I liked, and she was there roaming about with a pencil and a tablet and seemed to be some kind of attendant. I'll never forget these lapis lazuli grape leaves she was wearing. But I didn't know who she was. I thought she might be the gallery assistant or something; she was the only person there. So I asked her some questions about the painter, and she sort of laughed and answered them. I said, "I love that big painting of the snow on the barbed-wire fence." She laughed and laughed. It was one of the first Jackson Pollock throw-the-paint abstracts.

And then years later, we met again in Rome, and she invited me to stay for a week with her in Venice in her eighteenth-century palazzo right on the Grand Canal. A showplace. Her bedroom was a cerulean blue room with this oval bed. She had commissioned Alexander Calder to make her an old-fashioned brass bed. But at the time she commissioned it, World War II was starting and brass was absolutely forbidden to civilians. So she had him make it in sterling silver. The walls she had covered with her earring collection; the whole wall was gorgeous earrings, hung up on nails. What I most loved—she has a Marino Marini, a man on a horse sculpture. It's a naked man on a horse, throwing his arms back as though he were exulting and looking up at the sky. And also he had a big erection. Gorgeous. After the penis had been knocked off and stolen three times, she had one made by the sculptor that screws in. So the last thing she did in the evening was go and unscrew that penis and take it to a shoebox, where she kept it inside. Every morning, first thing she did in her negligé, she would go out and screw the penis in place to greet the morning sun.

In the Village, there was something called the Birdland bars. There were three bars. There was the Blue Jay, the Red Bird, and something else. If you wanted to indicate that you thought somebody was gay, you'd say "Bird-land." It was all the gay boys who were mostly in theater and the beginning of certain kinds of radio and advertisement. They were all from the provinces, and they were all more New Yorker than the New Yorker. They wore these Brooks Brothers suits, these white shirts, and these silk ties. They talked very properly. Every once in a while they'd forget, and you'd get Iowa or Missouri. Most of them had been in the army or the navy or the air force and were escaping small-town boredom. And the nonacceptance of anything that wasn't in a Bradley sweater or corduroy pants. But I found that closed gay world of New York impossible. They didn't have anything to talk about. They didn't read any books. They were just brainless wonders who thought they were getting New York gloss. And who probably had only two friends in

84

Viola, Iowa, and suddenly they could see hundreds from all over the United States. Mobile didn't have anything like the so-called gay set in New York. That was like a club in New York, a very private club, which was the saddest private club I've ever attended. Some of those people didn't see the so-called normal world for months on end.

There was this actress who had a huge loft apartment where she had parties for only gay males. I don't remember her name; I've had Alzheimer's all my life. She called and said, "I'm having everybody in to my loft apartment on Saturday night. Can you come?" I said, "Well, yeah," because I wanted to see a loft apartment. And I thought, Well, I'm going to give them something to think about. Because they would all be in those Brooks Brothers suits. So I wore my Prospero costume. It was a Mardi Gras costume with sequins and jewels, one of the old Mardi Gras costumes that really was silk and satin, not nylon. The sequins were real metal, and the rhinestones were real glass. It was a kind of Neapolitan nobleman's costume of 1500, mostly shades of blue, green, and yellow. Knee britches and tight stockings and a great jerkin sort of thing and a cape to the ground and sleeves to the ground.

I took a taxi, of course, and the driver said, "Oo-wee, you must be going to a party." I said, "I am the party. I'm going to a loft full of bores."

So I got there, and there were about thirty to forty elegant young men from the backwoods of Iowa, Minnesota, Arizona, Missouri; they were all in their gray Brooks Brothers being New Yorker. They fell in a faint when I walked in. Everybody was drinking martinis; that was the new drink at that moment of history. Everybody stood clenching a martini and watched me enter. And I pretended that I didn't notice that I was the only one properly dressed. And I went up to the hostess and shook hands and said, "What are you all drinking?" She said, "Well . . . I . . . we . . ." I said, "Well, I usually drink bourbon." She said, "Oh, yes," sort of like "I knew you wouldn't drink a martini. Not dressed like that."

So I went and sat on a sofa that was in the middle of this huge room and drank my bourbon. Everybody kept this respectful distance, kind of like "What is it?" Finally there was some boy from someplace in the South who had been saying something like "Have you seen the latest Paulette Goddard?" you know, but he dropped his loftiness and came over to me and said, "Where are you from?" I said, "Mobile, the mother of Carnival." He said, "I should have known."

When it came time to go, I realized I didn't have enough money and I was going to have to walk home. I'd come in this taxi and I'd tipped the driver generously because he was so amusing. So I just held my shoulders up, pretended I was dressed in native costume, and walked down Sixth Avenue.

Those cars would slow down, I'm telling you. Finally a police car slowed down. And they said kind of like "Hey there. Where are you going?" I said, "I'm going home." "Where you been?" I said, "I went to a party." I didn't tell them I was broke and why didn't they give me a lift. I didn't want any part of those New York police. One thing that makes a natural poet a natural poet is a dislike of military people and absolute fear and distrust of policemen. That's part of the born element of the poet. I always wish I had a water pistol full of Tabasco and could just shoot them in the eyes and blind them for twenty-four hours but do no permanent harm.

But anyway, I saw a loft. I went to a Birdland party in a loft. In the spirit of sociological research. I hope they are still talking about it somewhere. And I'm perfectly certain that more than half of them got sick of New York after three or four years and went back home and now are busy changing their grandchildren's diapers and mowing the lawn with that retired look on their faces. Others, you know, are probably dead of AIDS in Indochina or something.

I like parties where there's a cross section of the world. And if somebody brings a goat or a camel—like Patricia Highsmith once brought her pet tortoise to one of my parties—that makes it even better. But you have to have a cross section of the world. I always tried to have worlds in collision. Youth and old age, richness and poverty, painting and poetry, stock market and bordello. Worlds in collision. That's what makes a party.

I'd hate to be trapped in any little nasty world, whether it's the business world, the banking world, the garden club, the gays, the literary—I'd hate to be trapped in any little club. I belong to a union called international cats and monkeys. That's the union I belong to. So I see everybody. I can get through picket fences and over high walls other people don't. And I can dig out when I have to.

I was working in the daytime at the library and did theater at night. I was young. I didn't have to sleep. If I got to bed at two, I was ready to get up at seven. I had steak for breakfast with red wine. The climate in New York was such that I was never tired. I mean, I was raised in lizard land. New York wasn't humid in the way of Mobile humidity. And there was also this nervous energy in the air.

The first thing I did was for the Equity Library Theatre. Equity was trying to help all the unemployed actors, and they got some kind of grant to put on productions in the libraries. Most of the branch libraries had little auditoriums for lectures. For a production of Gorky's *Lower Depths*, I got up early

milking the moon

and went down to Clinton Street on the Lower East Side to those clean Jewish garbage cans and got my costumes from the garbage. After all, the play is about these people living in the slums of Russia. So I just took all the clothes that were thrown out, took them home, put them in a tub of Rinso with a little bit of lye wash, and made costumes for a cast of thirty. Everybody said it was one of the best *Lower Depths* they'd seen.

One of the persons I met in Equity Library Theatre was a struggling actress named Maureen Stapleton. She saw something or other that I had done with the library—I think J. B. Priestley's play *Laburnum Grove*. I did this tropical set in bamboo with all this bougainvillea in the back. I also made chandeliers for that—I made chandeliers for everything, including my own apartment. And I have specially trained spiders that cover my chandeliers with spiderwebs. Well, Maureen had this friend who wanted to do a private tryout of a play script he'd written. The play had opened on Broadway and was not successful, so he'd rewritten it thoroughly. Maureen was going to direct it, and she came to me and said, "You've got to do the set." Well, it was *The Merchant of Yonkers*, which became famous as *Hello, Dolly!* And that's how I met Thornton Wilder. He was cranky, but I liked him. He had a bitchy sister who was even more cranky. They were both proper cranks, with fighting among themselves. But I liked him a lot.

And I loved this Maureen Stapleton. She was Irish American, and she was animated and fun. We had the same sense of humor. She had come to New York from Troy to get into the theater, and lived on the top floor of this dreary thing on 51st Street. I used to go to her apartment sometimes after the theater when she had these wonderful parties with Marlon Brando and Wally Cox and all those critters. This was before Brando's big blowup to stardom; he'd only played Marchbanks in *Candida*, but he'd had much attention because of it. We played what was called "the game," which was the same game I played later in Fellini's garden. Charades. It was called "the game" then.

After that, I designed for a new translation of Ibsen's play *The Master Builder*, which was at the Cherry Lane Theater in the Village. That's the one I got the prize from *Show Business* magazine for the best Off Broadway set of the year.

It was because of that I was invited to the Robin Hood Theater in Arden, Delaware, for the summer. One of the plays they were going to do was Andreyev's *He Who Gets Slapped*, this wonderful play about a Russian circus. And I thought, Oh, to design those costumes. I knew exactly what I wanted to do. And I wanted to do *Angel's Tree* with a good Victorian London interior with a little curved stair in the back. The minute they said the names of the plays, I'd already designed them. And they were going to do *Hay Fever* by Noël Coward. Well, I got to do *Angel's Tree*. And we did that Depression-period play *You Can't Take It with You*. But then the director decided that the summer theater public wasn't good enough for *He Who Gets Slapped*, and I quarreled with her. Argued and argued and argued. We didn't come to blows, but there was a one-week break in the middle of the season, and I said, "Well, I don't think I can come back for the second half of the season." It was easy enough for her to find another scene designer in New York City for the rest of the summer theater season, because everybody wanted to leave New York for the summer. So I went back to New York.

Well, I'd sublet my apartment, so I couldn't get back into it for two weeks. Now, in the summer theater company there was an actor whose name you often see in theater magazines. He directs now. But he had this actor friend who came every weekend to see him when he was playing. It was this guy that I thought must be about forty. For me, forty was ancient. He always had these dark glasses and this crew cut. He helped a little with makeup. When I was doing Mr. Sycamore, the old eccentric who lives with the family in *You Can't Take It with You,* I was having trouble dealing with a bald wig. You have to get it just right so you don't see the join. I knew how to do it, but I was having trouble. "Oh," he said, "put the collodion on and then settle it. Don't do any makeup until you do that final gentle pull when the collodion is set. Then you put the base on and then the makeup." Anyway, he showed me how to do it, and I thanked him. Well, when he heard I was leaving and didn't have any place to stay, he said, "Oh, come and stay with me. I've got gobs of space." He said, "My sister lives on one floor and I live on one floor and there is another floor." He said, "Come on for those two weeks when you are waiting. It would be fun to have you."

Well, I arrived from the train station with a Rinso carton full of paint-brushes and tubes of paint. I had this battered suitcase from Mobile. And I was in these ratty summer clothes. I gave the address he'd given me. It was Central Park West. Well, I'd never been to Central Park West. I didn't know what that meant. We arrived at this very grand apartment house. And this doorman—eight feet tall, with ice mantling his summit—looked at my luggage and said, "Service entrance is on the side street." And I went. But anyway, this guy, whom I just knew as a friend of a friend, was the man who played the Shadow on the radio.

He was immensely wealthy. He'd been doing the Shadow as long as there was radio. Well, when I got there, it turned out that his sister had brought a whole bunch of friends in, so every room was taken, except a wonderful private room on her floor; I took that one. There was a john in my bedroom, but for the bath I had to go down a floor and go through a bedroom and the dressing room of the Shadow. Because he was always recording or broadcasting, I barely saw him except late at night when he was finished, and we'd have drinks together when he came in. The servants showed me how to go down and find the bath. His bedroom was two stories high. It had a bed with sterling-silver bedposts and black velvet curtains because he was the Shadow. And there were these two rooms of mirrored cupboards. After I'd been there four days, I had to open a couple of them. I had to.

It was all wigs. He had a crew cut and could go through all stages from no hair to longer than shoulder by twilight. He could go from pale blond to Italian black, through all the stages of Irish red, Sabine Hills red. And there was a hairdresser permanently employed who lived in the household.

But he had said to me, "Will you paint something over my bar? I'm having my bar remodeled. Paint something that was like your *Hay Fever* set or whatever you want to do." I said, "All right—that will be my thank-you note." So I did this little mural for him over his bar, and then I moved back to Greenwich Village.

That Rich Mix of New York in the Forties

Right after the war, before I left for New York, I had worked briefly in the Haunted Book Shop in Mobile, putting the poetry section in order. One day I came across an errata slip that had fallen out of the poetry bookshelf. Cameron and Adelaide, of course, had all the latest books of poetry, whether they sold or not. Some of them stayed ten years on the shelf, twelve years on the shelf. They always got what they thought sounded interesting. A Southern bookshop. Well, this errata slip fell out. It was on good paper and I liked the typeface and I was fascinated by what was on the page. So I went on safari. It took three days going through all those poetry books to find the one this had fallen out of. It was a book called *The Ego and the Centaur* that had just come out from New Directions. And I thought, Oh, when I go to New York, I'm going to have to go to New Directions and buy me a copy for myself. Because when I was talking about it, somebody was in the shop and right away bought *The Ego and the Centaur*. I was doing this big thing and talking about it with Adelaide and waving it. Then somebody in there said, "Well, I'll buy that." So I thought, Yeah, sure, it's a bookshop. I'll have to go to New Directions.

When I got to New York I kept asking the *View* people, "Have any of you-all met a poet from the French part of Indiana called Jean Garrigue?" I thought it was a man. Jean Garrigue. Well, life being what life is like, and the interwovenness of it all, somebody from somewhere—I can't think who, it may have been Seymour Lawrence—and I were strolling down Christopher Street, having dined in a little restaurant, and he said, "Oh, look, there's somebody you ought to meet." And there was this charming-looking little thing with egret nest curls. Huge blue eyes; you could see across the street they were blue. And she was wearing these dirty slacks, sweeping the sidewalk in front of this slum building on Christopher Street between Sheridan Square and West 10th. Anyway, he said, "You Southerners from the provinces." And he said, "Jean Garrigue, Eugene Walter." I said, "WHAT? What? I'm your errata boy." She thought I was saying erotic boy. Then I told the story about the errata slip. We became great friends. Her building almost backed up to mine in that block. We'd been two years vibrating at each other and didn't know it. All these things happen to everybody, but most people don't notice.

Jean Garrigue was Something Else Again. Even before I met her, I considered her America's only Baroque poet. She wrote her own free verse, except it wasn't free verse. Just as Walt Whitman has a secret meter, if you read Jean Garrigue aloud, you discover this secret American rhythm. And she was writing about everything: animals, vast landscapes, and vast concepts. She was not one of the race of professor lady poets, saying, "I don't feel so well, I'm unhappy, nothing goes right, America's a terrible place to live, there are no men in America or all the men are cavemen in America." They never have any idea of a civilized male creature. It's either the Neanderthal or the priss. Anyway, Jean Garrigue wrote big.

And that was surprising, since she was a lady of the old school. A lady. But also a bawd, as all the great eighteenth-century ladies were. Could carry on any kind of conversation. Loved the same sort of dirty jokes that I like. There were a lot of the beginnings of liberated ladies in New York who were tough and nasty. Bitchy, mean, sexually unsatisfied, and putting off the very men who were attracted to them because they had spirit. It was that beginning of the women's lib thing, though it wasn't called women's lib then. But then there were people like Jean Garrigue and a whole bunch of Southern girls who stayed ladies except they learned to say "fuck." They still had a certain graciousness and, above all, a sense of humor. What some of those New England girls didn't have was a sense of humor. The men called them the scissors girls. If you weren't careful, they'd cut your balls off. The scissors girls. Later it was called women's lib.

Jean Garrigue was just an exceptional creature. With this irresistible smile and these blue eyes. She was petite, and she dressed very well. Sometimes she wore slacks and a loose blouse in the bohemian way, but if she was going uptown, she had on a tailored Chanel suit. Her hair was some honey colored. She was adorable. Imagine Emily Dickinson after two glasses of elderberry wine.

It was only revealed much, much later that she was multierotic and the lover of Josephine Herbst, the novelist and revolutionary. But she also had a long list of male lovers. She was not an erotic whiz kid. She was not what was called a nympho. She had a feminine thing of comforting people. I think that kind of lady just goes to bed with guys they feel sorry for. "Oh, poor darling. Poogie, woogie, woo." And I think she was a passionate woman in the eighteenth-century sense. It didn't always show. She wasn't lighting one cigarette after another and hiking her skirt up to her navel. She was a lady, but eighteenth-century: she knew everybody had to have sex.

She died of cancer while I was in Rome. Everybody on earth called me long-distance. Everybody. "Eugene we've got— Are you sitting down? We've got some news." By the time I'd had twenty-four hours of this, I thought, People love catastrophe. Now I know why the Greek kings killed the messengers who brought the bad news. Just cut their heads off after they'd given their message. I wanted to bomb the Bell system because I heard so many times that she died of cancer. We had just been corresponding and talking about how we could meet in Paris.

You see, the world is very small. It doesn't matter how many millions more are born. It's still that 10 percent of people who reason, who are aware of larger issues, and it's only 3 percent of the total that's cats and monkeys. She was cats and monkeys. And I adored her.

I met Josephine Herbst through Jean Garrigue and all the Village set. She had intense blue eyes and graying hair, and she was much older than everybody else. Much older. She was very much of the thirties: a thirties protester. I don't know if she ever was a member of the Communist Party, but she was extremely leftist. Of course, nobody today can understand what that meant in the Depression period. During those poor, poor, poor years, when people literally were starving to death in the streets, ordinary people had a certain resentment of some of the big wealth. They thought the government was in the clutches of the rich. Indeed it was, still is. I mean Reagan—

Oh, my God. I said I'd never say that in the same room with the monkey.

I'm sorry, darling. I have to apologize. Never again. I'll say Baudelaire twenty-seven times as penance.

But anyway, nobody can imagine who wasn't alive, and seeing the problems of the Depression, the rabid leftism of someone like Josephine Herbst. She did not come of a poor family, but she was of a farming family that was self-supporting and proud and red-white-and-blue American.

As a young woman she was successful as a novelist and a journalist. She covered the Spanish civil war and knew Hemingway through all that. But she was rabidly left, and I disapproved of that. Because I had come through the Depression and had seen real poverty with a Southern accent, and I still had a sense of humor. And even the most revolutionary young men never were that hysterical or rabid, where they got absolutely tremulous in talking about it. Even in 1948 she could get all worked up and get "What do you mean by that?" She was one of those "What do you mean by that?" persons. Like high blood pressure. I didn't like that aspect of her. I always talked to her about gardening. I learned early on that was a safe subject. And I could make her laugh.

How did I make Josie laugh? How do I make anybody laugh? I don't know. By putting omega before alpha rather than alpha before omega. Who knows? I could make Josie smile with just impressions of other writers she didn't like. I only had to give her impressions of someone at a party and I'd get her off politics for a minute.

I remember she took a great exception to Truman Capote. She thought he was a little puff from the South. He was not. He had a mind as sharp as a fox trap. But she, seeing that famous photo of him lying on a sofa—the photo on the back of his first novel—thought he was a cream puff from Alabama.

Then years later when I was living in Rome, I went to meet her in Naples after she returned to Europe for the first time since she'd been covering the Spanish civil war. I went right there and met her boat. Took her to a waterfront restaurant for a dinner, and I lent her my raincoat because she didn't bring one and suddenly it was damp and cold. But she was too sensitive. I escorted her around and did everything and gave dinners for her when she got to Rome and all that and all that. But there was one evening she called me and she was feeling at loose ends. I said, "I'm sorry I can't see you tonight because I have the proofs of *Botteghe* and I'll be working all night to get these to the printer in the morning." And she was offended. That's the last I saw her.

Ruth Herschberger was also part of that rich mix of New York in the forties. I flipped for her first book of poems. She had that American idea of poetry at one end and social consciousness at the other. Then she wrote this really feminist book that was like the last gasp of Edith Wharton and before the crankiness of the fifties and sixties ladies. A very witty, wonderful book called *Adam's Rib*. She had these flashing dark eyes and chestnut hair. Dressed very simply, but with that understated something which is American chic at its best. Even with no money, she had a way of wearing a sweater. And her skirt fitted and moved. She taught some, but she was a poet and wrote marvelous poetry. Now she is an alcoholic. She's at Stuyvesant Apartments dead drunk right this red-hot minute. Went to bed at three A.M. with a last gin and got up at seven this morning and had a first gin. You know: the pressures of New York. Southerners were able to cope somehow.

All the Southerners in New York would get together about every ten days or two weeks and cry over Smithfield ham. There was a community, like a religious group except it wasn't a church. Southerners always, by secret gravity, find themselves together. If somebody got a Smithfield ham, they'd call a few other Southerners. If I got gumbo filé that was fresh gumbo filé from Bayou La Batre, I'd call a few Deep Southerners. You always knew, if there was any kind of trouble, that was like cousins in town.

One lived right up above me in my winter apartment on West 10th. One day I heard this thing hopping down the stairs in heavy shoes. I looked out and he said, "Good morning." I said, "Where are you from?" He said, "Hanceville, Alabama." "Mobile." Oh, Lord, here we are in the same building. From that instant we were lifelong friends. This was Donald Ashwander, who had come to New York to study orchestration with the composer Ben Weber, who was also a great teacher of music.

David Walker was a friend of Donald Ashwander's. They had some music classes together somewhere, and Donald introduced him. Said he wanted me to meet this boy from Georgia. He was an accompanist for Aaron Copland. In fact, I met Aaron Copland through him. I adored him. There's a Jewish sense of humor which always gets me. "We've been blitzed, but let's keep our sense of humor." Like Southerners: "We've been Yankeed, but we've kept our attitude." I think David, for the last three or four or five years before Aaron Copland died, just really gave his whole life to Aaron Copland. I hope now he is composing again. He set the first paragraph of my story "Troubadour" for tenor, viola, and piano. It was absolutely delightful.

When I left New York, I sublet my apartment to David, and he still lives there. Since it's the old rent laws, they have only been able to put it up to something like $30 in all these years. And the telephone is still in my name.

93

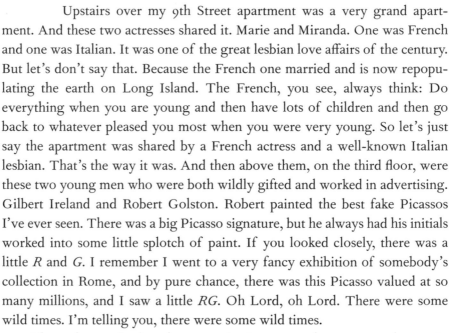

Upstairs over my 9th Street apartment was a very grand apartment. And these two actresses shared it. Marie and Miranda. One was French and one was Italian. It was one of the great lesbian love affairs of the century. But let's don't say that. Because the French one married and is now repopulating the earth on Long Island. The French, you see, always think: Do everything when you are young and then have lots of children and then go back to whatever pleased you most when you were very young. So let's just say the apartment was shared by a French actress and a well-known Italian lesbian. That's the way it was. And then above them, on the third floor, were these two young men who were both wildly gifted and worked in advertising. Gilbert Ireland and Robert Golston. Robert painted the best fake Picassos I've ever seen. There was a big Picasso signature, but he always had his initials worked into some little splotch of paint. If you looked closely, there was a little *R* and *G*. I remember I went to a very fancy exhibition of somebody's collection in Rome, and by pure chance, there was this Picasso valued at so many millions, and I saw a little *RG*. Oh Lord, oh Lord. There were some wild times. I'm telling you, there were some wild times.

Through somebody who came backstage at the summer theater in Delaware, I met some people from a community theater in Nutley, New Jersey. They turned up in New York a long time after I got back and asked me to come design a production of the old Kaufman play based on the Barrymores called *The Royal Family*. I did the set rather like an apartment I had seen on Park Avenue with a double stairway going from the first to the second floor. And I made this Baroque table that had two dolphins, with twined tails, all black and gold, all made of papier-mâché, with a marble top, to go on the little landing, with a mirror above. For when the young man comes back from Africa, I made these cages of slats and chicken wire that were colored to look weathered, and I made papier-mâché parrots. The bellboys carrying in the birdcages could pull a little string in the ring that they were holding the cage by and make the parrots do their things. I stood in the wings and went, *"Caw, c-c-caw, caw."* It was one of my favorite parts. And you know—that double dolphin. The tabletop was taken off and it turned up at Carnegie Hall in some woman's dance recital. She was playing a Greek nymph cast up on the shores of the Ionian Sea. Robert Golston called and said, "Eugene, you're not going to believe this. Your dolphins were at Carnegie Hall last night."

But anyway, while in New Jersey, I met a whole bunch of people. And there was this guy who helped backstage. He was a real tough. He was a truck driver, drove a big Mack truck. You know, New York is always—the world is always—full of surprises. He called me from New Jersey and said, "I'm coming to New York this weekend, and could I come by to speak to you for a moment?" So he came by to have a drink. He said, "Well, the gay boys in Nutley are having a big masquerade ball, and I want something really outrageous and spectacular because I'm the head of the ball committee. I thought you could design something." Lord love a duck.

I said, "What did you have in mind?"

He said, "Well, I'm blond and my hair is naturally curly, and I've always liked those photographs of Lillian Russell."

I said, "A hat. I'll make you a hat that will end hatdom."

I got this reinforced cardboard and glued some rather fine lightweight chicken wire to it. I made this sort of tree of life with all kinds of different fruits and different flowers and different little stuffed birds. I had these invisible wires that held the tree up.

The Nutley boys had rented a ballroom somewhere in Brooklyn for their gay ball. So we all gathered—everybody in the apartment house—the two actresses and a very old lady from across the street who had been a vaudeville star—and had a party on the top floor of Golston/Ireland because this guy was going to get into his wig and hat there. It took him an hour to do his makeup. So the boys made martinis and we were talking about a new show, and when he came out for me to adjust his hat, I was thunderstruck. There was this beautiful Lillian Russell. I mean gorgeous. With this blond, upswept, turn-of-the-century wig. Perfect makeup. I mean, Perc Westmore couldn't have done it better on Joan Crawford or Mae West. He'd shaved his chest, but then here were these fuzzy animal arms. He had a clean white shirt, tight blue jeans, and Keds. He won first prize. Lord love a duck.

Now Robert DeVries, the painter, lived upstairs over me in my winter apartment. He was tall and very handsome and very pleasant. A little quiet, a little shy. I introduced Marie, from my summer place, to Robert, this tall blond friend of mine in my winter place. And Marie and Robert had an oh so sensitive evening together and ended up in bed. Then they had this passionate affair that I knew about, of course, but pretended not to. I mean, if you are taking your garbage out onto 10th Street at seven in the morning and see your upstairs neighbor, the beautiful blond painter, coming out giggling with a French actress, who theoretically would have been sleeping in her own apartment on 9th Street, all you can do is say, "Good morning," and go on and put your garbage out. And after the morning giggles were heard over thirty times, I could only corroborate my initial impression.

I have a feeling that he might have had friendly sex with other art students, but that this tragic heroine—French, oh so sensitive, with a great sense of humor—might have been *the* love affair. This was *l'affaire du siècle* for him. She was not conventionally pretty. She was dead white skin. I mean, you could put her on Atlantic Beach for two months, and she'd still be dead white. It's that kind of French skin. Brown hair and huge, luminous eyes that could change from gray to almost blue, or be blue and suddenly change to almost amber, according to the room and the season. And she was an extraordinary actress.

Anyway, then Miranda caught on. She came to me because I had trunk-loads and trunkloads of dry lapels. People came to cry on my shoulder, because I'm a Southerner and I always know how to make that little drink and say, "Do sit down and here, have this; you'll feel better. Tell me about it." I think there's something, not about me, but about all Southerners. Call it patience and the willingness to converse. To say, "Sit down and tell me about it." It's a Southern thing.

Then I had Robert asking my advice. He said, "I really love Marie, but Miranda loves Marie." He said, "I think Miranda is going to hire some people down on Mulberry Street to knock me out. Because Miranda is beginning to follow me around New York." He said, "I see this figure with a very mascu-line stride in this raincoat with the collar up. This hat with the brim pulled down. I recognize Miranda from two blocks away, and she is following me."

Then Marie came, so I had all three. I had to make appointments to be sure they didn't meet coming in or out of my front hall. Actually I started a comedy play about it once and never finished it.

And I didn't give any advice. I just let them talk. If you just listen and guide them to tell more about this part, or more about that part, and never express an opinion, they'll come to a decision themselves. Advice is making people think for themselves, then they think you are brilliant. You don't have to say a word. Just pass the Jim Beam and smile and nod. And say, "Tell me about it." And if they reach a moment of dreadnought, put on music. Mozart's a better psychiatrist than Freud. Drown them in Jim Beam and Mozart, and it'll all work out. And they thanked me profusely for my wisdom.

The result was that since both of them protected this sensitive and deli-cate Marie, she woke up one morning and got tired of being the sheltered flower. Ran off to Long Island and got a job teaching English at Long Island University—she had all kinds of degrees. She married this delightful profes-sor and started making babies right and left. Miranda took up with a little blond Polish refugee. But she was still getting younger and younger actresses all the time. I think she is now doing Girl Scouts. Robert took up with one of his art class friends that he'd been dating before. And everybody lived happily ever after.

96

Combating Dailyness

Jean Garrigue and I used to love to go to the Museum of Modern Art garden on Sunday afternoons. They had all these little tables under the trees, looking very European. They had a proper alcoholic bar run by these Filipino boys, and they had a soft drink bar run by Baptists, I guess. We used to go there and sip gin and tonic and watch the students and professors who had come to New York for summer courses. They would always be looking sort of expectant, hoping they would see Picasso in the garden of the Museum of Modern Art. And I said to Jean one day, "You know, really it's so sad, these children from the provinces. They come here in August when everybody has left New York and nothing is happening." So I said, "Let's do something for them." It's because I'm a poet. When you say the word *poet*, there are people who think of something pale, frail, or a college professor with a bow tie writing sensitive verses. Or they think of something slightly mad. But the old Greek word for poet, *poiētēs*, means somebody who makes things or makes things happen. I make things happen.

This really was the first "happening." It wasn't called a happening. Other people later began to do this all over America, and they were called happenings.

We called ourselves the Apparition Group. It was José Garcia Villa, the poet Howard Moss, Robert DeVries, Ruth Herschberger, Josephine Herbst, this wonderful painter Ann Troxel, and the actress Marie Donnet. We rehearsed it for a week and timed it, because I wanted some things to happen simultaneously. Nobody else knew what we were doing. We sent little postcards to some well-known artists and writers, saying "The Apparition Group, Sunday at 3:00, August the so-and-so, Museum of Modern Art garden."

I had chosen my friend from Mobile Edith Zelnicker's birthday. I wrote to her and her husband and said, "I'm having a little party for you. You and Edwin come to the Museum of Modern Art and you'll see a little pink crepe-paper flower. That's your table." They thought I was just doing something silly like I might always do. That I would come dressed as Santa Claus in August or something like that. They came nervously and sat at the table indicated. They're old Mobile Jewish: conservative and no public display of any kind.

What happened was, at precisely three o'clock, a very beautiful little boy about ten years old, wearing a rather odd sort of blue hussar jacket and blue short pants, came into the middle of the garden, lifted his toy trumpet, and played a fanfare and then ran. That was the only sound we made. So everybody was looking. Then I appeared. I was the Very Sick Poet. My hair was jet-black, done with Kiwi shoe polish, and my face was dead white with black eyebrows and shadows under my eyes. I carried a large aspirin bottle and a bouquet of dead white roses. I was dressed in a Southern white linen suit with a flowing tie. My jacket pockets were full of diamond flitters—sequin dust. With this I made a little path behind me. Then Jean Garrigue came in as the witch of Christopher Street. She was no longer blond. I had dyed her hair jet-black, and we added ostrich plumes to her natural curls. She wore black to the floor and this fringed black cape with sequins. She carried a basket of four kittens wearing tiny little ballet skirts and came precisely on my path of sequin dust.

I went to the central table where some tourists were sitting. I put my aspirin down and my dead white roses and in my best Boris Karloff voice, I said, "I'm terribly sorry; this table is taken." They got up and ran. They ran. So I sat down, and Jean Garrigue came and sat opposite me. Turned the kittens in their ballet skirts loose under the table. We sat and talked in total gibberish. The Filipino boys running the drink booth were so enchanted they brought us drinks on the house right away. The soft drink people went to the armed guard and said, "They can't do this here. They can't do this here." The delightful German refugee guard who was always there said, "Well, they bought their admission tickets. . . ."

When Garrigue and I stopped our conversation suddenly, raised our champagne glasses, and clinked them, that's the moment when Robert DeVries got up from the table in the corner and hung several globes of colored paper in the trees and started blowing soap bubbles. He was dressed in a proper double-breasted business suit, white shirt, and necktie, looking as though he might be a young Wall Street lawyer. When he started blowing bubbles, that was the signal for all our cohorts dressed as ordinary citizens throughout the garden to do the same. Suddenly there were globes of colored paper in every tree and the whole garden was full of soap bubbles.

Everybody was in silent awe. I looked up and the whole glass wall of the second floor was smashed noses looking into the garden. Then people started sort of coming timidly out of the museum. Nobody was looking at pictures by then.

Jean Garrigue and I sat there and resumed our conversation in an unknown language. People were gathering around staring at us, but we didn't notice anybody. Then this woman in a raincoat with a hood appeared, staring at us. She was very pale with long green hair and a kind of mermaid's costume. This was Ann Troxel. I had copied the Graham Sutherland painting of a chartreuse, red, and white beetle. She was carrying it like a baby and rocking it and staring at us. Then the crowd was staring at her. Marie Donnet floated in like a dream figure in a bright red dress of chiffon to the ground and evening makeup, with rhinestone earrings to her knees and a cigarette holder three feet long.

At that moment, José Garcia Villa was supposed to come in the back door with purple hair, an old-fashioned movie camera, and start filming us and then pull endless yards of tinsel out of the camera and throw it around. But he lost his nerve. Howard Moss was supposed to come in and do something, but he lost his nerve and said, "You all are going to be arrested." We said, "No, we are not. We are buying our tickets. We are not making any noise." The only sound was the initial trumpet and our little nonsense conversation at the table. Everything else was done in silence. The whole idea was silence, except for the little fanfare and our conversation.

By this time the crowd was going mad, trying to talk to us, asking us, "What does it mean? Who are you? What does it mean?" The one guy I remember in the crowd—all the effort was worth it if only for him, this little fat man. He had to have been from somewhere way off. He was climbing onto his table and snapping pictures and shouting, "I just happened to have my camera! I just happened to have my camera!" You could tell he was the guy who sees a train wreck or a skyscraper collapse, and he's never got his camera when he needs it. He kept saying, "I just happened to have my camera!" For once in his life, he had his camera when he needed it.

At a given moment we all got up, went through the garden, and handed out miniature French playing cards. Everybody got a playing card. People said, "Oh, they are advertising something." Typical American reaction: the meaning is that they are advertising something. But our message was, the moral of the whole thing was, "You too can play."

Then we all slowly congregated at the back door as planned; taxis were waiting that had been called in advance. Josephine Herbst gathered up the kittens. Somebody in the museum had called the *New York Times* and there was a *Times* reporter who was tugging at me, saying, "What is all this? Who are you all?" Again, in my best Boris Karloff voice, I said, "We're the Apparition Group." He said, "What does it mean? What's it all about?" I said, "We are combating dailyness." Got in a taxi and was whisked off.

Afterwards I had a party in my courtyard in the Village. José came to apologize. He said, "I really thought we'd get in trouble." I said, "Well, since what we were doing was innocent, what trouble could we have? Seymour or New Directions would have bailed us out if we'd been arrested."

New York was full of it for weeks. Nobody quite knew what had happened. Nor did the *New York Times*. We never told them. We never let on.

99

And with the way fact turns into fiction with each retelling, a week or so later, I heard that the Museum of Modern Art had staged a preview in the garden to advertise Roland Petit's Ballets de Paris that was coming to town. Then years later—years later—I went to a dinner party in London and I had to almost bite my tongue off. There was a young woman there who said, "When I was studying in New York, I went to this wonderful birthday party in honor of Edith Sitwell at the Museum of Modern Art."

🙮

Oh, there were parties, parties, parties, parties. But for me, almost anything is reason for a party. The first tulips in spring: have a party. The first green peas are in: have a party. I just think that way. That's how I think. The reason I have never had more than ten dollars to my name—if I had ten dollars, I gave a party. If I had two hundred dollars, I gave a very good party.

So when Dylan Thomas came to New York, I had a party.

During the war, when I was in Alaska and the Aleutians, I subscribed to a magazine published by the University of Illinois at Urbana called *Accent*. That's where I read my first Eudora Welty story, about a black midwife, and I flipped. Then in the next issue there were these poems by this young Welsh poet named Dylan Thomas, and they said that his book had come out in '38 or '39 and was called *Fifteen Poems*. What I liked about those poems was that they were fresh and youthful. We get so much of that "I'm unhappy in the suburbs in spite of the steam heat and my new polka-dot tie." I get so sick of that kind of American poetry. It's as though the eternal themes are unavailable to some of these college professors and darling children. Oh so sensitive. Oh so unhappy in the steam-heated suburbs. I can't take it. What I loved about Thomas's poems was a kind of sideswipe quality, as though he heard words differently, as though he spoke words differently. He was born and raised in Wales; naturally his English would be different, as a Southern writer's English would be different. I flipped. I mean, wowee. So then I tried to find that *Fifteen Poems* or *Eighteen Poems* or whatever that book was called. Never could find it.

Well, there was this English poet who had taught somewhere in Alabama, who naturally ended up at my place in Greenwich Village to call on me and then also came to parties after. Ruthven Todd. People in Alabama had sent word to him, If you are going to New York, you have to meet Eugene. Well, one day he said, "You've probably never heard of him," because at that time, Dylan Thomas was known only to a few professors at Harvard who were keeping up with everything in them islands. But he hadn't published anything in America to speak of, and was unknown really. He said, "You probably don't know this Welsh poet, Dylan Thomas—" I said, "Stop right there. Know him? I LOVE him." He said, "Well, he's coming to New York." I said, "Coming to New York!" He said, "Do you want to meet him?" I said, "Do I want to meet him!"

There are some people I was friends with before I met them. Like Isak Dinesen. I knew I would love her. I knew she would like me. I knew I would get along with Dylan Thomas when I read those first poems in *Accent*. And I knew I'd meet him.

Ruthven Todd brought him one day, and there he was. A little old drunk. Just a little old rosy-cheek drunk. And as jolly a sense of humor as one would wish. Nothing professorial. Rather shabby. With all these Welsh curls and these wicked, wicked bright eyes. He didn't miss a trick. Harlech and leeks all the way, when so many American poets are hermits, or professors, or cranks, or show-offs. So I gave this party to welcome him.

I thought, Well, he's from the British Isles; that means rose gardens. So I went down to the Woolworth's in the Village and bought green-covered florist wire. It was summertime, so I was living in my "summer place" on West 9th. The day of the party I got up early in the morning and went down to the flower market and bought lots of roses. I came home and wrapped the stem of each rose in wet cotton wadding and then made these rose trees with florist wire and green wax paper. I wanted rose trees like those in the illustrations of *Alice in Wonderland*. I put a row of those trees against the brick walls on each side of this little courtyard. I had some other flowers that I put into fruit jars full of water and buried in the ground since that earth was so sordid after who knows how many years of New York soot. I had tried to work that garden, but nothing would grow; it was a desert. So I made an English garden. I had millions of candles. Millions. I looked out and I thought, Well, it needs a touch of Mobile. Of Carnival. So I got the last of those diamond flitters and spread them all over the flagstones. And in the candlelight, that twinkling pavement was rather something.

There was Curtis Harrington, the young film director, and his beautiful cousin Thamar. There was José Garcia Villa. Jean Garrigue. Oscar Williams, the anthologist who did so many anthologies of American poetry and included so many very young, practically unknown people. Ruth Herschberger. Josephine Herbst. Baby Andrew. Robert DeVries. And Gene Derwood, this rather serious lady poet, who came in a wool moor-stalking cape and brought a quart of milk. She said, "I know you won't be serving milk at this party." And I looked at this quart of milk. Nobody had ever brought a quart of milk to any of my parties. Then I took her out to the garden, and she said, "How spurious. I would never do a thing like this." Well, that and the milk: I never spoke to her again. Arriving with milk and saying my diamond flitter rose garden was spurious. Spurious. She was spurious. That moor-stalking cape—and this was August—and that quart of milk.

Anyway, it was a very good party. I had a little table set up where people could do their own drinks. I had Southern fried chicken, served in a big black umbrella turned upside down. Then along about three A.M., there was just Jean Garrigue, Dylan Thomas, Ruthven Todd, and myself. Thomas was pretty drunk and began to tell some great stories. You know, we all have a favorite character. Tallulah, I might say, was mine. His was old Queen Mary. He had hundreds of stories about her. All of her equerries were beautiful young men of grand families. She always had six young men attending her when she left the palace, and they were all bribed by every antique and jewelry dealer in London to let them know if she was going to visit the shop. The really valuable and beautiful things they'd go hide. Because if she said, "Oh, how perfect," "Oh, how perfectly gorgeous," they had to say, "Oh, Your Majesty, please take it." All of the people in the old country houses would hide the good paintings when she was coming on a royal progression. She'd come in and say, "Oh, I thought there was supposed to be a Van Dyck over the mantel," and they'd say, "Well, you know, it's at the restorer." "What restorer do you use?" She was a terror. But anyway, when she went to these shops and they knew she was coming, they'd have a folding screen, and behind it they'd have either a punch bowl on a little stool or one of those Oriental vases people use as umbrella stands, because she had nervous kidneys, and when she had to go, she had to go. So she would just drift in back of the screen, and all the equerries would start coughing and talking all at once to drown the sound of tinkling. So Queen Mary was Dylan Thomas's comic culture heroine.

And of course everybody adored him. He had an outdoor look in that city where everybody has an office look. He just looked English country animal. We had a lovely luncheon, just Dylan and I, at Charlie's Gorden, and talked about everything on earth. It was Alabama meeting Wales. Edith Sitwell was another one of his culture heroines, because she adored him and was one of the people to push his career. The minute she saw some of his poems, you know, she sort of screamed a bloodcurdling scream and said, "This is it." And Dylan loved her suite of poems for speaker called *Façade*, set to Sir William Walton's music. As we drank our wine, we reenacted for each other the story of its first performance in London in the 1930s, when Dame Edith recited the poems through a megaphone concealed in the mouth of a huge pink-and-white mask. For some reason, a crowd of prune faces had gathered outside to protest the event, and she had to have a police escort to get to her car afterwards. Before she got in she turned and said, "I have never, at any time, desired to pull the leg of the public." "I, however," Dylan said to me, "do. As often as possible."

I never saw him again after that. But of course, years later when I worked for Princess Caetani, *Botteghe Oscure* was the first to publish *Under Milk Wood*. The princess also loved his work. She had also screamed when she first read it. They had corresponded, and she published some of his most important works, like "In the White Giant's Thigh" and "Do Not Go Gentle into That Good Night." And she had given him an advance. He had said, "I have always wanted to write a play for voices, like a radio play." He had read Archibald MacLeish's *Fall of the City* and thought that this was a new medium for poets. Voice plays. Since you don't see actors or scenery, you can give total attention to the words. He said he'd always wanted to write one ever since he'd heard radio. So she gave him an advance, and off he went. Well, he was hard up, dead broke—I think his first child had been born by then. So he also got an advance from the BBC. Then he got an advance from a publisher. But since the princess had given him the first advance, she thought she should have the right to publish the work. So he sent her some pages, but it was not finished. And I was going from Paris to London for Christmas, so she asked me to get in touch with him and try to get a few more pages. I never saw him because he was down in Wales, but through John Davenport, who was something to do with one of the magazines, I tracked down a few pages more. I picked them up at a publisher's through the good offices of John Davenport and took them back. The princess and Alfred Chester and I read this thing out loud, the three of us, and we thought it was wonderful. We were just rolling. So she said, "I understand that the BBC can broadcast this, but since I was the first to commission it, I am going to go ahead and publish what we have." So about two-thirds of it was published in *Botteghe* under the title "Llareggub," which looks like a Welsh village. But being a cryptographer, I always read things backwards anyway, and I saw right off where it was called "Bugger All."

Then years later in Rome I became friends with his widow, the delightful Caitlin. Everybody says what a bitch she was and all that and all that. Well, I'm sorry. She had a hard time raising money to feed the children and pay the rent and clothe them. And she was never a bitch. She hounded publishers for royalties. She hounded the BBC. She nagged New Directions. But she was not a bitch. I liked her very much. She had some reddish hair and this white face. Finally she took up with an Italian.

At her invitation, I went to see her son when he was performing in *The Recruiting Sergeant* in this English school in Rome. He was playing the lead, and he was perfectly magnificent. He had a natural acting style and enormous charm. You didn't notice the other actors; he had that presence. Afterwards I was talking to the headmaster while we were waiting for him to scrape his makeup off. This very stern headmaster said, "Well, let's hope he doesn't end up like his father." And I couldn't resist saying, "You mean drunk or immortal?"

Just a Southern Boy Let Loose

There were twenty-five returning GIs who were given scholarships to the Museum of Modern Art special painting class. I was one of those. I studied drawing and painting with a wonderful painter named Bernard Pfriem, who was just a jolly soul. We had live models, and you could, on your own, throw the paint or abstract. But in the class we had classical technique, which is what I like. You learned how to use the pigments, learned how to use the brushes, learned how to draw the human face. Because the old idea is if you can learn how to draw a tree and a human figure, you can draw anything.

One of the students was Andrew Warhola. I don't think he was a veteran or in the veterans' class, but there were some other classes at that moment, and that's where I met him. I liked him. He had that indefinable sense of humor which makes people survive everything. He was rather polite and well combed. He wore this plaid cap—much too big for him—and this overcoat much too big for him. He had this blond hair like a little Dutch boy. He was terribly shy. We called him Baby Andrew.

The wig was not an affectation—at least not at first. I believe he had had a fever at some moment, and the wig was to keep his skull warm in cold weather. We became great friends, and I saw a lot of him. As a matter of fact, when I sailed for Europe, it was the composer Donald Ashwander, the playwright John Vari, the ballet dancer from the Balanchine Company Jeanne Mercier, and Baby Andrew who came to the freighter to see me off. They launched me. And in a sense, I helped launch him, because early on, when I was working for the *Paris Review* with George Plimpton, I asked him to do some illustrations for one of the issues. Then George met him after he made a point of going to the New York office later. So he got into George's world and all of that thing in New York. But he really was closer to what I would call provincial—good provincial, meaning not show-off. I never saw him even smoke a cigarette. He didn't smoke. Alas, he fell into that New York thing of "We're young and are going to try everything. Let's take another bit of this drug; let's try that drug." He fell into that crowd, as did Truman Capote. He was shy and probably went to those parties and saw that everybody sort of came out, so to speak—became exuberant. I think he took drugs maybe as a kind of insurance that he would be part of the party. He certainly did none of that then, in the 1940s. What he might have sniffed later, I don't know.

Of course, he created the whole school of grocery store art. I think he must have had fun doing all that Campbell's soup. Because he really was studying very seriously. He was a serious and good draftsman. He could really draw, and he could really paint. I think at some moment, he just wanted to tweak the nose of the Establishment. Who doesn't?

~

One of the things I most wanted to do in New York was to go to a performance by Martha Graham. For me she's Miss Mattie T. Graham. I thought she needed something in the middle. If she's going to be an honorary Southerner, she's got to have something in the middle, so I just put an initial *T* and a period. The first time I saw a photograph of Martha Graham, I flipped. That face: looking like a Japanese samurai warrior of the thirteenth century. And I love that story of how she started out with Ruth St. Denis, doing Oriental dance and all that, and then at a given moment she saw Picasso paintings, and suddenly she got rid of beads and high-heel shoes and castanets and got into these old gunnysack dresses and created a whole new vocabulary of dance, which was a very healthy antidote to Russian ballet, which had sort of fallen on cream-puffy times. They weren't doing any new works of great interest. Then here came Miss Mattie T. Graham down the highway just lassoing to left and right. Of course I wanted to see her.

Well, there was this young actress named Jayne Fortner in the cast of Thornton Wilder's *The Merchant of Yonkers*. We became great friends. She also wanted to see Martha Graham, who was performing for the first time in a big theater, the Ziegfeld Theater on Sixth Avenue. She didn't have any money, and I certainly didn't have any money. So we got into our best, and at the intermission we strolled in with the intermission crowd going back in from their cigarette on the sidewalk. We found us each a program off the floor. And we just went back every intermission for a week. We never saw the early works before the first intermission, but we saw all the important new works. And of course I flipped. It was so exciting. It was an absolutely new feeling of dance with this sort of bare stage and one or two Noguchi pieces from the sculptor who did these big crazy things she used onstage. She'd fall off of them, climb them, stick one leg through them. I thought, Oh, Lord, someday I've just got to meet that person. I want to see her up close.

Well, I think, since I've always been kind to birds and animals, Saint Francis of Assisi put in a little prayer with the Almighty. One day, when I was going to my French class, which was upstairs over the Fifth Avenue Cinema on that part of Fifth Avenue that suddenly dumps into Washington Square a block later, I came across this lady who had dark glasses and a flowered silk scarf covering everything. We got in the elevator together, and the elevator stuck between floors. It just stopped. She said, "Oh, I hope this is not going to take long." It did. So she took her scarf off and said, "Well, let's sit down." And when she sat, she just sank—with no bones—into one corner with her knees up to her chin. Cat and monkey: boneless. So I did the same, just slid down, and we just sat there corner to corner. When I saw it was Miss Mattie T. Graham, I said, "*Oh*, Miss Graham!" She said, "You know me?" I said, "Oh, and your work!" I said, "Oh, Miss Graham, that moment, when you put your head through that oval opening in that Noguchi, I almost wet my pants. I was in the third row." She laughed; we began to talk. If ever I should have had a little basket with an ice bucket and some champagne, that was the time. But the atmosphere was heady enough, just being with her. She was one of the grand people: she was interested in who I was. When she realized that I loved dance and had seen many living dancers including one week of her, she said, "Well, if you're all that interested, you must come to one of my classes. They are right up here."

About two weeks later, I went twice to her class. The students were girls of good family from the private schools. And she'd come to the point where she'd make them fall; some of them wouldn't fall. They would drop to one knee and then spread out, and she'd make them do it over. She would say, "Close off your mind and FALL! Shut off your mind, girls. DROP!" You could just see that she would have preferred to teach Italian slum girls or professional dance students, because these girls were well-bred young ladies, and some of those movements they just couldn't understand. There was one movement they could never get right. She repeated them and repeated them, and finally she said, "Oh, shit! Lead with your crotch, girls!" And I thought, All my life I've waited for this moment. I didn't go to French class that day. I just walked out in a daze and wandered around Washington Square looking at nature and thanking Saint Francis of Assisi. Thank you, Saint Francis, for favors granted. Thank you, Saint Francis, for crotch leaders.

These things don't happen just to me; they happen to everybody. But most people don't notice. Once I saw George Balanchine hurrying down

Fifth Avenue, biting his nails. Nobody seemed to notice him; I noticed him. Every day when I left Chaucer Head Book Shop to go to lunch at a little French restaurant down on 56th Street, I used to cross Fifth Avenue going west with Greta Garbo. Because she, heavily disguised, used to go to her tango lesson somewhere there. She was always coming across 57th Street from east to west at the Tiffany's corner, and I finally realized if I got there at five minutes to twelve every day, I could go a little bit behind this thing in a big hat with dark glasses and flat shoes which I knew right away was Greta Garbo because of those legs and big feet and the way she walked. She loped. But nobody else seemed to see her.

I think part of it is that I am observant, and most people aren't. Most people going from one point to another can't tell you afterwards what they might have seen. They're in their head. They ain't free. They just ain't free. They're still resentful of something that happened at point A or nervous at what's going to happen at point B. And being a backwoods little ole Southern boy going out into the wide, wide world, maybe I just kept my eyes open. Or it's the subtropics, maybe. You know, everything dies or rots. They die first and then rot or they rot first and then die: it's the humidity and the heat. If the malaria won't get you, the stink will. So you live in the moment. That's what the blacks can always teach us. They are very conscious of everything. Twenty-four hours a day. Rebecca would be cooking at the stove and humming to herself, and she'd say, "That's a mighty pretty june bug. Did you see it?" I'd say, "What june bug?" "Well, he's crawling between the screen and the sill." I'd go look, and here'd be this shiny blue-green june bug crawling along. She would have noticed because she noticed everything. Open eyes. And I suppose the people I really like are those who have their eyes open.

I remember one evening—it was one of those April days in New York City when there is a wind that blows these little playful clouds across a clear blue sky. This was just at twilight when there was an iris blue sky. New York can have these extraordinary moments. Not many. And everybody would sort of be smiling. Curtis Harrington and I were going across Fifth Avenue on 57th Street, and I saw Greta Garbo with this man I recognized as George—I can't think of his last name—a longtime companion. I don't think they were lovers. He was friend and gallant.

And I said, "Curtis, there's Greta." Being the movie fiend he is, "Oh! Oh! No! I don't believe it! You're joking! It's somebody else!" "Oh, no," I said, "that is Greta Garbo. I see her every day." "Where do you see her every day?" I said, "I cross Fifth Avenue behind her respectfully."

We strolled behind her, and when she looked over her shoulder once and saw me, I guess I smiled. What do you do? And I had realized that after a while, Greta knew that somebody was following her every day. Even though I stayed half the Fifth Avenue width behind her, I guess she saw me because she saw everything, too, looking behind those dark glasses. Anyway, she turned the corner on the next street going downtownwards. We followed. She stopped and looked in a jewelry shop window. She looked at us, and then she went in. And we went right away and looked through the jewelry store window. She saw us. And she knew we were not fans who would come up to her. Then she did a little act, trying on lorgnettes like you've never seen. And holding up necklaces. Always with her eye on her public. And that was another great moment of my life. We had our own private Greta Garbo performance.

And once I was on a bus with Dame Edith Sitwell. We were the only two people on a Sixth Avenue bus in a snowstorm. I had been downtown shopping for castanets. That's the story of my life: out shopping for castanets in a snowstorm. There were no taxis. So she got in the bus. I knew who it was; you cannot mistake people like that. She was twelve feet tall and extremely aristocratic. She had topazes this big and a garnet that big. She was all in black velvet and furs and this black velvet turban. She didn't sit down; she just held on to the two seats and had to bow her head because she was too tall with her turban. She was looking and looking. When she saw what she wanted, she just rapped with one of those stones on the metal partition that was between the seats and where the door opened. She said, "I will descend here, please." The driver was in the middle of the block, but he just stopped the bus and opened all the doors.

I actually met her once years later in London. I had been to see John Lehmann, who'd accepted my story "Love with a Drum" for *London* magazine, of which he was the founder and editor. This old Daimler pulled up as I was going out the door, and this chauffeur and footman reached into the back and pulled out what looked like a folding easel. It unfolded and unfolded and unfolded: Dame Edith. Her first line is one of the greatest entrance lines I've ever heard. She said to the secretary who was opening the door for her: "Has Mr. Lehmann found some more mousy geniuses for me to approve?" What a great line. I sort of fell at her feet. I said, "I'm not bold enough to call myself a genius. And mousy I'm not. I'm from Mobile, where the cows fly high." And she roared with laughter. Being the tall, ungainly girl with two brothers, she knew that Boy Scout song in England:

Oh, the cows they fly high in Mobile,
The cows they fly high in Mobile,
Oh, the cows they fly high

108

And they'll shit in your eye,
Oh, the cows they fly high in Mobile.

She just laughed and laughed. She said, "I've always wished to visit the American South."

I think another reason these things happen to me is because I have no cross to bear and no ax to grind. I'm not bearing a cross, and I'm not grinding an ax. I'm just a Southern boy let loose in the big world.

There was a man I met in New York named Joseph Cameron Cross, a Wall Street broker. His father was one of the founders of that famous men's club in San Francisco, where the guys all dress in Roman costume and get drunk, go swimming and all that. But he wanted to be an actor. And his daddy, who was a banker, said, "Oh, Joe, don't be silly. Nobody in the Cross family would ever be an actor. You are going to be a banker." So he was a banker. But he was stagestruck all his life. And he made a point of always knowing actors and actresses. He had a whole raft of forgotten actresses and ballerinas. Took a different one to every first night. He'd been courting the theater crowd since he was a guy twenty-nine years old who moved from San Francisco to Wall Street to do some of his father's brokerage business. I suppose he must have been sixty-five or sixty-seven at that moment.

Well, Joseph Cameron Cross always had two seats reserved in front row center for everything. I mean everything. Opening night of the Met, opening night of the ballet, opening night of this, opening night of that. If he wasn't going, he would call up some young actor or actress and just give the tickets away.

He somehow knew the two actresses who ran the Robin Hood Theater in Delaware and who later for one season ran the Cherry Lane Theater in Greenwich Village, where I worked on the Ibsen play. I met him through them. Then I also realized that he knew and went to the parties of Hazel McKinley, the sister of Peggy Guggenheim. The crowds all impinged on one another in a way I don't think would happen in London or Paris or Rome.

Anyway, I became friendly with Cameron Cross. And he said one night that we were going to the theater; he had three seats for Edith Evans in something—I don't remember what. He didn't say who was coming along, but it turned out to be this woman who was terribly tall. I mean, she was tall. Even though she occasionally sagged, she constantly remembered to stand straight. Joseph Cameron Cross came to about her shoulder. He was rather dapper and not too tall. But he was very well dressed always, very grand. And very rich. And she had dyed red hair which she obviously did herself because it was different shades in different patches of hair. There was one bit over her left ear which was almost purple. She must have gotten the wrong mix or something. She had dead white skin. And she must have put on that mascara with a teaspoon, you know. Just dug it up and went flip, flip, and dug little holes to look out of. And she had rouge in the old-fashioned way. I mean right on the cheekbones, a well-defined patch of rose red. And then seventeen shades of scarlet, orange, and one patch of purple hair. She was dressed in black, something silk or satin that was an old dress, cut on the bias. There was some black lace somewhere. And she had two wristwatches. She had a very fancy little wristwatch that was gold, and she had—it wasn't a Mickey Mouse watch, but it had something on it like that, with a plastic band. Right together these two watches. And she was wearing tons of pearls. To my eye, it looked as though half of them were real and half were fake. Then she had this flashy diamond ring. And she was carrying—God bless the lady; I had not seen one since I left Mobile—she was carrying a reticule. In the fabric that matched her dress. She was swinging her reticule. And she had a little brass-headed fruitwood cane, very slender, very elegant. She must have been ninety-five.

And Joseph Cameron Cross said, "Oh, Eugene, you know Nance O'Neil," which caused me to simply faint dead away on the pavement. I said, "Ohhhh." Crash. Because of course I had read the history of turn-of-the-century theater, and I had read about this American actress Nance O'Neil, who came from a village of three hundred in Iowa. One of those run-away-from-home tough teenage girls who became stars. And captured the civilized world. She had a voice she could bounce off the other end of Carnegie Hall without even trying. She could seem to be whispering, but it would knock the wall out of the theater in the back. And I'd read about how her real name was something like Phoebe Hebershloffen. Eliza O'Neill and Nance O'Field were those Restoration actresses who were among the first females to appear on the stage in Jacobean England. So she took Nance and O'Neil from Nance O'Field and Eliza O'Neill because she felt she was a new movement of liberation for women in the theater in America.

But there's something about that particular generation. I have a funny feeling that the Virgin Mary said, "God, let me into the act. You've been doing it long enough." So then She had some influence at court because when you think of Gertrude Atherton, Ellen Glasgow, Edith Wharton, Gertrude Stein, Alice Toklas, Nance O'Neil, and—oh, that's just the beginning. There are lots more. Think of some of the ladies who were all born roughly in the

milking the moon

eighties and nineties. There was just a bumper crop in America. There was something about extraordinary women coming up in America at that moment. Like a planetary conjunction or something.

Anyway, I didn't really fall to the sidewalk. Spiritually I collapsed in a heap and was speechless for an hour. I was absolutely floored. But my self-propel button made polite conversation. She was quite happy when she realized I knew who she was, because she had not appeared on the stage in a long time. She said, "Nowadays, I only do sitting-down roles. Duchesses in Henry James. I'm sitting down at parties being aphoristic." Because at first, with me, she'd been sort of: "Who is this little ape?" And after we got over the fact that I was from the Gulf Coast and had lived there all my life, I guess her thought was, Well, he's never been to the theater. But when she found out that I knew all about her and her history, she really softened up. She had a great sense of humor. Of course, you cannot be a great actress or a great actor without having somewhere, no matter how hidden, a sense of humor.

I couldn't watch whatever the play was. Who can watch Edith Evans when sitting next to Nance O'Neil? Afterwards we went to this very fancy restaurant where they obviously knew her and where obviously Joseph Cameron Cross had tipped them to do a sort of silent fanfare whenever she appeared in the door. I remember we went through this revolving door which the doorman in uniform pushed to start. She more or less did a star first act entrance. Joseph and I were trapped in the revolving door because she took a long moment to adjust her reticule, take her silk scarf off of her head, and take her cane from that hand to this hand. So Joseph and I were in separate compartments of this revolving door, and the doorman was waiting outside with two other people to see when he could push it. I'll never forget that entrance. Joseph and I stayed there trapped in the revolving door. And Joseph wasn't impatient. He was beaming. I wasn't impatient. I was beaming. We beamed at each other through our glass cages. And the headwaiter was saying, "Miss O'Neil, ah, Miss O'Neil," while she just did her first act entrance.

So we went to this table, and right away they brought a larger bouquet. There were bouquets at every table. They took away our little one on this table and brought a bigger one. And they were bringing the menus and she said, "Jacob, I'll have the same as always." "Yes, ma'am." Joseph ordered champagne, because when you entertain stars, you have champagne. She sipped a little, and they brought her a gallon of beer. What the usual was, was the biggest Welsh rabbit you ever saw in your life. A washbasin of Welsh rabbit. A pile of toast, I swear to God, over a foot high. She was smoking cigarettes two at a time. And someday I must do a drawing or painting of what I saw as I glanced down and saw the very beautiful gold Cartier watch and the Felix the Cat watch. The diamond ring, one cigarette lit, two pieces of toast, another cigarette in a little ashtray smoking there, and a fork. All the time saying, "Oh, I was crazy about Oscar Wilde. He wasn't a sissy at all." And I thought: They don't make them like they used to.

Then I said to her—I don't know where I read it or how I heard it, but I knew that Lizzie Borden was absolutely stagestruck, and so under another name and heavily veiled, apparently she went every night to the theater when Nance O'Neil was playing in Boston. She had sent flowers, you know, and finally she got somebody, some gallant who worked in the theater who noticed that she came every night, who said, "Would you like to meet Miss O'Neil?" And of course, she fainted on the sidewalk. So she was introduced, and she would go taking presents and oohs and aahs. And finally one season she invited Nance O'Neil and all of her company to her, Lizzie Borden's, mansion on the Hudson. And Nance O'Neil said, "I won't say I was nervous being in a house with Lizzie Borden. After all, there were a lot of us together. You can be sure we looked out for each other and made it a point never to be alone with her. And to notice how sharp her dinner knife was. But," she said, "there was one thing that I do remember as striking me. She would often make me repeat for her at teatime Medea's famous speech." And I said, "Which famous speech of Medea's?" At which Nance O'Neil suddenly was Medea right there in that restaurant. "Often the night of thunder I have a message from the gods on high. They ask me why I have not slept. Why in the morning I will touch no food. And then I'd tell them of my sleepless night and why I did not sleep. Because, I tell them, this house smells of blood. . . ." And the idea of teatime on the Hudson with the cucumber sandwiches and Lizzie pouring tea and Medea in the living room. It just gets to me. It just gets to me. Oh, Lord.

She was eating Welsh rabbit. And smoking two cigarettes and looking at two watches. Oh, Lord, I'll never forget it as long as I live. This was a great moment, a great moment.

She was like Tallulah. Using her powers for the greater good. Rewarding those people who happened to be in the same restaurant with a performance. She knew what she was doing. At least one fork clattered. But everybody else just put down their fork. She was a prima donna in the best sense. Prima donna usually means a certain self-centered or self-consciously defined center type, male or female. And usually unaware of other people's rights or reactions or necessities. But a real prima donna has that generosity of spirit which includes putting the shy at ease. Noticing the invisible. Putting down the bore gently. Tallulah was a perfect example. It has to do with cat and monkey

milking the moon

sense of humor. And this, Miss O'Neil had. I think Joan Crawford probably was really a bitch from all I've heard about how awful she was to everybody. Including all the stagehands and all the secretaries and everybody. She just was mean. But Helen Hayes was just too sweet. I don't think I could stay in the room with her. She was just so sweet . . . you're burping from the saccharine air in the room. But the real prima donna is something else altogether. I think the greater they are, the more generous they are. And one could spend one's life debating: Is it success and public recognition and a little bit of cash that sweetens the nature? Or is it the character which has made them able to deal with everything in a sweet-natured way when they arrived? I think it must be a natural thing, because there are so many marvelous creatures who are not at all known. I think it's only the second-rate who take pleasure in putting people down. I've found that the greater the talent, usually the gentler, kinder, and especially the more humorous they are.

I met—and I've forgotten how—through one of the theater groups—a young man who had just arrived in New York from California. He'd made a film, a surrealist film, 16 mm, about twenty minutes long, that had won a prize in some California amateur film contest, and so it got to some New York amateur film contest. And it was picked up by the critics. His name was Curtis Harrington. Later he went on to direct what has become a cult film with Shelley Winters and the little blond actress whose name I can never remember. When you have met as many thousands of creatures as I have met, you have to dive way down to the murk where the seahorses live to retrieve certain names. Anyway, it was Curtis who introduced me to Anaïs Nin, because her husband, Ian Hugo, was a highly proficient amateur filmmaker. So at the New York film festival, he'd met Curtis from California and introduced him to Anaïs. Then a year later I met Hugo at the Knickerbocker.

She was beautiful, but in a funny way. She had an 1840s face. It wasn't a twenties face. It certainly wasn't a fifties face. It was a wide oval and rather flat. Huge almond eyes that were dark but changed colors. Sometimes dark, but sometimes dark gray. And lots of eye makeup which exaggerated the expressive pupils so much that you didn't notice all the little crow's-feet. You didn't notice how old she was. Those ladies who learn in Paris go right on looking the same from 30 to 130. They emphasize the pupils in some way so it takes away from what's happening to the skin. She was slight and rather bony, really. Very rarely did she show any flesh. Sometimes in summer when she had a very light suntan, she'd show shoulders. But she was very careful her hands were busy. Or covered. That thing of age spots on the hands—

that's what the ladies say is first visible at a certain vintage. She was all over the place being young. Skipping about and shuffling on little flat-heel ballet slippers. And swirling skirts. And she would laugh a lot. She had charm. It was in her movement. It was manner as well as appearance. But one always had the feeling that she was totally false.

She did this little baby-talk thing. I think she had a tiny little impediment of speech. And so she put a little Spanish accent on top of it. She had made this myth about being raised in Spain. I don't know much about her early history, but I think a lot of what she said about it was invention. She was rewriting her life as a novel. I think she thought there'd been too many writers from the other countries, so she was going to be "Spanish." But she was not Spanish, she was not French, she was not American. She was this bitch from outer space.

I saw a little of Anaïs at parties. And there was a very charming bookshop right on Sheridan Square with a delightful man who ran it. I went to one autographing and made a crown for her. I think it was near Mardi Gras, and I made this gold-leaf-and-glitter crown and took it to the bookshop. She liked that. She liked any attention.

Anaïs was always surrounded by people. She was an eighteenth-century coquette. A *salonnière*. Someone who would gather artists and painters and encyclopedists for her Thursdays and rule charmingly. Except that she often put people down who weren't there that night. And we all do. It's natural. But she had a little nastiness about her. She was more often glitter than real gold. She was not fun, and that's the worst thing you can say about anybody, I guess.

I could see how she used people. I could watch her charm the pants off of anything: male, female, young, old. She had lots of lovers off and on and didn't always remain friends with them because they saw through her to the essential bitch. She liked to be cruel finally because—I don't know, I think she was trying to prove something—I don't know what—to her father, the famous composer Joaquin Nin.

At one point she went around with Anthony West, son of H. G. Wells and Rebecca West. I think they were lovers for a while. He was a real sourpuss. He was even crankier, nastier, and bitchier than she. You'd think that being the acknowledged illegitimate child of H. G. Wells and Rebecca West, he'd dine out in New York on it. But instead he was a sourpuss. I mean a SOURPUSS. I never saw the man smile. I never saw a glint of wit in his eyes. It was as though the shadow side of Rebecca West and the shadow side of H. G. Wells came out in him. It's like a man I knew in Rome who was half British aristocracy, half Italian aristocracy. He had the absolute worst qualities of both. And I think she got Anthony West into bed real soon, and she led him around as though there were an invisible ring in his nose. She didn't exactly say, "Tony, come with me." But that was the effect.

She was intensely feminine. And she led everybody on, male or female. The Italian actress Miranda really took a crush on her, and Anaïs led her on. She was the Circe. What in the South the boys would call a goddamn tease. But for everything alive, anything warm-blooded. I have an idea she was probably trisexual. She would go for male, female, and unknown spirits. She would probably have had sheep, dogs, and a camel if she could get one. Anything warm-blooded. I don't think nymphomaniac would be the right word—it's been used too much.

And she loved to be Circe to young men, young painters, young poets. Young men who were—I hate to use the word *sensitive*. Let's say young men who were conscious, something that young men in America aren't. When the last high school football game is over, they are just a potato for the rest of their lives. It's about time for the American males to be liberated. They're still living under that sort of football player and clever businessman role. And they never grow up. You know, get drunk on Saturday night and that's about it. But in every country, only 10 percent of the young men are conscious. And Anaïs loved to be Circe to these wayfarers. I think she liked to initiate sexually healthy young men. Plucking young men out of puberty and into adulthood was one of her hobbies. I can't say this is true; that is only my impression. As a student of human endeavors on this busy planet, I can only say that was the strong impression I had.

Anaïs quickly realized that I was thoroughly conscious. I'm not flattering myself, but by what I talked to her about, I think she saw that I was perhaps in spirit a little older than my statistic. And she sort of little by little ceased the coquetry and we really had a couple of enchanting conversations. For one of her birthdays, I organized a surprise party in her apartment. Of course, I called her and told her an hour beforehand so she could be properly surprised.

There was a whole bunch of young men and young lesbians and the man who had the bookshop in the Village. Whoever I could round up at the last minute, because the idea came at four in the afternoon and the party took place at seven. I think that her husband was coming back late that night and they were having something the next day. But she was a next-door neighbor and she was having a birthday, so I improvised a party.

When I did parties, I always had surprises, and I always made people wear funny things. Not silly. But, in other words, don't be yourself when you come to a party. That's the moral. Be an aspect of yourself we haven't seen.

Or be somebody else you think you might like to be for four hours. Because it's a party. It's not the end of the working day. It's a PARTY. But this birthday party was improvised at the last minute, so I gave everybody paper bags to put on their heads from the grocery store. Or a piece of crepe paper. It's always wise to have brown paper bags and tempera and a few feathers hanging about somewhere. You never know when you're going to need them.

There was one really boring girl at the party. There were a lot of lesbians who just fainted over Anaïs, and there was this one particularly boring, probably virgin lesbian—no makeup, straight hair. I made her wear these curtain pulls for earrings. "Why, I can't do that." "Yes, it's a party." By the end of the evening she was twirling those curtain pulls.

Well, as I said, I met Hugo backstage at the Knickerbocker Music Hall, where I was doing this marionette production. The surrealist artist Corte Seligmann had designed these crazy puppets, and I had made them. And Charles Henri Ford, the surrealist poet, had written this little thing about one puppet looking through a keyhole and describing what he sees. Anyway, Ian Hugo came backstage and introduced himself. That wasn't his name. And I carefully have avoided knowing his Morgan Guaranty name. For years he ran the Paris office of Morgan Guaranty. But when the war began he went back to New York, and they gave him an honorary post. But I only knew him as someone who made very beautiful engravings—little perfect engravings signed "Ian Hugo." He came backstage and said, "Oh—those marionettes— I've always been interested in marionettes. I always thought it would be such fun to make a film with marionettes." He said, "I do a lot of amateur films with my 16 mm. Would you be interested in writing a script?" I said, "Sure." A film with marionettes? Yeah, why not? So I gave him an idea of a story about a magician and his marionettes and he liked it and I did a script for him called *The Dangerous Telescope*, a phallic joke, of course. He liked it a lot, so he said, "We'll do it." So I started making the characters. Got the cardboard, the wire, and all that. He sent the script to Anaïs in California.

Anaïs would go to California for part of every year and live with this young forester who was one-third her age. And I was told by one authority that she arranged it so as never to meet him by daylight. She told Ian Hugo that she was teaching courses in creative writing at various establishments. She told everybody in California that she was there to do research, but she had to go back to New York very often because she had this ancient father there who was an invalid. This went on for years. I remember she had this little room at the top of her apartment building. It was the top floor of this modern building on 33 West 9th. I was 31 West 9th, in that old brownstone with the garden for the summer. On the second story of this two-story top apartment they had a little workroom, and she had this wooden cabinet marked LIES, so as not to forget what she had told.

Hugo knew perfectly well because he was no fool. He knew she was carrying on. He was a very intelligent man who put up with all of her shit for years. He loved her. But boy, did he have the blondes. He was already carrying on with any dizzy blonde he could get while she was carrying on the big passionate love affair with Henry Miller in Paris. The minute she left for California, he said, "Well, Eugene, I don't think we ought to work on this script today because I've got a conference at the bank." I remember once we were saying we've got to finish such and such. And he said, "Oh, come Friday, when you get back from work. Come and have a drink at seven and we'll look at the script." So I got there about ten minutes after seven. Rang the doorbell. No answer. So I rang the bell again. Then I heard voices in there, so I just sort of went down in the elevator and came back up and rang again, and he answered, quite flustered and flushed with all his hair—what was left of it—all in his face. Wrapping his robe around him. And here came this voluptuous blonde out of the bedroom. One of those, you know, who can't come through a door. She had to throw something out. She was wonderful. I never found out who she was. She looked country America. Probably she was a waitress or something. Usually it was actresses. She was dressed in rather Sears, Roebuck or Woolworth style. But she was a charmer. She had that natural gift. She just didn't come through the door. She threw something out. Oh, Lord.

Anyway, Anaïs read the script in California and said, "Oh. They have to be human actors, and I'll play the lead." And she rushed back to New York.

I've forgotten through whom I got permission to film in the Rhenish castle on the Hudson. The nephew of the man who sank the *Lusitania* had built a Rhenish castle which had been in ruins since World War I, and I got permission to film there, so we would go on Saturdays and do the scenes of the film in this ruined Rhenish castle on the Hudson, miles from New York City. But Anaïs came back and was directing Hugo how to direct the film. I can still see his horn-rimmed specs as he was looking down and figuring something out about the camera. And she would say, "Well, let's do this, and why don't I come down this path?" He said, "Now wait, Anaïs, we are not making the film yet. I've got to figure out the camera." You know, "Let me get this right."

There was one great party scene where I assembled thirty actors at this Rhenish castle. He filmed the whole day but forgot to put film in his camera.

She was so busy doing Anaïs that he got rattled. He shot all that day, and I had prepared a picnic for forty people. It was a wonderful day. But he didn't have any film in his camera.

So afterwards I sat at a little Moviola with him and made a new story using what footage there was. And of course it's very spotty. I did not have in mind a surrealist film. I had in mind a legend, a magic tale, with a logical development. Even though it was fantastic, it was logical. It wasn't juxtaposed images. So often those early surrealist films are surrealist only because they never had enough money to finish the story, or the weather went bad the day they wanted to finish it. So they just made something that jumps, you know, like a flea on a goat. Anyway, we edited it and it was shown in the experimental section of the Cannes Film Festival in 1947 or '48.

Anaïs was always asking to see my work. She liked to see the work of young writers and young painters and say, "Why don't you do this?" and, "Why don't you do that?" But I never showed her anything. Because my ego—which is classic, not twentieth century—is huge, you know. And she was not my idea of a critic or editor. She was highly quick. Very well read. And fluent in several languages. But she was not what I would call in the last analysis, and in the good sense of this word, intellectual. She wrote a couple of novels that I think are unreadable. They are so closed in. Always the subject is not what is happening, but the intense feminine consciousness. The vibrations as perceived by the intense feminine consciousness. It's like some of those secondary red clay Southern writers. There's no universal sense. They are genuinely backwoods. She belongs to another kind of provincialism, which is the provincialism of the party set of Rome, Paris, London, New York. Who are, in the last analysis, out of touch with life on this planet. I feel I'm my own best editor and critic. Because I know the different road I am taking. Which is a Southern backwoods road toward *Arabian Nights*. And how could she understand that? She wasn't raised in the South. She never went barefoot on black earth or red clay. She may have taken her shoes off at the beach once and said, "Oh, it's cold." But how could she understand somebody who took shoes off the day school let out and didn't put shoes back on until the day school started? As was the wont of my contemporary males. Boys took their shoes off. And a lot of little girls did when they got away from the house. Girls are divided into those who took their shoes off and those who didn't. I think Anaïs maybe took her shoes off once at the beach when she was a child. That's why I didn't want to show her anything I'd ever written.

Finally she got a copy of *Wake* magazine and read my poems. And she said, "Eugene, poetry is really a dead art. You should try England."

I went back home and never saw her again. To say that poetry is a dead art when there are still cats and monkeys in the world. Even if the human race dies, there are still cats and monkeys. Butterflies are still floating by. Even if the human race vanishes, there are still going to be poets because there are cats, monkeys, and butterflies. And ducks, who are infinitely graceful on the water and plump assed on the ground. So I politely said, "Good evening," but afterwards I faded out like a Cheshire cat, with my smile stamped on the air.

I became interested in Henry Miller because of a piece he wrote called "A Dream of Mobile." It was in *View* magazine, the surrealist quarterly. He had never been to Mobile, but he was saying, you know, Spanish moss hanging from the trees, humid air, blacks carrying bundles on their heads, going barefoot through the streets, Carnival parades at the next corner. I loved it. I bought millions of copies of *View* and sent them to everybody I could think of in Mobile. When I heard he was coming to New York, I wanted very much to meet him. Finally I did meet him, at a party given by Charles Henri Ford, the founder and editor of *View*.

I didn't like him. I suppose he was friendly enough and all that. I mean, I was nobody, just a little thing from Alabama that wanted to meet him. And I wanted to say, "Thank you for 'A Dream of Mobile.'" He laughed and said, "Well, I've never been to Mobile. I may never get there." I don't think he ever got there. He just went on dreaming. But he said, "I always had this idea about it. Just the name itself." I said, "Well, yeah. For a town that's sitting so still, the fact that it's called Mobile is one of our biggest jokes."

But he was sort of fake tough. If there is anything I hate, it's that fake tough American. That baseball tough, that fisherman tough, that woodcutter tough, that fake tough American. Because usually in Europe, in the Mediterranean world, the people who are the sportsmen or the fishermen or the woodcutters have a quiet gentleness. They are at one with nature, and they are not proving anything to their mamas or their wives or their daughters or their friends or their papas. They're just natural. But in America, there's that kind of fake hard-boiled thing which bores the pants off of me. He had a lot of that. I just don't like it.

Farewell, Farewell, Eugene

One night I went to see Edith and Edwin Zelnicker, my old friends from Mobile. He was working for the Limited Edition Club. It took an hour from where I lived on 194 West 10th to their place way up Riverside Drive. One hour underground. And I thought to myself: I'm not made to travel underground. It ain't my style. I had always thought I'd eventually get to Paris and live there for a few years. But that night I thought: I've got to get to Paris. I've got to leave. I don't like the smell of this thing. I don't like the look of this thing. I don't like being underground. I'd be perfectly happy shaking on a hayrick, but not alone, underground, shaking on that thing.

New York was always just a place I was stopping on the way to Paris. It's not my city. Even though I enjoyed it immensely, it was never my town. It was glamorous, it was fabulous, it was certainly a world capital. But I didn't like it. People always ask me: "Do you prefer Paris or Rome?" I say, "Whichever one I'm in." The only place on this planet where I didn't feel at home was New York City. There was something finally in the official New York that I didn't like. I mean taxi drivers, bus conductors, policemen, the people at the unemployment insurance office, some of the officials at the public library, some of the librarians. There was some coldness and irritation which was universal under the surface in New York.

I felt so alienated in New York because nobody smiles and nobody looks at each other. People in New York don't like it if you look in their face. They don't want you to look right at them. Eye contact—that's what they call it now. I wasn't making "eye contact." I was just looking at all the animals running around in the street. But if you really look at somebody a second time in the street, they'll go, "What do you want?" you know. Whereas in Mobile, sometimes we would just go and sit on the iron benches in Bienville Square and look at people. It was what you did. Especially on Saturday when all the people came in from everywhere to shop, to go to the doctor, to go to the dentist, go to the movies. Saturday was market day. The people came in from all the provinces to sell their stuff at market, to do their shopping. Proper country families with their starched shirts, neckties, and little hats and the young ladies in their little white gloves came into town to shop for dry goods and go to the pharmacy—all the things that all those little rural communities didn't have. It was the cross section of the South, in the big city of Mobile, on Saturday. Shopping, going to the dentist, going to the matinee at the Lyric or the Saenger. And then back home to Chinaberry Town. I used to love to go sit on a bench in Bienville Square and just watch all that. But you had to avoid looking people in the face in New York City—I just couldn't understand it.

And also the extreme heat and the extreme cold and the stench. There's a certain stagnant air that stays between the tall buildings. Only two or three times a year is there a wind from the Hudson that blows away the stagnant vapors: the smell of taxis and trucks and hot dog stands. Then you have an amazing day, and you see New York as a new city in a new world with a new concept. But only once or twice a year.

And New York is one of those places where if you give a party, you have to give a party. If you are going to a party, you have to be at a party. You know. You can't sit in the corner if you are tired or gossip with a friend where the bottles are if you feel like gossiping. All those poor Yankees never understood that a literary party is sort of the apotheosis of gossip. Southerners giggle and laugh and have a good time. But Yankees say mean things about publishers and other writers. I mean, parties were hectic. Nervous tension conversation. Little groups forming. Most people brought their office nerves with them because they wore their office nerves twenty-four hours a day. They never got out of them. "Upwards and onwards, I want to have enough money to retire at forty," you know. I could no more think in those terms than I could fly.

People in New York threw parties. I don't throw parties. I push parties gently forward. Most of my "Oh, come over tonight, I've decided to give a party" took two weeks to plan. Most of my sit-down parties that look terribly organized, I thought of that morning. I just like to do it that way. Like a famous Southern hostess said, "A formal dinner party can be done in ten minutes if you have silver and porcelain and put everything very straight on the table. Then," she said, "you can get out the can opener and go to work." If the linen is smoothed out, if the plates are exactly opposite, if the knives are straight and the forks are straight and the salad and dessert pieces are precisely straight across. It's quite true. A lot of Southern hostesses, in Reconstruction and the Depression, had more porcelain and silver and crystal on the table than food.

I remember once I had expected a check in the mail that didn't come, and I needed it for a party I was giving that night. Oh, Lord God, so I got some big jars of peanut butter and I went to the bakery where I had credit, and I said, "I want a sample of every kind of baked bread and roll that you've got." So I put red crepe paper on the table and in the middle I had a Victorian cake stand. I put two jars of peanut butter on that, then piled that table with every known kind of bread and roll. I had a big jug of Chianti. Everybody thought it was so original, and they ate every bit of everything, because all

Americans secretly love peanut butter. When in doubt, serve peanut butter. And I always carefully chose the guest list, so that even my oldest friend would have a surprise and even my newest friend would not feel out of place.

But New Yorkers are the people who have the least liberation, you know, because they are always claiming how free they are and how wonderful. They are all nervous-breakdown candidates. They talked so much about sex, you realized that not one of them had a sex life of any kind. Americans waste so much time worrying about sex and thinking about sex, and that's another reason I hated New York. In Europe, one of the first things you see is that sex is a part of daily life. Like gardening, and watching the sky, and gossip. It's not a secret suddenly. There is something about making it secret which the Puritans and the Baptists have done that just has taken the pleasure out of it, I suppose, and made it like something you have to do to prove you can beat the system. It's like cheating on taxes; it's not living.

And in Europe, everybody is polysexual. America has these funny ideas about having to live on one side of the line or the other. The only line I insist on is the Mason-Dixon line. The rest is individual cases.

In Europe, the men smile at other men. They smile at women. They smile at boys. They smile at girls. I guess they smile at Shetland ponies, too. They just do a kind of sideways smile and a little wink. That means, "Are you interested?" If the other person returns it, they are interested. People just say, "Wouldn't you like to go to bed?" They say no; they say yes. It's simple.

And I love that Turkish proverb: "For love, a beautiful woman; for pleasure, an adolescent boy; for sheer ecstasy, a ripe melon." I'm saving that for a last thrill. I have never humped a melon. But everybody I know has humped a melon. The various melons were always a great delicacy in Turkey. To eat or to hump. My grandmother used to say that when you buy a melon in the market, if it has a triangular hole cut in it, then it's all right. They've plugged it to see if it's ripe. If it has a round hole in it, don't buy it.

The Europeans know and remember something that people in the United States forget. Healthy males want some kind of relief, every eight to twenty-four hours, beginning at 12 and going on to 112. In America, people just don't acknowledge that, although behind the haystack, the Puritans could give us all lessons in perversity.

᪥

So I started making plans. I went to this travel bureau on Washington Square and there was this gorgeous Italian girl with violet-colored eyes. Francesca something. I gave her ten dollars. I said, "Now I want to find the cheapest possible freighter to get me as close as possible to Paris." And I said,

"You shop around and I'll bring you ten dollars every week, and when you've got enough, you tell me." I said, "Don't even talk about it. When you find a boat that's going that way, I want a one-way ticket."

Well, there was this friend of mine, John Vari, a very showy little number. Sicilian background. He had degrees from everyplace and taught English, but he was also an actor. He got enough money to take over a summer theater in Hampton Beach, New Hampshire. The Hampton Beach Summer Theater. I agreed to come there as his designer for his first season.

So about two months later, the girl with the beautiful eyes at the travel bureau in Washington Square called me at the 28th Street foreign exchange section of the library. She said, "Mr. Walter, I have an unscheduled Dutch freighter carrying a load of ice-cream mix to Antwerp. It's $110 for the trip. Ten days, five meals a day." Dutch: five meals a day.

So then I went to John Vari and took him to dinner, and I said, "You are going to hate me, but you've got four months to plan." I said, "I've got to go to Europe, and I can't come to you as a designer." He was furious. Italian. Sicilian. But we never ceased to be friends. Then came this moment maybe eight years later, I got a letter from John Vari and a clipping from a London newspaper. The letter said only "Revenge!" The clipping was from the London *Times* announcing the opening of a new play by John Vari starring Margaret Rutherford called *Farewell, Farewell, Eugene*. The offstage villain of the play is named Eugene. He said, "Revenge!" We remained great friends. He was one of the ones who came to see me, all the way to New Jersey, where the boat sailed from.

It was what they called unscheduled, but they know within three days when they will sail. As I told the Italian girl, "I'm from the South. If you tell me unscheduled, I would think you didn't know whether it was this year or ten years from now. But if you tell me within three days—in the South, that's scheduled." She laughed and said, "Well, for the Italians it is, too. But this is a Dutch freighter, so for them it's an unscheduled sailing." She said, "I will call you the day before. You have to be ready and have your papers filled out."

So I had three days of leave-taking in that apartment waiting for her call. Every day Donald Ashwander would come in that apartment and say, "You're not going. You'll never make it. You'll never raise the money. You're not going to get on that boat. You'll never go. You're just dreaming. You've got to get a good job here in New York." Finally I showed him the ticket, and he believed me.

Everybody said, "Oh, you are so courageous to go with only that bit of GI Bill. How will you get back?" I said, "We'll see. . . ." But I hated when they said I was courageous, because I had many misgivings privately. Will the

123

GI Bill be enough to live on? That was scholarship money for returning soldiers. The government paid tuition at the school and gave an allowance. I was going to the Alliance Française and then the Sorbonne. And I thought, Will that really be enough to live on in a capital city? I already knew I did not want to be a gypsy. I have never hitchhiked. Ever. It is not my style.

But I am really like old America: just get up and get in the covered wagon and go three thousand miles because you want fresh air. You know, most people analyze for all the wrong reasons. Some things you analyze. Some things you just hop. I think people hop at the wrong things, like safe investments. And analyze whether they should go to Alaska or not. It should be the other way around. Hop to Alaska. Analyze the safe investment.

With my friends, I was going in their stead. Most people really don't take chances, you see. They wanted to go. But they didn't have the—I don't know what it is. It's not courage. It's not ambition. It's cat and monkey spirit. Let's see what's over there. Let's just have a look.

Paris

PART FOUR

Bonjour, You-All

The crossing took ten days. But the bar opened at seven-thirty in the morning, and Dutch gin was ten cents a glass. Then there was a Dutch breakfast. Then there was warm broth and little hot crunchies of some kind of cheese in the middle of the morning. Then there was this lunch of twenty-seven dishes. Then they had afternoon tea, echoes of England. And then they had dinner. The bar would open for ten minutes between any of these five meals. It was like an old-fashioned roll-front desk. It would roll up and they'd beat this gong, and everybody would rush to get their gin. They had every kind of Dutch gin. The brand that I'd never heard of before that I really liked was called Wine and Fucking. Wynand Fockink. It was nothing but Wine and Fucking for me all the way to Paris.

I felt at home in Paris instantly. I got off the train at the Gare du Nord and thought, I'm back home. *Bonjour,* you-all.

There was a smell of coffee roasting, like downtown Mobile, and there was a sense of hubbub in the streets. It wasn't like New York at all. New York is *opéra serieux*. Mobile and Paris are opéra bouffe. And I just felt at home.

I knew that I wanted to be in the Latin Quarter, because it was an old, elegant, run-down quarter, mostly seventeenth and eighteenth century. I knew that Gertrude and Alice had lived in this quarter. I knew that Oscar Wilde had died in this quarter, that Molière had lived in this quarter. I mean, Gertrude and Alice, Oscar Wilde, and Molière were enough for me. That's enough recommendation.

I had asked everybody on earth who had been to Paris since World War II about where to stay, and at least three people of widely varying backgrounds, tastes, and requirements had indicated this little hotel in the rue de Tournon called the Hôtel Helvétia. They said, You realize that the john is in the hall and you will share it with the other three rooms on your floor. But, they said, it's scrupulously clean, because Mme. Jordan, who runs the Helvétia, is from the next-door neighbor to Switzerland, and they're the scrubbers and sweepers. They said, It's just in front of the Palais Luxembourg, and I knew that sat in the Luxembourg Gardens. And I knew there were fountains.

And I knew there were trees. And I knew there were flowers. So I had written ahead and reserved a room.

What I had was a bedroom that had been divided into two rooms. I had a washbasin and a bidet. And a wardrobe and a bed and a sweet little eighteenth-century marble fireplace. There was steam heat, so I used the fireplace as a wine cellar.

Mme. Jordan brought my breakfast tray every morning at seven with croissants still hot from the bakery next door, unsalted butter from somewhere in the country, and coffee and milk that they had heated and frothed. Very soon, this orange tabby whom I had befriended in the hallway learned to come up with my breakfast and sit next to me on the bed as I had my meal. And to leave the room when I put the tray outside on the floor, because he knew he would get some warm milk and a butter pat. He came every morning and sat right at my left elbow as I ate. He was a charmer. And that was my breakfast.

From my window, I looked across the rue de Tournon, which, after a block or so, becomes the rue de Seine, which is more famous. I looked out at the garde républicain across the street. I could hear them in the early morning when they marched and drilled with a brass band in their courtyard. Next to that was a rare-book dealer, and next to that was the Café de Tournon.

It had once been sort of an eatery, but the owners realized that, being around the corner from that French literary review *La Table Ronde,* there would be people needing coffee, coffee, coffee. So they made it into a café and had very good coffee. You could smell that coffee early in the morning. It was a real pleasure to wake up and smell the Café de Tournon. M. Alezard, the proprietor, opened the place in the morning with Arnauld, his red Irish setter, who, with one enthusiastic lashing of the tail, could send whole trayfuls of drinks crashing off the little round tables on the sidewalk. Later, Mme. Alezard would turn up; she made excellent fried or scrambled eggs on a hot plate not much bigger than a silver dollar.

There were tables and chairs and tables and chairs and tables and chairs where you could sit inside and look out, and a bar along one side with a mirror and bottles of every known thing, and a cashier's desk. Then around the back there were mirrors and a banquette that ran against the wall. In summer it had an awning that lowered and raised over the tables outside. I used to love to be there when the wagon pulled by the huge Percheron horses came by to deliver the ale and beer. They were big, shaggy, and very good-natured. You could almost say they smiled.

It was an all-Brazilian crowd when I first arrived, because the coffee was superior. And perhaps that is why it later became a literary café. The exchange of the franc and whatever was Brazilian was very favorable, so there were all these charming Brazilians, all coming because they wanted to learn French. French was still, even after the Second World War, the language of diplomacy and the language of literacy. Not for the Americans, but for everyone else French was still very necessary if you wanted to be a diplomat or in the State Department. A whole bevy of delightful Brazilians frequented the Café de Tournon. I loved them. I remember one song they sang in Portuguese: "The only way to live, ladies, is to try everything. . . ." One day the Brazilian currency was devalued, and one by one they vanished.

I started school the instant I was there. I got there, slept late the next morning, went that afternoon to the admissions office, and got myself into the next week's classes. I did it double, both morning classes and afternoon classes. I took the beginner's class in the morning, and I went to the beginner's class in the afternoon. Since the teachers were French, nothing was the same. I mean, Mme. Picard's beginning French was nothing like Monsieur whatever in the afternoon. Because they were French, they were individualistic. They each had their own ideas on how to teach beginning French at the Alliance. And I went to French films and puzzled over French newspapers from the day I was there. I knew enough to say a few things and read a few words. So I started buying the daily paper and reading French newspapers with my coffee every morning, going to French films every night and just talking to ladies in the market. In other words, I dived into French. I drowned in French. I bathed in French. Everything French, and avoiding my fellow American tourists at first. Because I had to have French.

A Chanel Suit and Keds

It was early in the summer of '51 that I arrived in Paris. About two days before I'd left New York, I'd seen a copy of *Botteghe Oscure* in the Gotham Book Mart. I thought, Wow, look at this funny thing from Rome. The cover was this thick, buff-colored expensive, heavy bond paper which is almost cardboard, with little letters that said *Botteghe Oscure*, number so-and-so in roman numerals. Naturally since I didn't know what it was, I pulled it off the shelf and looked at it. It had an English section, then an American section, then a French, then an Italian. Later a final section was added that alternated between Spanish and German. It was international, this little old League of Nations. And I thought, There are no notes. There are no introductions. There is no criticism. And no book reviews. There is just text, text, text. I'd gotten so bored with *Partisan Review* and *Sewanee Review;* they were so full of these professorial, long-winded things that as far as I could see added no clarification to any text. They only added a few dabs of mist for somebody else to decipher. And I didn't like them. I died for somebody to point out why he or she liked and/or enjoyed somebody's work. And show some depth or some hidden references or hidden forms that gave pleasure. Not that you had to take it apart to see whether the screws were oxidized or not oxidized. You know.

I recognized some of the writers in *Botteghe,* but I saw that there were a lot of obviously young writers. So I took the address of the publisher, the Princess Marguerite Caetani of Palazzo Caetani in Rome. When I got into the Hôtel Helvétia—like the first week I was there—I pulled out old Remington and copied some poems. I think I sent her six, and she took all six. I got this letter back. She answered everything in a free, very wild hand on blue notepaper. Thin blue envelope, blue notepaper, and a large, flowing hand. Not always legible, but most times so. It said: "Dear Mr. Walter, I like your poems. Who are you? Are you English or American? Do you wish to be paid in pounds or dollars? I am coming to Paris on such and such day. I shall expect you for lunch on June the so-and-so, at such and such a time." She spent half the year in Paris, because she was free there. In Rome, she was very much the grand lady. If you were going to send a message to a countess across the street, you didn't telephone. You wrote her a note, and your footman in uniform delivered it. That was Rome. So you see, when she went to Paris, she was just a thing let loose.

I thought, Wow, what have I gotten myself into this time? But you see, these are the kinds of things I pray for. God is so bored with people who pray to Him constantly for nasty little favors. He just wants them to have a good time. Now occasionally I have asked Him to help in moments of crisis. You know, "Gee, bubba, I'm having a rough time. Do what you can." I call him Skybubba. "Hey, Skybubba, if you're not too busy this weekend, see if the mail can get a check to my postbox." But He's grateful not to hear those stingy prayers all the time. Aristophanes did say it: God is a comic poet.

So I wrote back and I said, "I'm not English and I'm not American. I come from a country called the South. The dollar is our currency, since the Confederate dollar is devalued." And I showed up for that luncheon.

When I rang the bell I expected to see this tall woman with black hair going gray, and I don't know why I thought there'd be clanking gold jewelry. That was my idea. A great many of the Roman aristocrats are tall. I thought there'd be a bony nose and sharp black eyes and a humorous look with a wildly chic, underdressed style. Maybe a straight woolen dress with some sort of bolero or jacket or scarf. But clanking gold jewelry and heavy eye makeup. So I was trying to think what kind of smile I should wear. One-hundred-watt? Fifty-watt? I mustn't overdo it, but I mustn't underdo it. Then the door opened and glunk, my head fell because it was this tiny little thing with hair pulled back to a knot on the back of her neck. A very beautiful, obviously French suit and a silk blouse with some sort of froufrou at the neck and no jewelry at all except a very beautiful old Roman quartz set in gold, obviously antique, obviously either ancient or Renaissance. The Chanel suit was rust and gray and white wool with jaggy lines of those colors all mingled. Silk stockings. And good American Keds. I don't mean the latest model. I mean white, 1930s, tennis-shoe Keds. Imagine a Chanel suit with Keds.

She said, "Oh, Mr. Walter, you are so young." And I said, "But you are American." And she said, "Well, yes. Didn't you know?" And she said, "Come in," so we sat down and she served orange juice. I later convinced her that for poets, bourbon or Scotch was more effective. At five in the afternoon, after a difficult day at the Alliance Française, one doesn't want orange juice. Not that she was antialcohol, she just thought that was a nice thing to serve because she was brought up in an age when fresh oranges weren't always around.

Anyway, we got along from the first moment. She asked me what I studied and who my favorite writer was and where I stayed. We talked about my poems, and she told me why she liked them. "I should like to see more manuscripts from you," she said. Then we walked about three blocks—that's why there were Keds—to an Italian restaurant where she was known. And where they rearranged the flowers, the tables, the window curtains, the silver, on every table when she came in the door. "Ah, *buon giorno, principessa*. Today we have fresh wild asparagus. Not on the menu, but we have two servings in the kitchen."

That was a busy girl, that Princess Caetani. She was originally Marguerite Chapin from New London, Connecticut. Her family owned all the copper mines out west and had built railroads going to the mines in the last century. She was an only child of her mother, who died when I think she was young, and then her father married again. Since she had a very beautiful singing voice, she got Papa to send her to Paris, where she studied with the famous singer Jean de Reszke. And she stayed on.

As a young man, Roffredo Caetani also went to Paris. He was a composer and a very good one. He was born in wedlock of the duke and duchess of Sermoneta, but everybody knew that his papa was really Franz Liszt, the composer. The duchess of Sermoneta, in the 1870s or something, had a love affair with Franz Liszt. All of Rome knew it, but it was never mentioned publicly. And if the lady is married, the child is—let's not say "legitimate." Let's say "highly within the official bedroom." And nobody dared ask questions. But Roffredo Caetani was the godson of Franz Liszt, studied with Liszt until he was fourteen years old, and when Liszt was dying in Vienna, he sent for Roffredo Caetani. Everybody in all the biographies speaks of how Liszt, when he died, said, "Tristan"—that his true love was really Wagner. That ain't it. In the next room, Roffredo Caetani was playing the piano and was playing Liszt's transcription of themes from the Tristan and Isolde solo. Liszt was only recognizing a piece he'd written. Anyway, Roffredo Caetani was every inch a gentleman. And he was about seven feet tall, with snow white hair. He had gaga days and ungaga days.

Roffredo was the youngest son, and he was prince of Bassiano. One of his brothers was prince of Teano. The eldest brother was the duke of Sermoneta. That was the family title. The princess was Princess Bassiano when she was in Paris doing her first magazine, *Commerce*. She didn't use Princess Bassiano in Rome; she used that only in Paris. Then the only son of the duke of Sermoneta died, and Roffredo got the title duke of Sermoneta, and so she was officially duchess of Sermoneta for the last six years, perhaps, of her life. She's three personalities in Roman history, and you have to be sure which one. It's very confusing.

Anyway, Roffredo and the princess lived all the time in Paris in the twenties and early thirties. Their home was the Villa Romaine in Versailles. They gave glittering Sunday breakfasts frequented by many personalities of the day. Out of these grew a little group of friends who met every two weeks in a different Paris restaurant, and out of their conversations came the French-language review *Commerce*, published by the princess. She published new works of French writers like Paul Valéry, Jean-Paul Fargue, Valéry Larbaud, André Gide, and René Char. She more or less created the name and fame of René Char, who did not run in French literary circles. He was snotty and difficult and stayed outside Paris. Even though he published some delightful poems, nobody wanted anything to do with him. I think the princess was in love with him, because his name was God. You know. I don't think they were lovers, but I think she did have a real passionate crush. Because he was God. If he said something, that was it. I never met him, but there was something so unpleasant about his letters and the way I felt he used the princess. Of course, everybody should read his prose poems about the war. They are extraordinary. I think René Char is a great poet, a rare voice.

But he never left the war, never left the provinces. Never came to Paris, never joined any kind of literary thing. My thought was, along about 1957: He's a big boy now, and the war is over. But he just went on being underground.

She also published some very important famous texts in translation, and she published the first Pasternak outside of Russia and outside of Russian, the first Lorca outside of Spain and outside of Spanish, and the first Faulkner in Europe, "A Rose for Emily" in French in *Commerce*. Since she read and read and read and was so interested in what other people were reading and their reaction to new work, she just somehow hit it right every time. Every time. Bless her heart.

She was intelligent, so naturally she had an interest in literature. And the money for the magazines came from her own pocket. She had lots. Her husband owned a hunk of Italy about as big as Mobile County, but of course, keeping that up was expensive. It was not as if he couldn't have gone to the Vatican Bank if he needed cash and said, "I need a million dollars by tomorrow morning." But he never did because they don't do that over there.

Commerce had a ten-year life. The Germans were coming, were rumbling in the distance. Also, when the duke of Sermoneta died, they had to go back and do the administration of the estate. They owned all the land from Naples to Sermoneta: the middle hunk, the belly band of Italy, from sea to sea. The legend is that Aeneas landed there and said to his nurse, Gaeta: "For your faithfulness and the good care you've taken of me, I am giving you all the middle of this peninsula." The family name at one moment was Gaetanus; another was Caetanus. It was all considered myth until about 1957, when they were doing some repairs at the Vatican and dug up right under the chancelry tombs of the Gaetanus and Caetanus family, taking the Caetanis, who were historically known since A.D. 3, back to long before Christ. It makes our American history so short.

There was everything of the confusion of the war starting. The princess was very much against the war because Italy was joining with Hitler. She was very upset about all that. And she was coping with the administration of this huge estate. What she did was, she retired to the castle of Sermoneta, which is a medieval stronghold on a mountaintop in south central Italy, about two hours from Rome. She put in some plumbing and some electricity and got a kitchen going. Then, when the Germans occupied Italy, she got all the peasants on Caetani land, with their animals, into the courtyard and all the thousand wings of the castle and ran it. She got word through her half sister in Washington, Mrs. Francis Biddle, whose husband was attorney general under Roosevelt, that nobody should bomb Sermoneta because she had all the peasants there. She said, you know, Bomb the Germans, but leave Sermoneta alone.

And then she went into three years of coma when she got the news of her son's death. Her only son, being the heir to the title of Sermoneta, the oldest son of the oldest living son of a papal aristocratic family, had the privilege of not being drafted. But he was half American. He wasn't going to sit there while his contemporaries, whether peasant or prince, were off fighting. So he got himself into the army that was fighting in Greece. Not fighting any Americans. He died of gangrene on the battlefield. Apparently he was wounded and no one dragged him to safety. An unnecessary death. An unnecessary bit of American valor.

When Rome was freed she went back there, and she and some other grand ladies who were antifascist made something called Il Retrovo, meaning "the refindery," the refinding. It was like a reception center, partly sponsored by American intelligence, where all the people who'd had dealings or had relatives in the war could regroup and find out what they needed to know. It was for people who wanted to find out what had happened to all their friends during the war and to make contact. That went on for about a year.

Then she began to realize that the outer world knew little about all the young writers who had developed in Italy during the war. She'd had the idea of a polylingual magazine ever since leaving Paris, because she thought this ought to be translated into that, and that ought to be translated into this, and then there are some new writers there who should be alongside some new writers here. But she never got to it until after Il Retrovo. Then she started up.

She called it *Botteghe Oscure* because the Palazzo Caetani is in the Via della Botteghe Oscure. It literally means "the street of the dark shops." Once upon a time that street, in the Middle Ages, sort of passed by this semiruined small early Roman amphitheater. As I remember, it was older and much smaller than the Colosseum. In the Middle Ages there were shops in the promenade. The ground floor had these big arches and then this walk where there were doors going into little shops inside. Now there are bits and pieces of those walls built into some of the structures on the street, although there is nothing major left of that ruin. But the street is still the street of the shadowy shops. All her friends were scandalized when she called the magazine *Botteghe Oscure*. Everybody said to the princess, "You can't call it that because everybody will think it's the Communists or the Jesuits." The headquarters of both were on that street. People all over Europe would say "Botteghe Oscure" when they meant the Communist Party headquarters in Rome. But the Caetani palace predated both, so she said, "The Caetanis were here earlier. We've been here at least three centuries longer."

The magazine came out about twice a year. The first edition that I saw was number six. So it would have been the end of the third year that I first saw it in New York.

Then she began to ask me to help her. We just got along and had things to talk about. About the difference between Europe and America. She was interested in my first impressions coming from remote Alabama to New York. She was interested in my impressions of Paris, where she had lived since 1912. Little by little we talked about writers. So little by little I began to work with her. Suddenly I was working for her. I was not doing it for pay. She simply included me in all kinds of luncheons. In the middle of the day she liked to have young writers and newcomers and unknown quantities. And for a long time she served only orange juice, until I began to tell her about how writers really do absorb stronger beverages. Afterwards we'd look at manuscripts and she would say, "What do you think of this?" She loathed literary conversation, but she loved to see people's reactions to new work. She always had these things on her tea table. She would say, "I'm just reading this. Do you know who this is? What do you think of this one? I just love it." And so on. Everybody was always flattered to be asked advice by her. It was part of her act. But she published what she damn well pleased and didn't listen to anybody. And she would say, "Oh, Lord, I've got this pile of stuff. I've got it all mixed up. Will you just have a look at it and sort it out? Anything that's the least bit good, put it in one pile. If it's impossible, put it in another pile." She asked if I could come several afternoons a week and help her.

The princess liked my work as a writer, but she also realized that I was not a moonstruck writer, that I did have a certain knowledge of printing, paper, mailing, and all the dirty work of publishing. And I did some errands for her. I think that's what made her want me more and more. I almost worked full-time for her in Paris.

George Was the Hitching Post

The first year I was in Paris, just after I went to work for Princess Caetani, these young men came to her asking if she could give some financial assistance. They were thinking of starting a literary magazine in English, in Paris, and they were having problems getting it going. She said, "No, I can't give you any money." It took every penny she could spare to do her five- to six-hundred-page-long *Botteghe Oscure* twice a year. Then they said, "Well, do you know anybody who writes funny stories? Because we've set up this first number and realized that everything in it's about death." "Oh," she said, "I can give you somebody who writes funny stories. Money I cannot give you; but I can give you Eugene." So she sent me to meet them all.

It was George Plimpton, John Train, Peter Matthiessen, Donald Hall, and Billy Pène duBois. They had all just finished Harvard and were doing their *Wanderjahre* in Europe: a Harvard-to-Paris graduation ceremony. And they'd all had something to do with the Harvard *Advocate* in some way or another, and they just wanted to do a publication. They had the same attitude as Princess Caetani. No reviews. No critiques. Text, text, text. And they really started the interview in dialogue form. That's what I thought was so interesting: insistence on text and the interview with some living, breathing writer.

I had seen George Plimpton about in the neighborhood café. We may even have had a conversation without knowing who each other was. But then the princess told him about me, told me about him. So I just dropped in on the office unannounced. George was rather unsmiling at first, and then he said something like "Well, Eugene Walter, the princess speaks very highly of you." And I said, "I speak very highly of the princess." Ask me something, you know. I think the Harvard boys were nervous with me because I was an unknown quantity. I had never been to college but had published in snobby reviews, and the princess had praised me. But they couldn't figure out what wavelength I came from. What was I? Was I a sharecropper's child or the great-grandson of Robert E. Lee? you know. (I'm both, and more besides.) I think they thought they were fishing salmon and had suddenly caught something native to the Gulf of Mexico, you know, maybe a big catfish or something like that. I have a feeling that I was a rare bird. They didn't know how to place me. But they reserved judgment, with real Yankee politeness. They didn't go into my geographical origins or which university I had attended. Which most Harvard or Princeton or Yale boys would want to find out. I would say that each of those boys, in his own way, was liberated. These were all lively spirits. Instinctively, I think, they went to Paris to shunt off some of the tight bonds of New England and Harvard or Yale or whatever. And most of them were young. I'd had my thirtieth birthday and was older than most of them. They were five to eight years younger than I. In that age group then automatically there is going to be a certain exuberance. It's just nature. As Tchelitchew said, "Mrs. Nature is wonderful. Oh, Mrs. Nature, she is wonderful." He meant Mother Nature, but he said "Mrs. Nature."

Anyway, George said, "Do you have any unpublished material?" I said, "Yes." He said, "Well, we need a story that's a little lighter." And I said, "Well, I don't know if it's light, but I hope to God people will at least smile at certain passages." "Well," he said, "let's see it." So I showed them two stories,

milking the moon

and he left a message at my hotel saying, "We like your story 'Troubadour' and want to put it in the first issue of the *Paris Review*." So they took my story for the first number and it did all kinds of things, and I think that sort of corroborated what the princess had said about me. It went into the O. Henry collection, and then it was bought by *Atlantic Monthly,* and then it was a radio program starring Brandon De Wilde, who had just appeared on Broadway in *Member of the Wedding.* So I was not an original articulator of the *Paris Review,* but I was working with them before the first number came out. My name did not appear on the masthead until the second number. They said, "You help the princess, don't you?" and I said, "Yeah." And I said, "I think this magazine is a grand idea, and I'll give you my mailing list." (I always have a mailing list.) Then they said, "Well, gee, why don't you come and join us?" Somehow it just was natural for them to get me to help.

I liked all of those *Paris Review* boys right away. I got the right vibrations. Now George is as much a mystery to me as I am to him. I realize it was a Harvard/Boston thing. And he was more Harvard than Boston. I only saw his real humor the second or third time. Being New England, he fears exuberance or extravagance. I'm perfectly certain that if he were in the slums of Rostov-on-Don, and drunk on vodka, and it was Carnival time, we might see him take all his clothes off and dance in the street as a satyr. But I don't think he's gotten around to it yet. Thus speaks one who has swung from an iron bar three floors above the street and gone in Mardi Gras costume to a Brooks Brothers party in New York. He would not understand why I did it. And I would never understand some of his reticences. But he has the cat and monkey sense of humor. He is one of the 3 percent. He has that Yankee laconic sense of humor—that understatement—whereas Southerners tend to give colorful details, reinvented with each telling of the story. George sometimes mutters things under his breath just like my Mobile friend Emily Lynn. In the middle of that rackety-rackety and everybody talking about themselves, she was brushing white hairs off her navy blue velvet dress and saying, "What I really need is a navy blue cat." George has that kind of little muttered thing in the midst of cocktail parties and me-first publication parties, and I'm crazy about him. He is one of my favorite people on this planet.

They called me "Tum-te-tum." I did say that, I guess. It's one of those Southern expressions. Somebody says something with which you do not agree or disagree; you say, "Tum-te-tum," or "We'll talk about it later" is what it means. Or "Well, that's a piece of news, but let's don't dwell on it now." It's one of those useful noncommittal things when you have something else to talk about, like addressing envelopes. George never writes "Dear Eugene," he writes "Dear Tum-te-tum." At his age. At my age.

There had been a café in the rue de Tournon for one hundred years. But before the *Paris Review* crowd, there was no Café de Tournon. It was across the street from my hotel, so I naturally drifted over. Then, when the *Paris Review* was being formed, they were given space by Georges Duhamel's daughter, Colette Duhamel, who worked with *La Table Ronde,* which had its quarters in rue Garancière, which was the next tiny little street over, like a back alley, behind the Café de Tournon. So then somehow we all were there. Eventually the people from *La Table Ronde,* the clerks and underlings, all went to that café. So did the people from *Merlin,* which was a terribly serious, nonhumorous, avant-garde magazine financed by this girl from Limerick, Maine, Jane Lougee. Austryn Wainhouse was the big-deal editor of *Merlin.* There was a pretended rivalry between it and the *Paris Review.* They thought George and all of us were fools.

Upstairs, next door over the post office at the corner, lived an important Polish composer, and Stravinsky came to call on him, for example, and they sat in the Tournon sipping their drinks. The Palais Luxembourg was right there at the head of the street, so there were certain curators who would come there for their aperitif. The Pakistan actress Roshann Dhunjibhoy was staying in the Hôtel Scandinar, which was next door to where I stayed in the Helvétia, and she became the mistress of the Dutch photographer Otto van Noppen, who was also in the Scandinar. And Dominic Beretty, the Dutch photographer with the Italian name, was in the Scandinar, and Hans de Vaal, the Dutch journalist, was in the Scandinar, and up the street was Catherine Morison and William Gardner Smith and Vilma Howard, this black girl I had met at the Alliance from Davis Avenue in Mobile, who was one cute thing who wrote poetry. I got her first poems published in the *Paris Review.* She had written some poetry and asked me if I would look at it. I thought it was very good so I took it to George, and the other editors liked it, and she was published first in the *Paris Review.* So everybody just congregated at the Tournon, which was natural.

This was that moment five or six years after World War II when Paris suddenly just burst with exuberance. The *Paris Review* and what became the Tournon crowd was part of all that sweep to Paris. That was 1951. The war ended in '45, but people didn't come immediately after the war because it was miserable. Paris was a hardship center, broken-down and dirty, and the plumbing didn't work. There was a shortage of a lot of things: no heat, no food, no nothing, for quite a while. And long about 1950 is when it was livable, and people couldn't wait to get there. So all these young people who graduated from wherever they graduated rushed to Paris. Everybody's dream: Paris, Paris. Paris was the place.

I wouldn't say that I was riding the crest of the wave, because that sounds like it's planned or you've worked to be there. I'm traveling with the wave of the crest. It's accidental. It's triple Sagittarius cat and monkey.

Max Steele, the young man from North Carolina who won the Harper Prize for his novel *Debbie,* came to Paris. He got a cash prize, so he went to Paris. He lived not far away, and he came to the Tournon. I met him there before the *Paris Review* even started. He came in about the same time I did, when they found he was there and had heard about his book and all. He was shy: one of those people who didn't tell you everything. You could know him all your life and not know him.

He knew this girl from the South in Paris—she was one of those extras on the set. She had invited Max and myself as two literary figures to have dinner at her place. But of course, Southern girls don't really learn to cook. They had black cooks. And Max had explained that I was very fussy about food. So she was going to make what she thought was a kind of beef creole dish. She had this recipe out of a cookbook, and it said "flavor with bay leaf." She didn't know anything about bay leaves. She went to this herb shop in her neighborhood and said she wanted some bay leaf, and the clerk said, "How much do you want?" She said, "Oh, I guess a pound." Being French, he didn't question her. In France, you think, Well, maybe she does some funny sniffing thing. He didn't question. So he gave her a pound of bay leaves. She made a beef stew. And when we turned into her street, you could smell bay leaves in the air. She didn't put a whole pound in, but I think she took a handful and dumped it in the casserole. It smelled like Davis Avenue in Mobile when they are making catfish stew. We got to her apartment house and went in, and the concierge was out of his mind going, "What is that smell?" We got to her hall upstairs, and Max said, "Courage." When we went in, she was looking a little nervous. She had *that look,* which any perceptive male creature knows. When you go to an unmarried female's house and she's cooked, there's a look of the ends of the hair being damp and freshly combed. There's a dab of perfume she's just put on, always one button undone or one strap showing. You know that she's been slaving away in the kitchen and that she's had ten minutes to bathe, dress. So we sat politely and had our Dubonnet. When we were served, Max wouldn't look at me and I wouldn't look at Max. So we tasted it, and Max, who was really a quiet soul, said, "Um, bay leaf."

It must have taken ten years to get the smell out of the curtains. And of course Max and I, with laughter, rushed to the Tournon for drinks afterwards. And sat far into the night talking about girls who had scorched things and girls who'd forgotten to get the fish for the fish stew.

But curiously, Max Steele didn't write anymore. He went and became a teacher of creative writing at Chapel Hill. He is still at Chapel Hill. I would have expected him to go on. It's dangerous to fall into the world of academe until you've really thumbed your nose three times in all four directions. East, north, south, and west. Three times you must thumb your nose in those directions. That's an old Gulf Coast charm. Keep you out of trouble.

One of the crowd at the Café de Tournon was this model, from a very eccentric and marvelous family in the mountains of Tennessee. She had come to Paris, and she was a pert, charming creature: Pati Hill. For some reason, she wished either to drop or let lapse her accent, so she had learned to breathe in a different way. She'd been modeling for two years and was in *Vogue* and all that. One day she came out of the alcove and onto the runway at Schiaparelli's in a mink coat and immediately took it off and then dragged it down the runway behind her, showing off this evening dress. In the middle of this fashion show, she looked around and had this moment of revelation that Southerners have more often than other Americans of the total picture of where she was. And she said, "Oh, shit." Ran out and got a taxi and went into the woods near Paris and didn't leave for a year. Cut her hair off short and lived in one-piece peasant dresses in this shepherd's dugout in the woods. She just looked around and said, "Oh, shit," at the artificiality of the Paris fashion world, especially the backbiting and feuding. She couldn't take it. They couldn't see the humor of the whole thing. To her, the artificiality was basically humorous. At first. But they couldn't see it. She could. So she wrote a book called *The Pit and the Century Plant* that had a certain success. Max Steele had this big crush on her. They flirted, but I don't think she took him seriously.

I'm sure it was Max Steele who introduced me to another delightful creature, Miss Daphne Athas, also from North Carolina. Her mother was from Boston. Her father was from the wildest mountains in southern Greece. In fact, she used to say, "I have a double-barreled ancestry. I'm descended from Governor Winthrop of Massachusetts on my mother's side, and from the Zephs on my father's side." He immigrated to America because he was one of the younger sons and there wasn't enough land to go around. Miss Winthrop was doing some kind of work that great ladies do, like helping with people who didn't speak English who were coming in, showing them where they had to go, giving them their papers, and finding somebody who spoke their language. Miss Winthrop took one look at Pan Athas and fainted dead away when he got off the boat. He was this gorgeous young man with black curls and honey-colored skin and rosy cheeks. She said, "That's for me." That led to marriage. He didn't have any money, but he'd learned perfect English, and they came down to Chapel Hill and in no time at all he was teaching classical mythology, classical literature, and classical Greek at the University of North Carolina. He built the family house, but he never got around to putting in a front porch. They went in and out of the back porch, and there was only a long ladder from the ground to the front door.

Daphne wrote her first novel based on a school where she had taught—I think it was blind children—and it was much made over. She had this soft way of speaking and this immensely pleasing voice. Everybody stopped everything to listen to what she was saying. And she has those eyes that always look as though she hadn't slept last night. Natural shadows under the eyes that some people have. She wrote several very good novels, and the publishers were crazy about them, but for me—as much as I enjoyed them—knowing her, I felt she was holding back a little bit. I wanted her to go ahead and say, "Shit," because she was very realistic, and they really had a struggle: this big family and this house under construction at the tail end of the Depression. Every once in a while, amidst this Carolina softness and this true gentleness, there would come some word with a Boston accent to surprise you. That's what her novels needed. But oh, she was delightful.

Some friends of mine in New York said, "We are sending you someone very special. She will be writing you." She wrote me from London and said, "I hope my knight of the white rose will meet me on Tuesday the 11th at three P.M." So I went with a white rose. Some of those tourist people got out, the guys in shorts, women in those awful red and green clothes with everything hanging on little straps everywhere. I thought, Oh, what am I doing here? and my white rose was beginning to melt. Suddenly there was a lady in a Christian Dior long skirt and a hat with a little veil. I said, "Ooh, ooh." And in good eighteenth-century style she said, "La! There you are." And that was Catherine Morison. She brought only useful things with her to Paris, such as her grandmother's fan collection.

I liked her instantly. She was giddy, but she was also one of the 3 percent. She has one of those minds so quick, she finishes the sentence you're saying for you, even before the object has been revealed. It's that quick, quick mind. She was Admiral Samuel Eliot Morison's daughter, and he had exiled her to Europe for two years. She had this stepmother she hated. It was a very distant cousin who was a singer and lived in Baltimore and swooned into

Samuel Eliot Morison's arms the minute he was widowed. Catherine called her the Baltimore Oriole. They married, of course, and Catherine hated that because she had been her father's official hostess during the war years. She was only nineteen or something, but she sat at the other end of the table when Daddy was entertaining ministers of state from Washington. Admiral Morison and the Baltimore Oriole were off somewhere, honeymooning or something, when Catherine gave a party where all the Harvard boys dressed in her grandmother's ball dresses. And they burned the first floor of the house out on Beacon Street. When the firemen came they found all these beautiful ladies shivering in the snow, and it was all these Harvard boys dressed in her granny's dresses from the attic. So her daddy exiled her.

I guided her to the rue de Tournon, and she took a place about a block away, in a little hotel right where the rue de Tournon changed into the rue de Seine. The Boston crowd at the Café de Tournon grabbed her at once. She had known George Plimpton in Boston. She and Vilma Howard also fell into each other's arms, because there's a certain kind of Bostonian who is still doing antislavery. They have an attitude about making friends with intelligent blacks.

She was in Paris like a year and a half and then went to live in London. That's where she married Julian Cooper, this roaring boy from a British family that had lived in Argentina for a hundred years and had vast estates. She said, "I don't want the usual wedding. I don't want the usual dress. I don't want the usual wedding cake. What am I going to do?" I said, "Well, can I help you?" She wanted to be married in that Elizabethan mansion Crosby Hall, on the Thames. It had been bombed in the war, and she asked me to decorate the ruined chapel. So I decorated with garlands and cherubs and diamond flitters wherever I could toss them. She had musicians playing Elizabethan tunes. Then there was this great banquet hall Hadden Hall, in another building about a block away, where she had the wedding breakfast. So I hung garlands off the balcony and garlands off the chandeliers. Garlands, garlands, garlands. Flowers on the table. I went to Chelsea flower market at dawn and bought it out. She had said she wasn't going to wear white because white was only for virgins and there were no virgins left in the world. She had gotten this beautiful blue-and-white dress made to be presented to the queen, and she used that for her wedding dress. I had designed a wedding cake that had Eros skipping rope with seven cupids applauding. It wasn't your usual wedding.

But I told her, "Darling, you have gotten the wrong apartment, because there are no doors that slam. A newlywed couple has got to have a door that slams." I was right: they were divorced within a year. I think she and Julian fought from early on. I don't think he knew what he was getting into. He was getting a surprise package he didn't know about. Catherine liked men, boys. She just liked them. All of them. She had once been kicked out of a prissy proper New England girls' school because they found lipstick on a penis of a statue of Eros in the garden. Apparently Catherine would pass and just kiss it. They knew it was Catherine because nobody else in the school would have done it. She was a phallic worshiper. There are lots of ladies like that, and they call them all kinds of things—neurotic, abused, oversexed—but they are just phallic worshipers. It's fertility and fun and games, and I'm glad I'm alive. She had thousands of little friends—some not from the same social classes as frequented our café. Sometimes she got into what I would call a working girl's outfit—like a clerk in an office—a white blouse and a black skirt and a shoulder-strap battered bag—and head for truck drivers' cafés. She just liked men.

I think her mother died when she was at the wrong age for her mother to die. And her father must have been a severe gentleman—an admiral. Used to giving orders. Sweep the deck. And if she didn't do right, he'd sweep it with her. And with her father, I think a brother, uncles, and all of these government types in and out of the house, you can just see all of them saying, "Ooh, look at the little Kitty, sweet little Kitty. Where's your papa? We've got business." Living in a world of men admiring her and petting her.

I really don't know all the details, because I wasn't in the bedroom or the backseat or the barn or the beach or the thicket. And I always prefer not to know too many details. I don't mind prying into people's minds, but I'm very old-fashioned about some things, because as a poet and humorist, I can imagine better things than they really do. I mean, my idea of the very best sex is to be in a phone booth, naked, with a lot of butterflies.

I met Sally Higginson through Catherine Morison. They were not gossipy friends. They were sort of formal tea party friends, both being of old, high Boston. But once in Paris they gave parties on the same night and never spoke again. They were cool to each other at café. They may still not be speaking. On that night they both gave parties, that's when I left town. Because the world had to decide. I didn't go to either party. I left town. I don't know what George and the others did. I left town. I never wanted to talk about it with either of them. I left town.

Sally had come to Paris because all those Boston people go to Europe every year or so: the Boston trek to Europe every two or three years. And if you are going to go to London, you may as well go to Paris. Because they all had money. They weren't ruined in the Civil War. They made money in the Civil War. Sally is one of those who came for a few weeks and stayed on. She knew George Plimpton—both Sally and Catherine had known George Plimpton vaguely. Knew who he was and met him at Harvard and blah, blah, blah. All that, over the years. But I don't think they had really known him intimately or closely until Paris. They looked up one another and said, "Well, did you know So-and-so was here?" It was one of those things.

Sally's great-uncle or something was the Reverend Higginson—Emily Dickinson had the big literary crush on him. And Sally's mama was of the J&P Coats Thread. Southern cotton went up north and was spun into J&P Coats cotton thread that went around the world. Sally was a millionairess. And never made a show of it. I was very impressed when she tried out the little Hôtel Helvétia, just because all of us were there. She was not slumming. She was coming with great interest to be across the street from the Tournon. At one moment, everybody in the hotel was a friend of mine. That's when M. Jordan broke down and gave us all keys. When I first went there, you had to ring the doorbell to get one of them to come and let you in when you got back to the hotel at night after ten. That must have been all right when the hotel was kind of, you know, sort of quiet. But when all my friends were there, they got pretty tired of getting up every ten minutes at one in the morning and opening the front door to the street. We all came in around one, because we stayed at the Tournon until it closed. It was all buzzer system. Buzz, buzz. Buzz, buzz. They got sick of it and finally gave us all keys. But Sally couldn't really take the john in the hall shared by four rooms. Even I found that rather . . . and I'd been in the army with a latrine shared by twenty-five soldiers. After trying it for a few weeks, she went back to live in her fancy hotel at the place Vendôme.

She and I became great friends. Out of the 3 percent, she was of the 2 percent of the 3. The Boston sense of humor finally is as provincial and as international as the Southern. Boston and certain New England have the grandly provincial outlook that the Deep South has. Finally it ain't provincial. Like Princess Caetani, like Catherine, Sally had been raised in a world where ideas are coinage. So many people, from New England, especially from Boston, that I have met—we have become instantly *au rapport*. Whereas there are people from Chicago or Milwaukee who are as exotic to me as Tibetans. Anyway, I saw Sally off and on for a lot.

After her mother died of cancer, I went with her to Switzerland to get her mother's last bits and pieces that she'd left in this villa of a friend of hers. Sally really was pretty downcast and hated the idea of going through her mother's stuff in this room where she had stayed before she went into hospital.

Which is why I went as her comic relief. We left early so we could go and spend a few days at George's place on Lake Como. This is the villa that George Plimpton's family owned on Lake Como. Some grand cousin left it to all the family—by the time George came along, there were so many that they had to reserve it a year ahead. George only had it for two weeks every third year. So he had a *Paris Review* gathering there.

Then Sally and I drove right out through the mountains and got as close to Voltaire's birthplace as we could. We were afraid the emanations there might scorch us. And then we went to this place way over in the east on Lake Geneva, I think, where a friend of Sally's mother had this villa on the lake. With this delightful orchard and this wonderful garden and oh—the furniture and objets d'art in this house. It made you remember that the Swiss haven't had a war for several hundred years. Undisturbed was this eighteenth-century garden. Polished was this eighteenth-century furniture. Polished was this eighteenth-century floor. Little sterling-silver trinkets. Little bits of blown glass. Little bits of brocade. I mean: European civilization. It's like Cocteau said: "The Americans say, We can show you wealth. But the Europeans say, We can show you luxury." Anyway, it was a wonderful experience, that particular villa and that particular Swiss gentleman.

Now we stayed at the hotel where Hermann Hesse lived and wrote *Siddhartha*. I went to him and asked for an interview for the writers series in the *Paris Review*. And he agreed to do it. This Jewish lady from New York with the biggest ears I ever saw, and tiny little diamonds in them, was my interpreter. She was a wonderful woman, all in black, in old European Jewish style. Very intelligent, very well read, speaking seventeen languages. So I would go early in the evening when the bar first opened in the hotel. This three-piece Italian jazz band would tune up and play 1920s American music. But on the second day as we sat there, there came a bulletin on the radio that Thomas Mann had died in Holland. And Hermann Hesse got very flustered and ran from the room. I'm not sure he didn't say something like "Now there's only me!" as he rushed out of the room. He never finished the interview.

I thought he was an old pest. I didn't like him. He didn't like the Jewish lady, and I hated that in him. Because she was very amusing. She was obviously a grand lady, obviously a money background, but she made herself as invisible as possible as an interpreter. She made herself part of the furniture in the brief moments that we had, the three of us.

My only other encounter with Hermann Hesse was when I was sitting in some pine woods near the hotel. I was learning to play the alto recorder, and I would go every morning and every evening to practice. There's this

Couperin piece I'm queer for called "The Nightingale in Love." It has this heavenly up-and-down thing, and then it goes into twittering. And quick fingering. I was trying desperately to learn it. And I was sitting under these pine trees. Down the forest path came Hermann Hesse. I think he said, "What kind of bird is that?" Then when he saw me, I think he said, "Oh, it's you."

We did have some lovely times, all of us, in that period of time. Paris was good for everybody who had come from a somewhat closed world. My world was closed because I had never known the advantages of money. In fact, nobody told me about money. Money had never entered my world. I was twenty-something years old before I really and truly understood that if you left money in the bank, it drew interest. And then finally there was interest on the interest on the money you left in the bank. I've never gotten enough money to put in the bank and leave it there. I've never had more than ten dollars at once, ever. The idea of having an estate lawyer whose office you go to four times a year to look at the audit was completely exotic to me. Sally and Catherine and George and all those people had that closed world. I had the other closed world. That's why we were refreshing for each other and why it was good for all of us to go to Paris. It was children from closed worlds meeting not on a battleground, but a ruined garden. New York is a battleground. Paris is a ruined garden.

Tom Keogh had designed one of the productions of the Roland Petit ballets which I had liked so much when I saw it in New York before I went to Europe. It was not serious ballet; this was ballet bouffe. When I was in Paris, I made a point of finding someone who knew him so I could meet him. He wasn't well-known then; he was just beginning. So I did meet him, and we became friends. We were sitting at a café one day, and I said, "There she is again. Who is that fascinating girl?" She had a slightly nervous thing about her—not jerky—a little nervous. Very bony. Very elegant. Had this face that came to a little point like certain Victorian ladies. She had this auburn hair and these hazel eyes. There was something charming about her. I said, "Who is that girl? I've seen her at several of the cafés." He said, "That's my wife, Theodora. We often go our separate ways. We're very much a married couple, but we don't always like the same cafés. I like certain cafés; she likes certain cafés. Do you want to meet her?"

milking the moon

I just liked her right away; she was a very funny lady. Then I saw in a bookshop a novel by her about a man who leads a completely double life, and I saw she'd written three or four novels, so I got them all and read them, and I liked them. But nobody took her seriously, and her reviews were never very good, although she had the storyteller's art and a good sense of character. She had observed. But for some reason, she wasn't taken seriously, and at a given moment she stopped writing. Then after I'd known her quite a while, she said, "I live in two Parises because of my two names." I said, "I thought you were Theodora Keogh. Do you have a pen name?" She said, "No, I'm Theodora Roosevelt. I'm Teddy Roosevelt's granddaughter." And I said, "Well, Lord love a duck." Then I understood why New York critics wouldn't take her seriously. This was Teddy Roosevelt's granddaughter pretending to be a novelist. But I took her seriously and still do.

She had flown the coop and liked to have fun a lot and then always had an abortion afterwards. The pregnancies were not by her husband. Oh dear, no. These were by fun people. She and Tom had a kind of loose latticework marriage. It was not a brick house. It was a loose latticework summer cottage. But she did not take precautions of any kind. And once I went as her knight of the white rose to escort her to an abortion, and then afterwards to a restaurant for her to sip champagne and eat a roast beef sandwich. It was her third time. I took her to a café neither of us had been to, some other café far away from our usual bailiwicks. She wanted champagne and cheer. She wanted to be entertained. I did my best.

But I respected her. Having a little abortion now and then did not change the fact that she was genuinely a lady in the old-fashioned sense. And what is that? you ask. Well, part of it is the generous point of view. You give the benefit of the doubt to one and all until you're proven wrong, and then you retract your sympathy. She came later to live in Rome. She tried to convince her husband to take a year there. He said maybe later. She said now. So she just moved to Rome. We had a lot of fun. She was just very special.

Everybody turned up sooner or later at the Café de Tournon. My darling Jean Garrigue came shortly after I got there. Like '52, maybe. She caught Paris fever from my excitement during my preparation. She'd always planned to come and never made any arrangements, and then suddenly there were a lot of people she knew over there—other writers. She lived in my hotel for a while, and then she lived up the street for a while. She wrote a novel called *The Animal Hotel* which is partly based on the Hôtel Helvétia.

She was absolutely queer for animals, all animals. She had fallen in love with the bird market in Paris, and she had these rosy-colored birds in her room. You could go up and down the stairs in the Hôtel Helvétia and hear twittering birds.

Francine du Plessix was part of the crowd at one moment. Her daddy was one of the founders of *Vogue*. She was a friend of George's, part of that New York set that he knew. She was very, very beautiful and very, very French. Tiny waist, broad fanny, slim ankles, high heels. Exquisite coif, exquisite clothes. And educated beyond belief.

Alan Lomax came and stayed awhile. He had many versions of "The Jolly Tinker," but I had some that he didn't have, and so we would sit there and I would be singing "The Jolly Tinker" in one corner while Bee Dabney and Catherine Morison described the Dior show they'd seen that afternoon. It was great. One day I looked at Daphne Athas, Sally Higginson, and Catherine Morison sitting at a table together at the Tournon, and I thought, Oh, God, I wish I had a painting of this. Not a photograph. Only a great painter could do justice to the psychologies involved.

Then there was Christopher Logue, the English poet. I met him through Princess Caetani; someone had sent him to her—John Lehmann, maybe. He became part of the Tournon crowd. The *Paris Review* published a suite of his poems in which precious stones speak in the first person. He was disheveled and rather dirty looking in the way of young Englishmen of the period. Tweedy. A little stinky. He was always tough and always making a fuss. He was thoroughly outrageous, but I liked him. I would put him in my zoo of rare beasts. He had no money and survived entirely on what the princess gave him when she bought poetry from him. I think she slipped him some bits now and then.

And he also wrote some things for Maurice Girodias, who had the semiporn Olympia Press. All of the starving poets of Paris had written semiporn novels under other names. I had been approached by Girodias, but I was writing my own novel. Well, years later, in Milan, where I was shooting a scene for a film, I was strolling by this newsstand and I saw a familiar green Olympia Press cover. I went and looked at it, and there was a porn story by Eugene Walter. I opened it and knew from the first paragraph who wrote it. I put it back and said, No, I will not contribute one penny of royalty to that wicked Christopher Logue.

Evan Connell, the novelist, whom I absolutely adored, was part of the crowd. He was a friend of George Plimpton's—a delightful person. He was from Iowa or someplace like that; everybody liked him because he was for real. We had some fascinating conversations about life in America. This is

milking the moon

before he published the Bridge novels; he was talking about provincial life in America and how they are out of touch with the sun, the moon, and the rest of the world. I was always determined to get him to laugh because he looked like an old Hamlet. There's a picture of me making a fool of myself, dancing in the street. I finally got him to smile this shy smile, and you see he's a young man. He's not an old Hamlet.

I remember one day looking up from my Dubonnet at the Café de Tournon and seeing about ten people busy writing, staring into spaces, sipping endless black coffees or aperitifs. One was William Gardner Smith, the bestselling black novelist. He was very successful and very much spoken of. I don't know where he was from, but he had that sort of Central Africa look: a dark chocolate round face. He laughed a lot; he was one of the laughing spirits of the Tournon. One of the great moments was the morning that Vilma Howard, the charming and gifted black girl from Davis Avenue, and Renata Fitzhum, the Finnish art historian with very pale skin and pale hair, had a giggle fit together at the Tournon. They knew that William Gardner Smith was not in his room. So they went to his hotel and got in his bed—his little ole single bed—and pulled the cover over their heads. And when he opened this tiny bedroom door in this tiny hotel, this tiny bed was quivering with giggles. He ripped off the covers and there was Davis Avenue and Helsinki.

Alfred Chester was another character. He was a very gifted writer who was always hanging around the *Paris Review,* and I sent him to meet Princess Caetani. I think I took one of his manuscripts to show her. We published his first things in *Botteghe Oscure.* He'd had a fever as a child which left him without a single hair on his body. He had a good red wig, but people were nervous around him without knowing why. It was because he had no eyelashes and no eyebrows. Then he went off to North Africa and became part of that set with Paul and Jane Bowles: creatures that just got loose. They wanted to have hashish and many kinds of sex. They were all polysexual. Girls, boys, camels, watermelons. He was an innocent who'd been raised closely by a Jewish family in New York. I think he'd just never seen the greater world. Paris was one step out, and then North Africa was the full step out from the closed world to the open world. He committed suicide in the Middle East; that was the final step.

Amidst all of this there turned up an amazing creature. It was Gurney Campbell. Her family owned these fabric mills in Carolina, and she was very, very wealthy. Her husband was also, I believe, not exactly broke. She was enormously fat, but extraordinarily well dressed. Instead of being a fat lady pretending to be slim, she was a fat lady pretending that she liked good cloth and good jewelry. She and Daphne Athas wrote a play called *Sit on the Earth,* and everybody said, "Gurney, a plump girl like you shouldn't write a thing saying sit on the earth." I think she changed the title. Later she wrote that trilogy of plays about Gandhi.

Every Saturday night she did these readings at her apartment where all kinds of people read from their work. They were great fun. Once she had in Julia Randall, this serious poet. I saw at once that her braids were false, so I pulled them off. I put the braids on Gurney, and everybody laughed and giggled. The poor girl whose braids they were, she fled. She was too serious for that party. She'd been de-tailed, to some other task. Jean Garrigue wore the braids as a mustache. Then I wore the braids as a tail for two days. I walked through the Latin Quarter with Lady Angela Lady holding my tail.

Lady Angela Lady was an African princess who lived on this island off the Gold Coast which her family had owned since prehistory. She had come to Paris to study dressmaking. She always wore this red sari and red felt bedroom slippers set with broken mirror and rough-cut emeralds. (Now that's style.) I met her at the party given by the Aga Khan. So many of the people from Harvard and Boston said, "Well, do we dare invite Eugene to the party with this black girl because he's from Alabama?" And of course, we fell into each other's arms. They had three kinds of monkeys on that island where her family lived, including the kind called King of the Monkeys, which I had never heard of. Even though it's not the biggest monkey or the brightest monkey, all of the monkeys will do obeisance, bow, curtsey, and wait on this King of the Monkeys. If he comes into a group of three or four kinds of monkeys all picking little white slugs out of deadwood, they'll all stand back for the King of the Monkeys to come right up and help himself. So in the lobby of the plaza at that party in Paris, Lady Angela Lady was squatting down in her red sari and showing me how the King of the Monkeys does on her island. On the other side of the lobby, all these Bostonians and Harvards were just looking. They couldn't believe what they were seeing.

James Broughton was a part of all this. He'd been raised in San Francisco and belonged to that filmmaking group that included Curtis Harrington. I think he was in New York to do a program when I first met him. Then he turned up in Paris, and I introduced him to everybody I could. He was usually among the last few who closed the café at night. About two A.M. the weary waiter, Charles, would start sweeping up cigarette butts and making cheerful insults about "these bohemians."

Never a dull moment. You can imagine what a cross section of the world it was. It was all immensely young and fun in this establishment which was literary salon, permanent editorial board meeting, message center, short-order eatery, debating club, and study hall. There were several literary reviews in

milking the moon

English, one in French, and who knows how many books and other works springing forth from this noisy, smoky, clattery, raunchy, beat-up café.

⤞

We were doing something; we had a project. But we had no committees. We had no bookkeepers. We had no timekeepers. And we had no business managers. I think there was a New England girl that we called business manager. And there was a very tough Jewish girl from New York we called business manager at a different moment. But those were delightful individuals who were as much involved in the whole aspect of the magazine. I mean, it was certainly not my job to put up posters, but I probably put up more posters than anybody else in the group because, coming from Mobile, I realized the value of word of mouth: the little leaflet and the poster. There still is something human about those. Radio, television, and the paid ad still do not have the immediacy of the little handout, the word of mouth. If you are sitting next to the matron from Kansas City in the Tournon or the Deux Magots in summer, and you have the new number of the *Paris Review* in your hand, and you say—not to her, to the person at your table—"Have you seen this new issue?" . . . well, she might be a schoolteacher and she might go right to that newsstand and buy it.

Word of mouth comes first. Let's say the Municipal Auditorium is burning down. Bombed, I hope; it's so ugly. Burning down. Okay. A siren goes; nobody moves. Somebody beats a gong: boing, boing, boing: emergency. Nobody goes. Somebody does something else. Nobody goes. And then somebody leans out of a window and yells, "FIRE!" Everybody runs. Word of mouth. The voice on the radio will never have the same impact. You might hear on the radio that somebody let off a little bomb at Westminster Abbey. But the lady who was passing on a bus and runs to her next-door neighbor and says, "You won't believe it! I saw it with my own eyes! I was on the top deck of the number twelve, going from Chelsea Circle to Blackbird Lane, and I saw these guys leave a picnic basket in the front portal of Westminster Abbey, and it blew up!" And they could say on the radio, "A bomb believed to be perhaps a protest against the annexation of Ireland by Her Majesty's government caused minor damage to the west portal of Westminster Abbey today." It's that word of mouth that still gets attention in a way the BBC doesn't. I'm sorry; that's the way it is.

So I took posters around Paris to hang up. I addressed envelopes. I guided interesting manuscripts to them. I did a little of everything. Everybody who worked with the *Paris Review* did everything from emptying wastebaskets to serious study of manuscripts. We were busy trying to scrape up enough to get it through the press and pay the postage always. Everybody worked for nothing, and nobody expected anything.

When it looked as if it was going to go broke at the end of the first year, the Sadruddin Aga Khan popped in at the right moment and picked up the printing bill, bless his heart. The Harvard boys had known him at Harvard.

His father, the Aga Khan, was a delightful creature. He spent a lot of time in Paris. He was kind of London/Paris/Monte Carlo. He had more money than anybody could use in one lifetime. Once every year, his faithful subjects would give him gold equal to his weight. We'd see the newsreels of this huge Aga on these scales. These people would be sweating to crank it off the ground so the needle would say how much he weighed. Like three hundred. Then they'd stack up the gold bricks. I had one delightful conversation with the Aga once. He said, "You know, I've always wanted to be a writer. I really started writing short stories when I was very young." He gave me one of his short stories to read, and I took it to the *Paris Review* and said, "We ought to publish this because his son is paying for the magazine." But he died not very long thereafter.

La Table Ronde had given the *Paris Review* a small room in their offices in the rue Garancière, but it was not big enough to put everybody in. So early in the morning—like ten—we often met at the Deux Magots, not the Tournon, so that all the other people wouldn't hear what we were talking about. Because the French meet in a café to do business or to be friends. There are probably people in Paris who have been doing business for years who have never seen the inside of each other's offices. They meet at the Flore, the Deux Magots, the Montparnasse. I've seen big executives of the Gallimard publishing house and prominent lawyers spending two or three hours doing their business in a café. So strong is the tradition of "See you at the Flore." All cafés have some kind of grill, and you can get a hot sandwich of this or that or an omelet with heated French bread, butter, a piece of cheese, and some good red wine. And everybody has a secret café on some back alley. If they don't want somebody to see that they are discussing such and such a deal, they all have some other café or other restaurant or little bistro that they can walk to. So we met more often at the Deux Magots.

I don't think there ever was a meeting when everybody was there. It was a very loose-jointed editorial policy. Everybody was always coming and going, coming and going. George was the factor. George was the hitching post, and it was a portable hitching post. They were unofficial editorial meetings. Like "We are supposed to have everything at the printer next week and we haven't chosen the short stories" or "Did you have something you wanted to show?" I'd say, "Well, I got a real good one in my file." And George would say, "Well, Pati Hill has a new story. Maybe we ought to put that in." And somebody else would say, "Well, I got a story from Iowa the other day. I thought it was real good, and it has a lot of humor." Then, you know, "Well, what about poetry?" "Well, Donald Hall, you know, is at Harvard now, and we haven't heard from him. He did send us some things we didn't use last time." Somehow it got to the printer. I have a photograph of a *Paris Review* editorial meeting with Bee Dabney and George Plimpton and Alfred Chester and myself with our balloons at the Café des Deux Magots, having a serious editorial meeting. Serious. But we were not at all not doing our jobs. The *Paris Review* was a genuine publication of a salon, not a publication of a board of directors.

We might have all committed suicide if we thought we were doing something of global significance. Our whole point was the here and the now, Americans in Paris, in the tradition of Hemingway, Djuna Barnes, and all the Americans who were in Paris in the twenties. That sense of tending the fire of culture in the Old World. Here we are making sparks; that's why it was fun. Who knows what significance something has when they are doing it? Those Wright brothers really wanted to see what the shoreline looked like from the sky: the seagulls' point of view. They weren't out to revolutionize the world. They wanted to see what the seagull saw. And I think that Edison must have burned his fingers once too often striking matches to light a lamp. People who are doing earthshaking things often don't realize that. Anne Frank didn't know she was going to be an international name when she wrote in her diary. Proust thought he was doing *salon littéraire* gossip. Faulkner just had this sense about life in the provincial South. We were simply being a part of the here and now, Americans in Paris. Any group that would include South meets North and North meets South—by the time you shake that up in the popcorn popper, naturally you are going to have something lighthearted.

We thought we were trying to put out a readable and lively and first of all intelligent review that need not necessarily be defined as literary. I think all the people involved had a certain scorn for certain professorial literary circles in America, and I think they all had a sense of delight in the *salon littéraire*, which is such a different thing. The professorial get together to bitch. *Salon littéraire* gets together to gossip. It's as simple as that.

"Did you hear So-and-so had a book accepted at Doubleday?"

"Well, Doubleday, you know, that's not . . ."

"He thought he was going to go to Harcourt Brace."

"Harcourt Brace kept it for a long time, but then they sent it back to him."

"Well, he never would really finish it properly."

"That ending. He's got to do something with that ending. The last fifty pages . . ."

"Well, anyway, Doubleday is taking it. I guess he's happy."

"Yeah, but you know, Mary Louise says she's leaving him. She says she was ready to dry his tears until he got something published, but now she's going on to do her own thing."

You know. That's exactly what the French *salon littéraire* is. Gossip on a very high level. Whereas American professors theoretically discuss English ritual and all that, but they are really discussing salaries and tenure and who's been called up for fondling a student. It's not about books and manuscripts.

Ink and Paint

All the time I was working hard at my own stuff. I write always. I have always lived in a world of tablets, lined pages, and number 2 pencils. And I was always writing. Even before I could read, I was grabbing the colors and writing in my grandmother's ledger book. I can remember lying on my tummy on the floor, scrawling in one of her book-keeping books. I couldn't read or write; I was just scrawling. And she laughed and laughed and said, "What are you writing?" I said, "I'm writing an opera called *Dialogue of the Tulips*." So she got drawing pads and little notebooks and started teaching me to read the next day.

From the moment I was born, I knew that I wanted to write poetry and plays and that I wanted to use colors. There was just something about the idea of words. Words, words, words, words, words, words, you know. And making rhymes. If I were locked in jail, I would have a very long novel in two months. I just never thought of being anything other than ink and paint. I think I was ten when I wrote my first poem. It was printed in the public school *Courier*. I published regularly from my sophomore year. I did a column that was in every issue of the school newspaper. In my last year of high school, I won a prize for the best column written by a high school student in the United States. And I did a short story they published called "The Weird Sisters," about this woman and her maid who hate each other. But when the woman dies, a week later the maid dies because they can't live without their enmity. In the *Register*, I published some tiny little articles about the actress Alexandra Dagmar and Edmond de Celle, the painter. So I was always in print somewhere, little by little, from the beginning.

In New York I used to get up early before I would set out for the library and sit at my table and write. When I finished my first novel and looked back at it, I knew where it belonged: in the circular file on the floor. It was too close to gloom and doom. It's about a man who hates his parents and hates his wife and goes off for this long weekend and comes back and kills his wife. I was thinking of a news item I had read, and I wanted to contrast the kind of Baptist puritan small town with Mardi Gras. There was a famous story about this guy who vanished and then came home many years later and killed his wife, saying, "Think how many years you kept me here when I could have been in New Orleans." But murder is not my thing. I'm triple Sagittarius with a healthy liver; I couldn't do gloom and doom. It just ain't in me.

Although I love the works of Faulkner, there had been too many novels emulating him that were gloom-doom novels, almost as if the writer were insisting on gloom doom. William Styron's *Lie Down in Darkness* is a perfect example. I call it *More and More Darkness*. It's all going straight for the fall. From the first sentence you are on the way to the cemetery. Whereas it seemed to me that the human scenery contains more than the sustained note of gloom. People still tell jokes at funerals. Styron was part of the *Paris Review* crowd, and I liked him personally. He's a fine writer, but his books were too gloom doom for me. I never really got to know him or have a conversation, because what he wrote made me nervous.

I didn't consciously set out to write an antidote to the gloom dooms, but by just the way I feel about life and the fact of Carnival and the fact of the Gulf Coast, that's how it turned out. One night in New York, I came home late from one of the plays I was working on, had a steak and some red wine, and went to that Remington typewriter and wrote, "Down in Mobile they're all crazy." It just came from nowhere, outer space, five thousand years of ghosts of cats and monkeys saying, "Let's help Eugene." It didn't become a novel until about page ten. Then it wrote itself. I'd done my apprenticeship, in a sense. My theme was the difference of the Gulf Coast from the rest of the world—a little pocket of something special. I had about a hundred pages when I left New York; just shoved them in the trunk with all the stuff I needed for Paris. I'd been in Paris about six months when I put some paper in the Remington and picked it up again. Then when I had about two hundred pages, I sent it off to the Lippincott Prize novel contest.

I had been in Paris nine months when I read the news in the *Figaro* that Nicolas Nabokov and I've forgotten who else were doing a festival of twentieth-century music at the Théâtre des Champs-Élysées. I saw that Stravinsky was going to conduct his *Oedipus Rex*, this fabulous soprano from the state theater in Brussels was going to sing all three soprano parts of *Socrates*, and a production was coming from Juilliard doing Gertrude Stein and Virgil Thomson's *Four Saints in Three Acts*. And I thought, Oh, God, I wish I had the money to buy tickets. Then I got this telegram saying "To what address should we send your check? You have won the Lippincott novel contest."

Three weeks later the announcement was in the *Figaro:* Tickets go on sale at eight o'clock, Tuesday the so-and-so, for the twentieth-century festival. I bought a folding chair and a thermos bottle and a picnic basket and filled it with goodies from a fancy food shop. I had a notebook with little three-by-five cards. At midnight the night before, I went to the Théâtre des Champs-Élysées and I sat by the door closest to the box office. I stayed there all night. 'Long about three, a lot of students turned up. I didn't say anything. I just wrote numbers and gave them out. Because the French—nobody stays in line, they push, they climb over trodden dead bodies of other people in the queue, so I just wrote numbers and handed them out. I grunted when they asked things, so they just thought I was a rude French official. When the doors opened there was quite a mob, but since the line had stretched and formed itself correctly at least twenty back, those who would have rushed were held back by those who were numbered.

So I was the first. They had the floor plan of the theater, and I said, "First row balcony, these two seats for the first performance of EVERYTHING." It was like a few hundred dollars. Oh, God, how I loved it. I would always wait until the last minute and say to some friend, "Oh, incidentally, tomorrow night. What are you doing tomorrow night? Would you like to go to the first night of *Four Saints in Three Acts?*" "*What?* You have seats? How'd you get them?" Three-by-five note cards, a pencil, and a folding chair. Coffee in a thermos and a picnic basket which you could use as a blunt instrument if you had to.

My stock went up a great deal at the Tournon after the Lippincott. It was announced, I think, in *The New York Times,* and somebody who knew I was part of the *Paris Review* had clipped it and mailed it to George or Peter or somebody. There was a little hush when I went into the Tournon one night. I played it cool, of course. Is there any other way? They were all delighted, because naturally, the more fuss members of the *Paris Review* were making in the world, the better for the *Paris Review.* But everybody there was publishing things and winning prizes and getting contracts, and we were congratulating each other constantly. It was fun.

In New York, I had gone to every museum. At great leisure. Like do the Metropolitan for two months. Just do two or three pictures and get out. Just forever and forever and forever and forever. So I didn't get around to the Museum of Natural History until much later. Dinosaur bones or dinosaur reproductions have never meant much to me. King Kong, yes. Dinosaurs, no. But finally, one day, I didn't have a museum left. I'd done them. So I thought, Well, I'll just go and look at that Museum of Natural History that's off of Central Park.

Well, I saw some bones and some dinosaurs, and they had a model plane that was doing something funny—I've forgotten what. Then I wandered into the habitat groups. I looked at some hartebeests and thought, Oh, the dear things. And went on and saw some giraffes and the double-humped camel. And I thought, Well, yes, camels. Then I turned this corner and here were these most elegant monkeys. The white-mantled colobus. I mean elegance. Black, black, black with a dead white cape of silk fringe on their backs. The kind of black that is not the absence of color, but is the world of shadow and soot in a chimney, which is another concept. The white-mantled colobus was soot black with these perfect opera capes of snow-white fringe. They all looked as though they were going to the opera. Rather long tails. Delicate wrists and delicate hands, feet. And pure white eyelids in a black face. The little label said they rarely descend to ground level. It said they could inform each other when certain trees are ripe or when certain beetles they consider a great delicacy are available in their vicinity. They can communicate with other white-mantled colobus monkeys as far as half a mile away by employing a kind of Morse code which they blink. With those white eyelids and black face, they just do their own perfect monkey Morse code. You know, like "Get over here quick. The wild pomegranates are falling off the trees. Those green beetles are back in town. Get over here quick. Have a party tonight." You know. I flipped.

I'd never seen or heard of that particular monkey. I knew about monkeys. I had books about monkeys. I'd seen pictures of all kinds of monkeys. But I had never encountered the white-mantled colobus. They're rare. Nobody had ever seen them until fairly recently because they just don't come to the ground. And they also said that when humans walk through their grove, they remain absolutely motionless. The minute that person is a little farther on, they blink to the others, "They are on hand." I couldn't leave. I stayed till closing. I just sat there. In those habitat groups with stuffed animals, they have a curved painted backdrop—a panorama—that's very realistic. If you close even one eyelid slightly, you really think you're in an East African jungle. For that afternoon, I was in an East African jungle.

I walked away in this daze and wrote a sonnet about the white-mantled colobus, which got lost and only turned up much later, perfectly illustrating what Gertrude said to Alice: "Never never never never never NEVER throw anything away." Then, of course, I wrote poems about all the other kinds of monkeys. That's how *Monkey Poems* started. If something really strikes me, I guess I deal with it the rest of my life.

Later in Paris, Sally Higginson and I went one night to see the first time they'd had fireworks at Versailles in thirty years or something. We sat in our uncomfortable wooden folding chairs, gossiping about whatever party we'd been to the night before, and waiting, thinking, Oh, goodness, I hope this is worth waiting for, because those chairs were *un*comfortable. Suddenly, way up at the top of the steps came a fanfare of eight hunting horns. Now a French hunting horn is quite unlike the English hunting horn. Naturally. They were playing something very Baroque and full of frilly phrases, and then these little torches appeared at the top of the stairs, and then water began to trickle down this little waterway between the steps. Down the hill came these eight huntsmen, tootling away in eighteenth-century costume. Then, as if by magic, light came out of these eight urns along the side of the pond. Later we saw there were eight little boys behind these urns. Then there was this extraordinary bang—the caps being released by some mechanism in the fountains—and these jets of water began to grow very slowly in the air. Then the fireworks began, so you had water and fire going simultaneously. It ended up that there were fireworks coming out of the bushes, coming from the top of the stairs, and the water just all going mad with little sprays from little jets that you just couldn't imagine were there. I almost peed in my pants. I didn't. I didn't. But it was back to childhood. It was genuine awe. It was like those Italian acrobats and those little twinkling lights at the vaudeville. It was just pure magic. So I went right home and wrote the poem "The Fireworks at Versailles," which begins, "I'll celebrate all wayward things from man's mind born," and I realized that was the theme of the *Monkey Poems*.

The princess liked those first ones very much, and she published about eight of them. Then John Train read them in *Botteghe Oscure* and said that he would like to publish them as a book. And he did. I wouldn't say he was wealthy, but his father was a judge who wrote murder mysteries. He had all his daddy's mystery story royalties. And he had that passion for publishing that a lot of young people do who are readers—who are perhaps not creative writers themselves. So he published it.

But I made him mad. The book came out with this sort of olive green cover, and it looked like a literary pamphlet. It didn't look like *Monkey Poems*. It had this dingy green color that just turns me off because I have seen too many doctoral dissertations bound in that color. Dismal green. It's very close to army uniform color, which ain't a pretty color. It's green, but it's kin to khaki. Not a gleeful color. So I was raising hell and complaining mightily. I went to a shop that still made that gorgeous marble paper, and I got six colors:

yellow, pinky blue, blue, rose, red, bright green. I had a little jacket made with the King of the Monkeys pasted on that marble paper. I think I may have said something nasty. I'm afraid I insulted him. I wrote much later and apologized and said, "When I meet you next I will bow my head on the sidewalk and you can put your little red heels on my neck." I haven't seen him since. We've never been in the same city at the same time. I've lost three friendships with people who surprised me with that color.

By pure chance, when I went back to America to do broadcasts and interviews when my first novel was coming out, I met this dear, wonderful creature, Daisy Alden, who published this thing called *Folder*. She was one of the new crowd that had come up around the galleries—the new young painters, the new young poets—since the years I'd been out of America. She asked me what I was working on. Well, I had had this idea about doing a little essay on *Hamlet*, but when I went to the New York Public Library and saw how many professors had written essays on *Hamlet*, I thought, Well, I'd better write a new version of *Hamlet*. I cannot add another thing to that groaning board. So I told her, "I'm writing a version of *Hamlet* for monkeys." She said, "Oh, I'd love to see it," so I showed her some bits and pieces. "Oh, sure," she said, "I want to publish it." So *Singerie Songerie* appeared in this rather elegant thing called *Folder*. It really was a folder with poems and silk-screened prints in color from those young painters in the news in New York City. She had color serigraphs from them and new poems and again, no reviews, no criticisms. Just new work. So she published *Singerie Songerie*, and then I became the Paris editor of *Folder*.

Then I sent some poems to *Whetstone* in Philadelphia. They said, "Wouldn't you like to join us as a foreign editor?" Then I sent some to the *Wormwood Review* in Connecticut. And he said, "Wouldn't you like to join us as our European editor?" They were all beginning, and my name had begun to be seen in *Paris Review* and *Botteghe*. So, of course, I was delighted to do anything, because they were publishing creative people. They had some book reviews and some essays now and then, but the big thing was new work, new work, new work, new work, new work. So I just guided things their way. If I saw a poem that I thought was perfect for the *Wormwood Review*, I would say, "I'm sending you a manuscript on." A lot of people had begun sending me manuscripts just as an editor. Not as an editor with this or that. If I saw work from a young writer and it wasn't taken by *Botteghe* or *Paris Review*, I could always suggest other possibilities that they might not have heard of. It's more and more impossible for any young artist, the cost of printing being what it is.

Of course, *Whetstone* didn't pay, nor did *Intro Bulletin,* nor did *Folder,* nor did *Paris Review.* But it was publication. The princess paid ten dollars a page for prose and two or three dollars a line for poetry. No other literary magazine paid anything like that.

When I really went full-time with the princess in Rome, I more or less gave up the others except for *Paris Review* and the *Transatlantic Review.* I was with *Transatlantic* from the first number to the last. Joseph McCrindle, whose father was General McCrindle and whose mother was a novelist, was born with books. He was an apprentice at my publisher's in London, and they wrote me and said there was someone who wanted to meet me and he was coming to Paris and his name was Joseph McCrindle. He was this cherub. Now there are some cherubs that are childlike. This was an older cherub. He's round and he has a pink English complexion, but there is nothing childish about him. This was just an older cherub. He's shy, but not that shy. He has great good taste, and the *Transatlantic* was wonderful. People always think that when someone rich like the princess or Joseph McCrindle makes a magazine, it's just their money and they are having talent do it under the counter. But Joseph did edit it. He did know all the writers, and he did talk to them. He was the real editor, and he paid for the whole thing.

At a given moment—I think in its tenth year—the tax people said, "Well, you can't go on. This is a fluke. You are doing something crooked here." He wasn't. He took a tax cut on what he spent, but he sold subscriptions and sold it on the newsstands and made a big point of trying to make it support itself. But the tax people, who hate free thinkers or art of any kind, couldn't believe that Mr. McCrindle actually did it because he thought there should be a good literary review. They thought it was a tax dodge. They forced him to close it then; they wanted millions of dollars in taxes.

Banishing the Commonplace

I had lovely dinner parties in Paris. I don't really enjoy cooking for myself. I really cook to invite people in, do the gossip and the book reviews. And I loved to sort of alarm people by saying, "Would you come to dinner?"

"Where shall we go? Where shall we meet?"

"Well, in my room." Since nobody ever did anything like cook or even eat in those cubbyhole rooms, I liked to do it as a gesture. I worked hard at it.

It was strictly forbidden to cook in the rooms, but I had a one-burner stove—one of those wonderful alcohol burners they have in France. You just go to the corner store and buy a quart of alcohol, you put it into this thing, and you pour one drop on a little coal and take a match and light that. When that little drop is burning on the coal, you turn the little handle and then it goes blue and then you can cook.

By then Mme. and M. Jordan knew me. They knew that I never left one crumb in the room. Because they were afraid of rats, I carefully washed everything, carried everything down, and put it in the sewer hole in the street after cooking a meal in the room. All of Paris was rats. The Parisians always loved their cats, but they ate them in the last months of the war. Since all of the cats of Paris were eaten during the starvation period at the end of World War II, kittens cost like twenty-five dollars. That's why Mme. Jordan loved her orange cat that matched the woodwork. But they were afraid of rats in the attic of the hotel, which was full of luggage left by Jewish refugees who'd been hauled off to the camps. Although M. Jordan was a cranky Frenchman, he kept all of those things with the people's names carefully on them even though it was perfectly obvious what had happened to them. The attic was full. And it was full of rats. I kept something in the attic that later had deep bites out of it.

So when I gave these dinner parties, I very carefully took every scrap and I swept and I washed everything. I remember once I had forgotten something I needed, and when I got back into the lobby of the hotel, you could smell gumbo simmering somewhere. And of course, they pretended not to notice. I went to early morning market, and they saw me carrying those string bags of food. They never said anything, because I never left any food in the room. Never. In America, the rules would be the rules. But in Europe, rules can be bypassed if done gracefully, graciously, and logically. With logic, grace, and style, you could do anything in Europe. In America, the law is the law. You have to go underground to break it. Young Europeans are raised with the idea that they are themselves. They are not controlled by rules and laws. Rules and laws exist, but only to thumb your nose at.

Anyway, I did have some lovely parties. I could only really do four people because the room was so small. Catherine Morison once did a little dinner in her room prepared by a restaurant. One of the seats was the bidet; she put a sofa cushion on the bidet. Then there was a chair and a stool and a trunk. Those were the four seats at her dinner party. I had a marble-top dresser where I kept the stove in the bottom drawer and used that marble top when I wanted to cook with it. There was a fireplace with a metal front that pulled up, and I kept my wine bottles in that unused fireplace. Then there was a little washbasin behind a curtain hanging from the ceiling in one corner. But I gave rather elaborate meals.

Once I had a cocktail party honoring Stephen What's-his-name, the Polish writer and publisher who created his own press in London. He wrote these mad, wonderful novels and wonderful, crazy plays. Nobody in the *Paris Review* crowd had met him or his wife, who did these delightful books of cartoons. I thought, I'll try to see how many people can I get into this room. There was this vicious old bull dyke in the room next to me, but I was always terribly polite to her, and when she was ill, I did her shopping for her. I asked if I could leave a chair and a box in her room just for that night, so that gave a little space. Then I thought, Now how am I going to decorate this place? There is nothing you can do. It was faded floral wallpaper that obviously was put up before the Second World War. And dingy curtains. It was very clean, because Mme. Jordan was from the scrub-and-dust set. But it was dingy. It was sad. I thought, Oh, I have a beautiful sheet of rose red marble paper made by that bookbinder supply house that I loved just to go in, stand inside, and smell. So I took that sheet of rose red paper and put it over the lighting fixture in the middle of the room. I took my scissors and made little star-shaped holes out of the paper. Wherever that beam of light made a white star on the wall or the curtain, I made a red paper rose and put it so the spotlight was on a red paper rose in various places. It was a very odd effect. And it was a great party. I got twenty-five people into that tiny room.

Pati Hill always remembers one particular meal that I made for her. She was dead broke, down to absolutely nothing. And I was down to absolutely nothing. But she had three onions, and I had a bottle of wine and some crackers. So I put some olive oil in a frying pan, and I did onions in three ways. I did all this elaborate froufrou about giving it French names and pretending we were doing this very elaborate French meal. But it was onions thrown into boiling water just long enough to be crunchy and flavored with cloves; and then onions boiled until they were mush, flavored with something else; and then onions fried with a little sherry poured into them. Then crackers, and I think I had some peppermints. We were both absolutely penniless; we just had arrived at nothing. So I did this pretend snob French dinner of onions. Lord, Lord. It just goes to show it's not money that makes a party; it's imagination.

Sally loved to give parties in her room at the Hôtel Vendôme. They didn't have a restaurant, but they had kitchens that catered to the rooms. She'd arranged a beautiful party for George Plimpton's birthday. Or was it the party for Eddie Morgan, of the wealthy Morgan family, after he had failed the course in good manners at Long Island University? Those were two great parties that Sally gave. Anyway, I knew that everybody would come to the Hôtel Vendôme very well dressed. And my idea always was let's

milking the moon

make every party something else. So I took a suitcase of colored scrap paper and tinfoil and made everybody do something. Either on their own or I just bullied them and put something on them. I made Sally mess up her hair and put something on it. I made George put on a white jacket and be a Southern planter. Everybody was wearing little bits and pieces of different things. And of course, it makes a good party. The minute you leave the here and the now, it's a party. Whether it's in a ruined filling station in Pascagoula or the Hôtel Vendôme. When you've done something to banish the commonplace, it's a party. It really is a childish thing or a highly sophisticated thing, according to how you look at it. Children given a package of Hershey's silver bells and left to their own devices will get under a tree or climb a tree and eat them all and make something with the silver paper. You know. I can remember, with Mary Agnes Wolfe, eating a whole bag which we stole from my grandmother's kitchen. It was our bag, but my grandmother had said, "Now I've bought this bag of silver bells that has to last you a whole week. It's here on the shelf." So we each had a couple, and we looked at each other. We didn't think again. It was actually Mary Agnes who reached in and took it and put it in an apron pocket and we climbed a tree. We ate them all, and we covered our ears with silver paper. And enjoyed a morning in the tree with silver ears. There was no difference in that and the party at Sally's. It was banishing the commonplace.

On occasion, when I gave a dinner party, I'd have all the food the same color, like all white food. All purple food. All green food. Or serve a meal backwards. Like first you have the dessert. All the courses would be carefully chosen to be eaten in reverse order. The dessert would be something like avocado sherbet with tiny little almond cookies. Then a special, heavy yogurt for the cheese course. And then paper-thin ham when you get to the meat. But just making the meal backwards somehow has an effect. I've done all kinds of parties. It makes people a little giddy when you break the rules.

A Ticket of Admission to Everything in Paris

One day the Princess Caetani said, "Oh, Eugene, Carson McCullers is here, and Mrs. Alfred Knopf is bringing her over. You must come and join us." I said, "Oh, that would be so exciting," because I loved Carson's books. It was one lovely summer afternoon in Paris with all the windows open and the curtains blowing. And here was Blanche Knopf, a rather theatrical lady with a very New York cocktail party–type dress and lots of makeup although it was bright sunlight still. I belong to that upbringing in the South where ladies can put on all they like when the sun goes down, but in the daytime, belles only put on makeup that's invisible. Anyway, Blanche sort of dominated things. There was this little mousy thing with green skin and huge shadows under her eyes and looking like a lemur sitting next to me on the sofa. She was a charming Southern girl, but she was odd looking. If I were casting a sharecropper film, I would cast her. She looked slightly unhealthy. But she was animated and charming; she was one of those cats and monkeys.

After we talked for a while, she turned to me and said, "Where are you from?" It's a Southern question. I said, "I'm from Mobile." She said, "Oh, Mobile, I knew somebody from Mobile in school. . . ." Anyway, she and Reeves had taken this old ruined monastery about an hour from Paris that they were able to get through her publisher. And she said, "I'm going to try to start a Southern garden. I've got to get me some lantana seeds and some four o'clock seeds. But I don't want those bright pink ones. I don't want the ones that are all speckled and spotted. I want some pure white four o'clocks and some pale pink four o'clocks." I wrote home to some friends in Mobile who I knew had the four o'clock seeds themselves. A lot of people pick off the seeds when they are ripe to be sure they are put in the garbage because they don't want the whole land to be four o'clocks. I was able to get for her the pure white and the pale pink. And I got white lantana for her, and I got something else. I can't remember what. Anyway, she was very happy and invited me to come visit her. George Plimpton and I thought of driving there, but then Reeves committed suicide in a Paris hotel room.

Reeves had been in the hospital since the end of the war, having an aluminum stomach put in or whatever they do. His stomach was shot out in the war, and he had some aluminum parts. He had never been to Europe, and he kept a room in a little hotel about three blocks from my hotel. He was this blond Southern country boy from Georgia, soft-spoken. "Yes, ma'am." "Yes, sir." "Why, I do declare." You know. We met as Southern boys would to have drinks, have supper, and go out and get drunk. We had a marvelous drunk on B&B together once. We talked and talked and talked about the war and exchanged stories. We didn't talk anything about books. We just talked about things Southern boys talk about when they get drunk. He didn't seem suicidal to me at all. If I'd been asked to guess ten people out of a hundred that I would be sure would never commit suicide, he would have been one of the ten. That's why I think he was only doing it to get attention. Everybody made such a fuss—I mean a fus-s-s-s-s-s-s-s-s—over Miss Carson. And didn't even notice him. So he took to staying in town more and more and getting drunker and drunker because he was free from hospital and didn't have to go to bed at ten. He could go from bar to bar and see all those crazy people.

He took sleeping pills one night afterwards, but he telephoned everyone he knew in Paris. I was gone; I was somewhere else that particular weekend. But he telephoned everybody he knew, saying he was going to end it all. He'd had it. So he took those sleeping pills. Didn't take many, but he was so full of whatever he drank that it didn't do well, and he just passed out cold and died. I don't think he really meant to kill himself; I think he just wanted the attention. But I never saw Carson again because she just went into a state of shock.

I saw William Faulkner when they had that twentieth-century festival, and he came to Paris and made a speech. I had met him as a child in Mobile. On Government Street one day I was going along, and here was Faulkner and my grandparents' friend Mr. Lyons. Faulkner was a friend of the Lyons family and was there visiting. He was polite and charming, but he didn't say very much; never did. In Paris I saw him at Natalie Barney's. She had this grand party and invited the *Paris Review* editors. Mr. Faulkner was there, and I said, "You don't remember, but many years ago we met on Government Street with Mr. Lyons." "Oh, yes, well, I did go to Mobile several times." And I said, "Well, the news from Mobile is there was this big snow and it didn't melt. It stayed on the ground." He said, "Snow in Mobile. Think of that." Then I told him how much I liked the speech he'd made, and he said, "Snow in Mobile. Think of that. Snow in Mobile." And I said, "Well, have you been in Paris much before?" And he said, "Yes, I've been here before. Snow in Mobile and it didn't melt." That was our conversation.

Then, I knew this French gentleman who was one of the editors of the publishing house where Faulkner was published in Paris, and he invited me to dinner with Faulkner and Katherine Anne Porter at the Grand Véfour. We'd finished this extraordinary meal. The chefs had known who Faulkner was, and obviously they knew the French editor was a bigwig in one of the publishing houses and brought all kinds of white elephants and dead ducks to that restaurant. So they'd gone all out. You wouldn't believe what we'd had. It was a hot summer evening, and there was that moment as we sipped our 1870 cognac or Grand Marnier or whatever we had after the coffee, when Katherine Anne Porter said something like "Back home, first butter beans'll be coming in." And he said, "The baby speckled ones." After all the triumph of French cuisine. It's a warm summer evening, and they're thinking about the first butter beans back home.

Again, he didn't talk much. He never did. He had his pipe and he drank a lot and he ate rather properly. He would cut his meat, put his knife down, pick up his fork, pick up a piece of meat, put it in his mouth, put the fork back, pick up the knife, and cut another piece of meat. Miss Porter and the French editor just rattled on. I didn't feel she was Southern the least bit. She had a kind of pointed sense of humor, where you got the sting a little bit after she'd said it. I could tell by the way she handled the French editor and Mr. Faulkner—she didn't bother much with me—I could tell she was BOGB. Bitch on good behavior.

Archibald MacLeish was one of those serious thirties people. I had lunch with him a couple of times. The princess received him. He was a friend of her half sister, Mrs. Francis Biddle, who was very instrumental, very helpful, and very backing of the Library of Congress poetry readings. A real patron of the arts without a fuss. She sent Archibald MacLeish to the princess. He was of that world of Harvard professors. Some of them are jolly souls, but most are what I call the tenure commentators, the tenure critics, who don't have one idea to present. What half ideas they have they clothe in upside-down English, so you get the idea there's profundity, if you could understand it.

I've nothing against the dear boy. His jackets were so beautifully cut. He could afford a very good tailor. He did some wonderful poems, and he certainly was a charming man. But I don't think he'll be remembered for literary creativity. He was a literary society figure. In about thirty years some intelligent child graduating from someplace like Iowa State is going to do a grand book about literary society figures. People who sort of advised writers or advised publishers or presided over evenings in the tavern or in the saloon. Who wrote a lot—piles—but who will never be remembered as creators.

The Harvard boys respected him very much. He was on sort of that honorary board, or something, of the *Paris Review*. But he wasn't Café de Tournon. He was part of a more serious Harvard crowd that was in Paris. I'm not putting the man down. He had a sense of humor. I just never thought of him as creative. He was a promulgator. It goes back to what I liked about George and Peter Matthiessen and all those creatures and the princess. They wanted to publish texts. They had some essays, and they had interviews, but it wasn't that gobbledygook.

In Paris the world of literature was small and rather closed. You had to know somebody to be introduced into it. I had the highest introduction

on earth: I was the editorial assistant to the Princess Caetani. You can't do better than that. The fact that I worked for the princess was like a ticket of admission to everything in Paris. That was how I got invited by Natalie Barney to her marvelous weekly salon. She was a very wealthy lady, an undertaker's daughter from Ohio who'd come around the turn of the century and stayed on. She was a fixture in Paris. She wore squarish glasses and wandered about, beaming, looking a lot like Benjamin Franklin. You entered a dim, cluttered hallway and were received by an ancient servant and led back to a huge room with a big round table in the middle loaded with sandwiches and pastries. The food was wonderful, and everybody was yakkity, yakkity, yak about some new book or some new play. It was a zoo, with all those rare creatures. Many of those present had known Proust. Some were angry at having been used as models for characters in his novel. Some were angrier still for not having been used. There was a great divan in each of the four corners of the room, and some major personality or beauty presided over his or her court from the center of each divan. Once Colette was there; she sat on one of the four sofas, preening like a great pussycat. She was so crowded around by a cluster of people chatting over her and around her and under her and above her and next to her that I didn't really get to see her there.

But then one day this delightful man who was a publisher in Paris said to me, "Now I've got to stop in for a moment and see Madame Willy. Do you want to come?" Her married name was Willy. In fact, she was a ghostwriter for him until something she wrote was published under Willy's name and was so successful that she just started doing her own stuff. Anyway, we went there where she lived in those grand, grand residences in the Palais Royale. She was in bed then. She was old, and she had arthritis and this and that. It was not like other bedrooms. She slept there, but it was her salon. There were three or four cats on the bed and fresh flowers everywhere. Little sketches all over the walls from Picasso and Matisse. Lots of mirrors. Her hair looked as though one of those bristly baboons of East Africa had tried to imitate a human being. It was this bristly thing that stood up in every direction, like a Brillo wig. I would call it Colette red, which was a combination of mahogany and henna. But it was the mascara that really got me. I'm certain she flung her mascara on with a tablespoon, then took a toothpick to pry out a peephole. She had this fancy dressing gown of some sort, and then there was an animal skin thrown over her. It was a first-act entrance, although she was in bed, not entering.

~~~

There was this crazy man in Paris who was the heir of María Sert. She was the widow of the Spanish painter José Sert, who collected medieval stuff. He restored a lot of murals in medieval monasteries and churches all over Spain, and instead of taking money—since he was independently wealthy—he'd ask if he could have an old chest or an old crucifix or an old tapestry, and he had a collection that was just unbelievable. He left it to his wife, and then his wife gave it to this funny little Frenchman who looked like an enlarged tadpole. I can't think of his name. He took drugs. In the middle of a dinner or a cocktail party at his house, he'd suddenly start looking pale and tired. Then he'd run out of the room and come back looking all fresh.

It was at one of his parties that I met Greta Garbo and the old guy with the dead white face and eye makeup who was the original of Mighty Grain of Salt O'Connor in Djuna Barnes's *Nightwood*. Garbo was introduced as Harriet Brown. That's the name she went under. I also met her longtime lover, Mercedes de Acosta. I'm not sure, but I think Garbo was what we in the Old South called nympho. In other words, she didn't have a stamp collection. Some people have stamp collections. Some don't. Mercedes looked like a Madrid madam of 1890. A little fleshy, a little flabby, dyed black hair. I mean hair dyed so black that it was like a black hole in space. Big black eyes and a lot of black eye makeup and red lipstick. I mean lipstick they don't make anymore. They haven't made it since they closed the whorehouses in Madrid.

And the things in that apartment. His bedroom was about as big as a house. It was papered with studies of oil on canvas that Rubens had made for one of the famous tapestries. That's what he had for wallpaper. The dining room had a sixteenth-century Chinese table that had a top made of the scales of deep-sea turtles arranged in a fan shape. Then on the sideboard there were these temple guardians: one-third cat, one-third dog, one-third dragon. Not even the Met has anything like it. There was an old marble fireplace, but you couldn't see it because sitting in front of it were natural crystal formations from some unknown part of the globe.

We talked a lot, and it came out that I loved Tiepolo because of those drawings of Pulcinella. "Oh," he said, "come with me." We went into this little room that only had a wall of little drawers. In the little drawers were nothing but Renaissance to 1800 drawings, drawer after drawer after drawer. And a little table and a little magnifying glass. He left me there for about an hour before lunch one day, and if somebody hadn't come to get me, I might still be there. They might have found this skeleton of a fairly youngish man just leaning over a table of drawings.

I met lots of extraordinary creatures. I met Esther Arthur, the granddaughter of President Arthur. He was the one who signed the thing

Group photograph taken outside the Café de Tournon in Paris in the mid-1950s. In the front row, from left to right: Vilma Howard, poet; Jane Lougee, publisher of *Merlin;* Muffy Wainhouse, wife of Austryn Wainhouse; Jean Garrigue, poet. In the second row: Christopher Logue, poet and *Merlin* editor; Richard Seaver, *Merlin* editor; Evan Connell (with mustache), novelist; Niccolo Tucci, essayist and novelist; Eugene Walter; a young woman known as "Gloria the Beautiful Cloak Model"; Peter Huyn, poet, translator, and editor; Alfred Chester, novelist and short story writer; Austryn Wainhouse, *Merlin* editor. In the last row: George Plimpton, *Paris Review* editor; Michel van der Plats of *Het Vaderland,* a Dutch publication; James Broughton, filmmaker; William Gardner Smith, novelist; Harold Witt, poet. (© VAN NOPPEN)

Eugene, again with members of the *Paris Review* crowd, this time dancing in the street in an attempt to make novelist Evan Connell smile and prove he's not just "an old Hamlet." From left: Michel van der Plats, William Pène duBois, George Plimpton, Vilma Howard, Eugene Walter, Alfred Chester, and Evan Connell. (© VAN NOPPEN)

From left: Eugene Walter, David Hughes, Catherine Morison, and her husband, Julian Cooper, at a café in Paris, 1950s. (PHOTOGRAPHER UNKNOWN. COURTESY OF KATHERINE CLARK)

Eugene Walter and Christopher Logue at a café in Paris, 1950s. (PHOTOGRAPH BY RUSS MELCHER)

From left: Eugene Walter, Jean Garrigue, Gurney Campbell, Lady Angela Lady, and Jack Campbell. Note that Jean Garrigue is wearing as a mustache the braid Eugene stole from Julia Randall. (PHOTOGRAPHER UNKNOWN. COURTESY OF KATHERINE CLARK)

Lady Angela Lady, an African princess from the Gold Coast, Paris, 1950s. (PHOTOGRAPHER UNKNOWN. COURTESY OF KATHERINE CLARK)

Eugene at a party given by Gurney Campbell, with false braids he stole from the poet Julia Randall. He proceeds to play the monkey, his favorite of all animals, precariously balancing himself on a window ledge. (PHOTOGRAPHER UNKNOWN. COURTESY OF KATHERINE CLARK)

Catherine Morison and Eugene Walter in London, 1954, when Catherine married Julian Cooper. (PHOTOGRAPHER UNKNOWN. COURTESY OF KATHERINE CLARK)

From left: Hans de Vaal, Mary Lee Settle, Alfred Chester, and Eugene Walter, at a dinner party in Eugene's Paris apartment. (PHOTOGRAPHER UNKNOWN. COURTESY OF KATHERINE CLARK)

Pati Hill, a former model and an early contributor to the *Paris Review,* in her Paris apartment. (PHOTOGRAPH BY EUGENE WALTER. COURTESY OF KATHERINE CLARK)

Theodora Roosevelt Keogh, a member of the expatriate café society in Paris of the 1950s. (PHOTOGRAPHER UNKNOWN. COURTESY OF KATHERINE CLARK)

From left: Ollie Harrington and Richard Wright, American writer and expatriate, at a café in Paris. (© D. BERRETTY)

From left: Bee Dabney, Eugene Walter, Yvonne Pène duBois, and George Plimpton, at a birthday party for Plimpton given by Sally Higginson in her room at the Hotel Vendôme, Paris. (© VAN NOPPEN)

Sally Higginson at the party she threw for George Plimpton's birthday. (PHOTOGRAPHER UNKNOWN. COURTESY OF KATHERINE CLARK)

Princess Marguerite Caetani receiving the Légion d'honneur during the tenth anniversary celebration of *Botteghe Oscure*. (PHOTOGRAPHER UNKNOWN. COURTESY OF KATHERINE CLARK)

Eugene Walter and Princess Caetani in Ninfa. (© PHOTO BOSIO PRESS, ROME)

Virginia Campbell (Ginny Becker),
who lived in an apartment in the Palazzo
Caetani and performed marionette
productions with Eugene, Rome, 1960s.
(PHOTOGRAPHER UNKNOWN. COURTESY
OF KATHERINE CLARK)

A scene from "The Cat Cabaret,"
a marionette production by
Eugene and Ginny Becker, Rome.
(PHOTOGRAPHER UNKNOWN.
COURTESY OF KATHERINE CLARK)

Eugene Walter and Ginny Becker
picnicking in Italy with friends.
(© KOO STROO)

Eugene Walter and Princess Brianna Carafa enjoying a picnic outside of Rome.
(PHOTOGRAPHER UNKNOWN. COURTESY OF KATHERINE CLARK)

Eugene Walter and Isak Dinesen during her visit to Rome in the late 1950s. (PHOTOGRAPHER UNKNOWN. COURTESY OF KATHERINE CLARK)

A contact sheet (above) and detail (right) of photographs of Eugene and Isak Dinesen. (PHOTOGRAPHER UNKNOWN. COURTESY OF KATHERINE CLARK)

Concert in honor of Isak Dinesen

Rome:
Chez Brianna

7 November 1957

Calde sangue	A. Scarlatti
chiare onde	Vivaldi
I attempt from Love's Sickness To Fly	Purcell
nymphs and Shepherds	Purcell
Chevaux de bois	Debussy
L'Invitation au voyage	Duparc
La flûte enchantée	Ravel
Le vaincu	Aubert

Jeanette Pecorello, Soprano
Loredana Franceschini, Pianist

Cinq sonates inédites	Marcello
Cinq valses	Mozart
Trois intermezzi	Schumann

Alda Bellasich, Pianist

Babalù	Afro-Cuban
Drumi negrita	Afro-Cuban
Les feuilles mortes	Prévert-Kosma
¿De Ben?	Barberis

Wanani

Handwritten program by Eugene Walter for a concert in honor of Isak Dinesen, performed at a party given by Princess Brianna Carafa, Rome, 1957. (COURTESY OF KATHERINE CLARK)

Leontyne Price, American opera diva and a
good friend of Eugene, Rome. (© H. M. NULL)

Wanani, a nightclub singer at Bricktop's,
an establishment under the Via Veneto in
Rome that Eugene frequented. (PHOTOGRAPHER
UNKNOWN. COURTESY OF KATHERINE CLARK)

Eugene Walter on the set of Fellini's *8½*. (left: © MICHELANGELO DURAZZO; right: PHOTOGRAPHER
UNKNOWN. COURTESY OF KATHERINE CLARK)

Federico Fellini (foreground) and an assistant in a lobster trap during a charade at his house in Fregene, Italy. (PHOTOGRAPH BY EUGENE WALTER. COURTESY OF KATHERINE CLARK)

Eugene Walter as Mother Superior in Fellini's *Juliet of the Spirits.* (© FERRILL AMACKER)

The painter Mitty Lee Brown Risi in front of her "morgue" apartment, where she threw a party for the visiting Isak Dinesen. (PHOTOGRAPHER UNKNOWN. COURTESY OF KATHERINE CLARK)

that took Yankee occupying troops out of the South a decade after the Civil War. Northerners had occupied the South longer than the United States has occupied any country it has conquered. So she was naturally someone I enjoyed meeting. She was a passionate historian and a lady with nervous kidneys.

It was in the apartment of Charles Lovatt, whose family had the Bank of Singapore. I had come to Paris armed with two letters of introduction, one to Alice B. Toklas, one to Charles Lovatt and Thad Lovatt. They had one of the first grand art nouveau apartments designed by the architect who designed the entrances to the subway. It had this enormous oval window that looked out over the Montparnasse Cemetery where Baudelaire was buried. It was an extraordinary view, like an opera set. And Charles gave these wonderful dinner parties.

Charles would always seat Esther Arthur in one particular easy chair. "Oh, no, Esther, honey, you must sit— Esther, darling, I'm sorry, you must sit right here where you like to sit." Because he would put a sponge pad in the seat and put this old blanket over the chair. Because when she got started on subjects that impassioned her, she would just let go.

I remember a conversation that I shall never forget as long as I live about the famous poisoner in the late 1600s in Paris, Madame de Brovier. Esther Arthur was saying, "I disagree with von Ranke! Madame de Brovier had no intention of poisoning both her brothers!" And she stood up and her chair overflowed. Of course, everybody pretended not to notice. "She had no intention of poisoning them!" Drip, drip, drip, drip. She pretended not to notice. She was a president's granddaughter, and she had been doing it since she was a child. She had weak kidneys. President's granddaughters can get away with murder, or floods.

Eugene-ing

One day I heard that they were doing Rousseau's opera *Le Devin du Village*—*The Village Soothsayer*—in a courtyard of something at Tours. So I organized these friends in Paris and we tootled off on a Saturday and had a wonderful lunch. We went to the Hôtel de l'Univers and had the famous fish paste they make from the Loire River. It's a wonderful old restaurant. Then we went over to this courtyard. We were met at the door by a very sweet young lady who said, "We are terribly sorry, but one of the singers has been ill and we've had to put it off till next Saturday." I said, "Oh, well, I've got my *Baedeker*." And I looked and I said, "Well, we are only a mile or so from the church and the abbey where the poet Pierre de Ronsard was curator or a friar or a secular priest or something." And I said, "Maybe we just better stop by Pierre's place." We got there, but of course it had been destroyed in the war. The only thing left was one little piece of rubble standing. But they had found the grave of Ronsard and had a carpet of green around it and two rosebushes. There was this delightful old man who was the caretaker. He had a leather apron, and he was doing some kind of work on something. He said, "*Ah oui*. Nobody ever knew where Ronsard was buried. After the bombardment, we found a skeleton that could only be his because he had this misshapen spine which was examined by doctors and pronounced upon in his lifetime. There was a young doctor in Tours who was coming here gathering skeletons from all the graves to use for his medical students, and it was he who identified it. So we had a reinterment, and for the first time we know where he is buried." So I said, "Oh, what a story. I'll have to have a couple of those fallen rose petals to press in my complete Ronsard, where he says, 'This rose that opens with the morning and shows her purple garments to the sun.'" But I put it in something I was carrying—my passport or wallet or something—and didn't think anymore about it.

Now. In Mobile, when I was growing up, we loved catalogs. We used to send for catalogs, catalogs, catalogs. We always got the Macmillan Publishing Company catalog. Every spring it came. They always had one page about each new book. Well now, one time they had a book called *A Mad Lady's Garland* by Ruth Pitter. It had an example of mock Jacobean poetry, someone addressing a black cat. Anyway, I saved that catalog from when I was about ten. I had it with me when I sat on that dreary island in the Aleutians thinking of what books to order. I had read some comic pieces in *Punch* by Miss Pitter, who said that the duty of a poet was to make people laugh during wartime. And she wrote a poem called "The Rude Potato" about this farmer who digs up a potato that's like a big phallus and testes, and he hangs it over the bar in the village and everybody laughs and gets drunk. So I wrote to Heffer in Cambridge, England, and ordered *A Mad Lady's Garland*. Then I got this little note saying "You are lucky because there were only two copies left. It came out nearly twenty years ago, but Macmillan still had two copies left in their basement, and this is the original edition." It took about three months to get from London to the island of Atka. But not a book that I ordered from Heffer ever got submarined on the Atlantic during the entire war. The monkey gods were protecting them. I just loved the book. So I wrote to Miss Pitter care of Macmillan to tell her how much I approved of everything she had done and blah, blah, blah. I got this letter back in this tiny little cranky hand. So we corresponded.

Then when I was living in Paris, I met a creature that I loved dearly: Jeremiah James Sullivan Sherman. He was from some tiny town in Pennsylvania and obviously had money in the bank, because he collects old racing cars and Baroque organs. He didn't like the idea of working with his brain. He wanted to do manual labor so he could be free to read, play the organ, and race through the countryside. I had never met anything like that, from Pennsylvania, and he had never met anything like me, from the South. So we just sat there at the Café de Tournon night after night, exchanging worldviews. Well, he had this Bugatti racing car, and we were going to make a tour of southern England in a Bugatti racing car, which is too small for American boys. It was made for midget Italian drivers. We had to wear caps and goggles, and we both looked like Mr. Toad of Toad Hall because we stuck up over the windshield. So I wrote Miss Pitter and I said, "I'm coming with this friend of mine to England, and I'd love so much to stop in London and see you." She lived in Church Street, Chelsea. "Oh," she said, "I think I'll be in London that weekend, but I may go down to Black Chapel. Just be kind enough to telephone or come by Church Street. If I am out of town, by chance, I'll leave you exact directions so you can find me."

I called her number in London, and this terribly British voice said, "Ruth's gone down to Black Chapel. This is her friend, Miss O'Brien. She looks forward so much to meeting you. All you do is, you go down— Do you know Sussex?" "Ah, no, ma'am. This is the first time I've been in Sussex." "Well, it's very easy, you see. Just get a map and be sure that you go to New Haven, and if you take the road out of New Haven, you turn left and then go six kilometers and then turn into this little lane and then you come to the black chapel." "Oh, yes. Sure. Thank you, ma'am." So I turned to Jeremiah, and he said, "Do you think it's worth it? Are we going to make it?"

We got lost, of course. We searched, and we searched and then finally I found the address where she was staying and called. Miss Pitter said, "Oh, hello. Yes, Miss O'Brien called and said you had rung. Why don't we meet at the black chapel at twilight?" I said, "Well, what time?" "Oh, around eight o'clock." Well, it wasn't a black chapel, it was bright white. And it wasn't twilight; the sun was still in the sky. Here was this little thing in a tweed suit with gray hair. She had tweed-colored hair and hair colored tweed. She was cute as a button, a real wit, a real live wire. We went to see the house—it was a thatched cottage—and she showed me her garden, which was not at all big, but she took me through as though it were the gardens of Versailles. And she said, "I suppose you want to see my pond." There was a tiny little thing of water with one duck sitting on it. That was a pond.

Then we went to have drinks, and as we sat down, she pointed to something growing under the window. She said, "This is the bedroom of my friend, Miss O'Brien." I hadn't met Miss O'Brien, didn't know anything about Miss O'Brien. She said, "That's the true poet's myrtle. She loves that plant." And I said, "Oh, I don't know the true poet's myrtle. I've never seen that plant. I'd give anything for a cutting, and I'll pay for it in coinage of the realm." She said, "What do you mean?" I said, "I have rose petals that I gathered at Ronsard's grave, and I'll give you three of them if you give me a cutting." She turned quite pale, and she said, "Yes."

Then the minute I got back to Paris there was a letter from her. She said, "Dear Mr. Walter. What you cannot know is that Miss O'Brien is directly descended through her Huguenot antecedents from the young lady to whom Ronsard wrote that poem where you pressed your petals."

The P.S. to the story: I was minding my own business in Rome one day—or at least, I was sitting still in Rome one day—and there came a telephone call. "Mr. Walter? This is Miss O'Brien. We've never met, but you remember the friend of Miss Pitter? She gave me your address and your telephone number in Rome, and I'm here with a friend of mine. Of course, we'll have to meet you; you're responsible for the rose petals." I said, "Yes, it is a long and marvelous story." "Oh," she said, "isn't it? We'd love to take you to lunch." I said, "Oh, how wonderful." Then we had lunch, and she turned out to be Edna O'Brien, who writes historical novels.

A singer had to have a sore throat, a Rousseau opera had to be postponed, they had to have discovered Ronsard's body through a medical student stealing bones, I had to collect the rose petals, I had to get to the backwoods of England through many misstarts and finally get into Sussex and sit by Miss O'Brien's window and get a leaf of poet's myrtle and pay for it with rose petals from Ronsard's tomb. But things like that happen to everybody every day. They just don't notice. I do. And I have pleaded with the monkey to enlighten me and send me the wayward, the undefined, the unexplained, and he is doing his best.

It was Sally Higginson who said one day, "Well, I'm going this afternoon to see Alice B. Toklas. Do you want to come?" Sally knew her through the Harvard financial wizard and economics specialist Galbraith. And I said, "I'd kind of like to meet her because I do have this letter to her." Sally said, "You do?" I said, "Yes, Miss Ruth Haber from Mobile was her classmate in San Francisco and gave me a note of introduction. They used to say that Ruth was famous as the only person who knew what the *B* stood for: Babette." And Sally laughed, and so we went.

The street was the same one where Oscar Wilde died. Rue Christine. That's where they moved from Fleurus and where Gertrude died. She'd been dead, oh—four or five years when I got to Paris. In the apartment, the first thing I noticed was the needlework on the chairs was pure Matisse. It was Alice who had done the needlework, but Matisse had designed it. And of course, the paintings there we know now from postcards from museums. Every painting was by somebody, and you recognized it. But Alice wasn't making a thing about it. They were just pictures she enjoyed. The chairs were just chairs. You could sit in them. Naturally I did. The whole apartment had a strange mixture of twenties audacity, World War II privation, and natural exuberance.

Alice was tiny. And Sally looked down at this little lady, as I imagine she would in her Boston house, if a Pekingese of unknown provenance had suddenly walked into the house. A very well mannered, well-brushed, and combed Pekingese. "Oh, isn't she cute" was the look.

I adored Alice B. Toklas because she had this little mustache, and I swear she waxed it. I can just see people staring at it, so finally instead of shaving every day, she let it grow and waxed the ends. I'm sure she waxed it. It was a proper mustache. She was in this kind of hip-length, sleeveless garment of some strange twenties patterned wool with a velvet edge. Then this peasant blouse with big sleeves under this hip-length. She could have been anything from Catherine the Great's scrubbing woman to high chic of 1927 to underground French in World War II. I just adored her. Right away you could see cat and monkey. She had a very logical mind, but she also had the gift of the parenthesis. A lot of people start parentheses and never finish them. To me, it is the most maddening of all human characteristics. I don't say, Do unto others as you would have others do unto you. I say, If you must parenthesis unto others, finish the goddamn parenthesis. Now there are some who are mountain goats and jump from mountain crag to mountain crag. Like "Oh, I've got something to tell you. And then I saw Mimi this morning. Now, have you gotten a telephone call from Eleanor? It's next week, you know. He was coming down the street when I came out of Delchamps. And then I asked him, 'Did she call you?'" Those are not parentheses. That's mountain goat stuff. Cliff to cliff, peak to peak. That's different. But Alice B. Toklas had the gift, the true classical gift, of the parenthesis. I'm not sure but that's a French characteristic rather than Anglo-Saxon. If, in conversation, the French begin a parenthesis, they usually end it and finish the original thought. Anyway, I loved Alice the moment I met her. She had some wonderful tales about Gertrude.

My favorite was about the American professor who was particularly boring and who was writing a paper on Paris in the twenties. Gertrude and Alice obligingly invited him to lunch at some old-fashioned hotel that had very good food. And this man went on and on and on and on about semantics. And about the restructuralization of English. Alice said Gertrude was so well behaved. But this guy barely seemed to notice that Alice had asked the chef to do this, Gertrude had asked the chef to do that and this special for the occasion. So when this man had finished his long recitation aria, Gertrude said to the man very seriously, "Did you see that?" He said, "Huh? Who? What?" She said, "At the next table." Apparently these people had a white poodle that reminded Gertrude of her white poodle. And she said, "The white poodle sitting in a chair at this next table." They were giving it tidbits. And Gertrude said, "You didn't see it? A white poodle with blue eyes and a pink tongue eating a green grape?"

What she was saying was, The here and now is so important. We are having a good French lunch, and what is all this blah? Bless her commaless heart.

Alice told me some other stories, but that was the one that threw everything else out of my head. Of course, I should have been Boswelling all these years. I'm sure I've forgotten as many stories as I remember. I should have had endless Redbird notebooks and number 2 pencils. I should have been Boswelling. But I wasn't. I was Eugene-ing, which is different.

Low Bubbling Mark

Suddenly I had no more GI Bill of Rights. And I'd spent every penny from Lippincott. I was so broke. I finally moved out of the Helvétia and into a sort of slum area. A little hotel over close to the Sorbonne. I was at low ebb. Low watermark. Low bubbling mark. Because I was on beer by then, so it was low bubbling mark. I was as depressed as monkeys ever get, or cats. And the princess was always asking me to come to Rome. Little by little she would give me piles of manuscripts to read. Once she gave me a set of proofs. I said, "Well, you know, these haven't been proofread yet." "Oh," she said, "well, yes, there's this young lady who proofread them." I said, "Well, I don't think so. Look at this and look at this," and then I said, "The printer should not have broken this word in this fashion." Then she kept saying, "I wish you could be in Rome." She said, "I don't have an office. And I don't have any sort of subscription service. I can never find somebody who really can help me with all this. I do hope you'll come to Rome and help me set up an office." Finally I said, "Well, I'd love to." So I borrowed some money from friends and moved to Rome. Of course, the princess forgot to pay me for a year. And I was too shy to ask for a salary.

Rome

PART FIVE

An Orchestra Seat at a Comic Opera

Rome was a totally unknown quantity. I had already lived in Paris in my mind before I lived in Paris. But I had no preconceived idea of modern Rome. And I was surprised by the poverty of it just after the war. Which was what? '56. Just ten years after the war. It was a city of bicycles because not everybody could afford an automobile. And early in the morning, flocks of sheep crossed the town, driven by their shepherds to the Doria Parks on the Janiculum Hill, because they gave free grazing instead of hiring people to mow the lawn. The lawn was two or three square miles, so early in the morning, there would be these flocks of sheep filling the streets of Rome. When I left Rome years later, there were traffic jams tail to bumper of those Fiat 500s. You know. Honk, honk, honk, honk. But when I first arrived, there weren't that many cars. Everybody was broke. So every morning, streets were full of bicycles and flocks of sheep. Thousands of bicycles in the street; it was really a sight.

In so many ways, Rome was not so different from Mobile. It was a warmish climate, with street life—things spilling out into the street. People who didn't have porches just sat in front of their slum dwellings on little stools in the evening. Rome is flamboyantly Catholic, and I was raised Catholic. There were some processions that I enjoyed thoroughly, like the day of the Virgin, Ascension Day. It's an all-day parade through the middle of Rome with everybody in resplendent robes and choruses singing—it was another form of Mardi Gras, really. I just loved it. And on every block there were two or three cafés. You sat and watched the world go by, just like in Mobile in Bienville Square.

Now, the cafés in Rome were a little more democratic than the cafés in Paris. There was a café at the corner from me on Corso Vittorio where you'd get the street sweeper and the man who had the little newsstand and a high-ranking Jesuit from the Jesuit order and some politicians. You would never see a street sweeper sitting at the Café de Tournon. You would see only tourists, all the publishing world, all the government world, and all the intellectual world. You'd never see small-business men or street sweepers. Or firemen. In Rome it was much more mixed up; I had friends in every strata. And everybody knew everybody. Everybody spoke to everybody. I knew my neighbors on both sides even though there were thick Renaissance walls between us on Corso Vittorio. Unlike the French, who are so strange and withdrawing and snotty, the Italians have always welcomed intellectuals, painters, writers. In Paris nobody would ever invite you to their home. They'd invite you to a café, even after you'd known them for years. But in Rome, the second day you knew them, they'd invite you to their house for a drink. I knew a couple of very grand French people but never saw the inside of their house, ever. Whereas the Italians would invite you immediately. The more educated they are, the more pro-American they are. They were genuinely interested in young American painters, writers, and all that because they had had none for so long. And most of the noble Italian families have survived only because they have had a shot of either American blood or American money. If you were American and doing something interesting, they wanted to know you and all about the new. So right away there was this sense of being welcomed.

And I could walk everywhere. Since it's a medieval town built on Roman ruins, it's following the donkey trails and the sheep trails and the cow paths that went through the Roman ruins. It's not like Paris, where they tore down all the medieval sections and did avenues, avenues, avenues. Quite often at night, if I had to go a certain distance, I'd take a taxi. But usually I'd walk. Everybody else did.

One of my favorite places to go at night was the Tre Scalini, the famous ice-cream bar in the Piazza Navona, with the famous Bernini fountain. Just to sit there and watch the children roller-skating and the painters selling their paintings on the sidewalk and people hawking various things and tourists gaping—it was rather wonderful. It was like having an orchestra seat at a comic opera.

When I first arrived, I knew Rome only in theory. I knew the classical sculptures and all the classical architecture of Rome. The big surprise was the modern world superimposed. I mean, here was the Colosseum, and then about a block away, tucked away in some trees, was a dear little pizzeria. I never had thought of Fiat 500s and people on bicycles and street peddlers being between me and the monument. So I think the daily surprise of modernity amidst antiquity triggered something in me. And I loved it.

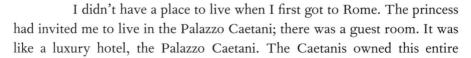

I didn't have a place to live when I first got to Rome. The princess had invited me to live in the Palazzo Caetani; there was a guest room. It was like a luxury hotel, the Palazzo Caetani. The Caetanis owned this entire palazzo; it was built for them in the 1550s. But they rented out various suites and apartments. It was never anything openly advertised. But there was Eulalia, her daughter, and Lord Howard, her husband, who lived on the roof garden of the main palace. Then there was the American ambassador to Italy and his wife and granddaughter in a very grand apartment. There was Ginny Becker and John Becker and their two children. Some sort of institute had a suite of rooms. The *amministrazióne* Caetani was in the *pianterréno,* on the ground floor. And all those palaces have an army—guards and a family police force—and they occupied the administrative offices on the first floor. And there was a room she would have given me, a very gorgeous, huge room about as big as a house. A salon. And then a little bedroom and bath off of that.

But I knew better than to be domiciled with the princess. I wanted to keep distance and have independence. I didn't want to be under auspices. I have never been under auspices since the age of sixteen. Even when I travel, I don't want to stay in a private house; I'll take the cheapest motel. I might want to skip around the house naked and get drunk at midnight, you know. I didn't want any private house. I didn't want to impinge on her or have her impinge on me. The princess was the type that if she thought I was living there alone, she would probably ask me to dinner, even though I lunched with her almost every day. Because we worked every day, and sometimes, if she had literary people or something like that for lunch, then I was always invited. I think she liked my entertainment value with certain professor types. But I knew I had to have another life.

So William Fense Weaver, the Rome editor of *Folder,* invited me to stay with him in his place about eight blocks from Palazzo Caetani while I looked for my own place. What I found was this huge room, rather like the ballroom of the Rubira House in Mobile, in an old palace in Via Giulia near the back door of the French embassy. I thought, Oh, what a wonderful place, Rome. This sunlight in the winter. The first night I spent there was the first time it had snowed in Rome in twenty years. The snow came in the window, and I woke up with a snowbank on the foot of my bed. And then I was saying, "Did I do the right thing, moving to Rome?"

I told everybody, "I have got to find a place to live. It has to cost nothing and it has to be in Centro, where I can walk to Palazzo Caetani." So one day this Venetian I'd met who was eight feet tall called me and he said, "Well, Eugene, I don't know if this would interest you. It's really very modest, and it's in Trastevere." I said, "What's Trastevere?" He said, "It's what it says: across the river." The Tiber is "Tevere." "Tras": other side. Other side of the Tiber. It's where the shepherd people lived when all those Sardinians and

Etruscans and all that came and took Rome in pre-pre-pre-pre-pre. So I said, "Well, let's go see it." I just loved it right away. It was a different atmosphere in that part of Rome, even though you were right there a few blocks from Piazza Argentina and a few blocks from Palazzo Caetani. The open-air market was somehow more giddy, closer to Naples in style. And there were lots of little restaurants and bars which were just sprawling out onto the streets.

So he took me to this back alley where we climbed the same number of stairs as the Spanish Steps. At the top of this hillside was this little gardener's cottage. It consisted of a bedroom, a dining room, a nice modern bath, and a kitchen with no stove, no anything. In front of it was the terrace, which was covered with gravel, and there were six wooden posts and a grapevine. You looked out over all of Trastevere and all of Rome. It was eighteen thousand lire a month; that was about, I guess, twenty-something dollars. So I said, "I'll take it." There was this cranky, cranky old landowner; this was his gardener's cottage. He lived on the Janiculum and entered from the Janiculum. He made the slaves climb 365 steps to the common folks' quarters. He was nasty and mean and absolutely miserly. But I did like sitting on that terrace and looking out over Trastevere.

On this hillside, there was nothing but weeds along the 365 steps. So I dug and planted fig trees that are still there, bearing by now, and lots of iris, iris, iris. In digging, I found the most extraordinary things, like pink slabs of red porphyry. Of course, my sculptor friends would faint dead away. This hillside had been the site of one of Cleopatra's kitchens. She had three separate kitchens. They all prepared the same thing, but starting an hour subsequent to each other, because she never knew when Caesar would get there from the Senate. So no matter when he arrived, it was freshly prepared, with three kitchens making the same menu. Those hunks of red porphyry I'm sure were left over from Cleopatra's kitchens. So I gave all that to the sculptors. I went out of my way to meet many of them, because I was fascinated by the fact of all the American sculptors living in Rome. There are the old foundries that have been casting statues since prehistory; we don't have that tradition in America.

The princess gave me a stove. She insisted that all my laundry be done by her washwoman at the palace. That the dry cleaning be done with the palace dry cleaning. They had a whole corps of servants, and there was a wardrobe mistress who literally looked after the dry cleaning and the laundry. The princess was very upset about the snow story, and she said she still wanted me to come and stay at Palazzo Caetani. But you know, I couldn't have. If I were a snob and wanted someday to be something fancy at Harvard, I might have lived with the Princess Caetani. But such as that never crossed my mind in all my life. I was out to explore the cat and monkey world. And you see, I could never have given dinner parties in the Palazzo Caetani. There was a hot plate or something in the corner of that huge thing she offered me. But some of the people I invited would have been looked upon askance by the *portiere* of Palazzo Caetani. Student types or artist types would have been considered inappropriate for the palazzo. I could just imagine that uniformed *portiere* looking down his nose.

There were a lot of people who would turn up. Like Allen Ginsberg turned up one day. If you could have smelled him. He had been hitchhiking in Italy, and I don't think he had changed his clothes in a week. He had these filthy shorts and this filthy shirt and this backpack. Of course, he wasn't famous then. He was somebody who'd heard about *Paris Review* and *Botteghe Oscure* and just dropped in on me at my office in Palazzo Caetani. I had seen his work in I've forgotten what little review. It had kind of an "up yours" attitude. This was long before the full flair of hippies. I liked his impudence. He had some poems that he wanted us to publish in *Botteghe,* and the princess just didn't go for them. Some of the words and phrases did not, to her, seem to occur naturally; sometimes you thought he made it raunchy or vulgar to make a point. I liked it, but of course she was from another generation and New England. After we talked, I decided I liked him a lot. He really is a very gentle, basically lonely soul, trying to be a tough Brooklyn Jew. He is just a gentle soul. But you see, I could never have invited him to dinner if I had been living in some *appartamento* in Palazzo Caetani. He, obviously, was just something from the streets.

Rome

I was always broke, of course; I had no money. I lived on what little royalties turned up now and again. I did the illustrations for the Grabbe book *Wit, Satire, Irony, and Deeper Meaning,* for the Gabberbocchus Press. And then they took a hundred copies of *Monkey Poems.* Then I got a check from whoever published *The Untidy Pilgrim* in England. Ten cents here, ten cents there. So I kind of eked out something. After I'd been about six months in this gardener's cottage is when the princess began to pay me a monthly salary. Of course, she always intended to pay, but she was absentminded and very involved with the printer and the writing. She wrote letters by hand, hundreds of letters a day. I would borrow money from her administrator now and again, and I think he finally said to her, "Well, you know, Walter's dead broke." Then right away I was put on salary. It was never anything worth talking about, just a pittance.

I was given an office in a medieval tower next door to this Renaissance palace. It was the Caetani tower from long before the palace. There was a stairway that went from somewhere in the palace into this tower, this gloomy thing. I was there until the princess came one day to look at it. It was winter, and she had dressed as though she were going to the North Pole. She had on a fur coat, and she had this shawl over her head, gloves. She had to go from her room to a stairway and down one stairway and up another stairway and through a thing in the wall to climb another stairway to this office in the medieval tower. She took one look around and she said, "You can't be very comfortable in here." Before I knew it, I was being moved into a room in the back of the palace proper, which looked out on the Via Michelangelo Caetani that ran along one side of the palace. That was my office the rest of the time I was there.

I had to baby-sit the princess, baby-sit Roffredo, make contact with people for various reasons. An enormous amount of material came. And her eyes were failing, so it was my duty to go through it. Finally, I was reading the manuscripts and shoving the best at her. And I really tried desperately not to promote my friends and not to low-rate the bores. I told myself, Now, Eugene, don't you dare push your friends or kick the butts of the bores. I wrote letters, wrote letters. She would tell me to write some woman. Or to send a certain note with a certain manuscript. And of course, I put the *Botteghes* into their wrappings and addressed them, for every number. Took them myself to the post office, and I carefully watched as closely as I could. One day it had been discovered that all of the last issue of *Botteghe* was piled up in a cellar. There was this idiot, Gino, who was from one of the peasant families that had been serfs of the Caetanis from medieval times. So what do you do? They let him sort of be like a footman in the palace, to carry notes from floor to floor because the Prince Caetani would never telephone anybody within the palace. Well, Gino was supposed to take the mail to the post office. So one day the princess was in the courtyard, getting into her car to go somewhere, when the chauffeur opened this storeroom to get a rag to do the windshield or something, and here were all these issues of the magazine, just dumped. And mail, letters—dumped. The princess threw a fit. She never raised hell with the servants. She was a lady. If something was really wrong, she would call the administrator and get him to talk to the offending party. But in this case she really let him have it, in very beautiful Italian. That was one of the only times I've heard the princess speak harshly to anybody on earth. So then he sent word that he was going to commit suicide. He walked forty kilometers or whatever from Rome to Ninfa, her weekend place which was the town hall of this medieval village where she restored and made famous the gardens. He turned up there, saying, *"Oh, principessa,"* kissing her feet and saying, "I know I've been wicked, and I'll jump in the lake." And she said, "Oh, no, Gino, for heaven's sake, behave." So he still worked at the palazzo, but I delivered the magazines to the post office.

And I quickly realized that the princess was someone who never sent manuscripts back. She stuffed the manuscripts she didn't like between her bed and the wall. And the maid just swept them out and put them in the garbage. Manuscripts she liked or thought had possibilities or writers she thought she would write and say, "Send me something else in a year," were piled up on her bedside table. The things she couldn't tolerate she just stuffed between her bed and the wall. I told her, "Well, you know, Princess, we really should send manuscripts back when they send those little international postage coupons." "Oh, is that what those funny little things are?" And I said, "In some cases when it's a known writer or even some very young one that you know who's poor, we still ought to send them back, even if they didn't send the coupons." So I would write little notes. I've often had them quoted back to me. "The Princess bids me return this manuscript to you with her gratitude, after having an opportunity to consider it for *Botteghe Oscure*. She hopes that within a year you will send another." Or, "Thank you so very much. The amount of material on hand is sufficient for two years of *Botteghe Oscure*." But I always said, "The Princess bids me." It was quoted back to me a hundred times.

Some days I would leave at three. Sometimes I worked twenty-four hours a day getting three or four languages proofread and through the printer. There were others who helped, somebody in every language. But Giorgio Bassani was no help at all. He was just a pompous little ass. He was theoretically, more or less, the assistant for the Italian part. And he was this novelist who had written *The Garden of the Finzi-Continis*. I thought he was a wonderful writer but a real monster. The princess invited him to Palazzo Caetani to meet me. She had this long room on the top floor. This was a kind of *soperattico,* a superattic that had been added in the last century to house French and English governesses. She'd had all those rooms thrown into one, with windows all around one side and bookshelves all around the other. Strictly modern, 1930s modern. A lot of white walls and white furniture. Only paintings painted since 1900. She didn't want the gloom of the Roman palace; she didn't want the weight of all those centuries of Caetani.

Anyway, she invited Giorgio Bassani to come and meet me there. Well, at the other end of the room, from where she had arranged little sofas, you stepped down a little step and there was a little door where you could just get through. When you went through it, you were just under the ceiling of this huge, huge red room. This was the noble room on the *piano nobile,* the noble

Rome

floor. Every palace has a *piano nobile*, and the Caetani was no exception. It's the grand floor that has state occasion rooms. It was a Renaissance room with a gilded ceiling and red damask walls and a grand piano and overstuffed furniture. When I say overstuffed, I mean Victorian overstuffed. I mean stuffed bursting. And gilded curves. The princess never went in there—she hated it—except when there were thunderstorms. She was afraid of thunder, and the curtains were so heavy and the walls so thick that when you closed the inner shutters and then drew the curtains, you could barely hear the thunder. I sat through many a thunderstorm with her there.

But anyway, anybody coming officially would catch an elevator that she'd had installed in the palace corridors and stairways. They'd catch it in the courtyard and go up to the sort of hallway where you entered the grand room. Then in the corner of that grand room, she built a funny little stairway that climbed up to the ceiling. And you went through this little cubbyhole and ended up in modernity. You went from Renaissance to twentieth century, just under the ceiling.

There was a rap on the little door. She said, "That must be Giorgio. Go and let him in." So I went and stepped down and opened the door. And this nasty little thing came in and did not acknowledge my presence. Being Southern, I thought no matter who opens the door, you would nod or say "Thank you." The princess was half a block away on that floor, and he obviously knew who I was. But he just looked right at her and put on this great hundred-watt smile. *"Principessa!"* And I thought, Well, what a piece of shit. Obviously he resented my arriving to be her assistant.

Then Giorgio Bassani published a book of all his stories that had been in *Botteghe Oscure*. Now it says in the beginning of the magazine that for anything reproduced from the magazine, acknowledgment must be made. Well, Inaudi, the big publisher in Milano, published Giorgio Bassani's book, and Giorgio Bassani did not put any acknowledgment of *Botteghe Oscure*. So I, little old bite ass, wrote a nasty letter as an assistant to the princess. She knew I was writing it, and she giggled and gurgled when I showed her the letter I had written, saying, "This is highly irregular; it is usually considered not only a courtesy, but a legality," and so on and so on, and I sent an actual cover where you see that written in the magazine. He answered to the princess in a rather huffy-puffy letter, and he loathed me because of that letter.

Then on another occasion, there was this manuscript that the daughter of Benedetto Croce, the philosopher, brought to show the princess. Eleanor Croce said, "I don't know what you'll think of this, but it was sent to me anonymously, as I am a friend of yours and of *Botteghe Oscure*. The writer begged me to show it to you." She said, "Well, I've read it, and I don't know.

It's Sicilian. It's beautifully written, but it sounds to me like one of those one-time writers writing about his family in Sicily. So here it is." The princess read it. She loved it. By then I had enough Italian, and I said, "Well, you know, Princess, I'm a novice at Italian, but it was fascinating." She said, "We'll publish it." She said, "I'd already decided, but I was curious to see what you'd make of it." But Bassani said, "Oh no, this is trash, this is some journalist. I advise you not to publish it, it's not worth it."

It was a chapter from *The Leopard*. Every Italian publisher had turned it down, and so he, the prince of Lampedusa, sent it anonymously to this lady he knew was intelligent, Eleanor Croce, and said, "You are a friend of the publisher of *Botteghe Oscure*. I should like so much to beg you most humbly to pass it to her." And it was a chapter of *The Leopard*.

So right away there was interest after the princess published it, because a new number of *Botteghe Oscure* was beginning to be meaningful. It was a British publisher who wrote first to inquire about it, because by then British publishers began to have their foreign readers, people in London who spoke French or Italian or German.

And then, of course, who takes credit for it? After it had been published in every language and was this huge success, Bassani would say it was he who received the manuscript. And after the prince of Lampedusa died and Princess Caetani died, it was Giorgio Bassani who was honored for discovering the manuscript. There was a ceremony in Milano where he went to accept the prize.

I don't know what sign of the zodiac he is, but he's one of those people that I get warning signals from. My hair stood on end that first day I met him. I happen to like snakes; there is no animal in the world with whom to compare Giorgio Bassani. Except the race of self-congratulatory editors. Editors in the grass. He made so many enemies because of the way he used his power as an editor of *Botteghe Oscure*. He had refused so many things or advised her to refuse so many things. I think the princess did not realize the extent to which he flicked his tail to right and to left as a literary lion. I think she saw through him, but she just saw this amusing little thing who was a very good writer. But he had little lines around his eyes that were tight. Like nerves or a false smile had gotten engraved. His literary-lion smile: *"Buon giorno, principessa!"* As though God had sent invisible lightning and those fake smile lines had gotten etched by invisible lightning. I'm sure he's still alive. He has to be. People like that never die young. Well, you know, you have to think about his upbringing in a moment when Italy was anti-Semitic. He was part Jewish or all Jewish and so sensitive and nervous about that. I would give lessons in neurosis if my life had been his. And it's a rough thing for an artist of any kind, anywhere, in the world today. Homer had it easy. He could sit by the fire, tell stories all night, and they'd feed him and drink him. Give him a place to sleep. But life's gotten more complicated. And I've often felt sorry for Bassani. But he was a monster. A monster. I put him on my shit list. I make a weekly shit list, and when it's finished, I burn it. I consign those names to oblivion.

Those Cats and Monkeys That I Collect

Once in a pile of manuscripts I found this story called "The Portobello Road" which I just loved. The princess didn't particularly like it, but I just loved it. Muriel Spark was totally unknown. She'd only done book reviews, and she was having a little book on John Masefield coming out. John Masefield was poet laureate, but he certainly was not a popular author or big figure in English letters at that time. He's since been seen to be indeed a major talent. But at that moment, he was just sort of old hat. But Muriel liked him, and she had done this little book. So she had been a critic and biographer but at a given moment turned to fiction. But somebody from England who knew Muriel bad-mouthed Muriel. The person said something like "Oh, she's this tiresome woman, tiresome woman." It may have been T. S. Eliot who said she was a mess. I've forgotten. I think it was. Because she'd interviewed him in some newspaper. He knew who she was. And the princess didn't like to get involved in anything with feuds. She said, "I've heard of this Muriel Spark. Cousin Tom says she is difficult." She was just going to throw it out. I said, "Princess, this is a great story," and we published it in *Botteghe Oscure*.

I wrote Muriel Spark, saying "The Princess would like to publish your story," and I said, "I must tell you how very much I enjoyed it." Then she eventually turned up in Rome. She was this little middle-aged lady with a very English skirt and jacket. A well-rounded Scots lady in a rump-sprung tweed skirt. That look of English ladies who've been in the city or on a plane or something and their skirt has that rump-sprung look. She'd been in the Holy Land covering that trial of one of the war criminals. And she had this red hair that was beginning, you could see, to have one little silver hair in it somewhere. And she had these delicate little freckles that had come out in that pale Edinburgh skin when she was in the hot sun in the Holy Land— little golden freckles. And sensible shoes. She was adorable. An animated creature. Cat and monkey.

Then she was off to New York at the invitation of *The New Yorker*. They gave her a room to work in there. She stayed in America a couple of years. Three years or something. Then I got this letter saying "I've decided to come and live in Rome for a while." The editor of *The New Yorker* said, "Why are you leaving New York?" Because they think it's the end of the world, you know. The be-all, end-all. And she said, "I want to live in quiet luxury in Rome like Eugene Walter." Because by then I was on the top floor of the palazzo where I lived for so very long with Leontyne Price on the floor below.

So I met her at the plane when she came back to Italy. And I looked and looked for Muriel Spark and couldn't find her. Then I saw someone waving at me. And there was this very chic lady in high-heel shoes, very Parisian, very coiffed, very made up and looking about twenty-nine or thirty. That was the new Muriel.

I've seen about seven or eight Muriels. I've liked them all.

That New York lady loosened up a little and became rather more English country. You know, terribly, terribly British countryside. And then that turned into a sort of very elegant bohemian in Rome. And then she found this apartment in the palazzo, one of the cardinal's apartments from the Renaissance. And I helped her arrange for this terrace to be enclosed with some trelliswork so she could sit out without all these close neighbors in these other buildings off the back of the palazzo. She wanted to make it grand.

That's when she became our lady of the palazzo. With a chauffeur-driven limousine and the simplest of clothes. The kind of simplicity that you know costs millions of dollars. I mean, what we in the Old South call "chic as shit." It means total simplicity that smells expensive a block away.

Anyway, all of her metamorphoses were enchanting because there is a lot of the actress about her. All poets and poetesses have much of the actor and actress in them. It seems to be a natural component of people who write in the concentrated style of poetry. And that was one of her greatest manifestations, our lady of the palazzo.

Now I remember when—oh, the actress, the one who was nominated for an Academy Award for best supporting player for *Auntie Mame*—I can't think of her name. Who played the secretary of Auntie Mame. Played on Broadway and in the film. I met her through Mary Chamberlin Harding, who appeared with her on Broadway in something. And introduced this actress to Muriel Spark. And also the painter Ferrill Amacker. And one evening Muriel invited us to her house, this actress and the painter from Poplar Grove, Mississippi, Ferrill Amacker. It was a four-acre room, and only one corner was furnished with some elegant sofas and chairs. The rest was just polished hardwood inlaid floors. It was this huge empty room, with a huge fireplace ten people could stand in. We were in this one corner. She had some very gorgeous Persian carpets that were about maybe eight feet long and rather narrow. And she had these cats she adored. So she suddenly came whooping into the room. She's a very tiny, active lady, is Muriel. She had one of the Persian carpets, and on it sat the two cats proudly. She was riding them. "Time for the evening drive!" she said. She just ran around the room dragging this carpet and singing to these two cats just sitting there. And she'd go out of the room and come back dragging one of these carpets with one or two cats on it. She'd dance around the room pulling this carpet. The cats just sat there loving it, just loving it. If you had come in the front door and had never seen or heard her before, you would have thought it was a child running around with this rug and these cats.

And then, of course—I can't think what this actress's name was—she got up and sang a song from some musical revue she'd been in on Broadway. Cannot keep a leading actress down. Whereupon Muriel got up and sang songs she remembered from variety shows she'd seen as a child. "Daddy wouldn't buy me a little bow-wow" was one of her hit songs. And Ferrill got up and sang some old Mississippi song with a chorus of "Rip, dippy, do da," and recited something about Winken, Blinken, and Nod he'd learned in the third grade. Then I got up and sang something, and we put on the music and just danced the whole night away in the cardinal's salon. We'd been to some restaurant and come back for drinks at Muriel's. And that was a great evening.

T. S. Eliot had come to Rome to receive an honor from some university. He was on his honeymoon with that lady who'd been his secretary and such a comfort to him after his first wife, who'd been slightly demented, went totally stark raving mad. The princess asked me to arrange a party at Palazzo Caetani. They were cousins. He was Cousin Tom. Some distant, distant way back when in Boston. And that's when I saw a good side of him. I had the feeling he was someone trapped, inside sixteen locked doors. I thought if I could get enough Jim Beam into him, he would really be great. So I made my 23rd Field Artillery punch. We brought up from the cellars of Palazzo Caetani a huge, magnificent old punch bowl that had not been used since around World War I. And I put a block of ice in it. And I made a little hole in the block of ice. And I put some sliced oranges and lemon in that hole. And then I poured two bottles of cognac over that. And then I poured two bottles of good white rum over that. And then I poured two bottles of very good English gin over that. And then I just filled up the rest of the bowl with cold champagne.

It tastes like the most delicious orange punch. You would never guess there is one drop of anything alcoholic in it. You think it's just this sweet little you-all fruit juice. The people who taste it say, "Oh, you have such sweet oranges." There are millions of punches like that on the Gulf Coast. For Mardi Gras. You know: "Want a little fruit punch, darling, before we set out for the ball?"

It'll make a party go. After a while, people achieve a rosy view.

The princess had invited all the literary figures of Rome: Alberto Moravia, Elsa Morante, Natalia Ginzberg. Writers, writers, writers, writers. She was nervous, since there were two or three famous feuds among the crowd. You know, literary backbiters are the worst. And Italian writers are always feuding with other Italian writers. And there were all kinds of Italian lesser writers begging for Eliot's attention just like the Harvard boys. We forget that *The Cocktail Party* was written God knows when, in the 1920s, and only got produced in the 1950s in London. That's one of the things that put him on the map all over again.

I was careful to see that all glasses were kept full. Feuds were forgotten, and toward the end of the evening Mr. Eliot remembered some football cheers from Midwestern colleges, which he'd heard in his youth. He had a yellow rose in one hand and a punch cup in the other, wielded like a pom-pom, and my favorite was:

Rah-rah-rah
Sis-boom-sah!
Go to war,
Holy Cross!
Bim 'em, bam 'em,
Skin 'em, scam 'em,
Rip 'em, ram 'em,
Holy Cross!

He was doing that cheerleader after just two glasses of 23rd Field Artillery punch.

But overall he was rather hoity-toity. I know that if you live in England and you are of the English language, sooner or later you speak English English. There is no way not to, because it has something which we just pick up. We can't help it. I would be doing it in ten minutes if I lived there. But he had the snob accent, not just the English accent. The snob-snob accent. It was a kind of artificial snobbism superimposed on artificial Englishness. After all, he *was* from M'zou. He was born in St. Looey. The hub of the bourgeoisie.

Yes, well, the Eliots of Boston. The one *l*, one *t* Eliots of Boston. There are laundresses named Elliott with two *t*'s and two *l*'s. But this was a one *l*, one *t* Eliot. You can discard the superfluous at a given moment of greatness. But still, he was born in St. Louis, Missouri. We mustn't forget that. M'zou. Born in M'zou. Being born in North Haiti is superior to being born in M'zou.

When he was on his way to speak at the university in Rome, there was a mob of students running along his car and screaming in the street. And there was a piece in *The New Yorker* about Eliot in Rome by one of our *New Yorker* girls who's become famous. We published her first short story, "The Statue," in *Botteghe Oscure*. Jewish girl in New York City. Funny name. Ozick. Cynthia Ozick. And she says that his car, as he left for the university, was accompanied by these cheering students, and what a lift it gave him to feel so acclaimed by the populace.

That wasn't the thing at all. I was there, fighting off journalists at the Palazzo Caetani. It was one of those sixties student things, and they were screaming for the director of the university to resign. There were a lot of younger students who wanted the university reorganized in a certain way and rather more free. And they were running along his car, and Eliot thought they were welcoming him. But they were saying, "Please don't make the speech, you fool." You know: Down with the university.

I've never understood the kind of sourpuss quality he had. He didn't have a little edge of good humor that is basically American, which all Americans have. It's very rare the American doesn't have that little "yeah, well, you know" somewhere. Even the crankiest. There is a kind of generosity of spirit which is American. Even with the most closed in or most miserly or whatever. I mean, T. S. Eliot was not my idea of fun.

It's all because he became such a cult figure. Just after World War II, all the Harvard boys—if you said T. S. Eliot, they got to their knees facing England, you know. They forgave him for being born in M'zou. I think he had too much of that adulation.

But his wife was a charmer. So intelligent, so polite, so humorous, so kind. The princess asked me to go with her chauffeur to take Mr. Eliot and Madame Valerie to the airport when they were leaving Rome. So, we were going to go, and he said, "I've never been to the graves of Keats and Shelley." I said, "Yes, we do have time."

Now this is one of those cemeteries where nobody is dead. It's like Père Lachaise in Paris. One day in Paris I saw this bus that was going to the Père Lachaise Cemetery. So I got on it instead of the bus I should have gotten on to go to school or wherever I was supposed to go that day. Rode right up to the cemetery and wandered through. There was Molière. There was Abelard. There was Sarah Bernhardt. There was Gertrude Stein. There was Nijinsky. There was Oscar Wilde. And I thought: This is not a cemetery. This is a cocktail party. There were no dead people there. So about once a week I would pack a picnic and just go to a different part each time and sit on somebody's gravestone and communicate. This particular cemetery in Rome was the same way: a great place for a picnic, because nobody is dead. Old friends gathered. Keats is there and Shelley is there and a Romanoff princess and other grand Russian refugees.

There are cats that live in the cemetery. There's this little caretaker's cottage, and they sit in front of it. Because they've seen so many people go to the grave first of Shelley and then of Keats, they accompany them like guides. And they walk a few steps ahead and look over their shoulders and say, "This way," and then they turn at the right corner and turn at the left corner. So first we went to Shelley, and we were taken by a black cat. At the grave of Shelley, there was a tabby cat waiting. The black cat went back to the caretaker's. The tabby cat took us to Keats, way over in a corner. And it says, "Here Lies One Whose Name Was Writ in Water." And Valerie was busy picking violets off the grave to take back to her garden in England, and T. S. Eliot was saying, "I've always thought that inscription was rather supercilious." And she said, "Dammit, laddered m'nylons!" It's one of my favorite moments. She was a very down-to-earth creature with a great sense of humor. She's cat and monkey. But there was something acid about him which I just couldn't take. And I'd always disapproved of his poetry because I come from a subtropical country. How could I know melancholy and the bleakness of winter?

Ingeborg Bachmann was another one of those cats and monkeys that I collect. She was born at Klagenfurt, Austria, which is only a small ride north of Italy. She really had a lot of Mediterranean, but she was very Austrian and wrote in German, and I loved her. She's quite hot shit in the world today; she's *the* modern German-language poet. She submitted some poems to the princess, and the princess took them right away. Then Ingeborg was coming to Rome, I think for the first time, so she came to the princess. And the princess asked me to lunch. She often asked me to lunch to fill up gaps when there were people, especially Americans, catatonic-ized by the word *princess*. Tongue-tied. Spellbound. Fallen arches. Everything because of a princess. So she often asked me for the Americans. But then sometimes she asked me when she was getting an unknown quantity to run interference and giggle at the right moment. So this was a terribly shy German girl. She had this dead white skin and was dressed in kind of a colorless way. She had no makeup except a tiny little lipstick. She had reddish hair, and she was nearsighted and wore these glasses. When I saw her across the room, I thought, Oh, Lord, it's the farmer's idea of the poetess. But then when we shook hands, I got this electricity. And when I really looked in her eyes, I got something else. When we began to talk, there was something about her I liked right away. So I escorted her out to an elevator and said, "Well, wouldn't you like to have dinner in Trastevere some night?" She was very shy. "I don't know. I'm not certain what my plans are. I have these proofs to correct." She was just too shy. She was Miss Vulnerable. The original Miss Vulnerable. But she was a rare creature. A rare creature.

She came again to lunch. Then she was a little bit more loose. The next time I met her by chance in a bookshop. There were two tough English ladies who had a bookshop in Rome. I mean tough. That cigarette hanging, you know, and that short hair and that sweater. I called them the dragons. Their name was Doggin or something, but I called them the dragons. Anyway, I ran into Ingeborg there, and she was more relaxed, so I took her to lunch at this little place around the corner and up the street from the bookshop. I guess she finally realized that I was just something that got loose from Alabama. We became great friends.

Much later she came and settled in Rome for a while. And when she came back, she was a very smart lady. She'd had this book published, which was a big success, and she was taken up by the German intelligentsia. So she was very smartly dressed. Her hair had been reddened more, and she was wearing a perfect lipstick. I don't know if she'd been in the sun or something, but she looked different and was a little more sure of herself. She had this big crush on Hans Werner Henze, the composer. He adored Ingeborg, but he has a lot of dancing boys in attendance. You know.

Anyway, we had a dinner one night. She said, "Now I have brought Bitsy with me from Klagenfurt." I said, "Who is that?" "Oh," she said, "we have been friends for a long time. Now I want you to bring Coco." So I went, and there was a table for four set. She was cooking up something. She said, "Now put Coco right there." And she went and got Bitsy. It was her teddy bear. And she was saying to Bitsy, "Now don't you start eating until I tell you because we have to say grace." She said, "Is yours table trained?" I said, "Oh yes, Coco is table trained." And she would say, "Now, does Coco want some of this?" Finally I got into the spirit. We did this whole evening with the children. She never dropped it. She held up Bitsy and waved her paw when I was taking Coco home.

It was while I was in Madrid that Ingeborg, reading late at night and sipping her gin, set herself on fire with a cigarette—she smoked like a fiend. She was wearing some sort of nylon or something and puff! She lasted in the hospital in intensive care for a month and then died. I just couldn't believe it. I tried to go to the hospital and see her, but there was no way. They wouldn't let you near her. I never knew if she got what I left for her or not. I never knew how out of it she was those last weeks in hospital. So that's the story of Ingeborg.

Now as I said, the German composer Hans Werner Henze was a friend of Ingeborg Bachmann's. I went to Naples to see her once and met him, and we had a lot to laugh about. Afterwards we became friends. I liked his music so much. It was modern, but it was not so modern that it put your teeth on edge. It had melody. It was like Aaron Copland, taken slightly a bit further into an acid quality. But I loved it. He was looking for a libretto, and he liked my *Monkey Poems,* so he asked me to write him a libretto. I started one about the town of Sybaris, from which we have the word *sybarite.* These are the people who got up at noon and who slept on mattresses of dried rose petals. Who taught their horses to dance a number of different steps to their favorite music. Who had everything: good food and good wine and love, love, love. Then there were battles with the more puritan tribes from the mountains. The spies learned of the tunes that the Sybarites played for the horses. So in the big meeting on the battlefield, the invaders got their musicians to play these tunes, and the horses started dancing rather than charging, so the Sybarites lost and the city was captured. I thought that was a theme for an opera. And naturally with a Sybarite princess and a little mountain boy who loved each other, like Romeo and Juliet. And how he tried to warn her, but she ran away, and when she heard the city was destroyed, she jumped off a cliff. He finds her body floating in the water in the last scene. Curtain. But I didn't want horses onstage. What a mess that can be. You know, in *Aida* there's always a moment when some horse forgets. Let's not have any animals onstage, thank you.

Anyway, I was writing that when I came down with a tropical virus and had to go in hospital. So then Hans Werner Henze got Ingeborg to do a libretto, and she chose a German tale of the nineteenth century about an Englishman who goes to this little town and he has his monkey with him. I sort of gave some hints. That's why there's a black cook from Mon Louis Island who sings my grandmother's ginger balls recipe in one scene.

I really wish I could have written my libretto, but I did appear in the gala Christmas production at the Rome opera of Ingeborg's *The Young Milord* instead; I created the part of the Englishman. The monkey was played by a ballet dancer, a tenor, and an acrobat. I was onstage for five acts; had to change in the wings. My role was all in pantomime. There were no lines to learn. Nothing to do but have fun. The greatest compliment I ever had, which really humbled and thrilled me—the wife of the director of the Rome opera said to me at a party afterwards, "Eugene, you know something strange?" She said, "I had a little chill about halfway through the opera." I said, "Was there a draft in your box?" "No," she said. "I went all that way before I realized you didn't sing or say anything. But I knew what you were talking about." So I thought, That's my diploma in the pantomime department. There were eight performances and a matinee on Sunday. Then I did the English translation, which was performed at Lincoln Center in New York.

Now, I got that tropical virus because I went once to Positano, where I had done a show of Lillian Whitteker's paintings. I had been told, "Don't drink the water," because they haven't changed the filter system in three years and it was supposed to be changed every six months. "Only drink bottled water." When I went into this little auberge, I ordered bottled water. It never came, it never came, it never came. I was so thirsty that I was about to die, so I turned on the faucet and let the cold water run forever, and I drank a full glass. The next day I started having this runny nose and strange headache, and when I got back from Positano, I had to go straight to bed. Then, I couldn't walk. I don't have things like that; it's not my style. But I was in the hospital two weeks so they could try and get the spine unparalyzed. They wanted to operate for a slipped disc, which they thought I had. Then the voice that sometimes speaks clearly to me, the monkey voice that I've tried to conjure all my life, said to me, "Don't be operated. Don't have the knife." Then this Dr. Heller, the famous surgeon from Milwaukee or something who doesn't like to operate unless necessary, was there for the summer courses with some famous sculptor in Rome. He came to call on me in the hospital and said, "I'd like to see your blood tests. I'd be very careful about being operated on." Well, that just corroborated it.

So finally I said to my dear friend Paul Wolfe, the harpsichordist, who came every day, "Couldn't you bring a board and get me out of here?" because I couldn't walk. And he said, "Well, I've got the harpsichord case lid, the lid of the crate the harpsichord travels in." He said, "I'll get three other guys, and we'll come and get you out." Then I bribed the Indo-Chinese nurses with Tabasco. I knew they loved Tabasco but couldn't get it from the shops. So I sent a friend to the American embassy commissary to get some, and I gave it to those nurses. And I said, "Now I want to get out that laundry door on Sunday afternoon when all the doctors are away." The Indo-Chinese nurses were glad to do it for Tabasco. So Paul Wolfe and three others carried me out on a harpsichord lid. There was a boy at each corner, and they just hauled me out. I got home and got some Jim Beam right away.

This American doctor finally saw my X rays and blood tests. What I had was a tropical fever called the Iceland virus which paralyzes the muscles that hold the spine. And if you are cut when those muscles are in spasm, you are dead. I would have died. It was identified by German and American doctors only after there was an epidemic of it in Iceland brought by sailors on some boat from the Mediterranean who obviously picked it up from North Africa. You have a high fever at first and this pain in the lower spine, and the muscles of the lower spine tighten. Then you have it a year later in a milder form, and a year after that it's almost unnoticed. The doctor said, "What you want is gallons of liquids." I said, "Is it all right if I put a little water in my Jim Beam?" He said, "Just take it easy for a while. It'll go away."

That's what happened. There was one night I got drunk enough—I drank a whole bottle of Jim Beam, and I crawled out of bed. I was wearing this steel corset that they'd put me in in hospital. I got loose from that, and I threw it over the balcony into the Corso Vittorio. I filled the tub with hot water and climbed into the tub and soaked. That was it. A year later, sure enough, I had a slight flu and a backache for three days. I was looking for it for a third year, but I didn't notice anything.

The funny part about being in a Rome hospital: I could not, being born and raised a Catholic, I could not let a nun in white with horn-rimmed spectacles shove a suppository up my rectum. I could not. Cultural history forbade it. I said, "Oh, Sister, put it there on my bedside table. I'll do it." Well, they didn't tell me you were supposed to take the tinfoil off. So I had a form of constipation after a few days. The doctor came and we talked and he said, "The diet is very carefully chosen. You certainly drink plenty of liquids, and we let you have your bourbon every evening. I don't understand this." After we talked a while, he finally realized and he laughed and said, "Well, what you need is what we call a depth charge." He brought back this foaming stuff which tasted like that citrate of magnesia or something I'd taken as a child. Stinky stuff. And finally I gave birth to a little modern sculpture made of tinfoil. It looked like a little man, so I called it "Tear Ass Tummy." I guess the moral lesson of that is: No matter what hospital, somebody who knows should insert the suppository. Oh, Lord.

        ❦

For the tenth-anniversary number of *Botteghe Oscure,* I wrote a lot of people that we hadn't heard from, like Alice B. Toklas; like Dorothy Strachey Bussy, sister of Lytton Strachey; like Isak Dinesen. Of course, I had taken *Seven Gothic Tales* in my barracks bag through the war. And I loved them, especially the story called "The Monkey," about the unpredictability of people and fate. I had carried the seventeenth-century classical Chinese novel *Monkey,* translated to English by Sir Arthur Waley, and *Seven Gothic Tales* by Isak Dinesen. Those were the two books in my barracks bag which I reread several times, over and over. I had a lot of other books, but those two went through the war with me. They were a great influence on my life. The minute the war in Europe was finished, I sent Isak Dinesen seeds of a new morning glory called Scarlett O'Hara and some Guerlain soap, as I did to the poet Miss Pitter in England and as I did to the lady who wrote under the name of Olivia, Dorothy Strachey Bussy. Thinking of those ladies of style and elegance stuck in war zones, I sent them all garden seeds and French soap. And then I sent a copy of my *Monkey Poems* to Isak Dinesen. I've forgotten how I got it to her. I think I sent it care of the American embassy in Copenhagen. There was never any reply. But then all those thousands of years later, I was writing all those people and said, "We'd love it if you have something that you would care to submit for the tenth-anniversary edition of *Botteghe Oscure.* It's going to be a delightful number. We're having a lot of young writers who've never been published, and we'd like to hear from people we haven't heard from in a while." The princess loved to publish work by famous older writers beside the work of younger, unknown writers. She always had everything from children to dodderers. Dorothy Strachey Bussy wrote back and said, "How kind of you. The only thing I write nowadays are laundry lists." And then Isak Dinesen wrote back saying, "What a thrill. What a delight. Your letter reached me the day I came out of hospital. And pleased me very much. Yes, I have a story I've been working on called 'The Country Tale.' I will send it along. I have not been in Rome since 1911." Blah, blah, blah. "If I came to Rome, would somebody show me a good time?" I wrote back and said, "Send 'The Country Tale.'" And I said, "Oh, yes, someone will show you a good time." It was the first time Isak Dinesen had published in ten years.

Three or four months after, she did come to Rome, and I met her at the

milking the moon

airport with this apple-cheeked secretary, Clara Svendsen. I had never seen a photograph of her. They didn't exist. There was a painting of the back of a woman's head that was repeated three times in a Book of the Month Club thing saying "Karen Blixen, Isak Dinesen, Pierre Andrézel. Who is which? Who is he or she?" I didn't know what I was looking for. Then I saw this thing in a bearskin coat in the summertime. Tiny lady, but a bearskin coat to the ground in summer in Rome and this hat. It had a brim she had to look out from under. And these eyes exactly like the monkey that's the frontispiece of *Monkey Poems*. Black, black eyes, mascara, and this little apple-cheeked secretary standing there with her. A tablespoon of mascara: plop, plop, and then took the handle and made a little hole to see out of. It's that Arabic stuff; she called it kohl. I forget what it's made from—charcoal paste and camel fat or something. But it was the real thing. I loved it. I rushed up to her and I said, "Baroness Blixen, welcome to Rome." She said, "And how did you know it was I?" I mean, who else would it be? That bearskin coat and that hat. I adored her immediately. We just sort of took to each other. Monkey and cat, cat and monkey. She quoted my monkey poem, the one that says, "We've eaten all the ripened heart of life / And made a luscious pickle of the rind." She knew it by heart, and she was reciting it to me at the airport. That was her greeting to me. She is one of the few people who really made my knees tremble, because she played the part so well. When she spoke, she cast her head back and she had this way of speaking slowly and emphasizing every word so you found all of yourself listening. She was frail and fragile, because she'd been operated on for this brain tumor and gone down to nothing. And in Denmark I met the doctor who had done the operation. He said, "Oh, Tanya Blixen has done many clever things in her life. But the cleverest thing she's ever done is survive my operation." But she was exuberant, a jolly soul. She was a monkey. She was totally a monkey. And the secretary/companion was a pussycat. When I saw those two at the airport, I knew it was my material.

On the second day she was there, I escorted the Princess Caetani and Isak Dinesen to an exhibition in a very flossy gallery. They were very cool to each other. There was the slight thing that a New England proper lady would have toward a wild Danish lady with that much mascara. And the Danish lady was not certain exactly what coinage was the American-born princess. So they were terribly polite and smiled a lot. In the gallery, the princess immediately went that way around the gallery and the baroness went the other way around the gallery. And I said to William Fense Weaver, "Well, that's what you would expect. That the Queen of the Northern Monkeys would go in a different direction from the Queen of the Southern Monkeys." He's the one that kept that going forever: the Queen of the Northern Monkeys and the Queen of the Southern Monkeys. And they both wanted an entourage of males only.

At that time, I still lived in this little box on the Janiculum Hill, but I did have her for dinner and got a special permit for her to come through the owner's garden on the other side of the wall rather than climb all those stairs. She was enchanted, of course, with this toy house. I had oysters, champagne, and candied violets, because I had learned that she lived entirely on oysters, champagne, and candied violets. That was her diet. There were four of us for dinner, but I cannot remember who the fourth was. She was always with Clara, her secretary, so she was there. The fourth may have been Michael Batterberry. He was in Rome at that moment, studying painting. He was a Dinesen fan, too, and he flipped when he heard that she was coming to Rome. Most people thought of her as either dead or buried in some castle. They just couldn't believe she was real.

Then I had arranged these three very elaborate parties for her. They were a day apart to allow everybody to recover and allow me to prepare food. On Monday night we were at this fabulous apartment on the Piazzale Tiburtino. The painter Mitty Lee Brown, from Australia, had taken what had been an old morgue, which no Italian would go near because it's where all the plague victims were laid out and all that. And she—mad Australian lady— got the priest from next door to come in and fumigate the place with holy water and psalms. She made it gorgeous. It was two stories and quite big. I mean, it was huge. She opened everything up, made everything white. You looked down to the Tiber on one side, and on the other, you went out onto this piazza in front of the little church on the island. When I told her, "Well, Isak Dinesen is coming and I want to give a party. Would you let me give a dinner here?" She said, "Oh, I loved her book. Wow, wow, wow." So we did this party there. That's where I had Sir William Walton and his darling little Italian wife. And all the painters, from Prince Henry of Hesse, the grandson to the last king in Italy, to the little boy who had just gotten out of jail that day. He was a street painter and a pickpocket. And I found some old folding fans that were perfectly blank because in Naples they used to manufacture those so young ladies could paint the fans at home. They had beautiful, very white parchment and scented wooden spokes—sandalwood, maybe. I found a few of those, so I was able to give her a fan for each party so she could have everybody sign a spoke. And she had the pickpocket paint his first of all. That shows you how she thinks.

Well, on the way to Mitty Lee's morgue apartment where all the painters were gathered, we stopped on the bridge to the island right at six o'clock in all of Roman traffic. That was to accomplish our private ceremony. You see, a

milking the moon

young man in Denmark who had been to her parties and listened to her stories wrote a book called *The Red Umbrellas*. He published it under his name, but since she was always changing names, and would use one name in one country and one in another, he let it be known that this was her new book. So around the world and back, the book was widely reviewed, always with the question "Is this Isak Dinesen?" you know. The minute I read it, I knew it wasn't. But some of it was stories she'd invented on the spur of the moment at a party. It really was a plagiarism. And she was furious. It came out like maybe a year before she came to Rome that first time. Well, I knew someone in Reuters who knew something about something and who could get the manuscript from the Danish publisher. So through bribes and unbelievable behind-the-scenes carryings-on, I had gotten the manuscript from the Danish publisher. Whether it was the forger's original manuscript, whether it was a copy—I don't know. We had talked a little bit about it when we first met the first day she was in Rome before the private festival began. She said, "I committed an error in a Latin phrase in one of the *Gothic Tales*. He even stole my error. There's a place in hell for . . ." I said, "We're going to do something about him."

I had told the driver before we started, "We're going to stop on the bridge only for a minute. We have to throw something in the river. You won't get in trouble. If anybody says anything, I'll take care of you, and you're going to have a nice tip." He said, "Oh, my God. You're not doing something illegal?" "No," I said, "it's this manuscript." "Well, go ahead," he said. "You crazy foreigners."

That bridge is rather narrow, and it's one-way. Nothing can pass anything. He stopped right in the middle. All the six o'clock traffic was honking as only Rome can honk. I went into my little carryall bag. I said, "Madame Tanya, I have here the manuscript of *The Red Umbrellas*. Would you like to join me in tossing it into the Tiber?" She roared, and she jumped out like a monkey. I said, "All right. We have to hold it so our hands touch and we make a magic circle." And I said, "Repeat after me: Rat shit, bat shit, three-toed sloth shit. O Tiber and oblivion, receive this manuscript and its author." Splash. We watched it float and sink and got back in the car. She was just laughing, laughing, laughing. She said afterwards that was the best part of her visit to Rome. Traffic was tooting for miles. It was not only the joy of throwing the manuscript into the Tiber. It was also the Southern joy of holding up traffic. And two weeks later, the author of *The Red Umbrellas* died.

Wednesday was the evening we performed a marionette play at the theater that Ginny Becker and I did in her apartment in the Palazzo Caetani. It's called *Tanya, Tanya, and Clara Too*. Her friends in Denmark called her

"Tanne" from childhood. It's some pet name in Danish, like Boo Boo or Bubba or Cutey. So she's become Tanya to a lot of other people. Anyway, in the first scene you're in Denmark and it's snowing in this little woods. She and Clara drive in in this Baroque sled drawn by two huge butterflies. She says, "It's cold here." Then she says, "How I would love to have some fresh wood mushrooms." Then she is saying, "I'm tired of snow." And Clara is just sort of hinting, saying, "Well, maybe you should roam." Then in the next exchange, Clara says, "It must be so nice in Rome. What mushrooms come from just outside of Rome?" It goes on like that. Then suddenly Tanya says, "I know what we'll do. We'll go to Rome." There's this fanfare and the coach goes off through the snow with these butterflies flapping. The next scene is Piazza Navona in Rome. A Miss Rome, a retired soprano, is there to meet her, and Ginny Becker and myself, and Harlequin and Columbine. Isak Dinesen is throwing out a ladder from this hot-air balloon, but the cardinal hasn't come in yet. Each time she descends and goes back up, somebody makes a little speech, a little something of welcome. She says, "Where's the cardinal? I was promised a cardinal. I will not descend until there is a cardinal." Finally the cardinal comes in late on his bicycle. He says, "Where is she? Where is she?" The soprano says, "I'll sing a high C," and she does. Isak Dinesen comes down and gets out, and she and the cardinal walk around. That's all there is to it. A little divertissement. But she adored it and wanted a copy immediately. That party was all musicians. Pianists and violinists and William Fense Weaver.

Then the Friday night was at Princess Brianna Carafa's. She didn't have a piano, so she had to buy one for the party. I mean, you need a new mop for the kitchen, get a mop. Need a piano for the salon, get a piano. That's just the way she thinks; she's a princess. She bought a Beckstein grand and had it hauled up to that top-floor apartment. The reason was that Wanani, the Afro-Cuban singer, was going to sing French and Caribbean songs. And Aldo Bellasich, a blond south Italian who was a concert pianist, had found in the British Museum some Albinoni sonatas that had not been played since they were written. And Jeannette Pecorello, a soprano from an Italian family long in Boston, was going to sing. So there were three sections to this musical program. Each musician had three numbers. It wasn't to take up the whole evening. Three unpublished sonatas, three arias, and then Wanani sang "Babalu." And that's when we had the prince of Lampedusa. I had heard that he was going to be visiting Rome, so he was invited to the party. Oh, he was a cutie. He was just a great old gentleman, and he was very deaf. And the conversation between Isak Dinesen and Lampedusa on this sofa—I wish I'd recorded it. It was like a rare monkey and a wild wolf, speaking languages

milking the moon

that neither one understood. But each realized who the other was, so they were being charming in unknown tongues. Oh, it was just a wonderful party. Wanani was wearing a white dress, strapless, skintight, with little pearls all over it. This gorgeous antelope body. She was something.

But when Isak Dinesen wrote and said, "If I came back to Rome, would somebody show me as good a time as I had the first time?" that's when I had a nervous breakdown. Because what could I do? So I did a different kind of thing the second time around. I didn't do any big parties because it seemed to me it would be an anticlimax. And she had just as good of a time. She said she wanted to see a good hillside castle, so I took her to see the castle of Sermoneta, the Caetani stronghold on the hilltop south of Rome overlooking all the province they've owned since before Christ. Later she used that as a setting for "Echoes," a novella in either *Last Tales* or the book that followed. I took her to see the prison where the Napoleonic soldiers were prisoners and had drawn and written all over the walls. And I took her to see the flower festival at Gensano. Well, coming back, we started a game. She said, "Let's write a book together." And I said, "What fun." She said, "Let's toss to see who sets the theme." So we tossed. And I won. I said, "We'll have to have a monkey in it, or a ghost. And a fascinating lady of European background." "Oh, yes, yes," she said. "Well, you write the first chapter, and I'll write the second." But of course, by the time we got around to it and reminded each other and all that, she was dead. But that became my novel *Love You Good; See You Later.* We corresponded until she died. I'd always wanted to go to Denmark, and she'd invited me, but I didn't have the money to go at that time, although I got there later, after she died. And she'd invited me to come with her to America when she was doing her first visit. For her first trip to America, she not only wanted her little secretary, but she wanted a gallant to go to the American Academy of Arts and Letters and to the weekend with Arthur Miller and Marilyn Monroe and Carson McCullers. But again, I didn't have the money to go. That's one of the times when you really want money in the bank: her first trip to America. I'm sure a lot of people in New York didn't know how to deal with her. She really was Queen of the Northern Monkeys. I've thought since I should have written everybody I know and borrowed the money to be her escort for that. What a dinner that would have been. I'll go to my grave thinking, What would the conversation have been like?

Shedding a Skin

The French ambassador wanted to do something to honor the tenth anniversary of *Botteghe Oscure*. But since there were still very powerful anti-German feelings among the French, and one of the languages in *Botteghe* was German, he decided to do something in honor of her earlier publication, Commerce, which was purely in French. So I worked with the French ambassador in Italy and with these two ladies who'd come from the French Ministry of Fine Arts. We emptied the Napoleonic Museum in Rome and made this exhibition. The idea was to have not just manuscripts but photographs and paintings as well. We also had odd things from people. For example, Paul Valéry had a collection of toy soldiers. So the glass case dealing with him had a photograph of him, manuscripts of some of his famous works, and his toy soldiers. Then I took one little room in this museum and tried to make it look like the princess's little corner at one end of that long room on the top of Palazzo Caetani. So I had a gardening basket full of manuscripts. I had packages of seeds. Seed catalogs. Piles of books. And some of her favorite paintings that I borrowed for the show. I just reproduced her private little sitting room. We had this wonderful opening, and the French ambassador presented her with the Légion d'honneur.

During the moment of all that, a bookshop in Rome did an exhibition of my drawings for Grabbe's *Wit, Satire, Irony, and Deeper Meaning*. I did those under the name of Dr. S. Willoughby. Well, people began to talk about my show, and the princess was sort of irritated that she had not received an invitation. But she had. And she had been told that I was Dr. S. Willoughby, but she'd forgotten.

Then the French poet René Char, who was her pet, wrote and said that the index for the tenth-anniversary edition was full of errors, principally that there should have been a death date for Peter Matthiessen. Well, he confused Peter Matthiessen, who was very much alive, with F. O. Matthiessen, the uncle of Peter.

Then there was the incident with the bank. For certain things like buying supplies for the office, the princess had said, "You should have an account." So they made a separate account for me because I sometimes would pay, for example, the proofreaders for the summer when everybody was away. And I would deposit the checks that came for subscriptions into that account. I was so careful about all of that because I didn't want any part of doing this. The minute you get into money, you're asking for trouble. So I, who am not good at accounts, was so prissy proper, getting receipts when I paid for postage or whatever. And I had this notebook: what came in, what went out. Well suddenly, the account was overdrawn. And I should have had something like $200 in there from the subscription checks that I'd put in the bank. It looked like I had gone off with some money. Which, of course, I had not. It was only $70 that was overdrawn. It turned out that some silly bank clerk had simply put the subscription checks into the Amministrazióne Caetani account instead of the separate Amministrazióne Caetani Rivista *Botteghe Oscure* account. But I didn't feel like even defending myself.

And there were a lot of people who really objected to my closeness with the princess. And with my American impudence. They didn't understand my friendship with the princess, and they thought I was too full of levity. There was this lady who was a friend of the princess's, and she thought I was too American and too flibbertigibbet. Which was what the princess wanted. Because she didn't have any of that quality. She liked a gossipy account of who was at what literary gathering the night before that she wouldn't dream of going to. You see, I was an American imp for her. That's why we were friends.

But others were jealous, especially Giorgio Bassani. I know that I had Bassani always working against me. He told her that I led this ghastly life. I was in this nightclub every night and drunk and dah, dah, dah. Of course, I wasn't. Many Friday and Saturday nights I closed Bricktop's. But that's when all those darling Spanish and Portuguese and South Americans were there. And Wanani was singing. Oh, it was a wild and wonderful crowd. But it could not have been more innocent. It was just jolly souls together. But suddenly everything was misinterpreted. I liked to find out about life in that crazy country. It's one of the reasons I wanted to live on my own. So of course, you can imagine, I was objected to by some of the prissy propers.

Bricktop was a pale mulatto lady from Philadelphia originally, I think. I'm not sure, but her name was something like Elsie Blodgett. But she was known as Bricktop, because even though she was a mulatto, she had this reddish brown kinky hair. And she sang. She had that elegant twenties style. Sometimes she'd talk a song, sometimes she'd sing it. She had a great success in the twenties and had a nightclub in Paris called Bricktop's. And she had a nightclub under the Via Veneto in Rome. You went into this hotel and down into the basement. That's where she had this nightclub. There were some cafés right on the Via Veneto which were very international, and you'd see movie stars and famous composers and all the tourists gaping. They were wildly expensive, and I didn't really like them. For me, there was no other nightclub besides Bricktop's. There was the diplomatic set, especially from South America and Spain. They were all there because of Wanani. She was part African, part Chinese, but from Cuba. And she was a gazelle—tall and willowy with this long neck and these arms that just unfolded. She couldn't put on a shoe without being a spirit of elegance. She did these glorious mambo-jambo things, and she sang a lot of old American twenties and thirties songs like "Love for Sale." But with her accent, it came out "Love per Tail." "I can give you fascinating love per tail . . ." She never knew what she was saying. She was a heavenly creature. Later, I introduced her to Fellini, who immediately grabbed her. There is a voice that you hear in the background in *Juliet of the Spirits* saying, "Ah-ah-ah-ah-ah-ah-ah." That's Wanani.

Theoretically, the club was supposed to close at midnight or one o'clock. So Bricktop would pull one of those expanding metal gates across the entrance at the legal hour and just let it stay open forever. All the Latin Americans and the Spaniards loved to stay up all night. At nine o'clock in the evening they are just starting, because they sleep long hours in the afternoon. In the summertime they don't eat before eleven or midnight.

Now one night, I was there with Theodora Keogh and Count Diego DeMasa. Big table at Bricktop's. Boozing it up and enjoying Wanani's Latin rhythms. And the count said, "I'll take you all home in my new car." And we went roaring down the highway to Naples. He wouldn't stop. We kept saying, "You can't do this." And I said, "The princess expects me at eleven tomorrow morning to look at proofs." "Oh," he said, "I'll tell her I did it." Well, she loved him, was very devoted to him. He did the Spanish section of *Botteghe*. But anyway, people were saying, "Well, you know, Diego and that Theodora Roosevelt meet Eugene in nightclubs," and dah, dah, dah. It was really the dreary ones who were always courting the princess. I was not courting the princess. I was enjoying the princess.

So, I had gotten some bad-mouthing. I don't even know all of it, and I never got the straight of it. But she sent her administrator to say that she no longer wanted my services and would give me passage back to America.

In a way, I was prepared for the abruptness with the princess because I had seen it with so many of her friends. She was like that, you see. All or nothing: that was her style. She would get impatient with people and just turn the faucet off. Years ago when I had first met the princess, I had done a piece in *London* magazine for John Lehmann, a "Letter from Paris," saying—oh, I don't know—what Jean-Louis Barrault and Madeline What's-her-name, his wife, were doing, and then I said, "The Princess Caetani is ringmaster in the

milking the moon

rue de Cirque." Because her apartment in Paris was on Circus Street. I made an image of a circus of her literary meetings. Then I had this ferocious letter from her saying "I didn't know you thought like that about me." I wrote back and said, "Well, after all, you do have a circus. You have so-and-so and so-and-so, and for monkeys, you have Alfred Chester and myself." Well, of course, that made her giggle, so everything was all right. But there were several people she dropped for strange reasons. So when it happened to me, it wasn't a surprise, and I never even knew all the reasons.

We had no words. I was supposed to go and answer to my sins about no death date for Peter Matthiessen and this, that, and the other. But I had worked so hard on all of that for the tenth-anniversary number and the exhibition for *Commerce* that I thought, Well, this is the swan song. I loved the princess very much, but I was feeling smothered. So then Countess Loynskarenska, a lovely lady and friend of the Caetanis, talked to the princess and said that she thought there was a big error and that a lot of people had bad-mouthed me simply because I was a piece of impudence. She came to convince me to go and talk to the princess. And I said no. You know, sometimes things have to change. And this was the moment, it seemed to me. We'd done the big exhibition. We'd done the tenth-anniversary number. All the proofs were read for the next number. I needed to do some of my own writing. Blah, blah, blah.

And I was so sick of all the problems. Now, I could get along with Gino, this peasant child, who was really a man of fifty. I can always talk to idiot children and animals. But the administrator was a tough military type. He'd been a big fascist military captain. He didn't approve of me because I was American and I didn't salute him. And he didn't approve of the princess publishing this magazine. Not that it was any business of his, but they were all penny-pinchers. He would howl and was always telling the princess to look out for this, look out for that. He was really an upstart country boy, not exactly a peasant. He could read and write, but how he got to be administrator, I don't know. And he was dipping his hands into a lot of things, apparently, as was learned much later. He had gotten Roffredo to sign papers that ceded certain unimportant vacant fields to him.

And Hubert Howard, the English Lord Howard, whom Marguerite's daughter had married, also didn't like the amount of money she spent on *Botteghe Oscure*. His mama was Italian, his papa was English, and he had the worst qualities of both. He would mark the olive oil jars in the kitchen to be sure the servants weren't taking olive oil out of the olive oil jars. And you know, I think if you are at a certain level, you don't worry about that sort of

Rome

thing. But it was always suggested that the princess might have fewer pages, you know. She never said anything. But when Hubert would go away for the summer and before she left for Paris, she would sort of say, "Good. Now we can add twenty more pages to the autumn number." It was her money. It was not Caetani money. It was Chapin money. But it was always uphill work because the administrator really didn't like anything to do with *Botteghe Oscure* and the son-in-law wanted to cut it down.

Anyway, I could see that just for thousands of reasons, this was the moment for it to end. Right then and there. And she made the gesture, not I. And the princess was tired. She was getting crankier and crankier, and her eyes were failing. She was going blind, poor darling. Toward the end, especially with poetry, I read a lot aloud to her. I realized that she was getting old and that she wouldn't be able to do it much longer. In a sense, I was relieved that I didn't see her decline. She had gone to Europe to study music in 1905, and she would have to have been twenty-something then, so she must have been entering her seventies in 1950-whatever. Or eighty. She might have touched eighty. There were only two numbers published after I left.

Of course, I had many regrets. You know: friendship gone sour. And not through her fault or mine. The hangers-on. But it was just cycles of nature; everything comes to an end. Sometimes I will draw up battle lines over one misplaced comma. Other times, when people have taken offense at something I've written, I refuse to defend what I've said. I've said it. It is there. And I didn't feel I wanted to go through "Yeah, but you see, gee, you know, gosh." Because I did my job, and I never wavered in my absolute fidelity to *Botteghe Oscure* and the princess. So I just didn't want to hear any of the crap.

That's when I sat down and finished *Love You Good; See You Later*, right there in my little gardener's cottage on the side of the hill. My French novel. There was this delightful man whose name was René Juilliard. He'd been a big underground chief in World War II in France. He had done underground publications—underground newspapers and bulletins. And he became a publisher after the war. I met him in Rome through the French ladies with whom I'd worked on the exhibition of *Commerce*. He'd read *The Untidy Pilgrim*, and he said, "Even though I'm fluent, I don't really get some of the expressions in this. Since it is so in the vernacular, it would be practically impossible to translate." And I said, "I will write you a French novel." And what is a theme for a French novel? Either a young man with an old mistress or a young girl with an old sugar daddy. And my last line: "Let's have another drink; we're not dead yet."

So I just went on into another world. Totally. It's not true, you know, that we have only one life to live. We are much more like cats than we know, and we have at least nine lives. They say that every cell in our body is replaced within a seven-year period. We shuffle off skin. The blood renews itself. Every seven years we are different. We shed a skin; we start a new life. And I guess that's how I look at it.

One Big Cocktail Party

Well, one thing leads to another, say what you will. The minute I had arrived at Palazzo Caetani, the princess had said, "There is someone who is dying to meet you. She's read your whatever it was that I published in the magazine." This lady also happened to live in Palazzo Caetani. So we were introduced, and it was Ginny Becker, who was from Plaquemines, Louisiana. She had been an actress on Broadway and had been taken to Hollywood to play in one of Ernst Lubitsch's films, the last one he made as a director. Ginny was to play a little French maid. But she came down with tuberculosis and was in hospital in Hollywood for a long time. And she said to her husband, John Becker, "I can't take another minute of Hollywood. I want to go to Rome." Well, people with tuberculosis were not supposed to go in or out of anywhere. So they dressed her in ski clothes and bandaged one foot and pretended it was a ski accident and that's why she was in a wheelchair. And got her onto a plane and into Rome. And John Becker found this apartment in the Palazzo Caetani that nobody but somebody from Chicago, where he was from, and Plaquemines, Louisiana, would want. It had been Cardinal Caetani's state apartment, where he received and gave audiences and all that. Red damask walls and a portrait of him, very severe, saying: "What is a martini?"

Because Ginny gave wonderful parties. She was a Southern girl. She would always do things in her offhand "Well, we'll have a little sandwich after." And a famous restaurant had been brought in with a twenty-course meal and a famous florist. And red damask dinner cloth. You know. Gilt-plated silver. A little sandwich. Then, "Oh," she'd say, "we'll have home movies." And there'd be Marcello Mastroianni and Iris Tree and a wide-screen thing in the parlor. The best of all was when she said, "Oh, we'll have a quick look at Ostia Antica and then we'll find a place down there some-where to eat." This was that famous Roman village that was dug up after the earthquake. So we made the tour and she said, "There's a little old restaurant around the corner. Let's lunch there." Of course, she had sent her butler to turn it into a fancy restaurant and a bar. There was champagne and a damask cloth and two large umbrellas arranged and food like you never imagined. "I've heard the food is very good here," she said. It's that Southern thing of even though you may have been boiling eggs for three days, it's nothing really. A little sandwich.

Anyway, Ginny had had made for her little girl, who was about five then, a very pretty marionette theater. The child wasn't interested. But the child would sit and watch Mama, because Ginny went mad, missing theater. Missing theater, she suddenly was spending all day every day making marionettes. And when she heard about my marionette background, we fell into each other's arms. She immediately had a much bigger theater made and we began doing, for grown-ups, satirical reviews and all kinds of things. What we liked to do was tape the voices and have them play while we did the marionettes and mechanical effects. We did two or three voices, and then famous people did voices, like Iris Tree, this great lady of the British stage. Alex North, the composer, wrote music. It was just something special. And so we did marionettes and marionettes and marionettes forever and forever. There was the performance we did for Isak Dinesen's visit to Rome. When Robert Graves was coming to Rome, it was the first time all of his children from both his marriages had been in the same room. So we did *The North Pole Party* for the Graves occasion. We gave a lot of famous performances. Everybody was there, sooner or later. Helena Rubenstein, Christopher Fry; we had an all-star audience for one of our openings.

Well, there was this young man from a very old family in Siena, Guidarino Guidi. I met him early on, like the first week I was in Rome. I don't remember how I met him; somehow I just knew him the minute I was in Rome. He was a friend of a friend; maybe William Fense Weaver introduced him to me. He was at every party in Rome. Anyway, he was casting director for Fellini. He was also casting director for Vincente Minnelli's *Two Weeks in Another Town*. He was casting director for all kinds of things. He had perfect English and French and a little German, and he knew everybody on earth. It was he who first asked Ginny Becker to invite Fellini for the marionettes when Fellini was contemplating a film on the high life and low life in Rome. He had told Fellini, "You've got to see this." Of course, Fellini loved marionettes. Only a fool would not like marionettes. The more intelligent the person, the more they enjoy things that are miniature. Everybody of intelligence has something that is miniature. And all the Mediterranean world loves puppets or marionettes or enormous carnival figures. That's a hangover from the pre-Christians. I suppose that on long winter nights in those caves, somebody would take dinosaur bones and make a figure that danced. You know. And see, when Fellini and his brother were too young to be soldiers in the Second World War, they were able to get permission to set up in a vacant shop in Milano, and they did caricatures. People would come in and have a caricature done for a dollar or something. But then later they had this van, and they did marionette productions. They both loved marionettes. So I met Fellini at a marionette performance that Ginny Becker and I gave when he was brought by Guidarino.

He then wanted Ginny and me to do our marionettes in *La Dolce Vita*. He said, "I've got this episode I want you to do your marionettes for." I said I was terribly sorry, but I had to see *Botteghe Oscure*'s autumn number through the press while the princess was in Paris. Ginny had visitors from Louisiana she was taking to her summer place down in Ostia. We were probably the only people in Rome who refused him. Everybody who lived in Rome at that moment was in *La Dolce Vita*. Everybody is in it.

He was being inspired by real life in making *La Dolce Vita*. So much so that he was inspired by some real happening or some real personality. And he wanted to put us in. Well, as it turned out, he used the idea of the Becker family as the Steiner family in the film. Copied their apartment. Steiner, who kills his children and commits suicide, is Johnny Becker. Not that Johnny would ever do that. Fellini saw that Johnny Becker, who is a sensitive, intellectual, immensely wealthy Jew from Chicago, was overly protective of those children. The boy was Ginny's child by an actor in New York, her first marriage. Johnny was even more careful with him since it wasn't his child.

Their apartment had been reproduced. Ginny is a very good painter, and Fellini went to the gallery that represented her and rented some of her paintings to dress the set. He reproduced the hooded thing that Ginny Becker always wore. You see, Ginny is one of those people with very little hair. And the older she grows, the less there is of it. She has about three hairs on her head now. She did get a wig once, but then she just said to hell with it. So she always wore those hoods, like the actress playing Mrs. Steiner is wearing in the film. So there is everything. And a lot of the people at the Steiner party are people who went to Becker parties. Iris Tree plays herself. There is an awful Irish poet that I hate who plays me. Fellini wanted us to do the marionettes in that episode, not telling us that he'd done the Steiner episode.

Ginny was quite shocked when she saw it. I think total shock: pleasant, unpleasant, flattered, insulted. She never acknowledged to anybody that she'd even seen the film. No comment, you know.

But there was no viciousness in it. Fellini is not vicious. Now, if a set's not ready when he comes on it in the morning, and it's supposed to have been ready, or if somebody repeatedly gets something wrong, he would lose his patience and slam his script down and all that. After all, he is Italian. But he was never vicious with anybody. Fellini on his off days is real cranky, but he is mostly good cranky. There is good cranky and bad cranky and everything in between. But very seldom have I seen him cranky and directorial. He really is a sweet, gentle, kind, slightly demented gentleman. I think he just needed a story like that as one of his episodes.

Since I was the only one in Rome who refused to be in *La Dolce Vita*, I was the third person cast for *8½*. I was doing a weekly column for the Rome *Daily American*, and I was always asking him for an interview. He finally called me and said, "Well, do you want to come out to the studio today? We'll talk about that interview." So I went out to see him at the studio. He said, "How are you? Are you still doing the marionettes?" Yes. "Are you still a writer?" Yes. Then he said, "What are you doing this summer?" I said, "Well, you know, in the summer I stay very close to Rome because I have to see the autumn number of *Botteghe Oscure* through the press. That was the reason I couldn't be in *La Dolce Vita*." He said, "Well, I've got this film coming up and I thought maybe you could do a little part in it. It's only a few days' work, but you'd have to be available. If you're going to be in Rome, you'll be available. We could do the interview while we are working on the film. Run over and see Guidarino and sign up."

Three films later, we still had not done an interview. So I just sat down one morning and made one up whole hog and published it in the *Transatlantic Review*. I described the party at his place at the beach in Fregene, where he fed all the cats in the garden first, then his servants ate, then the guests at the party ate. A Fellinian reversal. Now, every bit of that is fact. I was there at that party; we played charades. It's all his dialogue that I invented. I have him saying all kinds of things about films like "Cinema is just an old whore. They've got her propped up in the parlor with Freud in one hand and Ovid in the other, but she's just an old whore." And I have him say, "Anybody can have *la dolce vita*. All you need is hats and wigs." It's not the image of Fellini as the cranky maestro, the oh-so-sensitive, hard-to-talk-to artist, the surly imperialist, that is usually projected by journalists or reviewers. But even though he didn't say any of that, it's more his attitude. When it was published, I took it to him and said, "Thanks for the interview." He read it and laughed and laughed and laughed. He loved it. Then later when he came back from when *Juliet*—I think it was—opened in New York, he gave me a clipping of an interview he'd done with the *New York Times*, where he'd quoted all this I'd invented—quoted himself, so to speak. He said, "Thanks for the interview."

In *8½* I was playing an American journalist interviewing Marcello Mastroianni. So, oh, my God, I was in a state. My first major film. It wasn't my first film: I had worked with Edward G. Robinson in *Two Weeks in Another Town*. I had two lines. Then I'd done this *Teenagers in the Sun* because I could dance the new dance from America called the twist. I learned it from the black actor Roscoe Lee Brown, who came to Rome I think the year the twist began. So although I was a tired old thirty-seven, they glued up my jowls with fish glue, painted me with suntan makeup, and I danced with a Hindu girl doing a Hindu twist as a teenager in the sun.

But *8½* was my first major film, and I was very nervous about my lines. Not so much memory as pronunciation, since I'd been such a short time in Italy. There were no coaches or anything. And I'd only been given the lines when I came out of makeup, because since everybody had revealed the story of *La Dolce Vita* before it opened, nobody saw the script for *8½*, except the lighting man, the casting director, the makeup artist, and the designer. And of course, there had been riots in the street when *La Dolce Vita* opened. Nobody had seen it, but it had been preinterpreted by the press and given a bad name while he was making it. Word got out that this film was going to be an embarrassment to Italy. That it was obscene. That it was this, that, and the other. Then, of course, the film was a world success and they saw it as something else. But when Fellini was making *8½*, a lot of people were thinking it was going to be even more this, that, and the other. It was the lower orders of intelligence. And there was a terrible scandal at that moment because a girl had been found dead at the beach who had died at some party, overdrugged, overdosed. Some people had taken her to the beach and left her. So the Vatican was doing a moral thing, and the police were doing a moral thing. So Fellini didn't let anybody see the script of *8½*. There were armed guards at the entrance of the set to keep journalists out. None of the actors saw the script until they started shooting. You were given your lines a few minutes before you went on the set. And for somebody who was shaky in Italian, I was very nervous.

After I did that film, I could see why everything was dubbed in afterwards. They don't depend on live sound, as Hollywood does. Hollywood has a siren and a buzzer, and the assistant directors all yell "Silence!" and they do live sound. Well, if you have two Italians within a mile of each other, there is no way to have silence. They do record the live sound, but when you hear that sound track, it sounds like a riot in a prison. Like Mobile at Mardi Gras.

But I was so enchanted with everything. Everybody loves being in a Fellini film. It's not like work. It's like Carnival. It was one big cocktail party. When he began shooting *8½*, he took a little piece of brown paper and taped it near the viewer of the camera. It said REMEMBER THIS IS A COMIC FILM.

What I loved was that he—alone above all the directors I've worked with, and I've worked with a great many highly interesting, famous directors—was always watching everybody on the set. While the lighting people are doing what he told them to do—brighter over there, get rid of that back-lighting here—he's watching somebody on the set over there talking. And he'll make them reproduce a gesture when they are on camera that he saw them do. "Now when you came on the set, you were fiddling with your neck-lace. You kept pulling it around and pulling it around. Let's do that at the beginning of this scene." There is a scene that I love in *8½*, one of the moments everybody notices. There are these three ladies in sequined dresses all crossing the yard going to their table at the spa, and one of them is carrying this huge palm leaf. Well, those actresses had come back from having their midnight picnic, and one of these ladies was dragging this philodendron leaf. She was fanning with it, fanning the mosquitoes away on this place where we filmed that scene. When it came time to tell her what to do on the scene, he said, "Well, where is your philodendron leaf? What did you do with it?" She said, "I threw it over there." So he sent the prop boy to go and get it. "Is this your philodrendron leaf?" he said. "Hold it and drag it along exactly as you did coming back from your midnight meal." So this lady is twirling it and dragging it in the scene; you see her just for an instant.

Quite often he'd rehearse something eight or ten times, until the actor was really relaxed and doing it precisely. Then as he shot it, in this soft gentle voice, he would say, "Now this time, look over to the fireplace." So it became a little bit startled and a lot more natural. "All right, Alberto, instead of sitting down in that chair, go to the red chair next to it." Over and over he'd do that. "In this scene, instead of sitting down at that moment, walk over to the window." They'll shoot that, and that would be what he wanted all along. But he wanted that freshness of the unrehearsed detail. He would rehearse until he got the actors out of their camera fright. Then when they relaxed, he just put in one new detail. Or he would whisper to the cameraman, "When the action is over, keep shooting." So the person would wait for him to say "Cut," and they would not know what to do, and that would become part of the film.

There's one scene we rehearsed two days to make it look unrehearsed.

214

The doorman holds open the door of the hotel. In comes a grand lady. She's dressed in black and white, and she has two black-and-white Dalmatians. The bellboy takes them from her and goes toward the elevator. She stops at the desk and goes to the elevator. The elevator door opens, and an old priest and a young priest get out, arguing. In the background you see a famous leitmotiv of Fellini—workers plastering a wall. In every important scene in every film, he has somebody tearing something down or building something. It's like the set is never really finished. The priests move over to the foot of the stairs. Coming down the stairs is Guido Alberti, who was this big Italian industrialist. He was a friend of Fellini's and absolutely screen-struck. He played the movie mogul in the film. So he's coming down the stairs with a blond floozy on his arm, and then a blond lady journalist sees him and runs to him with her journalist husband. Right away he's doing a blah, blah, blah. Then the camera follows them over to the desk. That's all one shot. The camera was in the middle on a rotating platform. We rehearsed two days.

It wasn't like work. Working for Hollywood films—that was work. It's so hierarchied within a production. You know, the producer speaks only to the director. The director speaks only to the star. The star speaks only to her hairdresser. Well, in Italy they're still working as though they're all on the same project. With the Italians, the costume people are friends with the electricians. The electricians are friends with the actors. It's everybody working together, like an old-time stock company. The technicians, lighting people, sound people, and camera people are a team. It was like Hollywood must have been in the twenties and thirties. It wasn't all powerful unions. If they wanted to finish on that set and strike it tonight to build a new one for tomorrow, you went on and worked until midnight, sometimes without extra pay. But then the director was always nice, and so he'd give you an afternoon off. Whereas in Hollywood, the unions are all-powerful and the actors are gods. Some of the greatest Italian actors, like Marcello, will be the first one on the set always, even if he wasn't going to be filmed until the next day. He wants to see where the bright lights are coming from, to know whether to look this way or that way, to see where the chair was, where the ashtray was. He wasn't the egotistical "Oh, how I enjoy seeing my face in the mirror when I shave every morning" movie star. It was a rare experience, seeing that aspect of filmmaking in the sixties and seventies in Italy. It was a whole other world.

The only time I was ever involved in a strike was with the original *Pink Panther*. I played Peter Sellers's majordomo in this Italian villa. There was a big scene of a masquerade party, and all of the people had to be there at six in the morning for costume, makeup. Blake Edwards, the director, didn't turn up until one. He looked as if he had been drugging it up the night before. He

Rome

was a mess. We didn't start shooting until about four. A lot of those Italians were furious, and I joined them in a protest.

I never met Blake Edwards. The assistant director said, "That's Walter. He's playing Fabrizio, the majordomo." Edwards said, "Okay, Fabrizio, let's try it from the stair to there." So you see, I never met him. Whereas Fellini talks to every extra. He asks them what they do, where do they live, what are their favorite films. He's amazing in his kindness toward a cast of two hundred, for example. I've always found that the greater the artist, the more humane. He'll look around a set of two hundred extras and say, "Well, Madeleine can go. Alberto can go. Pasquetta can go." Knowing he's not going to use them again that day. He'll look at some of the old people in their costumes, and he'll say, "Well, I'm not going to need you this afternoon, so you can have lunch and go. The children, no, the children I'll need for one more shot. They can leave at three." And he knows everybody's name. Amazing.

Fellini chooses each and every extra. And talks to each and every extra. He's always grabbing a waitress or grabbing a little girl who's filling cars at a filling station. Just grabbing them up—people from shops and shoeshine boys—because he sees something in people. That's why there is no such thing as an extra, really. If you look at the people in the mob scenes, they are all faces. There is not a blank there. They're not part of the scenery. Each one is an individual face. Which is why his films are so interesting.

I remember once being with Fellini in his car. We were going from someplace to some office he had in a studio. We were rushing. But then he said to his chauffeur, "Stop the car. Oh, stop the car." This was in the middle of traffic on the street that goes from the Piazza di Spagna to the railroad station. And he ran out to this old man who was walking along and was shouting after him, "Stop! Stop! You in the blue coat! Stop!" The man didn't stop. Fellini finally got to him and was carrying on. Turned out the man was stone deaf. So Fellini wrote something on a piece of paper, and the man said, you know, "Fellini, ahh." He became one of the cardinals in *Juliet*. I don't think in Hollywood today anybody would stop somebody on the street and say, "Oh, I like your face. Come tomorrow. We give fifty dollars a day."

He can see in women who don't know how to do makeup, don't know how to do their hair, some movement or some expression or some smile or some look. Who have an air. And he can see right away what a good wig-maker, a good costumer, a good makeup artist, could do. I've seen nice girls turned into ladies of mystery or the tartiest of tarts. The first time he saw Sandra Milo, he got her into a blond wig right away. She was brunette, almost black, if not real Mediterranean black. And she was a lady who had never dyed her hair, would never have thought of dying her lustrous hair. But the

216

minute she saw herself in a blond wig, she began to see different parts. A lot of actresses who had played stupid roles under Fellini's tutelage began to be taken seriously as actresses. A lot of actresses who were soul and drama smiled for the first time in roles Fellini put them in. Claudia Cardinale was just an ingenue until he created her, and she became something else.

And Edra Gale: now that's a Fellini story. She was this immense, terribly shy blonde and a brilliant singer. She graduated from God knows what with high honors. Her mother was something vaguely central European Slavic, the father was Anglo-American, and she was from California. Immensely shy, but her voice was sensational. It was a big voice, as you would expect. She could cause the chandeliers to fall with one high note. Somehow one of her professors had got her off to Italy, and she sang with the Bolognese opera or the Florentine opera. Well, someone who owned the principal circus in Italy saw her and said, "My God, what a fabulous figure." And he hired her at an enormous price to ride an elephant and sing an aria from *Aida*. It was one of the sensations of the age, because Italians love elephants, they love opera, and they love fat women. And Fellini, who is absolutely demented for the circus, saw her and said, "I don't know what role you're going to do, but I've got to have you sign this contract right away."

Edra Gale had this great sense of humor. I mean, to be that fat you have to have a sense of humor to survive the world. Otherwise you become a recluse. But she was very shy and also a very modest creature. She more often had sleeves down to her wrists and things that were never too open. Her skirt came to below her knees. Well, Fellini thought about it a long time. Finally one day: "Ah, the whore who lives on the beach."

He said, "I want her to look Italian. She needs a black wig, and give her a dark base," you know. "And a very short dress, something that's open big in the front." At first she wore this negligé that she would take off only for the scene. But all of the crew adored her so. They were always bringing her a flower or bringing her a Coca-Cola. Or their mama had made up their lunch for the day and they would offer it to her. So finally she started leaving off the negligé and just marching around in that short dress—it was like a rag—she wore. But it took about a whole day for Fellini to get her the way he wanted her. He said, "It's not right. Put another wig on top of that one." So they put another wig. And he said, "Different eye makeup. Let some hair come down on the forehead a little more. Let's just do a test of this." So he did a test and he looked at it and he looked at her. He changed the eye makeup again. Finally he said, "Put a third wig on top of those two." Then he said, "That's it. We shall have all this black hair up here and straggly in every direction." That was it. That's the Saraghina. She became part of folklore. At first she was just the prostitute. The young boy and his friends spy on this prostitute who takes guys into this dugout of an old gun emplacement on the beach. Then Fellini decided to have her be Mother Earth. In every mythology, she exists. And this shy, modest thing from California was not so shy and modest afterwards. Fellini wanted something that would bring her out, and not just for the role. He was always watching everybody on the set, and he would seize upon one little gesture or one repeated laugh and question them closely about their history, their lives. And then he would use something of them and make them aware of it, make them aware of themselves and somehow different. Oh, what a film you could make about the making of any Fellini film.

Then, of course, there are the great jokes. There are private jokes in every one of Fellini's films. For example, he would have a famous lesbian doing a wild love scene with an Italian sailor. Or he'd have an absolute crook, a jailbird, playing a very devoted priest. In *Juliet of the Spirits*, at the end of the film when the husband is gone, all the furniture is gone out of the house. Fellini told me, "A lot of people won't even notice it, but it's my joke." One of his jokes in *8½* was, all the people who work in the luxury hotel are names out of the *Almanach de Gotha*. The elevator boys are of the Medici family. The desk clerk is Alfresco Baldi. The concierge is Prince Volkonsky. The lady violinist in the open-air café is the princess of Sanseverina. Somebody else is Albertini. Those are the bellboys, the housekeepers, the maids in the hotel. All the guests are from the old folks' home and were allowed to keep their costumes afterwards. The men, their dress suits, and the ladies, their evening dresses, so they could go on playing luxury hotel in the old folks' home. That was just a private joke. Nothing to do with the film, but just his subtle Lewis Carroll sense of humor, of a topsy-turvy world. Turn the world upside down. And of course, there was a sort of disgruntled thing on the part of those titled people playing servants, and there was giddiness on the part of the old folks' home people playing the aristocrats, which were exactly the attitudes Fellini wanted to have come across. So many American films have such a beautiful veneer and a strange lack of content. They don't suggest anything under the surface. With Fellini, there's always a little something more you don't quite understand.

In *Juliet of the Spirits* I had the part of a journalist, a mad journalistic photographer. My scenes were with Sandra Milo. The tart. She lives next door to Juliet, and Juliet finally wanders over to one of her parties. Well, the party opens and I'm explaining the sexual parts of flowers in these botanical photographs. I had this rose-colored shirt and sequined vest, and I'm flitting about saying, you know, "Notice how the large vulva seems to contact the pistil of the other flower," and all the whores are clapping. Boy, I loved doing it. But that whole sequence was cut.

Then there was a scene in a bordello. The idea was that Juliet's husband went to the bordello not for sex. He went for the foolishness of the girls. The giggly aspect. The bordello madam had started this program to educate her girls, and this poet was to lecture them on poetry. Federico said, "Will you do that?" and I said, "Sure." I said, "Where's my script?" And he said, "Oh, improvise." He loved to get people to improvise, to get them free and just see what happened. He was amused when I started improvising, so I went on and on and he went right on filming for two hours. He had miles of footage. But that scene was cut. The film was like five hours long and had to be edited down. And Giulietta herself—the actress, his wife—was irritated. What she thought were some of her best scenes had been just cut out of the film.

Then the connecting links were cut to make it American length. For example, you are in the beach house, and then suddenly you are in a tree-house. Well, you saw them strolling from the beach house to the tree house in the original version. A dozen little connecting links have been snipped for the New York distributors. They said it can't be two hours and twenty minutes. We can have two hours, but you can't have two hours and twenty minutes. That was back when they still were fitting three showings into an afternoon and night. Someday we'll have the whole thing.

In the movie, there's a flashback to Juliet's education in a convent school. He wanted me to play the mother superior. I don't have a single line; I'm just there. I remember we waited hours until the costumer found the shoes he wanted. I can't remember whether you see them in the film or not. But he wanted a kind of shoe that is laced up to a certain point and then buttoned. It's the kind of shoe that mother superiors wore. He had to have that. Just had to have it. But my real role as mother superior was having my own dressing room and listening to the conversations of all those girls.

There were all these girls who applied to him in casting practically naked. And girls who would drop naked out of trees onto his car and by his gate when his car stopped to go into his beach house gate. "Oh, Mr. Fellini." They wouldn't let him alone. And he would say, "Well, casting is on such and such a day." So he hired them all but made them all nuns. He gave them nuns' costumes that covered every bit of them, even their hands. That's another one of the thousand jokes that are in every Fellini film. He told the costumer, "Cover every inch." Only their fingertips show. Because he was so put off by these dozens of beautiful girls appearing scantily clad at his gate.

So one day he called and said, "I want you to do something." And I said,

219

"What's that, Federico?" He said, "All these girls, you know, that have pestered me and pestered me, I've cast them all as nuns. Now I want you to be a nun. I want you to report to me all the conversations that go on in that dressing room." I said, "Oh, Federico, what are you asking me to do? You are throwing me in with sixteen bathing beauties." He said, "Yeah. You go to makeup first and then run in with your head down and get into that nun costume. I'll tell the wardrobe lady to get her assistants over there and get you dressed first of all. You can sit in the corner." And that's what happened.

Each nun had a tiny alcove. I had my little tiny alcove, and I was supposed to sit there and listen carefully. And I sat there, and I couldn't believe some of the things I heard. I mean, it was a sex education. A whole world of feminine mythology. It was a lot of like "Well, his face looks like a dog turd, but did you see the cute way he moves those buttocks?" I couldn't believe it. And then they said about Fellini: "Look how small his hands are. I bet his thing is small, too." Ever since then, I've been looking at men's hands. Anyway, it was amazing.

And then one day some stupid third assistant director came running in and said, "Signor Walter, Signor Walter, Signor Walter," and I made myself small in the corner. But he knew me because of the special shoes Fellini had gotten for my big feet. So the guy went looking for my shoes and said, "Signor Walter, Federico wants to see you right away." The expressions of those girls as they froze, I'll never forget. There was this hissing as I left. I went out and I said, "Our cover is blown. I ain't going back in that room. I won't get out alive."

He had wanted to know what women talk about with other women. It was just one of his things. The director's curiosity. I told him almost everything. I told about the dog turd face and the cute buttocks, but I didn't tell him what they had said about the size of his hands.

But finally Fellini just couldn't get the girls to do what he wanted them to do as nuns. They would pipe up in their sweet voices, and they wouldn't stay covered. So he went and got a lot of boys from the beach at Ostia. He'd say, "Come along with me. You're working in a film today." Then he put these boys into the nuns' costumes. He felt they could do that scene where the nuns are huddled together and sort of running about and all that, and they did. They came out looking more like nuns than the girls had.

Now with *Satyricon*, I worked for a year on the film before it came out. I did research on food. I did research on dye stuffs. Fellini is the papa-daddy, and he said, "I don't want costumes where everybody looks at them and says, 'That's cotton, that's silk, that's velvet, that's nylon.' I want fabric like nobody's ever seen. I want it to look like something we never saw and never will see again, something that nobody can identify, not even in a close-up." So he had a silk weaver in Venice who wove raw silk and processed colored silk together, then tore it into narrow strips and wove the narrow strips together. That's Fellini making.

So first I did the dye stuff. Then I did food research. I did a whole little booklet about food for the feast at Trimalchio's house. Then I translated the story. Then the treatment. Then the script. Then the shooting script. Then I worked as his assistant. Since many of the principals were English speaking, my job was to hover, and when he couldn't find the word he was looking for in his head to direct, I could tell them.

There was this black girl in the film, a famous model in England who had never acted, and she was supposed to be African from some unknown island in Roman times. So I invented her African language out of my little ole Southern head and coached her at length. I thought, Suppose I was sitting on Mon Louis Island and heard what they were saying backwards. The old Mon Louis Island patois is English with a French and African accent, and it's hard to understand. It's almost vanished; only a few old people talk it. But my cousin Francis did record Joe Summerlin of Mon Louis Island once for about thirty minutes, just talking about fishing and storms and seeing big fish out in the bay. Well, I just did some of that. I would sit her down and say, "Now don't speak to anybody when you get up this morning or when you come to the set. All these people and the makeup people and the wig people—they are speaking Italian, which you don't know. Don't listen to them. One second before you are going to go before the camera, we're going to sit down and I'm going to coach you in what you are going to say." And she just had one of those minds. I would just go, "Ahbiupe kylmadu woquixa," and she would just pick it up and go on and say it.

And then the best of all . . . there were all these extras, all these extraordinary types, and these dwarfs from Naples. Because you see, Fellini has that sense that they are a part of life also. He's not worshiping abstract beauty. He's not a romantic, even though people think of his films as romantic films. He's in the tradition of Hogarth, Aristophanes. Classic Mediterranean. He has giants and he has dwarfs. Anyway, I begged the casting director to let me be in the limousine picking up the dwarfs and taking them to the studio and delivering them back to their rooming houses in the evening. I wanted to hear what Neapolitan dwarfs talked about. I just had to; I was just dying to. So

I sat there crowded into the backseat of this limousine with four or five dwarfs, just so I could hear their conversation. Well, they only talked about clothes. Because this was September and school was starting and the dime stores were full of children's clothes. And here were these tough little gangster dwarfs from Naples saying, "Listen, the Upim on the Via Nazionale has got this blue one with three brass buttons." The other one said, "I don't care. At the Rinascente on the Via del Corso I saw this navy blue one with four buttons and this braid around the collar." You wouldn't believe it. These ugly things with these leathery skins and stinking of unwashed human flesh. I'm convinced that dwarf flesh has a higher smell.

This happened when there were all kinds of student strikes against authority and against the rich and so on. So here was this Bentley, or whatever it was, and I was sitting in the backseat, the only thing visible. There was a chauffeur and two dwarfs in the front seat. There were two dwarfs on benches and about three or four next to me. But you couldn't see them because it was an old high car, and they were tiny. So here were these students hitchhiking rides into Rome. And I won't tell you what they called me, seeing what they thought was an American millionaire in an empty limousine refusing students a lift. . . . That chapter of my life is called "Eugene and the Seven Dwarfs." Oh, I'll never forget those dwarfs as long as I live. That was one of the most splendid moments of my life, I think. My first glimpse of the northern lights, my meeting with Tallulah—oh, a few other glorious moments—but being in that big chauffeur-driven limousine and looking as though I were a millionaire riding in the backseat. And those Communist students shaking their fists because I wouldn't give them a lift. I couldn't give them a lift because I was just crowded in with all those Neapolitan dwarfs. Well, oh, God, I enjoyed making that film. Oh, was it fun. It wasn't like work.

Fellini and I were not good friends. Just friends. We had dinner together and all that. I went to his parties. He came to my parties. Et cetera, et cetera. But as with all great artists, you were conscious of rooms within rooms. Like with Jean Garrigue, even though we had many a giggle together and many, many, many a time when we were sitting talking about poetry or life and all, I respected in her other rooms and she respected in me other rooms. I guess I shouldn't go into it because otherwise I'd have to do a seven-hundred-page treatise on "What Is Friendship?" But I suppose by conventional standards, he and I became friends.

One of the most extraordinary evenings I had with him was at the circus. All the circus people loved him because, of course, he dealt with the circus in several of his films. And he'd finished some film—I can't think which one it was—and there was an Italian family circus that invited Fellini with whoever he wanted to bring, to come to a dinner served in the ring after the performance. And he invited me. Of course, I was beside myself. Because there was a dinner table set up right in the sawdust and the dwarfs, dressed in ballet skirts, were waiting on tables. And they had a tigress who had whelped two weeks before. Of course, their fur is like velvet. The vet said, "Well, come on around." This tiger's name was Maria; she was so beautiful you could die. He said, "Well, feel it." I said, "Huh?" He said, "It's all right." And he said something like "Maria, honey, he wants to feel your fur." Then he took my hand and shoved it through the cage, and I stroked her little haunch and she just went "Mmmmm." She was velvet. It was a thrill. It was my first touch of a tiger. It was all so marvelous that night. Eating dinner in a circus ring. With dwarfs in ballet skirts serving. I thought: These are the moments worth living for.

There's a rumor about how Fellini ran away and joined the circus. Well, finally I got the true story from his—I've forgotten whether it was his mama I met or his aunt. I just can't remember. But it was some lady of the Fellini family, whom I met very briefly on the set, and we were talking about the circus. I said, "Is it true about Fellini and the circus?" She said the same thing Giulietta said. "The only time that Federico blushes is when he tells the truth." She said, "He was missing one Saturday afternoon and we couldn't find him and it started getting dark. And his father caught up with the circus that was just going out of town, and walking right behind the animal wagons was little Federico. He was just following them." She said he was only missing for about six hours. He tells the story that he ran away and toured with the circus for about a year.

He was a delightful country boy. Like me, he's a country boy gone to the big town. He's an educated provincial, as I am. And he comes from a little town that has its own craziness, as Mobile does. It's a small town up there on the Adriatic. So he's not Roman or Sicilian or Neapolitan. He's from the north of Italy. Somehow I could identify with him and his sort of hidden sense of satire. It wasn't as if he were a know-it-all Roman or a know-it-all Milanese or a know-it-all Florentine or a know-it-all Neapolitan or a know-it-all Sicilian. He was from a town that was Byzantine as Mobile was Byzantine. So we Byzantine types understood each other. It's cats and monkeys and the difference between what they think, what they say, and what they do. That's the Byzantine holy trinity, as it is the Southern holy trinity.

Full of Spine and Free as a Bird

After I knew Fellini and after we had talked awhile and all that, he began giving me things to translate for him. I didn't translate the script for *8½*, but I had done translations of various other things for him to send to Hollywood or New York. So on the strength of having worked with him as translator, I was immediately hired by other people to translate. I must have translated well over five hundred film scripts, a great many stories which are five to ten pages long, and a great many treatments which are 150 pages long. It must have gone into the thousands of texts. I did one script a week and whatever bits and pieces. It was automatic. At first it was exhausting—I lost sleep over the first few. I had every known dictionary propped up on the desk. I finally realized I wrote them better if I didn't even read them first. I would just put it there, put the typewriter here, a pile of paper and carbons there, and set out. It always came out better. With translating, you have to be both full of spine and free as a bird.

My job was to make the script accessible to illiterate American distributors who might invest. They weren't the brightest creatures on earth, so they had to be amused, and that's what I tried to do. I tried to explain things that were terribly Italian without seeming to explain them. Like family relationships and certain customs like Ascension Day. I always tried to make it available to somebody, let's say, who was born in Iowa. Not writing down in any way, but making things clear. If I came to a passage I thought dull or too long, I adjusted it, thinking always of the need to sell the script to investors in America, England, Scandinavia, and Germany. I never changed anything to push my own style, my own ego, my own insight. But I didn't mind touching up here and there because they had to be sold. It was like putting a cherry on top of a dish of ice cream. Or putting the parsley where it was needed. I didn't think that I needed to call everybody who was involved to ask whether I could do it. I just did it.

After I'd done three or four, they were always calling every ten minutes because So-and-so, a distributor, let's say from United Artists, was passing through Rome, and they would want, in a big hurry, something to show him. The more I was certain of what I was doing, the easier it became, and I was able to go rapidly. Quite often they gave me better prices if I could do a five-hundred-page script in five days. Some of them were desperate for something overnight, practically. So I really did thousands. I mean literally thousands.

Some were brilliant and perceptive. Some were really just outlines to make a film. Fellini was much wordier in a script than he would ever let one of his films be. There was more exposition and more dialogue. I think that was to help possible investors get the story. The actual shooting scripts were fantastic in their economy and in the intelligence, poetry, and surprising qualities of the dialogue. Some of the greatest writers on earth couldn't write a screenplay if they tried because they don't have that grasp of how much the camera can write. The camera can do three pages of introductory material with one shot.

Liliana Cavani was brilliant in her screenplays. I worked very long and most particularly on her. I'd never met her. I only met her after she made her first film. But some young lady, her secretary or something, brought this script for me to translate. Somebody else had translated it, but then it was said to be awful in English. So this young woman who worked with her brought it to me. I read it and was just sent by her quality and took particularly a long time and many pains over those first two scripts of hers. And I was publicizing her and beating the drum for her and praising her and saying, "Here was a new talent," and blah, blah, blah, before she made anything.

I also worked with Lina Wertmüller from the beginning. I knew her from when she was this strange child. She was an assistant director to Fellini on *8½*; that's how I met her. She came to me to do that *Swept Away . . . by an Unusual Destiny in the Blue Sea of August*. I did all the English versions of that for her. I worked with her a lot. She always came to talk to me about the spirit of the script. She would say things like "I want some laughs here, but I want the essential design of these two or three scenes to be clear." She just wanted to be sure that I was on her wavelength, and I loved working for her. Considering, you know, the position of the female in Italy, I thought any-thing that could be done to open the doors of their little cages would be a good day's work. Lina was one of the—shall we say—revolutionists in the true sense of the word: you'd never call her a revolutionist. Most genuine revolutions are quiet, like the radio, the sewing machine, Mozart, Michelangelo, Edison, you know. Somebody sitting up late puzzling over things. Blood in the streets is so often not a real revolution. It's letting the lid off of built-up steam, an outburst of national hysteria and irritation, but it ain't a genuine turnabout.

Women in Italy were caged by family life. Caged by the duties of the mother, the duties of the homemaker. Up at dawn and wash the diapers. Then wipe the cream out of their husband's mustache after breakfast. Send them all on their way into the world and then start cooking lunch. And then start taking the sheep to market. They hadn't even learned to be conscious of other possibilities for themselves. Well, after the war there was a new minor bourgeoisie in Italy. Those peasant farmers who dealt their butter, eggs, and

Rome

cheese on the black market all got rich. And the first thing they wanted to do was send their eldest son to university to be a doctor or a lawyer. So suddenly Italy was filled with people graduating from law school and medical school, and a lot of those young people were very vocal. And among them were some daughters of those farmers who got themselves off to school. So many of the young intellectual females had the same idea, at the same moment. It was just one of those things—a spontaneous uprising all over the nation. The time had come for what happened in England in 1900 or what happened in America in 1885, you know. The girls let loose. They bit through their chains. Lina was just one of them, a female intellectual. And I use that as a complimentary term for the people who are actively interested in life on this planet and interested in the situation in which they find themselves, beyond the walls of their house, the hedge of their garden, the town in which they live.

There was something about Lina I just liked. She was small, tough, had black hair in a boyish cut. She always wore trousers and enormous thick lenses, like the bottoms of Coca-Cola bottles. She had a devilish sense of humor. But she was north Italian, and a lot of people from Rome and below Rome just didn't understand her sense of humor. She'd say things with a perfectly straight face. Of course, I got them because it was like understated British humor. And so we began to have giggles together on the set.

We collaborated on that crazy film of Zeffirelli's about Saint Francis. After I had translated some scripts for her and she was very pleased with my work, she invited me to come and join her at Zeffirelli's house one day to talk about this project, a film of the life of the saint, but modern. A surrealist thing. Everything was building up to this eight hundredth anniversary of the birth of Saint Francis of Assisi. And we did this version, but Paramount, who loved the idea at first, decided it was too special, that it wouldn't sell. Then we worked on something that Paramount was going to call *Holy, Holy Francis*. That's when I said, "No film in America is going to get anybody in, not even for the popcorn, under the name *Holy, Holy Francis*." So I said, "Why don't we call it *Brother Sun, Sister Moon*?" So it was called that, and the film went on to be a great success all over the world.

I was not available to work on that second version, which was historic, although I wrote a bunch of songs for it that were never in the film. But Zeffirelli liked very much what I did for him, and that's why I was called back to do a song for his *Romeo and Juliet*. He wanted an Elizabethan ballad, and he'd already said that he'd like for me to do it. But the Paramount people were going to get W. H. Auden, from Vienna, where he lived, to come down and write it. And it was Fellini who said to Paramount, "Why get Auden from Vienna? Eugene's in Rome." Nino Rota, who wrote all the music for all the Fellini films, had already done the music, so I wrote this ballad called "What Is a Youth?"

Nino Rota was charming, demented, and absentminded. Once we waited an hour to rehearse the song "Go Milk the Moon," which I wrote for *Juliet of the Spirits,* though it was later cut from the final version. The pop group was there in the studio, waiting. Finally someone went searching for him and heard this little voice. He'd locked himself in the john and couldn't get out. He'd put the key in his pocket. He's dead now, poor darling.

Zeffirelli was much more impatient than Fellini and not as interested in all the extras and their stories. But he's humorous, has a quick mind, and is a very nice person. He was always giving delightful parties.

There were a couple of pills I did translations for. Antonioni always sent assistants. I didn't really deal with him. Usually, the greater the director, the more they would talk to me. I think he's a big bore. Thirty minutes of Antonioni goes a very long way. I never understood that artistic film idea of hour-long close-ups of flowers unfolding and unnecessary mystifying of the viewer. Hour-long close-ups of Monica Vitti in *L'Avventura,* about this girl who vanishes from the beach in Sicily. Monica Vitti looks at the sun rising over the sea and bites her lip. I guess you were supposed to think she's unhappy. Or maybe has a nervous tic. Or is hungry. But we don't know anything about her. We have a close-up of her watching her sunrise on a deserted beach and biting her lip. Then she vanishes. It was a great hit with the intellectual critics and then thereby got international distribution. Since all Hollywood films go too fast, when Antonioni slowed everything down to a funeral pace, they said, "Oh, art. High art." But it was just relief after the Hollywood zip, zip, zip, zip.

Fellini knows when to be quiet, but he moves quickly. It's a movie. It moves. You don't sit on the beach in Sicily for an hour wondering where that girl has gone. Did she drown or go to town? With Fellini you can start counting how many stimulating images there are in ten minutes. Compare Monica Vitti on the beach biting her lip with *Juliet of the Spirits,* where you enter a fantasy world; you enter the world of the whorehouse next door; you enter the convent school where the wife went. It's a cross section of Italy. Fellini is movie. Antonioni is cinema.

Costa-Gavras was very complex but not pleasant, really. I translated a film for him, and *Variety* quoted me as saying something like "Highly interesting film. Difficult to choose a location where it will be filmed." Every once in a while *Variety* would call and say, "What new projects are going on?" And I think I said, "One of the most fascinating projects at the moment in

Rome is Costa-Gavras's new film." I wasn't saying anything special, but *Variety* had said I was working on the film. I wasn't working on the film. The film wasn't being made. I was working on the script. I had been called in by the backer to do this translation. But then Costa-Gavras sent right away a cablegram to *Variety* saying "Walter has absolutely no part in this film. He's not part of the production." I don't know why he got his dander up. There was no reason. I just was saying what was going on in Rome and all that.

Of course, I stopped everything when the sun went down to have a dinner party or to go out to dinner. Because you can't be a slave to anything. You have to switch buttons. Turn something off, turn something else on. And meanwhile, I was being called in for parts.

It Wasn't Work; It Was My Natural Behavior

I went to Cairo to make this *Arabian Nights* film about Sinbad the Sailor. All the people in the film were Italian or Egyptian, so the villain, of course, was blond in a film in that part of the world. In films for dark-skinned, dark-haired people, the villain is always blond. I was the blond eunuch. I got the costume designer to put a pair of gold scissors for jewels on my turban. I thought the scissors would make it clear for those who didn't understand what a eunuch was: that the balls had been cut off. Nobody caught on. Anyway, I had this fabulous costume, this huge turban, all these ropes of pearls and rubies. And I did sail down the Nile in a galley with all these creatures rowing. I was sitting in this boat, fingering my pearls, you know, as I was rowed down the Nile. It's the only way to travel.

Of course, it was a tiny little fishing boat on which they had built a façade of this galley. It was rather rickety, and I was very nervous as we went rowing down the Nile. I just fingered my pearls and rubies. I remembered as I was coming down the Nile my seventh-grade geography book, one of those Rand McNally geography books, and it had been through so many printings that the photographs in the book were quite gray. One of them said "The Nile at Cairo." There were these palm trees, there were some guys with jugs on their shoulders, and there was a camel. In the distance was a Pyramid and the Sphinx. Well, as I came rocking down the Nile that morning, I looked over and what do you think I saw? I saw a field of cotton and a brick building exactly like Water Street in Mobile. And over the door it said "R. J. Reynolds Tobacco Company." America, the South, went right by me.

It was fun. I loved making that film. Who directed it? Nobody. Who produced it? Nobody. Who wrote it? Nobody. Who was in it? Nobody. But it gave me six weeks in Egypt and some time in the Sahara.

≈

I got to go to Tunisia because of a film *Il Giovane Normale—A Normal Young Man*. It had been a best-selling novel in Italy. Dino Risi was the director of the film, and he had seen me in some awful things, but he liked what I did. So I was a female impersonator with this blond, mile-high wig you could not believe and these earrings to my knees. It's about three Americans on vacation in Europe. They pick up this young Italian boy who's hitchhiking, and they invite him to come along. He has a different relationship with each of them, a changing rapport with these three people as they go down Italy and cross the Sahara into the island of Djerba—it's the Island of the Lotus Eaters in Homer. I played a writer who had left his wife and children, and he sees me as rather corrupt, as having designs on his virginity. So this hitchhiker has a dream in which he sees me in this low-dive café entertaining as a female impersonator. I was so tightly corseted in this costume, and I had a long cigarette holder. If you bit into that thing there, you could make it go z-z-z-z-z and extend. So when I see him in the crowd at the café, I go, "Oooh," and bite into that long cigarette holder. The idea was that young men are changeable and that they do have different relationships with everybody. And are likely to try everything. A normal young man will try anything. That's normal. It's about that old dichotomy between natural and normal. Which gets so confused. It's one of the great confusions of American civilization; they've confused natural and normal. I believe in the natural, not the normal.

This actor whom I hate, the famous young actor, the young leading man who was in *The Garden of the Finzi-Continis,* was the star who played the hitchhiker, the normal young man. Lino Capolicchio was his name. He was an ass. He's impossible to work with; he just mumbles the lines, and none of the other actors can get their cues. He said, "It has to be natural." And I said, "Lino, I have worked with a great many actors in theater and on the screen. The more natural they look, the more you can be sure they've rehearsed." He's just one of those actors who's living the part. There's always some actor or actress like that, who's living the part. Oh so sensitive, you know. They are the people who fall apart if anything goes wrong. I like people who rehearse and who are professional. It's the professional who'll rewrite the play if necessary, but they never let you down.

And Lino Capolicchio got so homesick for Rome that he wasn't eating.

He was suffering the heat and suffering the food. He wouldn't eat anything. Even though a Roman, he was so provincial Italian. So used to his mother hovering over him and feeding him with a spoon. He wouldn't eat the Tunisian food, and he was losing weight like mad. Poor Dino Risi was getting so cranky and saying, "He's going to be a healthy young man in one scene and a ghost in another. What are we going to do? I'm almost ready to throw the whole thing up." Lino's hotel room was next to mine at one location shot, and I could hear him crying. Can you imagine someone twenty-nine years old, missing Mama and Mama's cooking so much that he wasn't eating, was turning pale green, and crying in his bed at night? I shouldn't have told Dino, but Dino was a friend of mine apart from the film. His daughter married Ginny Becker's son, and his brother was married to my Australian friend, Mitty Lee Brown, who was a painter. So I said, "Why don't we get all the Italians who are good cooks into the hotel kitchen and make a couple of proper Italian meals?" I said, "I think it's the food, the homesickness, and missing Mama." So Dino, with Italian Machiavellian artistry, got the mama to call him. And there was one electrician on the set who was apparently a famous cook. Dino just took him off the film and put him in the kitchen in the hotel that day. They finally put that electrician onto just cooking.

Lino Capolicchio was the one that I killed at the end of a film called *The House with Laughing Windows*, in which I played a Brazilian lady who had come to Italy and disguised herself as a man, a country priest. I was the little parish priest who is really a Brazilian lady crook. We filmed it in the Adriatic, and I had one scene with Lino Capolicchio where we are in this tiny little boat on the Pontine marshes of the river Po that flow into the Adriatic. It's where all the eels in every restaurant in Italy come from. There are like three million eels. And I had to catch an eel and get it off the hook and carry on this long conversation with Lino wearing these hot priestly robes out in the sunlight amidst all these eels. And flies. It's one of the hardest things I've ever had to do. I had to pull in the line, catch the eel, hold the line, get the eel off the hook, and go on speaking my lines in this tiny little boat amidst all these eels. Hot.

In the last shot of the film, Lino Capolicchio is wounded and I rip off my priest garment and here are these tits. And I start singing this Portuguese fado. And bring out this knife to kill him. That's the end of the film. And I will never forget sitting in the church in this little country parish at six A.M., naked to the waist, and these three makeup artists gluing this wire-and-foam-rubber thing on me. It took about an hour because they really glued them on me.

In *The Girl in the Yellow Pajamas* I play this eccentric creature who had an apartment full of birdcages and birds flying around. It's based on a real murder in Australia. The young hero who was charged with murder at one moment takes refuge with this crazy guy who has all these birds. That's me. And that's when I had a nude scene coming out of the bathtub with Ray Milland. He was clothed. I was nude, coming out of this bathtub, mooning for the camera. And I'm a pretty white potato, naked, you know. But I figured that everybody there either had something similar to what I have or had seen something similar, so it would be no surprise to anyone.

Another time I played this crooked cardinal who is dealing with real estate. There's a scene where I get off this helicopter in this village in south Italy and all the mob is there throwing rotten vegetables at me. I remember those hot cardinal's robes out in the country and the stink of that helicopter from all the rotten tomatoes. And we shot that scene over and over and over. When I got back to my apartment after filming and read my horoscope, it said "This will be a day of many ups and downs." Lord, Lord. Well, everything for the sake of art.

Oh, I've lived. You can't say I haven't lived. I've been a eunuch floating down the Nile, a female impersonator, a crooked cardinal getting pelted by rotten vegetables; I've been stuck in the eels in the Pontine marshes. You can't say I haven't lived.

I don't think I played any really straight parts. They were always character parts. Mother superiors and cardinals and sexy priests. After I played mother superior for Fellini, then everybody wanted me for a mother superior. And after I played a sheriff for somebody, everybody else wanted me for a sheriff. When they realized I could fall, I had a lot of falling-down roles. I had studied ballet as a child and been in the Children's Theater, you know. I knew how to fall. I could just fall. You let go of everything and fall. Italians don't know how to fall. They are so self-conscious and stand with a certain pride and all that. And they love their own bodies. The Latin male ego is something that somebody needs to write a seventeen-volume study about. It's not as simple as we like to think in the Anglo-Saxon countries. It's much more complex. So they do not fall. The actors do not fall. If somebody is going to be shot and fall down, they'll do the shot several times and get in an acrobat or stuntman to fall down. When they realized I could fall, I found myself playing bank presidents and getaway robbers who were shot. Because I could fall. So I was a falling actor.

In one of my great falling roles I was an industrialist who gets shot by terrorists. I had a scene where I had all these people lined up at this table for a board of directors meeting, and the terrorists burst in and shot me. I was hired for my fall. In another film I was laser-gunned by a Martian and got to fall in this eighteenth-century villa in Adava. Another falling part I had was with Alberto Sordi. He was the lead, and I had the second male part. I've forgotten the name of it; precocious senility has set in. But it was Giulietta Masina and Anita Ekberg and two other great sirens of Italian films, and Alberto Sordi in the lead. I played the manservant from Liverpool of somebody who had died and come back but was invisible to me. I had to look right into his face and not see him and look right past him and all that. And I had to fall on the marble pavement.

My best falling-down role was in Lina Wertmüller's *Ballad of Belle Starr.* I was the safecracker Velvet Fingers in this spaghetti western. I didn't really have time to do the part, but she was in litigation with the producer and was having trouble getting the film made. He wanted it to be much more an American western; she wanted to make it intelligent. It's neither, actually, but it has a cult following now in Italy. I was paid eight years after I did it, but I love her, and I respect and admire her very much. I did all my own high-wire stuff for that, falling off of roofs and swinging on wires. I enjoyed doing that because it was hot summer and it was cool out there at Cinecittà, and they would bring the food and wine up to us on the roof. They said, "Now we've got these acrobats who will double for you." And I said, "No. I have never fallen off a roof before. I've never put an umbrella in my mouth and gone hand over hand on that wire before. I'll do it." It was hot. Those whiskers were hot. But it was fun. It's not hard to fall off a roof. You just relax. There was a whole pile of empty cardboard boxes on the floor, and I am upholstered, you know. There's a first time for everything. As I learned from Miss Mattie T. Graham, you just close your mind and fall.

I also did a lot of commercials, because television commercials in Italy are totally unlike those in America. All the great directors, all kinds of extraordinary actors and actresses, do all these short sketches, and you don't know what they are advertising until the end. The whole idea is to be witty and amusing and then at the end say, "Use such and such scouring powder." There was one where I played a grandfather. I'm in this white suit and all my grandchildren are milling about me in this garden. And they are saying, "Oh, Gramps, do you want us to do a dance? Do you want us to sing something?" "No, no, I know what I want." Then at the end I hold up a bottle of strawberry jam and say, "This is what I want."

There was one charming one I did set on the roof of this Rome apartment house. It's a hot day, and this guy comes out on his roof and he's got all

milking the moon

232

kinds of creams and oils and one of those little reflecting things to put around the face for suntans. He has this towel, and he has this blanket he puts out. It turns out that he's too broke to go to the beach for his vacation. So he stayed at home and didn't answer the telephone and goes up on the roof to get a suntan so he can go back to the office with a tan. Now you would think that's an advertisement for some kind of suntan lotion. It's for prepackaged fried chicken. At the end, he opens a basket and eats some fried chicken. I guess there's a relation. You fry in the sun; the chicken fries in the fat.

After I started, I never stopped working in films. I always got a lot of bits and pieces, more than I can remember. I worked as a coach in certain cases for the English language. As assistant director. As translator of everything. As subtitler. Dubbing dialogue. Or acting. And it was fun. I loved it.

I never saw half the films I made. Take the money and run, you know. I just went and signed the contracts. A week later or a month later they would ring and say, "Well, you are called for tomorrow. The car is coming at six." I'd say, "Sure." I'd work maybe a week, six every morning, and I'd be back home by five or six. Since it was so exhilarating for me to see all those crazy people doing all those crazy things, I was never tired. I was just ready to have cocktails and go to a good restaurant at night. I worked in about a hundred films. I loved it all. How else would I have floated down the Nile? How would I have gone to the island of Djerba? It wasn't work. I tell you there was nothing worklike about it. I guess what I consider work is not what other people consider work. And what I consider fun is not what other people consider fun. It's many a night I stayed up painting scenery or dyeing cloth for something in the theater or writing something for a magazine. But that's fun. I don't think that's work. The only time I almost died was in that bookshop on Fifth Avenue with those tough, awful people. Some people would say, you know, that swinging on a rope three floors above the pavement with an umbrella in your mouth while you're cracking a safe was work. But you see, for me it was my natural behavior.

One of the Great For-Reals

I was working in films and I'd just finished *8½* when I was looking for a place for Leontyne Price, who came to record in Rome every summer for RCA. I had first met her in Paris when she was still a student at Juilliard. She sang in a production of the Virgil Thomson–Gertrude Stein *Four Saints in Three Acts* at a summer festival in Paris which was cast almost entirely from Juilliard. I was with Alice B. Toklas, and she said, "I'm going backstage. Who do you want to meet?" There were no famous names in the cast at all. It was just young people of Juilliard, mostly black. I said, "I want to meet the lady who sang the Santa Cecilia, and that boy who danced the Archangel Gabriel." And if I do say so, that encouraged me to think I might be a serious critic, because the Archangel was Arthur Mitchell, the man who founded the Harlem Ballet, and Santa Cecilia was Mary Leontyne Price. I also saw her backstage when she did *Porgy* in Paris.

Then when she came to Rome much later, she looked me up. She said she was looking for an apartment and asked if I'd help her find one. She said, "Please, I am sick of hotels. I spend my life in hotels. If I am going to spend three months recording in Rome in the summer, I would like an apartment. Find me an apartment." So I'd taken her seriously and was looking. And I found, in this palazzo, one block away from Palazzo Caetani, on the Corso Vittorio Emanuele, an apartment for me on the top and one for her on the floor below. On the top floor was this huge apartment with a terrace half a block long in the front of it. It had a formal dining room that gave onto this terrace overlooking Corso Vittorio. I had just started translating, and I could see that with any luck, I could really make a living. So I could afford this apartment. Later I took another apartment as well which was half a flight higher on the back of the palazzo. I just cut a little door and there was a little stairway that you went up and went through into another apartment. There were four baths, two kitchens, a great deal of space. I filled every bit of it with paintings, books, papers, and cats. I had three different terraces. The one on the street had a great number of iris. I had about a hundred varieties of iris. I even had a child's wading pool so I could have aquatic iris. I had sand pear trees, all in pots, that had pears, and all kinds of greens and herbs and roses like mad.

Leontyne loved her apartment because it was facing east onto this court-yard overlooking a fountain. When she went back to New York after a summer in Rome, in order to sleep in her Greenwich Village apartment, she had to leave her bathtub running all night. The sound of a fountain. She wanted to be on a quiet courtyard so she could sleep late without any traffic sounds. She had a little dining room, and under the window I had painted a wicker basket of oranges. I had painted almost invisible lines of gilt into the wicker, so that when the sun shone at ten in the morning, which would be the time she would be having coffee, it would reflect the light so that the basket suddenly came to life. There was an old, polished honey brown floor, and on the wall I painted little standard trees in urns. I had an oval table that had come from a garden in the suburbs of Rome from a family that owned Corsica in the eighteenth

milking the moon

century and a funny little sideboard that I found. Leontyne loved it all. We had an intercom phone, a little private connecting telephone from her bedside to mine, and saw a lot of each other. We had some marvelous times. It had nothing to do with Leontyne being an opera singer or my working with Italian films. When you got her away from the Music Corporation of America people, and some rather dreary assistants and some dancing boys, she was still Mary Leontyne Price from Laurel, Mississippi. So it was just two Southerners. Whenever I cooked or whenever she cooked, we just did Southern. Leontyne was one of those who cooked fried chicken in a way that you thought it flew in, dropped its feathers outside the window, and jumped into the grease. Because there was no grease. Crunch and succulent, crunch and succulent, crunch and succulent. And Leontyne knew what to do with a bunch of turnip greens. Oh, she was a heavenly creature. She was for real. She was one of the great for-reals.

I tried to take her to a lot of offbeat, small restaurants on one of those little side streets near the Palazzo Barberini that didn't have tourists. She liked some of the places in Trastevere, and I took her to the museum at Ostia Antica.

One year Leontyne was singing *Aida* in this production designed by the artist that I just flipped for at La Scala in Milano. Leontyne has a wild and wonderful sense of humor, and she invited me, saying, "Oh, I'll get you tickets, now don't you worry. I'll get the tickets." I arrived in Milano. She had said just to come on to the theater. "I'm going to be there raising hell all day until that costume is right." They had designed a white dress for Leontyne to wear in the tomb scene, I think. And Leontyne had taken one look and said she would have blue or nothing. She said she would never wear a white costume onstage. She didn't say it, but of course a white costume will make dark skin look darker. So anyway, I went to the theater and sheepishly went up to this ferocious-looking doorman who had a pistol inside his jacket because the student leftist groups had done all kinds of terrorist things in Italy, especially throwing bombs in theaters. He said, "Who are you?" And I said, "Eugenio Walter. Miss Price invited me to come to the show this evening." He said something like "Why are you here so early?" "Because I'm having lunch with Miss Price and the president of La Scala at the restaurant around the corner." "Oh," he said, and picked up a piece of paper. He let me in, and there was Leontyne indeed surrounded by ladies with pins in their mouths and tape measures in front of the mirror, being fitted into a very pretty blue costume. And she said, "Oh, hello, Eugene. Go and sit down out there." She had this anteroom with a chaise longue and a little icebox of her own. So I sat down and waited, and she said, "Oh, your tickets are here somewhere. We'll find them." And then she opened a somewhat battered envelope on the table and said, "Here they are." I didn't look at them, just put them in my pocket.

That night I came to the theater early because I wanted to look around and see who arrived. And when they saw my tickets, they sent this little boy in uniform with me all the way to show me to my seat. In the very middle of the major circle at La Scala is a royal box with two thrones. And that's what Leontyne had gotten for me to sit in. We went up these steps and I thought, Oh, how nice, I like to be up always. Then he parted these curtains and we were in this little antechamber with these little gold chairs. Then he opened some other doors and here were these two thrones on platforms in this velvet box. I said, "There must be some mistake." He said, "No, it was on the tickets."

So I thought, Oh, my God. What about the other ticket? I have two tickets. I want to give somebody a thrill. It was early still. I took a quick gander at the chandelier and rushed out to stand next to the box office. There were some grand Milanese ladies with their pearls and their minks off their shoulders. "What do you mean, sold out?" This was not opening night, but it was a Saturday night the opening week of the production. I stood there and watched several of these ladies saying, "What do you mean? I'm Mrs. So-and-so." "I'm the contessa. There must be a seat for me." "Sorry." Then there was a very snotty journalist from England saying, "I've never had difficulties getting a seat for La Scala. I am the correspondent for So-and-so. And she said, "Well, I'm terribly sorry, but it is sold out completely." She said, "We had several tour buses and we've had students from the Swiss school. Every seat is taken. Standing room only." And he said, "I'm not about to stand to see an opera." She said, "I'm terribly sorry, but if you had called us a week ago . . ." He went off huffy. Then there were some American tourists saying, "Oh, Jesus, all the way to Milan and we can't see *Aida.*" They went off. Then suddenly here was this little man with graying hair and a gray suit, rather pale. Obviously not Italian. In heavily accented Italian which I knew right away had to be Norse of some kind, he said, "Oh, I've come all the way"—from wherever he'd come from—"to see this. I've never heard Leontyne Price, and I've always wanted to see *Aida* and La Scala." And I said, "Here's your ticket." He said, "Hunh? What?" I said, "Here's your ticket. Come with me. You've been designated by the Willoughby Institute to receive a ticket to tonight's show." He looked startled. I didn't look especially important or rich, but I did have the ticket. So he went with me.

The lights had gone down by the time all this had happened, and we just got to the seats in time. I said, "Now just step up and sit down there." He said, "Oh, it's really comfortable." We watched the first act and then the lights went up and he saw this oval-shaped red velvet royal box with this oval ceiling with gods and goddesses painted on it, and honey—you should have seen his face. He said, "Who are you?" I said, "I'm Eugene Walter from Mobile, Alabama. Who are you?" And he said, "I'm So-and-so from Bergen, Norway." I said, "Oh, Bergen. That's the part where all the black-headed Norwegians come from." He said, "You must have studied some history." I said, "No, but I've read about Norway because I have a Norwegian grand-papa." Anyway, this went on, and at the next intermission he told me, "I'm the president of the cheese manufacturers' association of Norway." I said, "Oh, that interests me strangely. I've always loved that bit in *Peer Gynt* where Peer is with those cider girls up there where they take the goats in the summer to those alpine meadows to get fresh green grass for that milk that makes the famous cheese on the mountains. I've never tasted that cheese. I'm dying to taste that cheese." He said, "You mean the *gjetost?*" I said, "Yes, it's *gjetost.*" He said, "Oh well, when you come to Norway, you can taste all the cheeses, I'll see to it." When the opera was over, we left on a jolly note and exchanged addresses. I didn't think any more about it because I was going off to a party with Leontyne after the performance. I said, "Now, Leontyne, honey—" She said, "I knew you'd like it." It was really a great moment.

About a week later, my doorbell rang in Rome and here was an equerry from the Norwegian embassy in Rome with a lovely *gjetost* that had just been flown in. And a beautiful little *gjetost* cutter with a boxwood handle. So I sat down and put on Mozart, and I had some of those whole wheat crunchies that they make in Norway. I crossed myself three times and made a wish and ate my *gjetost*. It was a religious experience. For one minute I was with Peer Gynt in those mountains.

Well, Leontyne had a kind of male secretary who had been a singer. He did everything to make her a prima donna. Hubert Dilwood. He would say things to her like "Oh, we can't accept that part. Those people aren't important enough." Leontyne is an immensely generous, kind person, and her natural self is exuberant, but he had done everything to make her standoffish. One reason I think Leontyne enjoyed her Roman summers is because she was free from the agents, the New York coach, and Hubert. But the minute the secretary arrived, you could see this total change.

When she knew she wasn't going to be in Rome for six months, she asked me to sublet her apartment. I found this very nice young man through the American embassy. I've forgotten what he did. Something interesting—a journalist or publisher. He was very neat. Some people living in somebody else's apartment would destroy it without meaning to. But he was one of those who left the furniture where it was and emptied the ashtrays. Well, that summer, Leontyne came to Rome for a week and stayed in a hotel. She wanted to see the apartment, and I called the young man and said I hoped he wouldn't mind, that Leontyne was coming to me for drinks and dinner, and she'd like to stop by for a few minutes to see her apartment. He said, No, he would be absolutely delighted to meet her. Leontyne was an hour late, being the prima donna, and had this secretary type with her. And the guy who was subletting had come back from someplace by air that day and had stretched out to take a nap. So when they finally arrived, he opened the door wearing a dressing gown. It's not as though he were in dishabille. He was in a very elegant dressing gown. They went in and saw the place, and Leontyne was delighted. Then afterwards this secretary said to her, "That's an insult that this man met you wearing his dressing gown. That's an insult." He just catechized her, coached her in this line. So she was disgruntled by the end of the evening.

Being Northern, he had this overcharged sense of black and white. I hate to divide white and black. As a painter, I see twenty-eight shades of white and three hundred shades of honey color, crème caramel, café au lait, chocolate, ebony, jet. But he was always pointing out purported slights to Leontyne and making her nervous. Leontyne is of the open mind and of a vast sense of humor, and she had no chips on her shoulders, but finally I think she believed some of them. He was a pain in the ass. And he really sort of put a wedge between us, because I said something like "Oh, he's crazy, you know. Don't listen to him." And she told me with a giggle one day, "He really would like to wear my costumes and sing my roles." And one of the more interesting points about him: You'd be talking to him and he would just fall asleep. It's that ailment only properly identified in recent years— narcolepsy. Anyway, I think he was jealous of anybody who got close to her. He fancied himself as a kind of Phantom of the Opera, running interference and making reservations on trains and planes. Because Leontyne is woman, child, and artist. More than that, she's Southern woman, child, and artist. So in places like Vienna or Stockholm, she needed a toughie to help her get in and out of hotels or flag taxis or this or that. But she finally got overprotected, and we just sort of had a "coolth." Instead of a warmth, a coolth. We never really stopped being friends. Just the minuet ended. You see, most of my Aquarius lady friends have a seven-year life. We have a close friendship for seven years, and then we sort of fade away. I've had about eight Aquarius ladies, and it was always that pattern. I know that on the seventh year, we'll have a quarrel. It's a Sagittarius-Aquarius pattern. But I know that someday, in a restaurant in Vienna or on the street in New York, or going in or coming out of Saks Fifth Avenue, I know we'll meet. And pick up. And start a new minuet.

I Loved That Neighborhood

The Corso Vittorio Emanuele was a main thoroughfare on the site of an old Roman road. It's a wide street, compared to many of the side streets which are medieval in their narrowness, since medieval Rome was built over the ruins of ancient Rome. Just at the corner from the palazzo where I lived, there is a very famous ancient Roman residence that somehow survived intact. Around 1900 they were about to build some apartment houses on that block, and they had to stop because here was a beautifully preserved, ancient Roman residence with kitchens and baths, a latrine and everything, way below sidewalk level. It had belonged to the Argentina family, a noble Roman family, so they called it Largo di Torre Argentina. It's a sunken piazza with a mosaic pavement, and it's full of stray cats, street cats.

At one moment, all the stray cats that lived in this sunken piazza discovered how to get into the theater that had been built on top of this Roman residence in the 1700s, where *The Barber of Seville* had its first performance. One cold winter night they just walked in. The theater was closed because there had been trouble with the ceiling, and it was about a year before they got all the funds and the restoration was approved by the city council. The usual story of city government. They went one day to open it, and the stench apparently could have caused a strong man to swoon. When they went into the theater itself, looking up over all these seats were these glittering eyes. They got a man who played the flute and was some pied piper who piped rats out of barns, and he tried to pipe them out, but with no luck. Finally he just dragged an old undershirt soaked in tuna-fish juice and got them all back out. Crazy Rome.

There was a Renaissance palace on the other side of the street, and it sat on a little piazza where there was a church, la Chiesa del Gesù, the headquarters of the Jesuit order with its lovely Baroque curls. That's what I saw at the end of my terrace, this façade. At the other end of my terrace I saw the Church of Sant'Andrea della Valle, which is where the first act of *Tosca* takes place. And next door on the other side was another Renaissance palace. Then at the corner was a turn-of-the-century Banca di Roma, the Rome bank. Catty-corner was the palazzo where Anna Magnani lived, and where Eugene Berman lived. John Cheever stayed there for a while when he lived in Rome.

Right across the street was the Puerto Rico coffee shop that sold chocolate and bonbons and coffee. All kinds of coffee. There was a fresh fruit and vegetable place where they went to some little town early in the morning to pick up their stuff. And it was he who told me, after I had been dealing with him for about a year, he said, "Signor Walter, you know, you make such a fuss, paying every time." He said, "Now everybody here, really, they have a running account and pay once a week or once a month." I realized, of course, that they charged a little fee for this, but you see, they delivered right to my apartment, even when they had to walk up five flights before the elevator was put into this Baroque palace. They delivered. As did the bakery. As did the mushroom shop. As did the wine shop. As did the butcher. As did the delicatessen. When the first sausages came, sometimes the delicatessen man would call me and say, "Signor Walter, the *salsicce di stagione* just came in from the country." Now, there are some sausages you age; they just hang in the storeroom forever because they're smoked and they're made to do that. But some sausages you eat instantly, like the blood sausages and some of the white sausages. You just eat them when they're ready. I'd say, "Well, send them over." And the young man and his mother who owned the wine shop went out into the country to buy wine, which they bottled and put under their own label. It was this country wine. Some of it was so good, because it was made on a farm in a small quantity in old wooden casks as they've done it for centuries. There was nothing added. It was all wine. Wherever they would go, they'd always bring me a bottle of whatever that farm wine was. Across from the wine shop was a mushroom shop. It had blue and white tiles and a gray tile floor. The tables were oiled slate, very shiny. And then there were just these little baskets with every kind of mushroom they'd gotten from their secret pickups. Nobody would tell what groves or what glades or where the mushrooms came from. They had their country people who would meet them by the highway. And they had all these baskets; you could get a hundred different kinds. And of course, that bakery. I mean, it was worth getting up early in the morning and going on the terrace because the whole neighborhood was filled with these smells of fresh bread. And when I say fresh bread, I don't mean cotton wadding and cardboard. I mean bread. And I could call the greengrocer and say, "Have you any—" It was these long, green fleshy leaves that were called *barba de frati*—monk's beards or friar's beards—these prickly green things. You boiled them and buttered them and ate them, and oh, God, were they good. They're like nothing else on earth. I always liked some crumbled bacon on mine. I never found out what they are botanically. They don't grow commercially. They grow somewhere in the woods, and people pick them. They just pull them up by the bunches when they're ready, and that's it. They're in the market for two weeks and never again and never before. That's one of the things that people tell each other as they pass them on the street. "Yes, the first of the season—they're in." I could tell my greengrocer, "I want three bunches. And ask the boy to pick up the paper at the newsstand and a loaf of bread at the bakery on his way." And that's the way it was.

The people in my neighborhood were all such fun, and they were all fascinated by me. They were my friends. The dear old lady and her dear goopy son who had the fresh fruit and vegetable market a block away from where I lived were my friends. The newsstand dealer was my friend. The barber was my friend. I liked to talk to them. At first they just thought I was this quiet and studious type living in their neighborhood. Then they began to realize that I was in movies, or they would see me in a commercial on television. Little by little they got a picture of me. They would linger when they delivered things.

Some of these shops were on the Via del Gesù, which is this narrow street of little shops with apartments above. Then in the middle of the block is a small Baroque palace, and across from it is a kind of tiny little piazza. Then on the other side of the Largo di Torre Argentina, the Roman ruin square, there was another narrow street, and it had a lot of little shops. It had the delicatessen. It had the greengrocer. It also had a couple of Baroque palaces. All of these things grew up around the palaces. I suppose once it was lean-tos or tents or something, and then little by little the people who swept the street in front of the palace were given space to build something. So there are all these strange little buildings. Then another street over you would have printers and engravers and craft people. Everything is all mixed up, you know, like downtown Mobile. I loved that neighborhood.

I immediately got a maid and, shortly thereafter, a secretary for three hours every morning. For a working day I had to have a maid and a secretary. The secretaries were all pretty young girls; no middle-aged ladies. The first was Margaret Aubrey Smith, a very pretty English girl with brown hair, brown eyes, pink cheeks. She was a cat lover—passionate cat lover—thank God. Then this very pretty girl named Theodora Lurie, a distant, distant, distant, distant cousin of Alison Lurie. Then there was a girl who lasted only a month. Her lover was a violinist in the London something orchestra, and she followed her lover from school and London to Rome. And he was going on down to Sicily, so she went off with my keys and petty cash. About a month later she came in and apologized and said she had to do it, had to do it. I said,

241

"Oh, youth." What do you say? "You crazy little slut, you didn't have to take the keys and the money?"

Then I had an awful criminal type, an Irish girl who was slightly demented. She was the friend of the girl who had been hired as a companion to Olivia Hussey, who played Juliet in Zeffirelli's *Romeo and Juliet*. The secretary-companion was about three years older than Olivia, and she went everywhere with her, took care of her, helped her, listened to her lines, and all that. Olivia had a tendency to get fat, and the film producers put her on this terrible diet, and that's one of the things the chaperone had to do: watch and see she didn't eat. But I always invited Romeo and Juliet for late dinners and always cooked up whole potatoes drowned in butter for Olivia, because she was working hard, the poor darling.

When *Romeo and Juliet* was finished, I was looking for a secretary, and this Irish girl came to apply for the job. She heard of it through Olivia. The first day she came, she was wearing a miniskirt that barely covered her pubic hairs. I mean, if there had been one bit of exhaust from a bus, everything would have been revealed. And she had makeup like a signboard for Pizza Hut. And of course, it was the day that there was an archbishop going to call on the countess two floors below. They came in together. I said to her, "I think you ought to wear a more secretarial costume, because there are clergymen around here, and this is a Catholic country." I think she thought that since I was of the film set, I would be racy, you see. Afterwards she always came in that English uniform for ladies: a jacket and a skirt with pleats and a sweater and a string of beads and just a little lipstick.

But she was demented. Time and again I would give her a script to deliver in a big hurry, and I'd give her money for the taxi. Well, she'd take the bus and keep the taxi money. Not only that, somebody was always saying, "Oh, I saw Marilyn in the such and such shop on the Via Veneto yesterday morning." She would have just wandered about, window-shopping, for hours. I would say, "Did it really take two hours to get there?" And she'd say, "Oh, it was another one of those traffic jams." Then, of course, there was her lover, a thoroughgoing crook. He worked for the Hindu embassy, and somehow he was able to smuggle precious stones through diplomatic channels and sell them in Rome. He came one day to ask if I would let him use my apartment to give a party. And would I invite my friends because he wanted to sell his precious and semiprecious stones? And I said, "Oh, I'm sorry, but I can't really do it." He was furious, and she was furious. So she quit and then tried to sue me for social security.

But most of my secretaries stayed until they found a better job that paid

milking the moon

more. It was three hours every morning, and they typed, answered the telephone, did the accounts, collected bills from film studios, paid the light bill and the gas bill and the maid. And did some shopping. Occasionally—not always—they took my laundry to the laundry, dry cleaning to the dry cleaner's. It was an easy job, and I always asked them to lunch, which wasn't part of the contract. For two of them, they would come to me from nine to twelve and have lunch, then go to Muriel Spark from two to four. For Margaret Aubrey Smith, I found a penthouse apartment on the old servants' wing of the palazzo where I lived. She had a charming artist's studio with a huge terrace. I tried to treat them as family rather than hired hands.

After I had moved to Corso Vittorio, Miss Calico adopted me. I didn't adopt her. She lived in the block, this tabby, calico cat. This shoemaker had taken her in when she was pregnant because she didn't have any place in the street to have kittens. He used this tiny alley not far from where I lived. He gave her a box where she would take these kittens out to sit in the sun. One day a truck, which under law was not supposed to go in that alley, came sailing through and killed all four kittens. Smashed them flat. And she went around crying all over the neighborhood. So I got her into the courtyard of the palace where I lived and fed her and gave her a wooden box in one corner of this courtyard where she could stay at night. Once a day I'd feed her, and she more or less realized that the palazzo where I lived was her domain.

She eventually found her way up five flights of steps to where I lived on the top floor. That was before there was an elevator. Then later the countess put in an elevator. The elevator had only been in twenty-four hours when Miss Calico started using it to get to my floor. And she would never get in the elevator with anybody going to any other floor. Nobody knows how she knew to get in with somebody going to the fifth floor. It was a source of wonderment to all concerned. This dizzy countess who owned the building would always say, "I do not understand how Miss Calico chooses the person who goes to you." Nobody could figure it out. Well, she knew where the cooking was going on, bless her heart.

She came to me to eat and to have kittens. She'd tell me when she was going to have the kittens, and I had this screen I'd set up in the corner of the landing with two boxes behind it, one for her to have them and one for her to put the kittens in. I'd lay out a smorgasbord arrangement, you know. And oh, she had beautiful kittens.

But she was a strange and biggity street cat. She never would come in my apartment. Wouldn't come in. She found her way over the roof of the palace to my terrace. And at night, in the winter when the doors were closed and my cats weren't on the terrace, she'd march up and down my terrace. Go back over the roof, and she went through some other palace. Down the stairs to the courtyard.

She was something. And I loved her.

Well, one day there was this guy out walking his dog. He'd taken off the leash and the muzzle. The muzzle was hanging on the dog's collar, and he was swinging the leash. In Rome, there is a law that if you take a dog out of your house, or if you have a dog at all, when it is in the street, it has to have a muzzle and a leash. It cannot go free. That's because of the prevalence of rabies in Italy.

Calico had begun, at that time, to sit in this vast *portone*, the huge carriage door in the Roman palaces. It's in several sections and opens. There is always a little door for people. But usually in the daytime for cross-draft, they open the huge *portone*. She would sit there watching traffic and saying, "Actually, I'm the countess. There's another pretender living on the fourth floor, but I am the countess."

Well, this dog attacked her. Lunged for her. Calico was a very quick street cat, and she rose like an angel of song and bit the man's chin and fled. And the man, of course, realizing that he'd caused this fuss, quickly got his dog leashed and all that. And left in a hurry. But his wife apparently convinced him the cat might have rabies. So he hired these two thugs to go and catch Miss Calico. They were apparently skulking about the neighborhood because later someone told me they had seen these two guys at the corner and then at the other corner. They finally followed her into the courtyard and caught her and took her off in a pillowcase they were carrying. Took her off to the pound. At the pound, they always kept them for ten days in quarantine to see if they had rabies and then sold them to laboratories and all kinds of things—fur factories and everything.

Well. She didn't show up for dinner one night. And she was regular. She came right up to my floor. Either caught a ride or walked those flights. And she wasn't there for breakfast the next day, and I was really beginning to worry. So at noon I went to this nice lady who had the Puerto Rico Coffee Company across the street, which is a bonbon shop that sold freshly ground blends and all kinds of candies and chocolates, some of which she made. Very old shop. Now, every block in Rome has a kind of secret service agent. Someone who knows everybody's business. So I went over to this shop and told her that Miss Calico was missing and asked if she'd seen her. She said, "Miss

244

Calico is missing?" She was a great cat lover, this lady. "Oh," she said, "we'll find out. She has to be somewhere in the neighborhood because she never leaves this block." So she closed the shop and sent the three girls who worked in the shop out to canvass the neighborhood, door by door. And they reported, yes, in fact, they had talked to a street sweeper, and the street sweeper told me the whole story. But nobody knew where she'd gone.

Well, the bonbon lady got on the blower and called Anna Magnani, who was at the other corner in another Roman palace with her twenty-three cats. Just like my grandmother: twenty-three cats. Anna Magnani was the great Italian actress who was in several of the great Italian films that came out of Italy just after the war. She made *The Rose Tattoo* in Hollywood. She was a big international star and was a friend of Fellini's, so I met her when she visited on the set of *8½*. She had a three-story apartment. Her son, who had infantile paralysis, was about nineteen then, in a wheelchair, paralyzed from the waist down. He had a flat of his own with this lady who looked after him. He had cats. Then she was the floor below and had more cats. There was a top floor where there were servants and some more cats.

So the bonbon lady called Anna Magnani. Anna Magnani said, "Not that pretty tabby, red-and-white cat at number eighteen?" The lady said yes. "She belongs to a nice American writer who lives there." "Oh," said Anna Magnani. "Well." So Anna Magnani called the mayor of Rome. She said, "You know, excellent sir, this is Anna Magnani. I need a favor." Of course, he fell on the floor, you know, and swooned. And she said, "There is this cat, this timid little house cat, belongs to this nice American writer here in number eighteen Corso Vittorio, and somebody has stolen it, and we think—we fear—that she might end up at the pound. And we've got to find that cat." And he said, "Oh, yes, we'll put a plainclothesman on it."

He found Miss Calico in this particular pound. They had taken her, and maybe they'd gotten a few lire for it. And the plainclothesman told the mayor, and the mayor called Anna Magnani, and Anna Magnani called the bonbon lady. The bonbon lady sent one of the girls over to my apartment. Well, I dropped everything. That was when I had this delicious English girl Margaret Aubrey Smith as my secretary—pretty, Yardley lavender child. She was also a great cat lover. We jumped in a taxi, rushed to this place. And we just went in; we stormed in. The doorman was saying, "You can't go in. You have to get a pass from the director. He's over that way." But we had to find Calico.

We couldn't find her. There were hundreds of dogs barking. Three tiers of cages. All of the dogs were barking. The cats were all silent. A rather gray atmosphere. Finally we passed back again for the third time, and Calico's unmistakable voice spoke. This raucous voice. From the bottom level. She was on the ground. The cage was full of water because they flooded the cages to wash them. She was sitting in the corner, half leaning on the wall.

I didn't recognize her AT ALL. Her red had faded. She was a calico, but she was tabby, white and red. And the red had faded. The shock of being snatched, stuffed into a pillowcase, hauled off, and put in a cage and then watered—the sheer shock. She was also in the beginning of pregnancy.

We were both absolutely destroyed. And we had rehearsed. I had said, "I want to tell how she's this kitten that we found and how we've raised her. But when I get to the point where I have to stop, then you go ahead with the story." Well, of course, we went into his office and we both burst into tears. Margaret and I just both burst into tears. He was saying, "Oh, my . . ." But we had to fill out these forms. We had to tell our names, our parents' names, our four grandparents' names, dates of birth, birthplaces, our education, our occupations. I couldn't remember any of it. He said, "There will be a fine, but you can come at the end of ten days and get her."

We went every day. I would go one time, and Margaret would go another. To take food and milk and to talk to her. Then we organized a lot of grand people to call on her. The very grand Sicilian princess Her Serene Highness, the Princess Topazia Alliata de Sallaparuta, would go. She had a battered car, a beat-up old Fiat, because she didn't have any money. None of the Sicilians have any money. They owned vast acres. Her properties were big enough to show on a map of Sicily as a little province within a province. That's what "Serene Highness" means: you are not the ruling monarch of a country, but your properties are big enough to show on a map of the world. The idea is that if you own that much real estate, you are serene. But she didn't have any cash. So she borrowed from some fancy doctor in her neighborhood a big black car and got the boy from the chicken market in her neighborhood to drive her. She dressed, wore jewelry, and she arrived and asked at the door for Miss Calico. We had the Countess Gnoli, and we had a couple of actresses, including Barbara Steele, the English actress. She was one of the young actresses in *8½*. Willowy and demented and always dressed in something very outré. And we had the Baron Saint-Just, the painter that I introduced to Hans Werner Henze and who became the great stage designer of the Hamburg Opera and La Scala and everything. We had all the grand-looking people we could get. And Mary Harding, of course, who wrote *Dear Friends and Darling Romans*. Mary Chamberlin Harding is this little lady who played children on Broadway when she was thirty-five years old. Because she was so tiny. She's petite and of that French type eternal female. She had three

milking the moon

husbands and eighty-five lovers and was a success on Broadway. She came to Rome for two weeks and stayed twenty-five years.

About the seventh day, the director calls in and says, "Well, look, I suppose you all could take this cat." He said, "There are so many people who seem interested in her." And he said, "We really can't have this traffic coming in and out of the pound." I noticed the last two days her cage was dry. I learned later that Her Serene Highness had complained to the director.

Anna Magnani never knew that the young man she'd met on the set of *8½* was the same as the American writer whose cat was stolen. Who, at the same time as she every night, threw food scraps to the cats in the Piazza Argentina. I was three different people in her life.

I've always had animals. One should never lose contact with growing things or furry things. Never. Because they say, "Well, look here," you know. "You are so busy with your problems and your thoughts, and it ain't like that. We live in a huge, varied world." When I'm feeling at my worst with some of the disasters that have occurred, I only have to look at these darlings to be reassured. Because they say: "You fool." They say: "You human fool."

I had my first cat when I was in Trastevere. Paul Wolfe the harpsichordist and myself and I've forgotten who else went to meet this wonderful soprano, Emelina di Vita, at the train station when she came back from her triumph in Germany. I got all the composers and musicians I could gather to make a party at the station and greet her coming back to Italy. I wanted this cheering section because she'd had such a struggle and then triumphed in Germany as Elektra. I thought she deserved a mob scene. That evening we had a party at somebody else's place up on the top of the Janiculum Hill. My place was too small. When it was over, there was a lot of food left, so I was taking some home. On my way back, this strange animal—I couldn't tell what it was—jumped out of the bushes. Then it said, "Meow, I'm hungry." It was this poor cat who had gotten into tar or oil and then sand and was just a mess. So I fed it and walked on. Then half a block later, I heard these little velvet paws in the grass. "I'm hungry." So I gave it some more and went on. The third time I said, "Oh, for Christ's sake, just come with me." And I picked it up and took it home, and with an old towel and some warm water, I tried to clean it up. It was a perfectly beautiful tabby with some white. That was Felix. He stayed with me forever, died just before his eighteenth birthday, shortly before I was going to leave Rome.

Opening the Windows and Throwing Those Lire Out

Well, two decades passed while I wasn't noticing. Between acting and translating, I lived high on the hog. And since nobody ever told me that if you put money in the bank it draws interest, I just had a two-story apartment and a maid and a secretary and opened those windows and threw the lire out. And gave parties.

You might say I'm professional. I profess to give interesting parties. And I work to give an interesting party. I like to make people meet people. I like to make people have dishes they never tasted before. So, since I profess all of this, I guess I'm professional. I tried hard; I worked at it. After all, fun is worth any amount of preparation.

I don't make lists or anything, but I think it out some days before. Then I get up early on the day and do everything that can be done. At a given moment I like to say in Hindu, "Thus far and no farther." Then I stop and go have a bath. I put on talcum powder and a little cologne, comb my hair real good, and sit down and have some Jim Beam. I pretend that the servants did all the work. Pretend that I came in from riding the limits of the plantation. Had a quiet bath with two slaves scrubbing my back, saying, "Yes, massa." And bringing that bourbon on a little servant tray, and then the butler comes and says, "I hear the doorbell. The first guest is arriving, sir." For a perfect party, you see, the host should always seem to have the use of twenty servants and be absolutely as though you had come to the party after a long afternoon nap, a bath, and a good splash of Yardley. That wasn't the case, of course. Quite often up until five minutes before the first guest I was running around like mad. I did have my maid and my secretary, who were great help in the morning preparations. I usually had the table set in advance, because the kitty cats were more often on the terrace and in a front room that they seemed to like, so they didn't climb on and rearrange the table setting.

I loved arranging surprises, and the food was never really complicated. But I always had something that nobody expected, that startled people. My kind of antipasto dish was an English tea muffin very lightly buttered and very lightly toasted. Then with a light thing of mustard and a thick thing of peanut butter. Put back in the oven till the peanut butter was almost bubbling, it was so hot. Then on top of that you put ice-cold bread-and-butter pickles and bring it to the table. Everybody startled out of their wits, you know. One time I just cooked up some eggplants, took the peelings off, and lined them in a buttered casserole. I made this divine mixture of all kinds of things and baked it and turned it out on a plate. I had buttered the thing so heavily that it came out looking like patent leather. So I called it patent-leather pie. It's not patent-leather pie. It's an eggplant casserole. That doesn't matter. The title was catchy. They loved it.

I'm not a chef. I'm an experimental scullery boy. I like to eat. I'm a greedy guts, and any greedy guts becomes a good cook after exposure to simple utensils, a knowledge of heated coals, and a knowledge of seasonings. I never gave up the idea of having twice as much food as you need for the number of guests. That's Southern hospitality. If you are having four people for dinner, you always have enough for eight. Unlike New York, where they will have four lamb chops for four people. And a Renoir on the walls of this lovely dining room, French porcelain, French crystal, a servant in uniform. But four people, four lamb chops. Suppose somebody was hungry. You always have to say: "Take two; they are small." Never say, "Do you want some more?" It's, "You must have a lamb chop," as if they hadn't had one, you know. It doesn't matter whether you have fancy food or not, there's got to be enough for everybody and some left over. You might be inventing leftover dishes for a week. The servants might come to loathe lamb chops. But it's just a law of hospitality. Lord, Lord.

And I always had different courses. I never did buffet. I happen to hate buffet. If you're going to have a dinner, somebody should serve it. Only a couple of times did I get servants in when I had like twelve at the table. But I could handle ten easily. And I always liked to have flowers in the place, always tried to help people who have never met people, always liked to make a mixed batch for any gathering. If everybody knows everybody at a party, then it's not a party. It's only a family reunion. And you always have to have some surprises. I tried to have a surprise attraction at every party, like once I had a horse trainer from the circus. And then I had that ancient Swiss vocal teacher who had taught Gwyneth Jones and Leontyne Price. Once I just put a bowl of Silly Putty on the table. I don't think anybody went away from one of my parties and put it out of their mind as they left my door. Nobody has ever left my hospitality totally depressed.

One night there were these dreary professors who were sent to me from some university. They were brilliant and had published all kinds of things, but they just weren't party people. They didn't realize that unserious is much more serious than serious. It was difficult to get through to them and say, "You are not in Minneapolis tonight. You are south of the salt line." So often it's professors who have gotten to a certain stage in their academic careers that they have put their minds in cold storage. They have no curiosity about the new books or the other side of town or what's blooming at the botanical gardens this week. Or what they talked about at the party last night. That sort of mind's in cold storage. Some of them are very intelligent, but they have just stopped being in touch with the world. So that party of professors was not what I call a party. It was like unrelated spirits. Then I suddenly remembered that a friend of mine had left a phonograph machine at my apartment. So I plugged it in and got out all my 1920s records. And they all died. They slipped slowly out of their carapaces.

I had a party once for Gwyneth Jones, the Welsh soprano, who was coming to Rome with her first husband, who was a Welsh poacher. Gwyneth told me that she learned her roles outdoors. She would sit on the banks of this river watching for the woodsman or whoever owned the property while her husband was poaching wild fowl and rabbits. I can't remember now how I met her. It's one of those things. Some people I've known forever from other lives. We may have come down the Nile together on a barge early on. I don't mean in a movie. But I guess I met her at a party. There was something about her. I just went right over to her. We talked, and she said she was a vocal student. She was just beginning to sing. I told her, "I can see you as Aida." Said it right there at that party. She kind of laughed. And then of course, years later—years later— she was brought to Rome to sing Aida. And she invited me to the gala.

Anyway, Gywneth said that she, her husband, her mother-in-law, and her Hungarian singing coach all were coming to Rome around the same week, and she thought it would be amusing for them to see my Roman palace. That was one of the most amazing parties I've ever given. I just had those four, and then I had some scene designer who did opera. I can't think who. So there were six at the table.

I had decided since the leek is a Welsh symbol and since you can almost always get beautiful little fresh leeks in the market in Rome, I was going to have caramelized leek as a separate dish by itself to begin. You take a little bit of sugar which you use to make the coloring this lovely shade of honey as you cook them very, very slowly in the skillet in unsalted butter. Then I had some real Hungarian paprika, which is a mild paprika with a different flavor. It's made from a slightly different pepper. Since the lady was Hungarian, I was having a chicken with that paprika. There were fresh beans—some little dark beans. I didn't know what they were. Still don't. They were unlike any other beans, dark brown and little. I had gotten up early and gone to market and shelled three millions, because that was the moment of those beans. And of course, a salad. Everybody always wanted salad when they came to Rome because the greens sat with mama in the country until that morning.

Well, now, my stove ran on a *bombola*. What do they call those iron containers? It's a *bombola* in Italian. My stove ran on a big one of those that fitted into a compartment in this very modern stove. I would never use the gas system, because in Rome, if you live on the top floor, at a certain time of the morning, noon, and evening, everybody is cooking. And the pressure just doesn't reach the top floor, because it's ancient piping from the turn of the century. It's much better to have one of these *bombola*s, you know. It's exactly like any gas stove, but these were attached to the tanks.

While everything was cooking, I shaved and jumped in and out of the tub. Just as I put on my shirt, the *bombola* ran out. The *bombola* has a life of about a month. All I had to do was call the corner and the *bombola* woman would send the *bombola* boy. But it was a day in the week that they were closed. There was an emergency *bombola* place, but it was across town. There was nowhere. So I hastily dug out of the closet my little hot plate. I said, "My God, what am I gonna do?" I had this vat that I put on the hot plate, and I dumped everything in there. I put the leeks, the peas, chicken, and the paprika. I said, "I think I'm going to call this Hungarian stew." And I thought, I'll just open black olives and green olives and little French gherkins and have hors d'oeuvres *variés* to begin, and then go right away to a big plate of Hungarian stew, and then salad and then fruit. And hope for the best.

But there was something about the weight of this huge vat on this tiny hot plate that it blew a fuse. All the lights went out. I had candles on the table, but I quickly dug out every box of candles I had and put them all over the place. I hastily pulled myself together, was just sticking my shirttail in, when the doorbell rang. I opened the door, and here were these two little old ladies from Wales. They were wearing their Sunday-go-to-meeting best and they had these little fur stoles and they'd been to the beauty parlor and had their hair crimped. Behind was Gwyneth and her husband, the poacher. I was this wild-haired figure leaning out of this dark apartment, saying, "Welcome, welcome. I'm trying to do a real Roman evening for you. Come in." I quickly served sherry, and bourbon to the poacher. I said, "You will think it's strange our main dish is warm rather than hot. But in Rome in the warm weather, we always prefer the food lukewarm. As you will notice in restaurants, it's never really hot." "Oh yes," they said, "we noticed that in London in the restaurants." I had taken all the tomato slices out of the salad and put them on these plates with the green and black olives and those little cocktail onions. And thank God I had some breadsticks and a beautiful wine. And I carefully opened a lot of bottles. Like a bottle almost to every place.

Then when I served my stew, the Hungarian vocal teacher tasted it and put her fork down. I'll never forget the color of red on her hair. She had henna like you have never seen, and enough mascara to do India-ink drawings for generations. You would have had to take orange Easter egg dye, henna dye, and red drawing ink to get that red. And the white skin and the black, black, black around the eyes. She tasted it rather gingerly—I mean, rather paprikaly. She put her fork down and said, "Eugene, I haven't tasted this since I was a little girl. My grandmother used to make this stew." I said, "Oh yes, I've always loved Hungarian food." That was a great party. It was a great party.

One day I was sitting minding my own business in Rome and the telephone rang. This charming voice that I thought sounded familiar said hello. "Is that Eugene Walter?" "Yes." "Is it true your cat Felix wags his tail like a dog?" And I said, "Well, he does have a special wave, but I don't think it's like a dog." I said, "Who is this?" She said, "If I came to Rome, would someone give me a party?" I said, "Well, yes, but who is this?" And she said, "Well, this is Judy Garland." I was about to say "Come again?" but then I recognized the voice. "Mark says that your cat Felix wags his tail like a dog. So if I came to Rome, would someone give me a party?"

Well, sure. Someone would.

She had married this actor Mark Herron, who was in *8½*. I had met him on the set. He must have told her about my cats.

So she came, and I met her at the airport with two dozen American Beauty roses—I did it right. I would never take American Beauty roses to anybody on earth except a movie star because I don't like those long-stem hothouse roses. They wilt after ten minutes. I would have taken flowers from my terrace for anybody else, but American movie stars have to have two dozen long-stem American Beauty roses or they'll look sniffy. I alerted the press because she likes that attention. There were a lot of flashbulbs going and all that. I know how to handle prima donnas.

And we had this wonderful evening, just Judy and her husband and myself. Wonderful evening. We sat on my terrace and watched the sun go down and drank mint juleps because I had mint right there on the terrace, and we talked and talked and talked and then went and had dinner at a wonderful little restaurant. An offbeat restaurant where a lot of doctors and lawyers went, where everything was still cooked on a woodstove in the back. It was a famous restaurant among upper-class Italians, but not a tourist in sight. Had a little terrace on the street side. There was no traffic on that street ever—it was a side street. So we ate on the terrace, and she liked that.

About halfway through the meal she said, "Excuse me," and got in the limousine and went back to her hotel and went to the bathroom and came back. There was a chauffeur-driven limousine parked right outside. And she couldn't use a public rest room even in the fanciest of restaurants. The chauffeured car would drive her back to her hotel, which she had to do several times in the course of a six- or seven-hour evening. I was so struck by all that. And I noticed that under her three rows of real pearls on each wrist— adhesive tape. She must have done the Gillette act. But nobody said anything about it, you know. And I certainly didn't look twice after I noticed it. I looked at other things.

After our dinner at the restaurant we went to the Piazza Navona, which has this famous ice-cream place. We sat there and a lot of people were nudging each other, but nobody made a fuss. There is something curious about the Romans—even if they recognize somebody, they won't crowd them. In Naples, my God, you'd be killed in a minute from the lack of oxygen. But the Romans—after all, they've been seeing celebrities since long before Christ. Cleopatra did sail up the Tiber and get off, you know, in Rome. So they are used to it.

She did tell some good stories. Especially about Louis Mayer—what an old shit he was. She was only—what? fifteen, thirteen—and was under contract to MGM. They always closed down for a couple of weeks in the summer. So she was called to Louis Mayer's office. She hated him and was afraid of him. Apparently he called her the no-neck monster, because she had a very small torso, long legs, and not a long neck. And this nice lady was there who coached her in singing and was kind of an assistant. And he said, "Well, Maybelle"—whoever the singing instructor was—"what are we going to do with the no-neck monster this summer?" And the singing teacher said, "Well, you know, Joan Crawford has gone to spend the summer in New York. Why don't we send her to New York, and she could go to some museums and see some musicals, and we'll ask Joan to look out for her there." And he said, "Yeah, it's a good idea. Call that tart and see what she's planning for this summer."

Joan Crawford—that tart.

So with fear and trembling, Judy went to New York. And it was just like my going to call on the Shadow with my box of paintbrushes. She had an old suitcase—this battered thing—that she had taken along with her. And she went to the doorman at the Ritz and said, "I've come to see Miss Crawford." He thought it was some demented fan that had hitchhiked from Iowa or something. And he said, "The service entrance is over there." But some bellboy or something who had been told to look out for this child traveling alone said, "Oh, that must be Miss Garland," and they sent her up to Joan.

Judy said there was this secretary/companion that Joan had who was a very masculine lady with very short hair and a very masculine suit with a little bow tie and smoking one cigarette after another. Judy rang the doorbell, and this woman answered the door and said, "Oh, for Christ's sake, child, get in here quick before somebody sees you." Because she was dressed in a costume she had worn for one of her films. She had a green angora sweater on and a chartreuse green skirt with appliqué black-and-white music notes.

The woman said, "We're going to take you to the theater tonight, but you can't go like that." And she said, "Joan, we'll have to find something for this child to wear, because when you see it, you're not going to believe it." Joan was back there showering, and her voice came, "You mean they didn't fix her up?" And the woman said, "I guess they didn't."

There was a long corridor lined with double clothes racks. Joan would have six of the same dress in slightly different tints, starting with pale blue and ending with indigo. And as for jewelry, there was apparently a whole wall safe you could walk into. But anyway, the woman found her something very simple and got down and looped up the hem a little bit. So Judy was in this very plain dress, no jewelry, no makeup. Then Joan came in and said, "Well, they said to take care of you. We are going to the theater."

Joan got this fur coat, big thick longhaired fur with big shoulders. This thing was from her shoulders to the floor. Longhaired fur. It was August in New York. August in New York. Judy said it was yellowish and looked rather like some kind of collie.

The tough one said, "Well, Joan, do you want to slip out the back way, or do you want to brave the fans?"

Louis Mayer always hired twenty people to go wherever Joan was in New York and shout, "Joan, Joan, Joan," until everybody else on the streets joined them. You know: the star. The star was in New York.

And so Joan said, "Well, look, Mabel"—whatever the tough's name was—"we're supposed to take care of this child and teach her the game. We'll have to teach her how to fight our way through the fans."

So they went out the main door with two bellhops and one doorman, you know, saying, "Please let Miss Crawford through." And all these fans had assembled because the paid extras were shouting. There were twenty that started it and fifty more that just turned up in the street. "Joan, Joan." They were reaching and pulling out handfuls of fur. Finally, Judy was saying, you know, "Oh, don't ruin Miss Crawford's lovely coat. Please don't do that." She even took one woman's hand away. And Joan turned around and said, "Get your fucking hands off my fans." They got in the car, and Joan immediately got out of that coat and into this elegant silk coat that was in the car for her to wear to the theater. And the toughie would lightly sew more tufts of fur in for the fans to rip out the next time.

Oh, I just loved it. "Get your fucking hands off my fans." I died laughing. So they went off to the theater, and that was Judy's introduction to New York.

~~~

My big party for Judy was the next night. I gave some great parties in Rome, and one of the best was for Judy Garland. That was a gang bang; I don't usually give parties as big as that. I had groaning boards of food. And a little bar with a bartender. I had this Hindu couple—they were a famous dance team, and in my entrance hall they had arranged an exhibit of their dance costumes and jewelry and masks which was very amusing to come in to. Then on the terrace, which was about half a block long, I had all kinds of torches and hundreds of little tables amidst the trees and flowers. Fellini was there, and the composer Hans Werner Henze, and the Baron Saint-Just, the painter, and Leontyne Price. I just threw them together, a lot of people who hadn't met each other. Bringing dreamy-eyed youngsters to beam at celebrities. Bringing bored celebrities to fight with each other. It was a great party.

But Judy wasn't there. And nobody noticed that Judy wasn't there.

She had lost her nerve about attending the party for some reason and, in the afternoon, flown back to London. Leaving her husband and her trained nurse, this lady-in-waiting whose name was so happily Mrs. Snow, to attend the party. I think she couldn't face meeting Fellini and Leontyne and all that and just fled. Couldn't face the big party. The little girl couldn't face the grown-up party. She could belt it out onstage, but she was really very shy. She could play with an audience in a way she could never play with people at a cocktail party. She had that wide orchestra pit between them and her. I had the feeling that she was basically a sad person. Judy, you see, had been in a vaudeville act with her mother and sisters when she was a child. Her real name was Frances Gumm, and the Gumm Sisters was their act in vaudeville. She was always a little shy because her mother and sister were the flashy ones, apparently. And she'd never had a childhood. You know: "Get up, hon, we've got to catch the train, we play Kalamazoo this evening." Vaudeville. And just never, never a doll, never a puppy, never digging in the mud. Just on trains singing those songs with Mom and her sisters. There was just something sad about her.

She called me in the middle of the party and kept me on the phone for an hour to apologize and give me all the reasons why she had to leave. She said she wasn't very good at facing crowds, and besides that, she really had to get back and rehearse these new songs for a record. And she went on and on apologizing when I should have been circulating, seeing that everybody had something to eat and something to drink, you know, doing my headwaiter bit.

Oh, well, everybody remembers the party, and not many people noticed that she wasn't there. With Fellini and Leontyne Price, who's going to notice that Judy's not there? They'll think either she hasn't come yet or she left early, or they'll assume they'd fall over her sooner or later. But that one evening we had together was so marvelous that I accepted it, you know. And it was a great party.

A Never-Ending Traffic Jam

Well, it began to look as though the Communists would take over Italy. There were some provincial Communists who were Communist only because they had for centuries been peasants on farms, and they were the first generation in their families to be educated. Their fathers were the butter, eggs, and cheese people who smuggled all that into Rome during the war and made a fortune. There have always been the intellectual Communists who wanted to change the status quo. "Let's have a complete change and clear the air." But the intellectual Communists are different from the grudge Communists in every country. A lot of the ones who were coming up from the provinces were rather unpleasant. They were grudge Communists. There were bombings and street demonstrations constantly. Terrorists, poor darlings—all they can think of is a big noise and breaking something. Poets have words they can bombard with.

Finally, I did get tired of soldiers and police on my roof right above my bedroom running around every night. And gunfire. And I got so tired of street fights and traffic jams. I hate traffic jams, and Rome had become a never-ending traffic jam. The air was so thick with car fumes, and nobody smiled like they used to. The postal service didn't work, the telephones didn't work, and the banks were closed more often than they were open. Rome had just gotten impossible. I lived literally next door to the political power in power, the Christian Democrats, and there was a demonstration or street fight every day. One day when I was walking back to my apartment from the mushroom shop across the street, a policeman raised his billy club to conk out some demonstration going on, and knocked out my two front teeth. This was right in front of where I lived. I thought, I'll bet it's so peaceful in Mobile. I decided to start packing.

I had two beloved cats at the time, and of course, they had to come with me. I talked to the head of the Italian division of American Airlines about the best way to do this. He said, "Oh, yes, of course you can take your cats on the plane." So I reserved three places because I did not want the cats away from me in this great upheaval in their lives and mine. But then, a couple of days before I was going to get on the plane, I learned that if any passenger within three seats in any direction objected to my having cats, they would have to go in luggage. Now, some luggage compartments are pressurized; most are not. I wasn't about to even think of the possibility. One of the darlings was my beloved Rufo, the son of Miss Calico, who always let me know when she was going to have kittens. On one last litter, she put out a paw and said, "Don't go. Don't go." She was a very old lady, she'd gone through many litters, and I guess her muscles were not as flexible as they had been when she was young. I heard this kitten speaking inside of her. "Meow, meow." When he came out he must have heard me talking to her, because he came right toward me, this little thing. Dragging. I picked it up carefully and put it back with her. Well, she was busy with the next one, so this little thing turned around and came back to me. So obviously it was my cat. He had been with me many years in Rome, and I was not about to be separated from him on the trip to America.

So I hastily got in touch with a Mobile shipping line that's been doing freighters for thousands of years. Then I had this telephone call from Milano. The man said, "You don't know me, but I've just had a long-distance call from our head office in New Orleans. On whichever freighter we can arrange, you are to be given a cabin for two for the price of one plus five dollars for your cats. So you can have them with you in your cabin." He didn't even mention the possibility of putting them in the hold. They were going to be in this stateroom. Deck level. That's why I took a freighter, so they could be in the cabin with me, not in the hold, not somewhere else. With me.

There was a strike in Rome, and I walked carrying those cats two miles to the state vet to get the proper papers. Then I walked to the American embassy to get them notarized. I had a portfolio that was given me. Well, great is the power of the shipping lines. When I got to the travel agency, they had called two motorcycle cops to escort me to the boat. Nobody looked at any papers. Somebody stamped my passport. That was all. I went roaring off with a motorcycle escort right to the steps of that boat. Then this black man helped me with the luggage because I was holding the cats. He said, "Are you going to America?" I said, "I'm going home to Mobile." "What's your name?" "My name is Walter." "Did you folks live on Bayou Street?" He was born two blocks south of Bayou Street. Crazy: the interconnectedness of it all.

I had thirty days' worth of food because I didn't know what they would serve us on the boat. I wasn't about to be caught in the mid-Atlantic with something inedible. Thirty days of wine, thirty days of typing paper and a typewriter, thirty days of drawing paper and watercolors. When I got to Marseilles I learned that the ship was not going to go to Mobile as planned; it was going to Texas. I got as far as—whatever the port in Texas is. I had to buy another passage from there to Mobile. So I drifted up the St. James River. Went to all kinds of fascinating places, up the Mississippi River, and then home.

Of course, in some ways it was hard leaving Rome, but not as hard as you would think. The cats and monkeys, you see, they do get around. They always meet again. I mean, when they really have bus service to the moon, I imagine getting off that bus and seeing George Plimpton and Federico Fellini and Leontyne Price, and we'll say, "Oh, what are you doing here?"

milking the moon

Mobile, Again

The city of Mobile had lent me a house that had been lent to them. They didn't have enough money or help to restore it. I was to have ten years there in exchange for restoring it. It had been inhabited by vagrants and it smelled like a piss pie. Every single window was broken. So I went to work getting all my stuff in there and I did a lot of restoration. Then Hurricane Frederick came and blew everything up.

My cats were in it with me, the two beloveds who came with me from Rome. I spent a lot of time crawling around putting out buckets and moving books, moving books, because leaks sprang everywhere. At one moment the wind was so great on the east side of the house that a window suddenly just blew open and the rain came into the front room and I had very quickly to move a lot of things and then crawl on the floor with a hammer in mouth and nails to get under that window where the wind was coming in. The screen was like a green stained glass window because there were so many leaves smashed against it. I finally could reach up and first nail one side to the bottom of the window and then nail the other side.

It blew from something in the morning till very late that night. Of course, there was no telephone, there was no electricity. I had thought of putting the cats in the closet under the stairs. They wouldn't go. The minute it started they got under the carpet in the hallway. So I took an easy chair and put it in this middle hall right in the middle of the house and poured my Jim Beam. Finally I just went to sleep. I woke up with this big crash, so I made myself another drink and sat there and then heard another big crash. And I thought, "Well, I'm bored with it." So I moved my bed from where it was closer to the inner wall and went back to sleep.

I found out when I got up in the morning that the magnolia tree was the second crash I'd heard. It had cut right across the front porch against the front door. I couldn't get out the front door. And half of an oak tree in the yard had taken the back porch off and was against the back door, so I couldn't get out of either door. The most amusing thing: There was this cat that lived in the yard that I adopted. He'd once lived in the house; the couple who owned him moved away, and a year later he came from somewhere back to this house. When I first got into the house he was this skinny old tom. Actually he was a chartreuse, and a good one, all gray with green eyes. Beautiful cat.

By the time I fed him up he was pretty gorgeous. I always fed him on the back porch; he came precisely at nine every morning. He came out from under the house at dawn the next morning after Frederick when the wind had stopped. He totally ignored the fact that the back porch was not there. He climbed up the oak tree and clawed up the screen to the kitchen window, and he said, "Meow, Eugene, meow. What's for breakfast?" He ignored the hurricane totally.

I'd put everything I could into the freezer compartment. The guy across the street always had his deep freezer full, so after about eight days he was desperately giving presents all around the neighborhood. He gave me a ham that was still frozen. I just put that thing in the freezer, and that was my block of ice for another two days. I had several dinner parties as soon as I could find a way for people to get around the magnolia in the front and the oak in the back. My friend Nell Burks was coming back from Atlanta, and she thought, Oh, who knows what things will be like for them there? She stopped off someplace like Greenville on her way back down and bought candles and ice. She arrived and banged on my door. She came in, and I was having a dinner party. There was this elaborate meal and all these candles everywhere, because I keep bottles of water, bottles of wine, and boxes of candles, always. As a child of the hurricane, I always have basics. And colored paper to cut out for games.

All that with moving in and the hurricane was such a complication that I didn't notice anything at first. I had not realized how much the bulldozers and the Baptists had destroyed in the three decades I'd been away. The Baptists really are the greatest menace to art and culture. When the soldiers and sailors were off fighting World War I, and those temperance ladies finally got through the Eighteenth Amendment to the Constitution, that was the beginning of the end of downtown Mobile. The great restaurants—they were world famous—closed when they couldn't sell wine. That's when my cousins', the Schimpfs', restaurant closed. When I was three or four years old, I saw the last gasp of old Mobile, which was basically European before the First World War. Downtown was twenty-four hours a day. There were bordellos and all-night cafés and waterfront cafés with embossed iron ceilings. The great restaurants were bar restaurants. The ground floor was a saloon with a free lunch. If you had enough drinks, you got a free lunch from the buffet. Help yourself. One of the great things was pickled eggs, which is one of those forgotten dishes. There was every known seafood because a pound of shrimp cost about a penny then. All the theatrical people—Sarah Bernhardt, James O'Neill, father of Eugene—couldn't wait to get to Mobile.

milking the moon

All the theater people loved Mobile because it was Catholic and European, and after all the famine they'd gone through in America, they loved to come to Mobile and have a good meal. That's why Mobile was a great theater town. And people in Mobile went to the theater every night. Curtain at nine and dinner at midnight. All those places had midnight dinners. But that Mobile died when Prohibition came in. The great restaurants couldn't make money when they couldn't sell drinks. Some of them survived as places that sold oyster loaves, but only two or three of them. And when the great restaurants closed, the theater people didn't want to come to Mobile.

I will never forget, when the news came that Prohibition had been repealed, Mobile went on a three-day drunk. There was a three-day carnival in Mobile. All that stuff that had been in the back closet and under the house came right out in the open. Everybody went into their hiding places and brought out everything, and pop, pop, pop, pop, pop went the corks. The streets flowed. Go downtown; no shops were open. There was a two-week hangover. I mean, we have to remember Christ's first miracle. Why do you think he turned water into wine? He did it to help people, especially people past a certain age.

But then in the Second World War, all those peasants from the fields came to work in the shipyards. *Forbes* magazine said that Mobile was one of the towns that grew the most during World War II. And those peasants did not go back to the fields when the war was over. They stayed in town and built Baptist churches on every corner. The temperance movement and the Baptists have destroyed Mobile totally. So what was once a Caribbean ward has become a white-trash city. What was once a European port is now a Baptist colony.

To me, World War II is really the great frontier; it started the vulgarization of everything. That's when people downtown were all getting old. Everybody younger was off to the war, and they were renting out empty rooms. There was a citywide appeal from the Red Cross: If you have a room you can rent out, please do, because we have an airfield and a shipyard, and we need a place for these people who've come to town to work for the war effort, as it was called. So many places had partitions put up and rooms divided. Things sort of got run-down. And where everybody had a patch of something, some tomato plants and herbs, in the backyard, that just all stopped in the Second World War. Downtown went dead.

What's really got to me since I've been back is that Bienville Square, which had formerly been like a street salon, with everybody downtown on Saturday, was absolutely empty. Nobody is downtown on a Saturday. And that was for me like a party, a street party, on Saturday, downtown. I remember one Saturday when I came back taking a walk in Bienville Square. There was nobody in there. And I thought, Oh, my Lord, what's happened? I mean, most pleasant cities do have markets and bookshops and a street life and a kind of "Here we are."

And so many of the grand, glorious buildings on Water Street had been torn down to make places with lots of small efficient offices. They had been commercial buildings, except they were made like Baroque masterpieces. You know, *baroque* is from a Portuguese word meaning "misshapen pearl." When people began to do art and architecture that was not classical, that is not even on each side but has curves and all that, *baroque* was the word they chose for it. When I use it, I usually mean Southern exuberance and a delight in ornament. Disliking a flat façade in people, animals, trees, houses, works of art. It is natural for human beings to like baroque, especially if you live in a climate where the sunlight is hard and clear. That's why modern buildings vanish on the Gulf Coast. Some of these modern buildings that you might see if they were in Denmark or Hamburg just vanish in Mobile. You cannot see them. They are blanks. You could pass them three hundred times and not notice them. They're not there. Because the vegetation is baroque; the people are baroque; everything is baroque. So what's a perfectly plain box going to do on Water Street?

And so many houses I had known as a child, and known the people who lived in them, were simply not there. It was a great shock to go to the corner of Conti and Bayou Streets and see this little-prick Baptist church covering every inch where my grandmother's house used to be. I mean, right to the sidewalk, this cement building with a tiny steeple. Have you ever noticed how the Baptist churches have the smallest steeples?

And a great many trees had been cut down. I mean, they had just been cut down. Those primitive types with low foreheads have just gotten loose, and too many things have been bulldozed. They've cut down all along Government Street magnificent huge old oaks and old magnolias and planted those sappy little things that don't mean anything. Mobile once had a better climate; it was so covered with trees that it was not so hot then as it is now. If you stand for a minute on the sidewalk where there are no trees, then go stand under the oak trees on the sidewalk, you will instantly notice six or ten degrees difference. If all the things they cut down were still here, you wouldn't feel this heat. A full-grown oak gives out something like two hundred cubic feet of moisture. It's Mother Nature's air-conditioning. And the protection of many kinds of wildlife. But the balance of nature has been destroyed in the name of the dollar. Not to mention the people who destroyed downtown so they could sell their swampland in west Mobile and have malls, malls, malls.

And there has been a whole change of atmosphere. The idea of enjoying life has faded. The nine-to-five world has made it to Mobile. In Europe there is still not any idea of the nine to five, where an ambitious young man or woman has to have their personalities compartmentalized into waking up, quick coffee, then nine to five. And then you get drunk after the pressure of the day. Maybe you have sex, maybe you have theater, maybe you read a book at night. But you still have before you that drawbridge. The nine to five. I mean, theoretically, offices have schedules in Europe. But it's understood that schedules are kind of like a fence; inside you can grow any flowers or vegetables you like. Here it's a barbed-wire fence to the cement ground.

In Europe they have an idea that you're going to have to work hard if you're going to have anything, if you're going to eat, if you're going to have any comforts on this planet. You've got to work. It's just taken for granted. But it's not a religion. Europeans will stop anything to see something extraordinary in the street, or if they see an old friend, they go to a café to have a drink together at once. They go to the office at eight and stop everything at eleven to have a drink at the café. Then they have lunch. Then, along about two or three, they go back to the office. That's not true in America. Not true even in Mobile, although everybody used to go home for what was called dinner and then a nap. In the old days, when it got hot, you would hear guys say, "Well, I've sweated through my seersucker. I guess it's time to go home." They put on a fresh seersucker suit in the morning, and by twelve or one o'clock they had sweated through the armpits. So it was time to go home. Too hot to work. Finished for the day. And they got everything done. They got all their work done by ten in the morning. Then an hour of male gossip at the coffee shop or just sitting on the wharf or in the cool produce house. At eleven go back to the office and maybe write a few letters, do a few phone calls. Start home at eleven-thirty for midday dinner. Afterwards a nap, and when it was starting to get a little better, like at four, back to the office for an hour or so and close up and start home. Just like Italy. They got everything done, and nobody was ever in a bad temper. They walked slowly, because we were always told, "Don't get hot. Take it easy. Don't run. Walk. Take your time." They weren't rushing out in their cars and fighting for a parking space. They were walking slowly and seeing what was out there. But since World War II there has been air-conditioning and regular hours. You don't leave early, and you don't come in late. Eight to five. Ghastly in a climate like this. It's not possible. It's against human nature. While in the tropics, why fight them? Go along with them. But somehow the easy approach to life has ended.

Since my life has always been free-form, I live three days in one day without haste, without hurry. I stop when I'm tired. I have a glass of wine when I feel faint. I have no schedule, although I work every day. The idea of going to an office—I think I'd slash my wrists the third day. It's the plastic

Mobile, Again

265

clothes and the plastic neckties. The necktie, the necktie, the necktie. We've gotten these stereotypes in all things. There's a stereotype man, a stereotype woman. There's a stereotype child, a stereotype dog, a stereotype cat, a stereotype automobile, a stereotype vacation, a stereotype Christmas dinner, a stereotype Thanksgiving dinner, a stereotype grandparent. It's this fear of anything other than the approved. There is a kind of nylon suit, plastic shirt, plastic necktie, identical haircuts, identical shoes. You have to belong to identical clubs, drink identical drinks. These are the yuppies, the puppies, the hubbies, and the bubbies. That's the norm. So anything outside of it is abnormal.

When I was growing up in Mobile, there was no such thing as an eccentric, because individuality was permitted. It's only with the moment the dollar became God and the flattened-out culture of the mass media which has happened since World War II that the people who formerly might have been called—at the most—colorful or opinionated, now are thought of as eccentric or something. Somehow the television has created a race of morons. People in Mobile just sit around and blink, like lizards do.

And sex in America. In Europe they take it for granted. That's one of the things God has created to keep us from being bored in our stay upon this planet. In America they still haven't decided what it is. The Catholics think all of it's all right. The Episcopalians think you can do anything as long as your fingernails are clean. But the fundamentalists think it's all perverse, and they're trying to take over the country. The Europeans laugh and never talk about it and do it all. I'm telling you, when I came back here, I had to adapt to life in a barbarian country. Barbarian.

But I'm glad to get back and into that traditional American mock battle: artists versus Philistines. In Europe the arts are considered something usual, for daily consumption. In America there is still the old Puritan suspicion that it's all hothouse stuff. So I'm back where I started, sharpening my pen, my brush, my spade, my scissors, my pruning shears, my cheese parer, and the taps on my new tap shoes.

Sooner or later Southerners all come home, not to die, but to eat gumbo. And you see, I never really left home. You couldn't say I was ever an expatriate, because I never left home. I was just traveling. And I was always on Alabama soil. I had taken a Thom McAn shoebox full of red clay from a Spring Hill gully to New York. I had it under my bed. So I always slept on Alabama soil. And when I packed that trunk to go to Europe, my Thom McAn box of red clay went with me. I always told everybody: If anything happens, just throw this in the coffin with me.

There was only one moment in all those years when I was not on Alabama soil. In Paris I loved going to some of those gardens where they have these gorgeous roses. And I went to the lovely villa of Joséphine de Beauharnais, Napoleon's wife, and stole some cuttings, because stolen cuttings always grow best. Even the most strictly moral British steal cuttings. Dear little old ladies take out these fingernail scissors and steal cuttings. Anyway, Joséphine was famous for her roses and did all those famous paintings of them. She had all kinds of roses from all over the world. So I went and stole some cuttings and had them in a window box in Paris. Then I smuggled them across the border and had them on my terrace in Rome.

Then when Hans Werner Henze moved from Naples and bought this villa in the hills outside of Rome, he wanted some roses. So I gave him these roses. Well, one of Joséphine's roses was doing poorly. He said, "What shall I do, Eugene? It's the prettiest one, and its bloom is palky. The others are doing okay." So I said, "Oh, well." I knew I'd be going home at some moment, so I gave him that clay, because roses like red clay. And that rose climbed up to the top of the first floor, on Spring Hill gully red clay. Since that was a rose that belonged to a lady originally from the Gulf of Mexico, the Caribbean, that rose knew red clay when it saw it.

So that's the only time I gave away my Alabama soil. Otherwise I was always on Alabama soil. I never left home. Except for that time I spent in New York. One should have some exotic experiences in one's life, I guess. But I've always told everybody: Don't call me an expatriate. I am not. I went to Paris and Rome to get something I couldn't get at home. But I did not change nationalities. Although I lived in Rome all those years, I never took residency. My residence is Mobile, Alabama. I went every three months to the police station to have my visitor's permit renewed. Every time I got a job in a film, I had to go have my passport stamped and get a certificate. I did not want foreign residency. I just didn't want it. I wanted Mobile as my residence.

I never rejected the South. There are many things that are maddening, but since I was born with a certain cat and monkey detachment, I look at some of these morons as a cat or a monkey looks at an idiot fox terrier. Like I just know things they don't know. When I was getting ready to leave for New York, I thought, Well, am I doing the right thing? Maybe I should just stay. I said no. You've got to get to New York. Got to get to Paris. Got to do it. You've promised yourself since the cradle.

I never intended to be gone so long. But that's Southern. Like people who were invited to Termite Hall for a week and stayed a year. It's just Southern. You see, I'd made no plans. In that, I'm not American. I listen to teenagers today saying, "After I've taken my bachelor's, then I'm going to get a master's,

Mobile, Again

267

then I'll do this and that, and then I'll buy a house in Point Clear." You think you can plan a life? I've always thought you must improvise daily. Today may bring money in the mail. Today may bring a hurricane. You have to be ready for either one. In either case, give a party. But I never make plans. I just blunder ahead successfully. Now, a good party has to be planned. You can't improvise a party. You can improvise a life, but you can't improvise a party.

When I was in seventh grade and saw that faded photograph in the Rand McNally textbook with the palm tree, the Sphinx, the Pyramid, and a hunk of shore of the Nile, I didn't say to myself, Maybe someday I'll go, or, I'd like to go. I thought to myself, Now, when I'm coming down the Nile, that's what I'll see. Of course, what I saw was a redbrick building with an R. J. Reynolds Tobacco sign looking exactly like Water Street in Mobile. But anyway, I had a certainty that I had set enough energy rolling into the world, it would roll back and roll me to where I wanted to go. It was not a plan. You can't plan a life. So many people think they can, but then, they don't even see where they are. They don't see a strange bird in the sky. They just don't see. It's those blinders that the American educational system and the big dollar value on everything have put on most people. And they just don't see beyond. Somehow by pure good luck, by a combination of the nationalities meeting in me, by being triple Sagittarius, I was spared blinders. I haven't been smashed by the educational system, the financial system, the political system. So many people have. I'm so glad I never wanted to be an adult. I've stopped smiling on certain occasions, but I don't claim adulthood.

Sometimes you just have to get up and go. Most people make plans; they don't understand the importance of impulse. If you have a strong impulse, obviously there are some waves coming at you from way out there. You're at this end of something. Way out there from the other end of something, waves are coming towards you. And most people just don't pay attention. They say, "Oh, someday I'm going to Paris." "Someday I'll go to New York." But they don't go; they plan. It was not that I was so secure or fearless; it's just that I had this sense of get-up-and-go. The music is playing. It's my music. It's my cue. I'm due in Paris. Or Rome. Or North Africa. Or Egypt. Or wherever. It may be that people who have not been suppressed by education have some set of shadow instincts, so that they just hear something, smell something, feel something. I think everybody has it and they don't use it. All that goddamn eighteenth-century love of logic has squashed a lot. The current American educational system and television are squashing a deal more. Most people don't listen to their own bodies or their own supraconscious. They just don't listen.

I suppose that really, if I had planned my life, I probably would be in a well-cut gray suit with a black necktie in some office. And I'd have a lot of money in the bank and own real estate. And probably be miserable and not know why. Well, I'm broke. But I know why. I'm happy, and I know why. Of course, I have regrets. I'm human, so naturally I have several fireplaces full of regrets. But I have more delights than regrets. And I'm always thinking much more about next week than I am about last year. You can't relive what certain things meant when they were happening. I look back upon my life as something I read about in a book. There's this mad creature called Eugene who goes from Mobile and sets out. I don't recognize him as me at all. It's something I read about.

Well, it all goes too fast. But basically, it's been a success. Not in the usual American sense of success, but in my sense of success. Picnicking on Oscar Wilde's grave. Riding in a Bentley with seven dwarfs. Getting three pubic hairs from Tallulah Bankhead. I haven't gone to see those ants in Patagonia who make anthills higher than a man and who raise mushrooms in the cellar in the winter. I want to see those ants. Because any civilization based on mushroom culture has to be highly interesting. And I've never been to Peru. I've never been to Persia. I've never been to any of those places that start with "P." I want to go to Portugal, where they've got that fountain of rose-colored marble in Coimbra with those monkeys in eighteenth-century costume in rose-colored marble. I've got to be photographed *in* that fountain. And I want to go to Finland. I want to meet my 253 cousins in Norway I've never met. And I've got to get a good red wig and a white grand piano, because I want to tap-dance into the next century.

Cast of Characters

ALBERTI, GUIDO (b. 1909) Italian actor. Alberti made his first film appearance in Fellini's *8½*. He has continued to act since, though his career slowed down to a large extent after the 1970s.

ALBRIZIO, CONRAD (1894–1973) American painter and teacher. Born in Baton Rouge, Louisiana, Albrizio left his mark around Louisiana and Alabama in frescoes and murals commissioned for such buildings as the Louisiana State Capitol Building. Albrizio taught at Louisiana State University.

ALEXANDER, MADAME (1893–1990) American dollmaker. Alexander began her doll company in 1923, and it has since become a major toy corporation. Some Alexander dolls are considered more than toys, however, and are collected by doll enthusiasts. Alexander was given an FAO Schwarz Lifetime Achievement Award as "the First Lady of dolls."

ANTONIONI, MICHELANGELO (b. 1912) Italian film director, producer, and screenwriter. Antonioni is best known in the United States for his English-language film, *Blow-Up* (1966), for which he earned Oscar Award nominations for best director and best screenplay.

ATHAS, DAPHNE (b. 1923) American writer. With several novels to her credit, Athas is best known for her novel *Entering Ephesus* (1971). From 1944 to 1945 Athas taught at the Perkins School for the Blind in Watertown, Massachusetts. Her 1947 novel, *Weather of the Heart,* was based on her time there. Athas collaborated with writer Gurney Campbell to create the play *Sit on the Earth* (1957).

BACHMANN, INGEBORG (1926–1973) Austrian writer. Bachmann was a poet and a fiction writer who achieved immense critical acclaim and literary status in post–World War II Europe, especially for her poetry. The book to which Eugene alludes as the one that brought her the initial critical attention is probably her first book of poetry, *Die gestundete Zeit (Borrowed Time)*. Beginning in the 1950s, Bachmann collaborated with the composer Hans Werner Henze. Examples of their work together include librettos for the operas *Der junge Lord (The Young Lord)* and *Der Prinz (The Prince)*.

BALANCHINE, GEORGE (1904–1983) Russian-born American choreographer of ballet. Balanchine co-founded the School of American Ballet (1934), the American Ballet Company (1935), and the New York City Ballet (1948), for which he also served as artistic director from its creation until his death. He choreographed over two hundred ballets, including *The Nutcracker* (1954).

BANKHEAD, TALLULAH (1902–1968) American stage and film actress born in Huntsville, Alabama. Beautiful, sexy, outrageous, and immensely popular, Bankhead found her greatest success on the stage on Broadway and in London. Her performance in *The Skin of Our Teeth* (1942), the play that Eugene saw, won her the New York Drama Critics' Circle Award. Although her film career was less successful than her theater career, Bankhead did achieve critical acclaim for her role in Alfred Hitchcock's *Lifeboat* (1944).

BARNES, DJUNA (1892–1972) American writer of verse, fiction, and dramatic literature. A prolific writer and frequent contributor to newspapers and magazines, Barnes was an important figure in the literary and intellectual culture of Paris in the 1920s. While in Paris, Barnes had a tumultuous affair with another American expatriate, the sculptor Thelma Wood. The affair ended painfully and served as a psychological source for Barnes's novel *Nightwood* (1936). In 1930 Barnes returned to New York City, and in 1940 she moved to 5 Patchin Place, where she lived for the next thirty-two years, battling depression, alcoholism, illness, and her family's attempts to commit her to a sanitarium. Although she continued to write, she became fairly reclusive. Some believe that this tendency, combined with her refusal to permit reprinting of her earlier work or to grant interviews, accounts for her current lack of renown.

BARNEY, NATALIE (1878–1972) Born in America, Barney spent most of her life in France, where she established a salon in her Paris home that attracted major writers and intellectuals of the nineteenth and twentieth centuries. Although she was a writer, editor, and translator, and was noted for her many lesbian love affairs, the predominant source of her fame was her salon, to which she gathered such notable figures as Colette, James Joyce, Jean Cocteau, Gertrude Stein, Oscar Wilde, Ernest Hemingway, Edith Sitwell, Marcel Proust, Djuna Barnes, Rainer Maria Rilke, T. S. Eliot, Mata Hari, Ezra Pound, F. Scott Fitzgerald, Sherwood Anderson, Greta Garbo, Truman Capote, Thornton Wilder, and William Carlos Williams.

BARRAULT, JEAN-LOUIS (1910–1994) French writer, actor, director, producer, and mime. A star of the French stage, Barrault also had a strong career in film. He appeared in twenty-five films, including *Hélène* (1936), which costarred Madeline Renaud, who became Barrault's wife in 1940.

BASSANI, GIORGIO (1916–2000) Italian writer and editor. In addition to writing several novels, novellas, short stories, and verse, Bassani was an editor of *Botteghe Oscure* from its founding and an editor for *Paragone* from 1953 to 1971. Eugene mentions that Bassani is credited for "discovering" Lampedusa's *The Leopard*. Indeed, his April 14, 2000, obituary in the *New York Times* states, "In 1958, while working as an editor at the Feltrinelli publishing house, he discovered the work of Giuseppe Tomasi di Lampedusa and is widely credited with having championed the author." In 1962 he published *Il giardino dei Finʒi-Contini* (*The Garden of the Finʒi-Continis*), which was later adapted for film. He was an Aries.

BATTERBERRY, MICHAEL (b. 1932) British-born food writer and critic who currently resides in New York City. Editor in chief of *International Food and Wine* since 1977, Batterberry has contributed several articles and illustrations to popular newspapers and magazines, including *Travel and Leisure* and *Playbill*. He is also the editor of *Food Arts*.

BECKER, GINNY, *aka* VIRGINIA CAMPBELL (dates unknown) Stage and film actress. Campbell played the character Theresa in Ernst Lubitsch's last film, *That Lady in Ermine* (1948). Lubitsch died during its production.

BERMAN, EUGENE (1899–1971) Russian-American painter. Berman was part of the surrealist art movement in Paris in the 1930s. In addition to painting, he designed sets and costumes for the Metropolitan Opera.

BERNHARDT, SARAH (1844–1923) French actress. Considered one of the greatest stage actresses of the twentieth century in Europe and in America, "the Divine Sarah" was extremely charismatic on and off the stage. Her contributions to the stage included writing some of the plays she acted in and revising standard texts to great artistic success. She was not restricted in her acting by her gender; male roles included Hamlet and the title role of Napoleon's son in *L'Aiglon* (*The Eaglet*), a part written specifically for her. She was best known in the United States as a result of nine tours she made there from 1880 to 1918.

BIDDLE, FRANCIS (1886–1968) American lawyer. Served as attorney general under President Franklin D. Roosevelt from 1941 until Roosevelt's death in 1945. During World War II, Biddle oversaw the registration of aliens and the internment of Japanese Americans, responsibilities he later regretted having performed. In 1945 Biddle resigned his post as attorney general and was appointed by President Harry S. Truman as the American member of the International Military Tribunal in Nuremberg.

BIDDLE, KATHERINE GARRISON CHAPIN (1890–1977) An American poet, Chapin married Francis Biddle in 1918. She was the half sister of the Princess Marguerite Caetani, née Chapin.

BORDEN, LIZZIE (1860–1927) Although acquitted (after a well-publicized trial) of the crime of murdering her father and stepmother in their home in Fall River, Massachusetts, Borden remained suspect in her New England community and infamous in the public eye. After her acquittal, she and her sister inherited their father's fairly large estate and moved into a mansion at which Borden threw extravagant parties for theater figures, most especially the Boston actress Nance O'Neil.

BOWLES, PAUL (1910–1999) and JANE BOWLES (1917–1973) American writers. Paul Bowles, who was also a composer, is best known for his novel *The Sheltering Sky* and Jane Bowles for her novel *Two Serious Ladies* (1943). Apparently both Paul and Jane considered themselves homosexual, though they did have a sexual component to their relationship for a time. In 1947 they moved to Tangiers, where they became an important part of the expatriate scene during the 1940s and 1950s. They were visited there by many other writers, among them Alfred Chester.

BRICKTOP (1894–1984) American entertainer, nightclub owner. Born Ada Beatrice Queen Victoria Louisa Virginia Smith in Alderson, West Virginia, Bricktop opened Bricktop's in Rome in 1951, having worked as an entertainer in various nightclubs in the United States and in Paris from the time she was sixteen. It was at the age of sixteen that she was given her nickname, because of her flaming red hair, by a Harlem nightclub owner. In 1924 she went to Paris to work, meeting Langston Hughes, F. Scott and Zelda Fitzgerald, Man Ray, Pablo Picasso, Josephine Baker, and Cole Porter and his wife, Linda. The Porters befriended Bricktop and asked her to teach the Charleston at their Charleston parties, where she was introduced to the elite of Paris. She died in Manhattan, and more than three hundred people came to her funeral.

BROUGHTON, JAMES (1913–1999) American filmmaker. Broughton's films have been independent rather than mainstream. He won several international film awards for his work.

BROWN, ROSCOE LEE (b. 1925) African American film and television actor. While Brown's early work was on the stage, the bulk of his work has been as a character actor in film and television. He has made numerous guest appearances on television shows, including *Barney Miller, Soap, Magnum P.I.*, and *The Cosby Show*. His films include *Superfly* (1973) and *Logan's Run* (1976).

BURKE, BILLIE (1886–1970) American stage and screen actress. Burke's career began in vaudeville, and she had over sixty films to her credit. She is perhaps most popularly known for her role as Glinda the Good Witch of the North in the film *The Wizard of Oz* (1939).

BUSSY, DOROTHY STRACHEY (d. 1960) British writer and translator. Although she wrote only one novel, *Olivia, by Olivia* (1949), it was critically praised, as were her fine English translations of the work of her friend the French writer André Gide. She was the sister of Lytton Strachey and the wife of impressionist painter Simon de Bussy.

CAETANI, PRINCESS MARGUERITE, née Marguerite Chapin (1880–1963) Founder and editor of the literary journal *Botteghe Oscure*. Born in New London, Connecticut, Caetani studied singing in Paris until her marriage in 1911 to Italian nobleman and amateur composer Roffredo Caetani, prince of Bassiano. She edited the literary review *Commerce* from 1924 to 1932. Eventually she moved to Rome and established, in 1948, *Botteghe Oscure*, a literary review to which most of the leading writers of Europe and America contributed works in their own languages.

CALDER, ALEXANDER (1898–1976) American painter and sculptor. Calder was one of the few American surrealist artists given international critical acceptance. A lifelong friend of Joan Miró.

CAPOTE, TRUMAN (1924–1984) American writer. Born Truman Persons in New Orleans, Louisiana, he was sent at the age of four by his mother to live with older relatives in Monroeville, Alabama. His parents divorced, and both essentially abandoned him. His mother eventually committed suicide. He was a childhood friend of Harper Lee, who is also from Monroeville. Capote's first published novel, *Other Voices, Other Rooms* (1948), brought him the fame and fortune he had craved as a young writer. After Capote published *Breakfast at Tiffany's: A Short Novel and Three Stories* in 1958, he found himself even more famous and wealthy. In 1966 he published *In Cold Blood: A True Account of a Multiple Murder and Its Consequences*, which he called a nonfiction novel, a work that married "the art of the novelist together with the technique of journalism." Capote's abuse of drugs and alcohol, which began during the six years it took him to write *In Cold Blood*, finally caught up with him, and he died of liver disease and multiple drug intoxication. Eugene's interview of Truman Capote was ultimately published not in the *Paris Review*, but in *Intro Bulletin*, December 1957.

CARDINALE, CLAUDIA (b. 1939) Italian actress. Her beauty was frequently compared with that of her French contemporary Brigitte Bardot. Her work as leading lady in many films by important Italian directors, such as *8½* by Federico Fellini, made her a star in Italy and internationally. In 1964 she appeared in *The Pink Panther*, directed by Blake Edwards.

CARPENTER, THELMA (1920–1997) American singer. Carpenter was a big-band singer who worked with many jazz greats, including Coleman Hawkins and Count Basie. In 1968 she was Pearl Bailey's understudy in the Broadway production of *Hello, Dolly!* She appeared in the film *The Wiz* (1978).

CAVANI, LILIANA (b. 1936) Italian film director and screenwriter. Her first feature film was *I Cannibali* (*The Cannibals*, 1969). Her best-known film in the United States is *Il Portiere di Notte* (*The Night Porter*, 1974).

CHAR, RENÉ (1907–1988) French poet. Albert Camus stated in 1952, "I consider René Char to be our greatest living poet." One of his best-known works of poetry is *Feuillets d'Hypnos* (1946), written while Char was fighting the Nazi occupation in a resistance group in Vaucluse in southeastern France. Char lived for most of his life in Vaucluse, away from the literary and cultural center of Paris.

CHESTER, ALFRED (1928–1971) American writer. Edward Field, who edited Chester's *Head of a Sad Angel: Stories 1953–1966*, called Chester "a neglected but difficult genius." Chester was a reviewer and critic for a time in Paris. He worked as a book review editor for the short-lived literary journal *Merlin* and submitted essays to other literary journals as well, including *Paris Review* and *Botteghe Oscure*. A collection of his reviews was published in *Looking for Genet* (1993). Eventually he felt that his talents as a writer were being wasted in this work, and he dedicated himself to writing his own fiction. He went to Morocco as part of the literary colony that surrounded the Bowleses so that he might concentrate on his own writing. Unfortunately, he quarreled with them and with others in the group, including his boyfriend. Finally he moved to New York, where he wrote the novel *The Exquisite Corpse*, which was published posthumously. Chester, who suffered from increasingly debilitating emotional instability, ultimately committed suicide.

COLETTE (1873–1954) French novelist. Considered one of France's great novelists, Colette wrote over fifty novels. Her 1954 novel, *Gigi*, was adapted for the Academy Award–winning film in 1959.

CONNELL, EVAN (b. 1924) Born in Kansas City, Missouri, Connell is best known for his novels *Mrs. Bridge* (1958) and *Mr. Bridge* (1969). He has also published many other novels, short stories, and some poetry.

COPLAND, AARON (1900–1990) American composer and conductor. Copland is credited with popularizing classical music in the twentieth century in the United States. He won the Pulitzer Prize in 1944 for the score for the ballet *Appalachian Spring* and an Academy Award in 1950 for the musical score of the film *The Heiress*.

COSTA-GAVRAS, CONSTANTIN (b. 1933) Film director and screenwriter. Born in Athens; nationalized French citizen. He has won many international film awards. In the United States he is best known for the 1982 film *Missing* costarring Jack Lemmon and Sissy Spacek, which earned him an Academy Award for best screenplay.

COX, WALLY (1924–1973) American film and television actor and comedian. Cox is best known for his starring role as a quiet and introverted science teacher in the TV show *Mr. Peepers* (1952–1953).

CRAWFORD, JOAN (1908–1977) An American film star of dozens of movies, Crawford won an Academy Award for best actress in the 1945 film *Mildred Pierce*, in which she played a woman who martyrs herself for her no-good child. The role is an ironic one, considering Crawford's reputation for being spiteful, jealous, and nasty. Her adopted daughter's tell-all biography, *Mommy Dearest*, helped to codify Crawford's persona as a colossal bitch. However, she was purported to have never let a fan letter go unanswered.

CROCE, BENEDETTO (1866–1952) Italian philosopher. Croce was a prolific writer. His four-volume *Philosophy of the Spirit* is considered his seminal work. Eleanor was one of his four daughters.

CUMMINGS, E. E. (1894–1962) American poet. cummings's poetry is most recognized for its innovations of syntax and punctuation. The lack of punctuation in his poems and his insistence on lowercasing his name are examples of his resistance to mechanical convention. Although his writing career began in the 1920s, cummings was not recognized as an important poet until the 1950s. cummings moved into 4 Patchin Place in 1924, just after his wife left him for another man. Patchin Place is described by his biographer, Robert S. Kennedy, as a "quiet, tree-shaded court near the old Jefferson market at Sixth Avenue and 10th Street." He lived there until his death in 1962.

DAGMAR, ALEXANDRA (dates unknown) Famous British music hall queen. She was sponsored by the Schuberts in America, where she performed in operettas. She is buried in Mobile. She should not be confused with the famous variety actress and friend of Noël Coward's known as Gertrude Lawrence, whose real name was Alexandra Dagmar.

DAVENPORT, JOHN (dates unknown) British journalist. Davenport was an editor for a couple of literary journals in England just after World War II. He coedited *Arena: A Literary Magazine* from 1949 to 1951. He also worked on the journal *Circus: The Pocket Review of Our Time*, where he was one of three editors. *Circus* was quite short-lived, running only three issues from April to June 1950.

DE ACOSTA, MERCEDES (1893–1968) American bon vivant. Although de Acosta wrote some poetry, she is better known for her love affairs. She had affairs with dancer Isadora Duncan and with film star Marlene Dietrich. For years de Acosta was rumored to have had an affair with Greta Garbo. Her letters from Garbo were unsealed in April 2000, ten years after Garbo died, and are generally held to have verified the rumor that they had an affair but that for the majority of their relationship they were friends.

DE RESZKE, JEAN (1850–1925) Polish-born operatic tenor. De Reszke performed to acclaim in leading roles in most of the French and Italian operas. He performed in some Wagnerian operas as well.

DERWOOD, GENE (1909–1954) American poet; married to Oscar Williams. A collection of Derwood's poetry, entitled simply *Poems*, was published posthumously in 1955.

DE WILDE, BRANDON (1942–1972) American actor of stage, radio, and film, best known when he was a child. De Wilde's role in the play *Member of the Wedding*, his first at the age of eight, earned him the prestigious Donaldson Award for best debut performance of the 1949–50 season. De Wilde performed in several plays on the radio program *Theatre Guild of the Air*. As he got older, he lost much of his appeal. He had some forgettable roles in a few films before he died at the age of thirty.

DINESEN, ISAK (1885–1962) Danish writer. Isak Dinesen was the pen name of Baroness Karen Blixen, author of several works including *Out of Africa* (1937). Dinesen married Baron Bror Blixen in 1914 and moved with him to a coffee plantation in Kenya. Although they divorced in 1921, Dinesen continued to live on the plantation for the next ten years. *Out of Africa* is based on her life and experiences in Kenya.

duBOIS, WILLIAM PÈNE (1916–1993) American writer and illustrator of children's literature; founding editor of *Paris Review*. DuBois, who was the son of the art critic and painter Guy Pène duBois, won several awards for his work in children's literature.

DUHAMEL, GEORGES (1884–1966) French physician by profession; novelist, essayist, critic, dramatist, and travel diarist; director of *Mercure de France*, a literary magazine, 1935–1937. Among the dozens of works published by Duhamel is a collection of essays entitled *La Possession du Monde* (1919; English translation: *The Heart's Domain*). *La Table Ronde* was a subsidiary of the publishing house of Plon, whose offices were at 8 rue Garancière.

DU PLESSIX, FRANCINE (b. 1930) French-born American writer. In addition to several novels and works of nonfiction, du Plessix has contributed articles, stories, and reviews for periodicals including *The New Yorker*, the *New York Review of Books*, and the *New Republic*. She published *At Home with the Marquis de Sade* in 1998 and is currently at work on a novel.

EDWARDS, BLAKE (b. 1922) American film director and producer. Some of the films that Edwards directed are *Operation Petticoat* (1959), *Breakfast at Tiffany's* (1961), *Days of Wine and Roses* (1963), and the Pink Panther movies, beginning with *The Pink Panther* (1964). He had a lull of hits until 1979, when he directed *10*. In recent years his best-known work was *Victor/Victoria*, in which he directed his wife, Julie Andrews.

ELIOT, T. S. (1888–1965) Anglo-American poet, dramatist. Although a native of St. Louis, Missouri, and a graduate of Harvard, Eliot was an Anglophile who lived the majority of his life in Great Britain. Many of his poems, such as "The Love Song of J. Alfred Prufrock" (1917) and *The Waste Land* (1922), are masterpieces of twentieth-century literature, and his essays have become standards of literary criticism. In 1948 he won the Nobel Prize for Literature. Eliot's first wife, Vivien Haigh-Wood, suffered from severe mental illness, and Eliot's efforts to support her contributed to his own breakdown in 1921, when he spent six months under psychiatric treatment in Switzerland. Ten years after Haigh-Wood's death, Eliot married Esme Valerie Fletch, who had been his secretary for six years and was almost forty years his junior. The marriage is believed to have been a happy one.

ELLISON, RALPH (1914–1994) African-American writer. His novel *Invisible Man* (1947) won the National Book Award. From 1955 to 1957, Ellison was a Fellow at the American Academy in Rome, where he meet Eugene.

EVANS, EDITH (1913–1976) English actress. Although Evans acted in some films, her career was most successful in the theater. She made her New York debut in 1931 and began a career of performing in Shakespeare comedies and tragedies, in Restoration comedy, and in plays by Oscar Wilde and George Bernard Shaw. Her films include *The Importance of Being Earnest* (1951), *Tom Jones* (1963), and *A Doll's House* (1973).

FARGUE, JEAN-PAUL (1876–1947) French journalist and poet. In the beginning of his career, with the publishing in 1894 of *Tancred,* Fargue's literary focus was on poetry. In the 1920s he published in *Commerce* with Paul Valéry. In the 1930s his writing and focus had turned to journalism.

FAULKNER, WILLIAM (1897–1962) American novelist. Born in Mississippi, Faulkner wrote novels that were formally innovative and that focused on the social and psychological complexities of the American South, such as *The Sound and the Fury* (1931) and *Absalom, Absalom!* (1937). Faulkner won the Nobel Prize for Literature in 1949 and a Pulitzer for *A Fable* (1955) and another for *The Reivers* (1962). During the 1950s Faulkner did a great deal of traveling in America, Europe, and Japan on the lecture circuit.

FELLINI, FEDERICO (1920–1993) Italian film director, screenwriter; considered a major auteur. Although he was born in Rimini, a resort town on the Adriatic Sea, Fellini said that when he moved to Rome in 1938, it felt like going home. From a young age, Fellini had a fascination for performance and theater. His mother once said that he "always loved comic things and crazy, unexpected things" like carnivals and circuses. As a child he would stage his own puppet shows.

Fellini became an internationally renowned director and won a string of film awards, including six Oscars: five for best foreign film for the movies *La Strada* (1954), *Nights of Cabiria* (1956), *La Dolce Vita* (1960), *8½* (1963), and *Amarcord* (1973); and a special Oscar for his body of work in 1993. Critics have used the term *Felliniesque* to discuss the unique quality of his cinematic vision and the coherence of his work, which was said to be autobiographical, but not in a conventionally narrative way.

According to Fellini's biographer Edward Murray, the quality of spontaneity and naturalness in his films upon which so many critics have commented may be, in part, a consequence of his childhood belief that movie actors made up the film's plot and dialogue spontaneously. As Eugene points out, Fellini was a great student of humankind, and he was able to elicit innovative and fresh performances from his actors. He said that "faces are more important to me than anything else" and that casting is "the most important element of filmmaking." That he cast his wife, Giulietta Masina, whom he married in 1943, in six of his films suggests how important she was to his work.

It is interesting to note that in Murray's biography of Fellini, *Fellini the Artist,* he mentions Eugene's "interview" of Fellini and "quotes" Fellini as saying, "Cinema is an old whore like circus and variety who knows how to give many kinds of pleasure."

FIELDS, W. C. (1880–1946) American comedian. Fields, who began his career as an expert juggler, worked in the Ziegfeld follies from 1915 to 1921. From 1923 to 1935, Fields performed in revues across the country; Eugene apparently saw him in one of these. Fields's work in films began in the 1920s and includes *My Little Chickadee* (1940) and *Never Give a Sucker an Even Break* (1941).

FORD, CHARLES HENRI (b. 1913) American poet born in Brookhaven, Mississippi. Ford has been called the first American surrealist poet. In 1940 he founded the publication *View* as a vehicle through which to introduce American readers to the work of surrealist authors like William Carlos Williams, e. e. cummings, and Wallace Stevens. He was editor of *View* from 1940 to 1947. His sister Ruth Ford is the actress for whom William Faulkner wrote the play *Requiem for a Nun*.

FRY, CHRISTOPHER (b. 1907) English playwright. In the postwar period, Fry enjoyed popularity with his plays *Phoenix Too Frequent* and *The Lady's Not for Burning*, both 1949. By the mid-1950s, his drama fell out of vogue, which may explain his uncredited work on the screenplay of *Ben-Hur* (1959).

GALBRAITH, JOHN KENNETH (b. 1908) American scholar of economics. Galbraith has been a Harvard economics professor since 1949 and has been an emeritus professor since 1975. He has written many books, including *The Affluent Society* (1958) and *The Culture of Contentment* (1992).

GALE, EDRA (b. 1921) American actress. Gale appeared in Fellini's *8½*.

GARBO, GRETA (1905–1990) Swedish actress who retired at age thirty-six and became rather reclusive. She was the highest-paid actress in Hollywood at the time. She received an Honorary Academy Award in 1954. Her affair with Mercedes de Acosta was intense but short-lived.

GARLAND, JUDY (1922–1969) American film and recording star made famous by her role as Dorothy in *The Wizard of Oz* (1939). By the time Eugene met Garland in (what was probably late) 1967, she had been suffering years of well-publicized problems with drugs and ill health. Her reputation for emotional instability made her something of a pariah in show business in the latter half of her career. Garland made her first of several suicide attempts after being fired from a movie. Eventually she could no longer function professionally, and in 1950 MGM suspended her contract. She made what was her final performance in a London nightclub in late 1968, and perhaps this is the show to which Eugene alludes as the one for which Garland was rehearsing. She died several months after of a drug overdose.

GARRIGUE, JEAN (1914–1972) American poet. Critic Stephen Stepanacher described Garrigue's first collection of poems, *The Ego and the Centaur* (1947), as a work that "deals with the world everyone knows, . . . yet [has] the otherworldliness of experience raised several degrees above the expected and ordinary. It has a musicality, a refinement, and an elegance of phrase that are appealing and rare." Her 1959 poetry collection, *A Water Walk by Villa d'Este*, was also admired critically, but her later efforts were less well received.

GIDE, ANDRÉ (1869–1951) French writer. Gide, who won the Nobel Prize for Literature in 1947, wrote fiction and verse, translated literary works (*Hamlet*, for instance) into French, was a prolific letter writer, and kept a journal from 1899 to 1949. New Directions published many of Dorothy Bussy's translations of his work into English.

GINSBERG, ALLEN (1926–1997) American poet; born in Newark, New Jersey. Ginsberg was a central figure in the Beats, the underground circle of friends, artists, and intellectuals that included novelists Jack Kerouac (*On the Road,* 1957) and William S. Burroughs (*Naked Lunch,* 1959) and muse Neal Cassady. He is best known for his long poem *Howl*, which contains explicit homosexual themes and imagery. By the mid-1960s, Ginsberg was a celebrated and popular figure of anti-Establishment politics and poetic accomplishment.

GINZBERG, NATALIA (b. 1916) Italian novelist, essayist, translator, and playwright. Among her works is the novel *Tutti i nostri ieri* (1952; English translation, *A Light for Fools*).

GIRODIAS, MAURICE (1919–1990) French publisher and editor. Girodias is best known as the founder and editor of the Olympia Press (1953–1964), which published erotica, banned literature, and experimental literature. Some of the titles he published in the 1950s are Vladimir Nabokov's *Lolita*, J. P. Donleavy's *Ginger Man*, and William Burroughs's *Naked Lunch*.

GNOLI, DOMENICO (1935–1965) Italian artist. For having lived a very short time, Gnoli produced a body of work that is substantial and considered important.

GRABBE, CHRISTIAN DIETRICH (1801–1836) German playwright. Ridiculed or ignored in his own time, Grabbe found critical sympathy and respect in the early twentieth century. Chief among his works that gained legitimacy on the twentieth-century German stage was *Scherz, Satire, Ironie und tiefere Bedeutung* (*Wit, Satire, Irony, and Deeper Meaning*, written in 1867 and translated into English in 1955). His work has never become well-known internationally.

GRAHAM, MARTHA (1894–1991) American dancer and choreographer. Graham's innovations in dance made major contributions to the creation of what became called modern dance. She departed radically from the conventions of traditional ballet in her abandonment of what she called "decorative unessentials"; her costumes had a marked plainness, and the sets of her dances, if existent, were understated. Her work has been called "cubist." She established the Dance Repertory Theater in New York in 1930.

GRAVES, ROBERT (1895–1985) British writer and poet, best known for his historical novels *I, Claudius* and *Claudius the God* (both 1934), which were adapted by the BBC for dramatization. Graves's personal life was rather complicated. He had eight children from two marriages, between which he had a sometimes sexual, long-term relationship with the American poet Laura Riding.

GUGGENHEIM, MARGUERITE (PEGGY) (1898–1979) Wealthy art patron and collector. Guggenheim was the daughter of a copper heir who died on the *Titanic*. After gaining control of her fortune in 1919, she went to London, where her friend Marcel Duchamp tutored her in modern art and introduced her to many artists. In Paris at the end of the 1930s, she bought a great deal of art from important artists, including Pablo Picasso and Georges Braque, who were eager to get cash in hand because of the Nazi threat to France. Guggenheim removed her collection to the French countryside just three days before the Nazis occupied Paris in 1940. She returned to New York, where she opened the gallery Art of This Century to great critical acclaim for the works and artists she introduced to the United States. By 1947 she owned one of the greatest collections of modern art. She gave financial support to many artists and was instrumental in establishing the artists of the New York school of abstract expressionism—Jackson Pollock, William Baziotes, Mark Rothko, Clyfford Still, and David Hare. In 1949 she bought an eighteenth-century palazzo on the Grand Canal in Venice, in which she lived and displayed her collection. By her death in 1979 the collection she had bought for $250,000 was worth $40 million.

HALL, DONALD (b. 1928) American poet. In addition to being one of the founders of the *Paris Review*, Hall served as its poetry editor from 1953 to 1961. He was a Pulitzer Prize nominee for poetry in 1989 for his long poem *The One Day*, a poem of 110 ten-line stanzas divided into three parts whose subject is the crisis of midlife.

HARRINGTON, CURTIS (b. 1928) American director and producer in film and television. Harrington's "cult film" that Eugene mentions is entitled *What's the Matter with Helen?* (1971), which costarred Shelley Winters and Debbie Reynolds (whom Eugene refers to as "the little blond actress whose name I can never remember"). Film critic Leonard Maltin describes the movie as "a campy murder tale set in the 1930s." Other films directed by Harrington include *Queen of Blood* (1966) and *The Dead Don't Die* (1974). He directed the made-for-TV *Killer Bees* (1974) and episodes of such television shows as *Charlie's Angels, Logan's Run*, and *Wonder Woman*.

HENZE, HANS WERNER (b. 1926) German composer. Henze is an important and critically acclaimed composer of the twentieth century, with a reputation for industry and innovation. His operas include *Boulevard Solitude* (1952) and *Der junge Lord* (1965), for which Ingeborg Bachmann wrote a libretto. In 1958 he wrote the ballet *Undine*, a recording of which, performed by the London Sinfonietta, was released on CD in 1999 to enthusiastic reviews.

HERBST, JOSEPHINE (1897–1969) Radical American journalist and novelist. Born in Iowa, Herbst moved to New York City in 1920, where she began her career in journalism working for H. L. Mencken and George Jean Nathan as a reading editor. In 1924, she went to Paris and met Ernest Hemingway among the American expatriates. Back in the United States during the Great Depression, Herbst, whose politics were already sympathetic to the Left, became more radical. She published eight novels, each of which treated the injustice of social and economic oppression. Herbst is best known for her journalism during the 1930s. She covered Cuba's underground movement, German criticism of Hitler prior to the war, and the Spanish civil war. No corroboration has been found for Eugene's contention that Herbst and Jean Garrigue had an affair.

HERRON, MARK (1928–1996) American actor. Herron was married to Judy Garland from 1965 to 1967 and was her fourth husband. A biographer of Garland described Herron as "an inconsequential actor." After he acted in *8½*, his career stalled.

HERSCHBERGER, RUTH (b. 1917) American writer. Herschberger's poetry, dramatic literature, and nonfiction frequently explore feminist perspectives. Her best-known work is the nonfiction *Adam's Rib*, which was published in 1954 but is currently out of print. Her poetry has appeared in many collections.

HESSE, HERMANN (1877–1962) German writer, author of the novels *Siddhartha* (1922) and *Steppenwolf* (1927). In 1919 he moved to Switzerland, where he lived the rest of his life in seclusion. Hesse won the Nobel Prize for Literature in 1946.

HIGHSMITH, PATRICIA (1921–1995) American writer of crime fiction. Highsmith wrote twenty-two novels, including *The Talented Mr. Ripley* (1957), recently adapted for the film starring Matt Damon and Gwyneth Paltrow (1999). In 1962 Highsmith won the Crime Writers Association Silver Dagger Award.

HILL, PATI (dates unknown) American novelist and poet, born in Kentucky. Her journal, *The Pit and the Century Plant*, was published in 1955.

HOWARD, VILMA (dates unknown) African American playwright. Howard was associated with the Southern Association of Dramatic and Speech Arts (SADSA) during the 1950s. Her play, *The Tam*, was published in the *SADSA Encore* in 1951.

HUGO, IAN (dates unknown) American banker, amateur filmmaker. Ian Hugo is the pseudonym of Hugh Guiler, a successful banker and the husband of Anaïs Nin. The marriage was widely known to be an "open" one, and Nin had an eight-year affair with the American writer Henry Miller. Hugo's second career was experimental filmmaking. He also illustrated some of Nin's literary works.

JONES, GWYNETH (b. 1936) Welsh opera singer. Jones, an internationally renowned soprano, made her Metropolitan Opera debut in 1972. Her voice is described as "naturally beautiful" and "very feminine."

KNOPF, BLANCHE (d. 1966) American editor and publisher. Wife of publisher Alfred Knopf (1892–1984) and vice president of the Knopf publishing company. In 1917 she helped her husband establish Knopf, and in 1921 she became vice president of the firm. Although her husband did not always agree with her opinions, her interest in foreign literature helped strengthen the reputation of the firm. She created the Borzoi imprint, which won eighteen Pulitzer Prizes and six National Book Awards. By the 1960s, Knopf had published works by André Gide, Thomas Mann, D. H. Lawrence, Jean-Paul Sartre, and Albert Camus, and the firm had published eleven Nobel Prize winners.

LAMPEDUSA, GIUSEPPE DI (1896–1957) Italian prince; writer. Giuseppe Tomasi, prince of Lampedusa, began his literary career in earnest just a few years before his death. His novel, *The Leopard*, was published two years after his death and was internationally acclaimed as one of Italy's best modern novels.

LARBAUD, VALÉRY (1881–1957) French novelist and critic. Among other works, Larbaud wrote the novel *Fermina Marquez* (1911) and a collection of essays entitled *Aux couleurs de Rome* (1938).

LAUGHLIN, JAMES (1914–1997) American publisher. Laughlin's wealth came from his family's steel interest in Pennsylvania. After graduating from Harvard, Laughlin tried his hand at poetry until his mentor, Ezra Pound, suggested that he publish works of important contemporary writers, many of whom lacked the opportunity to publish in the poor economic conditions following the Great Depression. Laughlin took Pound's advice, establishing New Directions publishing house. The first book the firm published, in 1936, was an anthology that included works by e. e. cummings, Ezra Pound, Gertrude Stein, William Carlos Williams, Elizabeth Bishop, and Henry Miller. Laughlin focused on publishing not-yet-established authors whose publishing opportunities were limited by their lack of commercial appeal. In addition, New Directions is largely responsible for introducing foreign-language authors to the American public. Some of these authors are Vladimir Nabokov, Jorge Luis Borges, Thomas Merton, Dylan

Thomas, Rainer Maria Rilke, Franz Kafka, Baudelaire, Paul Valéry, and Jean Cocteau.

LAWRENCE, SEYMOUR (1927–1994) American editor and publisher who worked at Dell/Delacorte, E. P. Dutton, and, ultimately, Houghton Mifflin. Throughout his career Lawrence maintained a reputation for publishing what he considered to be important works that did not always bring immediate commercial success. Many proved to be profitable in the long run. A few of the best-selling authors he published are Kurt Vonnegut, Katherine Anne Porter, and Tim O'Brien. Lawrence published many others, including the Nobel Prize–winning authors George Sefaris (1963), Pablo Neruda (1971), and Miguel Angel Asturias (1967).

LEE, HARPER (b. 1926) American writer; literary mystery. Lee is best known for her beloved novel, *To Kill a Mockingbird* (1960), which won a Pulitzer Prize and was adapted for the Academy Award–winning film starring Gregory Peck. It remains something of an enigma, then, that she has never written a novel after *To Kill a Mockingbird*. She has contributed to the mystery by avoiding discussion of the reasons for her silence. She lives in her hometown of Monroeville, Alabama, where she and Truman Capote had been childhood friends.

LEHMANN, JOHN (1907–1987) English editor. John Lehmann has been described as "England's dean of creative editors." A founding editor of *London* magazine from 1953 to 1961, Lehmann helped many writers establish themselves through editing, anthologizing, and publishing their works. A few such writers are W. H. Auden, Jean-Paul Sartre, Saul Bellow, and Gore Vidal.

L'ENGLE, MADELEINE (b. 1918) American writer. L'Engle has written nonfiction and fiction for adults but is best known for her children's literature. Two of her many children's titles are *A Wrinkle in Time* (1962) and *A Ring of Endless Light* (1980). She has won many awards, including the Newbery Medal.

LISZT, FRANZ (1811–1886) Hungarian composer and piano virtuoso. Celebrated as a pianist, Liszt toured Europe playing piano while he composed. Some of his works include *Fantasia on Hungarian Folk Tunes* (1853), *Les preludes* (1854), and *A Symphony to Dante's Divina Commedia* (1857). A tall and dashing figure, Liszt was the much sought after idol of countesses, actresses, and princesses; his reputation for sexual liaisons is legendary. Christopher Porterfield commented on this, writing in *Smithsonian* that Liszt "was a notorious lover and bon vivant [whose] escapades have tended to obscure his genius."

LOGUE, CHRISTOPHER (b. 1926) English poet. Logue adapted Homer's *Iliad* in four separate books: *Patrocleia* (1962), *Pax* (1967), *Kings* (1991), and *War Music* (1997). He has also adapted and retold children's stories in *The Crocodile* (1976) and *Puss in Boots* (1977).

LOMAX, ALAN (b. 1915) American folklorist. John Avery Lomax, Alan Lomax's father, was a pioneer in the field of folklore and served as a curator for the Library of Congress. His son has continued the work of preserving folk culture, recording music in England, Scotland, Ireland, the Caribbean, Spain, Italy, and around the United States. He has also written several books on the subject of American folk music.

LUBITSCH, ERNST (1892–1947) American film director. As a director of comedy, Lubitsch has been compared and ranked with his contemporaries Charlie Chaplin and Buster Keaton. His best-known works are probably *Ninotchka* (1939) and *To Be or Not to Be* (1942). He died during the production of *That Lady in Ermine* (1948).

LURIE, ALISON (b. 1926) American writer. Lurie is best known for her novels *The War between the Tates* (1974) and her Pulitzer Prize–winning novel, *Foreign Affairs* (1984).

MACLEISH, ARCHIBALD (1892–1982) American writer, poet, dramatist, statesman, and professor. MacLeish won the Pulitzer Prize for Poetry in 1933 for *Conquistador* and again in 1953 for *Collected Poems: 1917–1952*. He won the Pulitzer Prize for Drama in 1959 for *J.B.* He served as Librarian of Congress from 1939 to 1944 and as assistant secretary of state from 1944 to 1945. From 1949 until he retired in 1962, he was a professor at Harvard.

MAGNANI, ANNA (1909–1973) Italian actress. Magnani is best known in the United States for her Academy Award–winning performance in the 1955 film adaptation of Tennessee Williams's play *The Rose Tattoo*.

MANN, THOMAS (1875–1955) German novelist. The author of *Death in Venice* and *The Magic Mountain*, Mann won the Nobel Prize for Literature in 1929.

MASEFIELD, JOHN (1878–1967) English writer. Although Masefield wrote short stories, novels, and dramatic literature, he was best known as a poet. He was Poet Laureate from 1930 to 1967.

MASINA, GIULIETTA (1921–1994) Italian actress; wife of Federico Fellini. Masina's work in Fellini's *La Strada* (1954), *Nights of Cabiria* (1956), and *Juliet of the Spirits* (1965) gained her international critical acclaim. She made many more films with her husband and other important directors and won many international film awards, including best actress at the Cannes Film Festival in 1957 for her performance in *Nights of Cabiria*. Her last film, *Ginger and Fred* (1986), was directed by Fellini and costarred Marcello Mastroianni.

MASTROIANNI, MARCELLO (1924–1996) Italian actor. Mastroianni, who was described as a modest man, was nevertheless one of Italy's premier leading men, and he appeared in over 120 films. He won many international film awards celebrating his performances. He earned Academy Award nominations for *Divorce—Italian Style* (1962), *A Special Day* (1977), and *Dark Eyes* (1987). Mastroianni, who was Fellini's favorite actor, appeared in several of that director's films, including *La Dolce Vita* (1960), *8½* (1963), *Roma* (1971), and *Ginger and Fred* (1986).

MATTHIESSEN, PETER (b. 1927) American writer; co-founder and editor of the *Paris Review*. Matthiessen has written several novels, including *At Play in the Fields of the Lord* (1965), which was adapted for film in the 1992 motion picture of the same name. In addition to novels, he has published several nonfiction works, including *The Snow Leopard* (1978), an autobiographical narrative of a journey he took to Nepal.

MCCRINDLE, JOSEPH (b. 1923) American editor and writer. McCrindle has served as editor for the *Transatlantic Review* since 1959. He is currently editing a collection of poetry published in that same journal.

MCCULLERS, CARSON (1917–1967) Southern novelist from Columbus, Georgia. Many of her characters have been called "grotesques." Some of McCullers's novels are *The Heart Is a Lonely Hunter* (1940), *The Ballad of the Sad Café* (1943), and *The Member of the Wedding* (1946). In 1937 Carson married Reeves McCullers, and in 1940 they were divorced. They remarried in 1945. In 1947 Carson suffered a series of strokes that left her depressed, and she tried to kill herself in 1948. Her husband became increasingly suicidal himself, despairing over his lack of direction and their tumultuous marriage. Reeves eventually killed himself in 1953 in a Paris hotel. The rest of Carson's life was difficult; she lost her mother in 1955, underwent surgery for breast cancer in 1961, and died soon after of another stroke when she was fifty.

McKINLEY, HAZEL (b. 1916) American artist. McKinley is Peggy Guggenheim's sister.

MILLER, HENRY (1891–1980) American writer. Miller's *Tropic of Cancer* (1934) and *Tropic of Capricorn* (1939), autobiographical novels written while he was part of the Paris literary scene, were initially banned in the United States because of their raw treatment of sexuality. Miller wrote several other novels, including those in the Rosy Crucifixion trilogy: *Sexus* (1949), *Plexus* (1953), and *Nexus* (1959).

MILO, SANDRA (b. 1935) Italian actress. Milo appeared in Fellini's *8½* (1963) and *Juliet of the Spirits* (1965).

MIRÓ, JOAN (1893–1983) Spanish painter in the surrealist style. Miro is considered one of the most important and influential painters of the twentieth century.

MITCHELL, ARTHUR (b. 1934) African American ballet dancer and choreographer. Born and raised in Harlem, Mitchell was one of the first black classical ballet dancers to succeed professionally. He was a premier danseur in New York City Ballet from 1955 to 1972. He founded the Dance Theater of Harlem in 1969.

MORANTE, ELSA (1918–1985) Italian novelist. Morante published her first novel, *Menzogne e sortilegio*, in Italy in 1948. It was abridged and translated into English in 1951 as *House of Liars*. Her novel *L'Isola* (1957) was published in 1959 by Knopf in the English translation, *Arturo's Island*. She married Alberto Moravia in 1941. They divorced in 1963.

MORAVIA, ALBERTO (1907–1990) Italian novelist. Moravia was one of the best-known writers in Italy and is credited with ushering the Italian novel into modernity by writing in the Italian spoken by the people, rescuing Italian prose from what came to be seen as the artificial prose of the nineteenth-century novel. Poor translations of his work have kept him from being better known outside of Italy.

MOSS, HOWARD (1922–1987) American man of letters; editor, poet, and literary critic. As the poetry editor of *The New Yorker* for almost forty years, Moss took the opportunity to help important poets get established while they were young: James Dickey, Galway Kinnell, Anne Sexton, James Scully, Theodore Roethke, L. E. Sissman, Richard Wilbur, Sylvia Plath, and Mark Strand. Moss has published substantial amounts of his own poetry and literary criticism, such as the highly esteemed *The Magic Lantern of Marcel Proust* (1962). In 1972 Moss won the National Book Award for Poetry for *Selected Poems* (1971).

NABOKOV, NICOLAS (b. 1903) Russian-born composer. His compositions include *Sinfonia Biblica* (1941) for the New York Philharmonic, *SymboliChorestiani* (1956) for the Venice Music Festival, and *A Prayer* (1968) for the New York Philharmonic under Leonard Bernstein.

NIN, ANAÏS (1903–1977) American journal writer and novelist. Although Nin wrote novels, short stories, and erotica, her journals stand as her most acclaimed literary achievement. These journals are collected in the seven-volume *The Diary of Anaïs Nin,* which spans the years 1931 to 1974. *The Diary* has not met with universal approbation. Susan Heath, for example, in *Saturday Review,* described Nin's journal as "the tiresome work of a querulous bore who cultivates neurosis in hopes of achieving self-realization." One could argue that Nin's many affairs, including a brief incestuous one with her father, may have been part of such cultivation of neurosis.

NORTH, ALEX (1910–1991) American film composer. Among the many films for which North composed the score are *A Streetcar Named Desire* (1951), *The Rose Tattoo* (1955), *Who's Afraid of Virginia Woolf?* (1966), and *Prizzi's Honor* (1985). North was nominated fifteen times for an Oscar for his scores. In 1986 he was the first composer ever to receive an honorary Academy Award for "his brilliant artistry in the creation of memorable music for a host of distinguished motion pictures."

O'BRIEN, EDNA (b. 1931) Irish writer. O'Brien has written fiction, nonfiction, poetry, and dramatic literature. Her works include *The Country Girls* (novel, 1960); *Tales for the Telling* (for children, 1986); *A Cheap Bunch of Nice Flowers* (play produced in London, 1962); and several plays for television.

O'NEIL, NANCE (1874–1965) American stage actress. O'Neil, whose real name was Gertrude Lamson, was an admired leading lady whose famous roles included Leah in Augustin Daly's *Leah the Forsaken* and Juliet in *Romeo and Juliet.* She was a major touring star of the turn-of-the-century stage. Her career, like that of many stage actors, languished when motion pictures began to dominate popular entertainment. She did continue to perform, however, into her sixties.

O'NEILL, JAMES (1849–1920) Irish-born American stage actor. Despite playing many roles early in his career, O'Neill became typecast as Edmond Dantes in a traveling stage version of *The Count of Monte Cristo,* in which he first appeared in 1882. He played the part over six thousand times. He was also the father of the Nobel and Pulitzer Prize–winning playwright Eugene O'Neill, author of *Long Day's Journey into Night.*

OZICK, CYNTHIA (b. 1928) American writer. Author of the novel *Trust* (1966), she has been a frequent contributor of essays, poetry, reviews, and translations to such periodicals as the *New Republic, The New York Times Book Review, Ms., Esquire, The New Yorker,* the *American Poetry Review, Harper's,* and *The New York Times Magazine.*

PFRIEM, BERNARD (b. 1914) American painter. In addition to presenting exhibitions of his work, Pfriem taught in the MOMA Educational Program.

PITTER, RUTH (1897–1992) English writer. Among her titles of poetry collections, the best known is *A Mad Lady's Garland,* published in 1934 with a foreword by the Poet Laureate John Masefield. *The Rude Potato,* which Eugene mentions, was published in 1941.

PLIMPTON, GEORGE (b. 1927) American writer and founding editor of the *Paris Review.* Plimpton has been with the *Paris Review* as an editor since its inception and has been instrumental in shaping it as a literary journal that focuses on contemporary creative writing rather than on criticism. One of the journal's most popular features is its interviews with writers, which poet Donald Hall has described as "literary history as gossip." Many writers published first in the *PR*, such as Philip Roth, Jack Kerouac, Henry Miller, and John Updike. Plimpton is also popularly known as a writer of sports anecdotes culled from his experiences as an amateur in different professional sports. *Paper Lion* (1966) is a collection of his football anecdotes.

POE, EDGAR ALLAN (1809–1849) American writer. In his story "The Gold-Bug," a cipher containing instructions for finding a buried treasure must be decoded.

PORTER, KATHERINE ANNE (1894–1980) American writer, originally from Texas. Porter was most noted for her short fiction, and she won a Pulitzer Prize in 1966 for *The Collected Stories of Katherine Anne Porter*, which included the stories "The Jilting of Granny Weatherall" (1930), "Flowering Judas" (1930), and "The Grave" (1944). She published one novel, *Ship of Fools* (1962), but most critics consider her earlier short fiction to be her best work. She was married and divorced four times, which may corroborate Eugene's assessment of her temperament.

PRICE, LEONTYNE (b. 1927) African American operatic soprano. Price, who has won thirteen Grammies, attended the Juilliard School of Music from 1948 to 1952, so Eugene must have seen her during this time, perhaps when she toured Europe performing in *Porgy and Bess*. Price was the first black prima donna soprano and the first black singer to become an international star of opera. She was most acclaimed for her performances of Verdi's work. Beginning in 1958, she had an exclusive contract with RCA for twenty years, during which time she made an impressive number of recordings. She retired from performing in 1985.

RANDALL, JULIA (b. 1923) American poet. Randall's earliest collection of poems, published in 1952, was *The Solstice Tree*, and her most recent collection from 1987 was *Moving in Memory: Poems*. She has contributed poetry to *Botteghe Oscure*, *Poetry* (Chicago), *Kenyon Review*, and *Sewanee Review*.

RISI, DINO (b. 1917) Italian film director. Risi has directed dozens of documentaries and commercial films since the 1940s. In 1976 he was nominated for an Oscar for best writing, for his screen adaptation of *Profumo di donna* (1974). *The Normal Young Man* (1969), the film Eugene mentions, was the only one Risi directed in which the actor Lino Capolicchio appeared.

ROBINSON, EDWARD G. (1893–1971) Romanian-born American actor. Appearing in literally dozens of movies, including *Little Caesar* (1931), *Double Indemnity* (1944), and *Soylent Green* (1973), Robinson often portrayed a tough guy or a gangster. He won a special Academy Award posthumously.

RONSARD, PIERRE DE (1524–1585) French poet. The poem to which Eugene refers is "A sa maîtresse," published in *Les Amours de Cassandre* (1553), a collection of Petrarchan sonnets. The poem was written for the twenty-two-year-old Cassandre Salviati.

ROREM, NED (b. 1923) American composer and diarist. In 1976 Rorem won the Pulitzer Prize for an orchestral piece called *Air Music* (1974), which he wrote for the Cincinnati Symphony. He studied privately with Aaron Copland for some time. In addition to composing, Rorem has published five diaries spanning almost twenty years and recording his life in Paris, New York City, and Nantucket.

ROTA, NINO (1911–1979) Italian composer. Although Rota composed for other film directors, such as Franco Zeffirelli and Francis Ford Coppola, most of his composing was done in service of Federico Fellini's films. From 1951 to 1979, Rota either wrote or selected the music for most of Fellini's films. Fellini and Rota's collaboration was often spontaneous and symbiotic. Fellini would give Rota an image or a feeling, and Rota often could spontaneously compose a piece that elaborated Fellini's nascent concept. In 1972 Rota's work on Francis Ford Coppola's *The Godfather* won him an Academy Award nomination, but it also brought an accusation of plagiarism that, although eventually disproved, nevertheless blighted his nomination. He did eventually win an Oscar, in 1974, for *The Godfather, Part II.*

RUBENSTEIN, HELENA (1870–1965) Polish-born cosmetics tycoon. Rubenstein built a financial empire on cosmetics for women and in doing so had to overcome the prejudice against ladies wearing makeup, which was thought to belong onstage only. Her beauty products brought her not only fortune, but also the social patronage of society people, artists, and actors.

RUTHERFORD, MARGARET (1892–1972) English stage and film actress. Rutherford was known and acclaimed most as a lovable comedian. She played the role of Miss Prism in the 1952 film version of Oscar Wilde's *The Importance of Being Earnest*, a role she had first performed in 1939 on a London stage. She won an Oscar for best supporting actress in 1963 for *The VIPs.* Many know her from her film portrayals of Agatha Christie's Miss Marple.

ST. DENIS, RUTH (1877–1968) American choreographer and dancer. It has been said that St. Denis has "influenced almost every phase of American dance in the twentieth century." With her then husband, Ted Shawn, she established the Denishawn School of Dancing in Los Angeles, the school where Martha Graham studied at the beginning of her career. St. Denis toured with the Denishawn Dance Company extensively until the school closed in 1934. She continued to perform on her own and remained an active performer into advanced age.

SELLERS, PETER (1925–1980) English actor. Sellers, who began his career as a radio actor, found transatlantic popularity thanks in large part to his work in the role of Inspector Clouseau in five *Pink Panther* movies, one of which was released posthumously. His work in American films like Woody Allen's *What's New, Pussycat?* (1965) and Stanley Kubrick's *Dr. Strangelove* (1964) brought him critical acclaim. He received an Oscar nomination in 1979 for his performance in *Being There.*

SERT Y BADIA, JOSÉ (1874–1945) Spanish painter. The mural Sert painted in the cathedral of Vich is considered to be his most important work. He also painted murals in Buenos Aires, Geneva (Assembly of the League of Nations), London, New York (RCA Building in Rockefeller Center), and San Sebastian.

SHADOW, THE. Popular radio show of suspense which always opened with the famous line "Who knows what evil lurks in the heart of men?"; on the air from 1930 to 1954. Several actors played the part of the Shadow, including Jack La Curto, Frank Readrick Jr., Orson Welles, Brett Morrison, Bill Johnstone, John Archer, and Steve Courtleigh. It is likely that the Shadow Eugene met was Brett Morrison (1912–1978), who played the part for the longest time and is best known in the role. Morrison moved to New York from Hollywood when a career in films failed to pan out. He did well in radio, playing roles in several other programs such as *The Guiding Light.*

SITWELL, DAME EDITH (1887–1964) English poet. Aristocratic by birth, Sitwell was either ignored or blasted by critics for her poetry. In her seventies, however, she finally received not only attention, but praise and honors as well. Dylan Thomas was considered to be a disciple of Sitwell's. In 1947 she published *The Shadow of Cain* in response to the ushering in of the atomic age with the bombing of Hiroshima by the United States. In 1948 she came to the United States on a lecture tour, which is possibly when Eugene saw her on a New York bus.

SMITH, WILLIAM GARDNER (1926–1974) African American writer and journalist. After World War II, Smith was a reporter for a couple of U.S. newspapers, including *Afro-American.* In 1952 he immigrated to France, where he lived for the rest of his life. From 1954 to 1974, he was the news editor of the English Language Services for Agence France Presse. He published several novels, including *Last of the Conquerers* (1948) and *Anger at Innocence* (1950).

SORDI, ALBERTO (b. 1919) Italian actor. Sordi's acting career, which spans the years 1938 to 1990, has been dedicated mostly to comic roles. In the later part of his career, Sordi also became active in cowriting and directing.

SPARK, MURIEL (b. 1918) Scottish writer. Although she began her career as a poet and a literary critic, Spark has found the greatest success with her fiction. Spark has published over twenty novels and several collections of short fiction. Her best-known work is *The Prime of Miss Jean Brodie.* Her 1990 novel, *Symposium,* was a bestseller. The critical work on John Masefield to which Eugene refers is entitled, simply, *John Masefield* (1953).

SPENCER, ELIZABETH (b. 1921) American writer. Although Spencer lived in Italy from 1953 to 1958, and then moved to Quebec province, Canada, her roots as a writer remain in her native Mississippi. She once commented on an epiphany she had regarding her Southern identity, saying that she realized that "there wasn't any need in sitting at home in the cotton field just to be Southern, that you could be Southern elsewhere, in Florence or Paris, or anywhere you found yourself." She published the novel *The Light in the Piazza* in 1960 and *The Salt Line* in 1980. She is currently working on another novel.

STANLEY, MARIE (1885–1936) American writer. Born and raised in Mobile, Alabama, Stanley early in her life observed the race divide of the early-twentieth-century South. Her novel, *Gulf Stream,* created some controversy in her hometown because of its frank discussion of race relations, but it was well received critically.

STAPLETON, MAUREEN (b. 1925) American actress. Stapleton made her Broadway debut in 1946 as Sarah Tansey in *The Playboy of the Western World.* She has also appeared in several movies, including *Bye, Bye, Birdie* (1963) and *Cocoon* (1985). She has made several television appearances. She played the role of Big Mama in the television film *Cat on a Hot Tin Roof* (1976).

STEELE, BARBARA (b. 1938) English actress. Although Steele is English, she has appeared in several Italian films, including Fellini's *8½.* She appeared in *I Never*

Promised You a Rose Garden (1977) and *Pretty Baby* (1977). Steele made quite a few "B" horror flicks, such as *The Castle of Terror* (1964), *They Came from Within* (1975), and *Piranha* (1978). Most recently she appeared in *The Prophet* (1999).

STEELE, MAX (b. 1922) American writer, from South Carolina. Steele has served as an advisory editor for *Paris Review* since 1952. His only novel, *Debbie* (1960), won the Harper Prize. He has submitted short fiction to *Atlantic, Harper's, The New Yorker, Collier's, Esquire,* and *Quarterly Review of Literature,* as well as other literary journals. Steele's academic career at Chapel Hill, where he is currently a professor of English, began in 1956.

STEIN, GERTRUDE (1874–1946) American-born writer and cultural critic. In 1903 Stein moved to Paris, where she lived for the rest of her life. She shared a home and salon with her companion and secretary, Alice B. Toklas. For the early half of the twentieth century their salon was a center for the Paris art and literature scene and was instrumental in defining the course of modern art, literature, and thought. Picasso and Matisse were among the painters Stein encouraged. She named the young American writers immigrating to Paris between the world wars, among them Ernest Hemingway and F. Scott Fitzgerald, "the lost generation." She advised that modern art, literature, and thought required a structural revolt from the aesthetics and assumptions of the nineteenth century. In her own writing she explored such a revolt through her use of language and narrative. Once she remarked that her move away from narration toward pure description was an attempt to realize in writing a "continuous present" that was at the heart of human existence. The story told to Eugene by Alice B. Toklas is interesting to consider in light of this concept.

STRACHEY, LYTTON (1880–1932) British biographer, essayist, and critic. Best known for his book of biographical portraits entitled *Eminent Victorians,* Strachey was a member of the Bloomsbury group, a circle of important British intellectual and literary figures in London in the 1920s and 1930s whose members included John Maynard Keynes, E. M. Forster, and Virginia Woolf.

STYRON, WILLIAM (b. 1925) American writer. Among several novels Styron has written is his controversial Pulitzer Prize–winning *The Confessions of Nat Turner* (1967), which some critics argued was exploitive and which perpetuated white stereotypes of African Americans. His 1979 novel, *Sophie's Choice,* was adapted for film with Meryl Streep playing the title role. In 1990 he published an account of his battle with depression, *Darkness Visible: A Memoir of Madness.* Styron has served as an advisory editor of *Paris Review* since 1952.

TANGUAY, EVA (1878–1947) Vaudeville performer. Billed as "Girl who made Vaudeville famous," Tanguay was known for her revealing costumes and her risqué songs. The songs "I Don't Care" and "It's Been Done Before but Not the Way I Do It" are especially associated with Tanguay.

TCHELITCHEW, PAVEL (1898–1957) Russian-born American painter. *Hide and Seek* (1940–1942) is considered by many to be Tchelitchew's masterpiece. It is housed in New York's Museum of Modern Art.

THOMAS, DYLAN (1914–1953) Welsh poet. Although Thomas wrote and published short stories, essays, and a radio play entitled *Under Milk Wood,* he is best known for his poetry. His collection *Eighteen Poems* was published in 1934. Thomas also had a reputation for hard drinking and for always being broke. Between 1950 and 1953, he made four reading tours in the United States, which helped establish his popularity. Unfortunately, his personal problems with drink and finances continued until he died of alcohol poisoning in New York.

THOMSON, VIRGIL (1896–1989) Film composer and music critic for *Vanity Fair* and the *New York Herald Tribune*. Some of the films for which Thomson composed scores are *The Plow That Broke the Plains* (1936), *Louisiana Story* (1948), and *The Goddess* (1958).

TODD, RUTHVEN (b. 1914) Scottish writer. Todd has published many novels under the pseudonym R. T. Campbell. Under his own name he has published several collections of poetry, with *Mantelpiece of Shells* (1954) his first to be published in America. He has written several children's stories. From 1950 to 1954, Todd taught creative writing at Iowa State.

TOKLAS, ALICE B. (1877–1967) American companion, secretary, and publisher of Gertrude Stein. Toklas was with Stein for almost forty years, until Stein's death. Although overshadowed by her lover, Toklas was integral in organizing the salon the two women ran and was also important to Stein's literary career. Indeed, when Stein could find no publisher for her work, Toklas began a press called Plain Edition, which published only Stein's work and for which Toklas served as publisher, director, and managing editor.

TRAIN, JOHN (b. 1928) American writer. An investment counselor by profession, Train has also authored several books in what is called the Remarkable series— for example, *Remarkable Names of Real People* (1977), *True Remarkable Occurrences* (1978), *Remarkable Relatives* (1981). He was a cofounder of the *Paris Review* and served as its managing editor from 1952 to 1954. He has been a trustee of the *Harvard Lampoon* since 1974.

TREE, IRIS (dates unknown) British actress. Tree had an uncredited role as Poetess in Fellini's *La Dolce Vita* (1960).

VALÉRY, PAUL (1871–1945) French poet associated with the symbolist group. Among his collections of verse is *La Jeune Parque* (*The Young Fate*), published in 1917.

VIDAL, GORE (b. 1925) American writer. Known for his (sometimes biting) wit, Vidal has been called "the Gentleman Bitch of American Letters." He has written novels, plays, screenplays, essays, and reviews. His maternal grandfather, Thomas Gore, an Oklahoma senator, influenced his passionate interest in politics. Among Gore's titles is the play *The Best Man: A Play of Politics*, first performed on Broadway in 1960, as well as the novels *Washington, D.C.* (1967) and *Empire* (1987).

VIDOR, KING (1894–1982) American director. Vidor directed over fifty films, including *Hallelujah* (1929), the first film with an all-black cast, and *War and Peace* (1956).

VILLA, JOSÉ GARCIA (1914–1997) Filipino poet. Villa came to the United States in 1930, and his first book of poetry to be published here was *Have Come, Am Here* (1942). He was an editor for New Directions from 1949 to 1951.

WARHOL, ANDY (1928?–1987) American artist and cultural figure. He was born Andrew Warhola, the youngest son to Czechoslovakian immigrants in Pittsburgh. In 1949, after graduating from the Carnegie Institute of Technology (now

Carnegie-Mellon University), he headed to New York, where he worked in advertising as a freelance designer. In the illustration credit for one of his first assignments for *Glamour* magazine, his last name was accidentally shortened to Warhol, and he kept the shortened version ever after. He dropped "Andrew" for "Andy" early in 1950. No confirmation has been found that Warhol took painting classes at the Museum of Modern Art.

WARREN, ROBERT PENN (1905–1989) Southern poet and novelist. *Night Rider* (1939), the novel Eugene mentions, was Warren's first. He won a Pulitzer Prize in 1946 for his novel *All the King's Men,* which was adapted into the 1949 Academy Award–winning movie. From 1935 to 1942 he edited the literary journal *Southern Review.* In 1986–1987, Warren became the first official Poet Laureate of the United States.

WEAVER, WILLIAM FENSE (b. 1923) American writer and award-winning translator. Weaver has translated many novels from Italian into English, including Giorgio Bassani's *The Garden of the Finzi-Continis* (1977) and Umberto Eco's *The Name of the Rose* (1984). Weaver has contributed articles and reviews to many periodicals, including the *Saturday Review, Harper's Bazaar, Opera News, Vanity Fair, Vogue, Architectural Digest,* and the *New York Times.*

WERTMÜLLER, LINA (b. 1928) Italian director. Her two best-known films in the United States are *Swept Away . . . by an Unusual Destiny in the Blue Sea of August* and *Seven Beauties.*

WEST, ANTHONY (1914–1987) English writer. West was the illegitimate son of the authors H. G. Wells and Rebecca West. Although he published several novels and nonfiction works, his works that either alluded to or directly treated his unconventional family and background have received the most attention. His autobiographical novel, *Heritage* (1955), is likely his best known. In 1984 he published *H. G. Wells: Aspects of a Life,* which chronicled his unhappy childhood, his relationship with his mother, and his father's relationship with West.

WEST, MAE (1893–1980) American vaudeville comedienne and stage and screen actress. Having performed in vaudeville since she was eight, West made her Broadway debut in 1911. She continued to tour in vaudeville after this debut, but this time with star billing. She was known for her unconventionally explicit sexuality. In 1926 she performed on Broadway again, this time in *Sex,* a play she wrote herself—and her notoriety as a femme fatale eventually earned her a film contract with Paramount Pictures. She made her screen debut in 1932 in *Night After Night.*

WHITTEKER, LILLIAN (1895–1978) American painter. Eugene introduced her to Italy by helping to organize shows for her in Rome and Positano.

WILDE, OSCAR (1854–1900) Irish writer. Wilde wrote a great deal of poetry, dramatic literature, and fiction, including the novel *The Picture of Dorian Gray* (1890) and the play *The Importance of Being Earnest* (1895). After serving two years upon his conviction for sodomy, Wilde wandered in exile on the Continent for a few years. He died penniless in Paris.

WILDER, THORNTON (1897–1975) American writer. Wilder wrote novels as well as dramatic literature. His novel *The Bridge of San Luis Rey* (1927) won a Pulitzer Prize, as did his plays *Our Town* (1938) and *The Skin of Our Teeth* (1942).

Another of his plays, *The Matchmaker* (1954), was adapted in 1964 into the musical *Hello, Dolly!*

WILLIAMS, OSCAR (1900–1964) American poet, editor, critic, and anthologist. Williams was the general editor of the Little Treasury series, poetry anthologies that have become standard textbooks in colleges and universities across the United States. He contributed writing to *Atlantic Monthly, Harper's, Harper's Bazaar,* the *Saturday Review,* the *Southern Review, The Nation,* and the *New Republic.* He was married to the poet Gene Derwood.

WINTERS, SHELLEY (b. 1922) American actor. Among the dozens of films, television appearances, and stage performances on Winters's résumé are the films *A Place in the Sun,* in which she costarred with Elizabeth Taylor and Montgomery Clift (1951), and *Lolita* (1962), directed by Stanley Kubrick.

WOLFE, PAUL (b. 1926) American violinist, oboist, and composer. Wolfe still directs the New College Music Festival, which he founded in 1965 in Sarasota, Florida.

ZEFFIRELLI, FRANCO (b. 1923) Italian director. Zeffirelli is best known in the United States as the director of the films *Romeo and Juliet* (1968), *Brother Sun, Sister Moon* (1973), and *The Champ* (1979).

ZEV (1919–1987) American artist. Born Daniel Harris, Zev took his family's original name, which means "wolf" in Hungarian. Zev created a kind of sculpture in architecture, called *Crazy Crescent,* at Big Sur in California. Eventually this structure was condemned, but before its destruction, architects and students came from French and English architectural institutes in teams to record it. Zev illustrated Eugene's *Singerie-Songerie,* a version of *Hamlet* for monkeys.

Acknowledgments

There are many people without whom my collaboration with Eugene Walter would have come to naught, or never happened at all. Matt McDonald is the one who first told me about Eugene, and arranged for me to meet him on the very night of my move to Mobile. This meeting took place at the house of Ted Dial, who became a great friend and was a supporter of the project from its earliest inception. It was Ted's friendship that sustained me during the fiendishly hot summer in Mobile when I interviewed Eugene. And it was my father's money that literally supported me and made those interviews logistically possible. I am also indebted to my father, Lawrence Clark, for the legal advice and assistance he has rendered. Mary Lillian Walker and Sean Smith are two others who have given both financial as well as legal assistance to this endeavor.

Then there is Frank Daughterty, whose continuous encouragement and feedback, along with various odd jobs of research and fact-checking, ensured that this project came to fruition. Frank is the one who relit the fire under me when my own faith had dwindled after various setbacks and rejections. One of the many services Frank rendered was to introduce me to John Sledge, then head of the Mobile Historic Development Commission. John made sure that the fire Frank had rekindled did not go out, as he quickly became my mainstay for the duration of this project. Without John, my interviews with Eugene would have remained just that, and would not have been transformed into this book. It was John's idea to approach Palmer Hamilton, a Mobile attorney and dedicated preservationist of his city's history. Although usually given to preserving architecture, Palmer rose graciously to the occasion of helping preserve Mobile's history in another way by donating the services of his extraordinary secretary, Doty Lowe. In addition to her usual tasks of transcribing depositions and typing briefs, Doty quickly set to work transcribing the tapes of my interviews with Eugene.

It was Doty's tireless and outstanding work that helped me secure the services of my agent, Jessica Jones, whose faith in my incipient manuscript has led ultimately to its publication. JoAnne Prichard was the one who acquired the manuscript for Crown, and I am beholden to her vision and insight. Lucky am I that the manuscript landed in the lap of Doug Pepper, who became my actual editor at Crown. Doug was ideally suited for this job, both rigorous and judicious in his use of the blue pencil, both hands-on and hands-off at just the right moments. The book could not have had a better editor. I was also blessed to obtain the assistance of Georgette Bisson, who researched and compiled the material for the Cast of Characters at the back of the book. Without her superior and indefatigable efforts, this portion of the book would not exist. Althea Bennett took up where Doty Lowe left off, and transcribed the remaining tapes with remarkable speed and accuracy.

There are still others. Eugene's cousin, Francis Walter, was so kind and generous with his time and knowledge, and I am grateful to him for the use of the photograph that adorns the book's cover. Tom Loehr also gave valuable assistance with photographs. Tom Uskali served as reader and unofficial editor, friend and handholder. Mary Alma Durrett lent me a recording of her interviews with Eugene and kindly allowed me to use that material. Tom Mason was always ready to help at a moment's notice and offered his house as my hotel in Mobile. It was to Tom's lovely house that I brought Eugene after he'd been rescued from the bathroom floor for the dinner party he wouldn't *dream* of missing. This was my last real encounter with Eugene, and I am grateful to Tom for making it so beautiful, with votive candles flickering on all the transoms above the doors, and camellias swimming in bowls on mantles and tables all over the house. Eugene was right not to miss that party.

It goes without saying, but I will say it anyway: without my husband, Brandon Dorion, I could never have finished this book.